REED'S GENERAL ENGINEERING KNOWLEDGE FOR MARINE ENGINEERS

by
LESLIE JACKSON, B.Sc. (Lond.).
C. Eng., F.I. Mar. E., F.R.I.N.A.
Extra First Class Engineers' Certificate

and
THOMAS D. MORTON
C. Eng., F.I. Mar. E., M.I. Mech. E.
Extra First Class Engineers' Certificate

THOMAS REED PUBLICATIONS
A DIVISION OF THE ABR COMPANY LIMITED

First Edition – 1966
Second Edition – 1971
Reprinted – 1974
Reprinted – 1976
Third Edition – 1978
Reprinted – 1979
Reprinted – 1984
Fourth Edition – 1986
Reprinted – 1990
Reprinted – 1994
Reprinted – 1995
Reprinted – 1997
Reprinted – 1998
Reprinted – 1999

ISBN 0 947637 76 1

THOMAS REED PUBLICATIONS
The Barn
Ford Farm
Bradford Leigh
Bradford-on-Avon
Wiltshire BA15 2RP
United Kingdom

Email: tugsrus@abreed.demon.co.uk

Produced by Omega Profiles Ltd, SP11 7RW
Printed and Bound in Great Britain

PREFACE

The object of this book is primarily to prepare students for the Certificates of Competency of the Department of Transport in the subject of General Engineering Knowledge. It also covers the syllabus for Engineer Cadet courses in the subject.

The text is intended to cover the ground work required for the examinations. The syllabus and principles involved are virtually the same for all examinations but questions set in the Class One require the most detailed answer.

The book is not to be considered as a close detail reference work but rather as a specific examination guide, in particular most of the sketches are intended as direct applications to the examination requirements. If further knowledge from an interest aspect is required the student is advised to consult a specialist text book, e.g., lubrication, stabilisers, metallurgy, etc., as the range of modern marine practice has superseded the times whereby all the subject can be accurately presented in one volume.

The best method of study is to read carefully through each chapter, practising sketchwork, and when the principles have been mastered to attempt the few examples at the end of each chapter. Finally, the miscellaneous questions at the end of the book should be worked through. The best preparation for any examinations is the work on examples, this is difficult in the subject of Engineering Knowledge as no model answer is available, nor indeed any one text book to cover all the possible questions. As a guide it is suggested that the student finds his information first and then attempts each question in the book in turn, basing his answer on a good descriptive sketch and writing occupying about one side of A4 in 20 minutes.

In order to keep as closely abreast as possible to the latest DTp examination questions the book has been extensively revised.

The Department of Transport publish examination question papers and have given permission to reproduce questions from them.

L. JACKSON
T. D. MORTON

CONTENTS

CHAPTER 1— **Materials**
Manufacture of iron and steel — processes. Cast iron. Simple metallurgy of steel and cast iron. Properties of materials — ductility, hardness, etc. Testing of materials — tensile, hardness, impact, etc. Nondestructive tests. Treatment of metals — hardening, tempering, annealing, etc. Forming of metals — casting, forging, etc. Elements in irons and steels. Effects of alloying elements. Non-ferrous metals. Nonmetallic materials. Table of properties and uses of various metals. Welding — electric arc processes, preparation, faults. Soldering and brazing. Gas cutting .   PAGE   1—46

CHAPTER 2— **Fuel Technology**
Liquid fuels — petroleum, distillation, refining. Testing of liquid fuels and oils — density, viscosity, flashpoint, calorific value, etc. Combustion of fuel — combustibles, hydrocarbons, flame temperature, additives. Analysis of flue gases — Orsat, CO_2 recorders, Clean Air Act, dissociation, heat balance. Combustion equipment — burners, air registers, fuel system, viscosity control. Gaseous fuels — compatibility, LNG and LPG, toxic vapours, explosive vapours, tests ...   47—91

CHAPTER 3— **Boilers and Ancillaries**
Safety valves — types, materials, adjustment, testing. Water level indicators — direct, remote. Other boiler mountings — soot blowers,

feed check valves. Boilers — waste
heat. Cochran. Scotch boiler, construction, defects, repairs, tests.
Packaged auxiliary boiler. Reducing
valve. Evaporators — scale, treatment. Evaporating and distilling
plants — flash evaporator, drinking
water ....   92—140

CHAPTER 4— **Corrosion, Boiler Water**
Treatment and Tests
Corrosion — metals in sea water,
graphitisation, de-zincification.
Other corrosion topics — fretting,
pitting, fatigue. Boiler corrosion —
pH values, electro-chemical action,
causes of corrosion, galvanic action,
caustic embrittlement, etc. Sea
water — solids, lime and soda treatment, gases. High pressure boiler
water treatment — coagulants,
deaeration. Treatment for laid up
boilers. Boiler water tests —
alkalinity, chlorinity, hardness, etc.   141—174

CHAPTER 5— **Steering Gears**
Telemeter (transducer) systems —
hydraulic transmitter, bypass valve,
receiver. Telemotor fluid, charging,
air effects, emergency operation.
Electric telemotor, control, local,
terminology. Power (amplifier)
systems — electric, hydraulic.
Variable delivery pumps. Hele-
Shaw, swash plate. Actuator (servo)
mechanisms — electro-hydraulic
steering gears; ram type, emergency
operation, control valve block, fork
tiller, four ram units, rotary vane
type, comparisons, automatic 'fail
safe' system. Electric steering gears;
Ward Leonard, single motor,

emergency operation. Rules relating
to steering gears. Ship stabiliser —
electric control, hydraulic actuation, fin detail, etc. Auto control —
block diagrams, steering,
stabilisation. ....   175—210

CHAPTER 6— **Shafting**
Alignment — general, in ship, in
shops (crankshaft and bedplate),
telescope, overall, pilgrim wire.
Crankshaft deflections — data,
bearing adjustments. Shafting
stresses — calculations, intermediate, thrust, crank and propeller
shafts. Shafting rules — shafts,
liners, bush and bolts. Propeller
shaft and sterntube — water and oil
types, withdrawable stern gear,
propeller bearing type, roller
bearing design. Controllable pitch
propeller. Shafting ancillaries —
torsionmeter, dynamometer, thrust
block, ball and roller bearings.
Simple balancing — revolving
masses, inertia forces. Simple
vibration — transverse, axial,
torsional, dampers. ....   211—255

CHAPTER 7— **Refrigeration**
Basic principles — phase changes.
Refrigerants — properties. Freon.
The vapour compression system —
operating cycle, faults, thermodynamic cycles, intermediate liquid
cooling, critical temperature. Compressor — reciprocating (veebloc),
rotary, centrifugal, screw,
lubricant. Heat exchangers —
condenser, evaporator, heat
transfer, liquid level control. Direct
expansion — automatic valves,

control. Absorption type. Brine circuits — properties, battery system, ice making, hold ventilation. Air conditioning — basic principles, circuit, heat pump, dehumidifier. Insulation, heat transfer. .... 256—300

CHAPTER 8— **Fire and Safety**

Principle of fire. Fire prevention and precautions. Types of fire and methods of extinguishing. Fire detection methods — patrols, alarm circuits, detector types. Critical analysis of fire extinguishing mediums — water, steam, foam, CO_2. Fire extinguishers (foam) — types. Foam spreading installations. Fire extinguishers (CO_2) — types. CO_2 flooding systems. Inert gas installations. Water spray systems. Merchant Shippng (Fire Appliance) Rules — extract. Breathing apparatus. .... 301—349

CHAPTER 9— **Pumps and Pumping Systems**

Types of pumps — reciprocating, centrifugal, axial, screw gear, water ring. Central priming system. Emergency bilge pump. Comparison of pumps — suction lift (head), cavitation, super cavitation. Associated equipment and systems — heat exchangers (tube and plate), central cooling systems, modular systems, domestic water supply and purification, hydrophore systems. Prevention of pollution of the sea by oil — Oil in Navigable Waters Act, oily-water separators. Injectors and Ejectors.

Sewage and sludge systems. Pipe arrangements and fittings — bilge, ballast, rules. .... 350—403

CHAPTER 10— **Lubrication and Oil Purification**
Gravitation separation. Filtration methods — types of filter, streamline, filter coalescers, oil module (fuel and lubricating oil). Clarification and separation — disc and bowl centrifuges. Sharples, De-Laval, self cleaning. Lubrication — fundamentals, additives. Bearings — journal. Michell. Definitions — pitting, scuffing, oxidation, etc. Lubricating oil tests. Bearing corrosion. Grease. .... 404—439

CHAPTER 11— **Instrumentation and Control**
Instruments — sensors and measuring elements for temperature, pressure, level, flow etc. Calibration. Telemetering — display, scanning, data logging, terminology. Components; amplifier, transducer. Signal media. Control theory — terminology, closed loop system. Actions; proportional, integral, derivative. Pneumatic P and P + I + D controllers. Electric—electronic P + I + D controller. Control systems — diaphragm valve, electric telegraph, fluid temperature control, automatic boiler control, unattended machinery spaces (UMS), bridge control IC engine. ... 440—473

CHAPTER 12— **Management**
Management processes. General

industrial management — organisation of divisions, planning, production, personnel, development etc. Further terminology, queueing theory. IDP. O & M. OR. Some practical applications, critical path analysis, planned maintenance, replacement policy, ship maintenance costs, optimal maintenance policy, co-ordination. On-ship management — shipping company structure, administration. Report writing — English usage, examination requirements, specimen question and answer, test examples technique. .... 474—490

SPECIMEN EXAMINATION QUESTIONS (DTp)

Class 3	**Miscellaneous**	**491-494**
	Specimen Paper	**495-496**
Class 2	**Miscellaneous**	**497-502**
	Specimen Paper	**503-507**
Class 1	**Miscellaneous**	**508-514**
	Specimen Paper	**515-519**
INDEX		**521-528**

CHAPTER 1

MATERIALS

MANUFACTURE OF IRON AND STEEL

Iron ores are the basic material used in the manufacture of the various steels and irons in present use. In its natural state iron ore may contain many impurities and vary considerably in iron content. Some of the more important iron ores are:
(1) Hematite 30 to 65% iron content approximately.
(2) Magnetite 60 to 70% iron content approximately.

Iron ores are not usually fed direct into the blast furnace in the natural or as mined condition, they are prepared first. The preparation may consist of some form of concentrating process (*e.g.* washing out the earthy matter) followed by a crushing, screening and sintering process.

Crushing produces even sized lumps and dust or fines. The fines are separated from the lumps by screening and then they are mixed with coal or tar dust and sintered. Sintering causes agglomeration of the fines and coal dust, and also causes removal of some of the volatiles. The sinter along with the unsintered ore is fed into the blast furnace as part of the charge (or burden), the remainder of the charge is principally coke—which serves as a fuel—and limestone which serves as a flux. Preparation of the iron ores in this way leads to a distinct saving in fuel and a greater rate of iron production.

In the blast furnace the charge is subjected to intense heat, the highest temperature is normally just above the pressurised air entry points (tuyères), being about 1800°C. The following are some of the reactions which take place in a blast furnace:
(1) At bottom, Carbon + Oxygen = Carbon Dioxide.
(2) At middle,
Carbon Dioxide + Carbon = Carbon Monoxide.

(3) At top,
   Iron Oxide + Carbon Monoxide = Iron + Carbon Dioxide.
From (3) the iron which is produced from this oxidation—reduction action—is a spongy mass which gradually falls to the furnace bottom, melting as it falls and taking into solution carbon, sulphur, manganese, etc. as it goes. The molten iron is collected in the hearth of the furnace, with the slag floating upon its surface. Tapping of the furnace takes place about every six hours, the slag being tapped more frequently. When tapped the molten iron runs from the furnace through sand channels into sand pig beds (hence *pig iron*) or it is led into tubs, which are used to supply the iron in the molten condition to converters or Open Hearth furnaces for steel manufacture. Pig iron is very brittle and has little use, an analysis of a sample is given below.

Combined Carbon	0.5%	Manganese	0.5%
Graphite	3.4%	Phosphorus	0.03%
Silicon	2.6%	Sulphur	0.02%

Open Hearth Process
   In this process a broad shallow furnace is used to support the charge of pig iron and scrap steel. Pig iron content of the charge may constitute 25% to 75% of the total, which may vary in mass—depending upon furnace capacity—between 10 to 50 tonnes. Scrap steel is added to reduce melting time if starting from cold.
   Fuel employed in this process may be enriched blast furnace

	Constituent	When Melted%	6 to 20 hours later Finished Steel%
Metal	Carbon	1.1	0.55
	Silicon	—	0.1
	Sulphur	0.04	0.03
	Phosphorus	0.4	0.03
	Manganese	—	0.6
Slag	Silica	19.5	—
	Iron oxide	5.6	—
	Alumina	1.2	—
	Manganous oxide	8.7	—
	Lime	50.0	—
	Magnesia	5.0	—
	Phosphorus	9.0	—
	Sulphur	0.2	—

TABLE 1.1

gas (blast furnace gas may contain 30% CO after cleaning) which melts the charge by burning across its surface. Reduction of carbon content is achieved by oxidation, this may be assisted by adding a pure iron oxide ore to the charge. Other impurities are reduced either by oxidation or absorption in the slag.

At frequent intervals samples of the charge are taken for analysis and when the desired result is obtained the furnace is tapped. Analysis of metal and slag in a basic open hearth furnace. (See Table 1.1)

Bessemer Process

In this steel making process a blast of air is blown through a charge of molten pig iron contained in a Bessemer converter.

The refining sequence can be followed by observing the appearance of the flames discharging from the converter, since the air will bring about oxidation of the carbon, etc. After pouring the charge, a mixture of iron, carbon (usually in the form of coke) and manganese is added to adjust the carbon content, etc., of the steel.

The principal difference between Open Hearth and Bessemer steels of similar carbon content is brought about by the higher nitrogen content in the Bessemer steel and is also partly due to the higher degree of oxidation with this process. This leads to a greater tendency for embrittlement of the steel due to strain-ageing in the finished product. Typical nitrogen contents are: Bessemer steel 0.015% approximately, Open Hearth steel 0.005% approximately

Modern Processes

Various modern steel making processes have been developed and put into use, some extensively. These include the L.D., Kaldo, Rotor and Spray processes.

The L.D. method of steel manufacture—the letters are the initials of twin towns in Austria, Linz and Donawitz—uses a converter similar in shape to the old Bessemer, and mounted on trunnions to enable it to be swung into a variety of desired positions.

Fig. 1.1 is a diagrammatic arrangement of the L.D. converter. Scrap metal and molten iron, from the blast furnace, would be fed into the converter which would then be turned to the vertical position after charging. A water-cooled oxygen lance would then be lowered into the converter and oxygen at a pressure of up to 11 bar approximately, would be injected at high speed into the molten iron causing oxidation. After refining, the lance is withdrawn and the converter is first tilted to the metal pouring position and finally to the slag pouring position.

If the metal is of low phosphorus content oxygen only is used, if however, it is high in phosphorus, powdered lime is injected with the oxygen and the blow is in two parts, the process being interrupted in order to remove the high phosphorus content slag.

The Kaldo and Rotor processes have not found the same popularity as the L.D., even though they are similar in that they use oxygen for refining. They both use converters which are rotated and the process is slower and more expensive.

B.I.S.R.A. (*i.e.* the British Iron and Steel Research Association) have developed a process in which the molten iron running from the blast furnace is subjected to jets of high speed oxygen that spray the metal into a container. This gives rapid

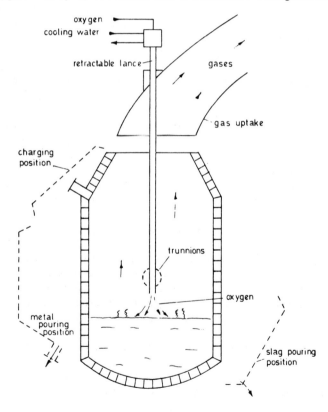

L.D. PROCESS
Fig. 1.1

refining since the oxygen and the metal intimately mix. The main advantages with this system are that the intermediate stage of carrying the molten metal from the blast furnace to steel-making plant is eliminated, and the steel production rate is increased.

Open Hearth furnaces have been modernised by the fitting of oxygen lances in their roofs. This speeds up steel production and the process is becoming more and more similar to the L.D. process. Eventually open hearth will be superceded.

Acid and Basic Processes

When pig iron is refined by oxidation a slag is produced. Depending upon the nature of the slag one of two types of processes is employed. If the slag is siliceous it is the acid process, if it is high in lime content the basic process is used. Hence the furnace lining which is in contact with the slag is made of siliceous material or basic material according to the nature of the slag. Thus avoiding the reaction:
ACID + BASE = SALT + WATER.

Low phosphorus pig irons are usually rich in silicon, this produces an *acid* slag, silica charged, which would react with a *basic* lining, hence silica bricks are used, which are *acidic*.

High phosphorus pig iron requires an excess of lime added to it in order to remove the phosphorus. The slag formed will be rich in lime which is a basic subtance that would react with a silica brick lining. Hence a basic lining must be used *e.g.* oxidised dolomite (carbonates of lime and magnesia).

Both acid and basic processes can be operated in the Open Hearth, Bessemer, L.D., and Electric Arc furnaces, etc.

CAST IRON

Cast iron is produced by remelting pig iron in a cupola (a small type of blast furnace) wherein the composition of the iron is suitably adjusted. The fluidity of this material makes it suitable for casting; other properties include; machinability, wear resistant, high compressive strength.

SIMPLE METALLURGY OF STEEL AND CAST IRON

Carbon can exist in two states, crystalline and non-crystalline. In the former state, diamond and graphite, the latter is pure carbon.

Pure iron (ferrite) is soft and ductile with considerable strength, when carbon is added to the iron it combines with it to form a hard brittle compound. This compound of iron and carbon called iron carbide or cementite (Fe_3C) lies side by side with ferrite in laminations to form a structure called pearlite, so called because of its mother of pearl appearance. As more carbon is added to the iron, more iron carbide and hence more pearlite is formed, with a reduction in the amount of free ferrite. When the carbon content is approximately 0.9% the free ferrite no longer exists and the whole structure is composed of pearlite alone. Further increases in carbon to the iron produces free iron carbide with pearlite reduction.

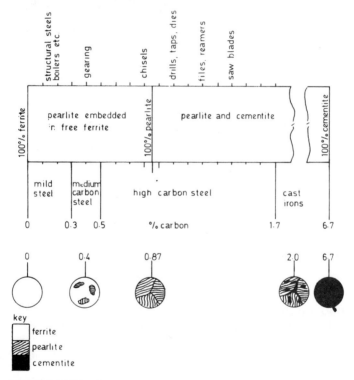

MICROSTRUCTURE VARIATION WITH INCREASING
CARBON CONTENT
Fig 1.2

The steel range terminates at approximately 2% carbon content and the cast iron range commences. Carbon content for cast iron may vary from 2% to 4%. This carbon may be present in either the form of cementite or graphite (combined or free carbon) depending upon certain factors one of which is the cooling rate. Grey or malleable cast iron is composed of pearlite and graphite and can be easily machined. Pearlite and cementite gives white cast iron which is brittle and difficult to machine and hence is not normally encountered in Marine work. The following diagram (Fig. 1.2) analyses the above in diagrammatic form.

PROPERTIES OF MATERIALS

The choice of a material for use as an engineering component depends upon the conditions under which it will be employed.

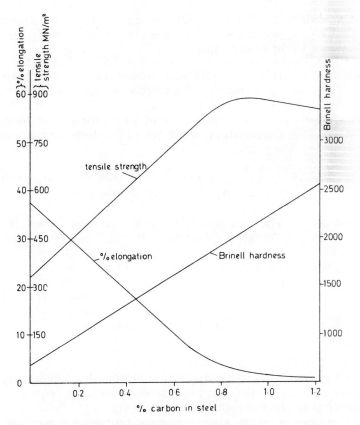

DIAGRAM SHOWING EFFECT UPON MECHANICAL PROPERTIES BY INCREASE IN CARBON CONTENT

Fig. 1.3

Conditions could be simple or complex and hence in choosing, the engineer requires some guidance. This guidance is invariably in the form of a material's mechanical properties and those of principal interest are as follows.

Ductility: Is that property of a material which enables it to be drawn easily into wire form. The percentage elongation and contraction of area, as determined from a tensile test are a good practical measure of ductility.

Brittleness: Could therefore be defined as lack of ductility.

Malleability: Is a property similar to ductility. If a material can be easily beaten or rolled into plate form it is said to be malleable.

Elasticity: If all the strain in a stressed material disappears upon removal of the stress the material is elastic.

Plasticity: If none of the strain in a stressed material disappears upon removal of the stress the material is plastic.

Hardness: A material's resistance to erosion or wear will indicate the hardness of the material.

Strength: The greater the load which can be carried the stronger the material.

Toughness: A material's ability to sustain variable load conditions without failure is a measure of a material's toughness or tenacity. Materials could be strong and yet brittle but a material which is tough has strength and resilience.

Other properties that may have to be considered depending upon the use of the material include; corrosion resistance, electrical conductivity, thermal conductivity.

Questions are often asked about the properties, advantages and disadvantages of materials for particular components, *e.g.* ship-side valve, safety valve spring etc. A method of tackling such a problem could be to (1) consider working conditions for the component *e.g.* erosive, corrosive, fatigue, stresses, thermal, shock etc. (2) shape and method of manufacture *e.g.* casting, forging, machining, drawing etc. (3) repairability, *e.g.* can it be brazed, welded, metal-locked etc. (4) cost.

Hence for a ship-side valve, sea water suction:
(1) working conditions: corrosive, erosive, little variation in temperature, relatively low stresses, possibility of impact. Material required should be hard, corrosion resistant with a relatively high impact value. (2) shape and method of manufacture: relatively intricate shape, would most probably be cast. Material could be spheroidal graphitic cast iron, cast steel or phosphor bronze. Taken in order, they are increasingly expensive, easier to repair, increasing in corrosion resistance and impact value.

TESTING OF MATERIALS

Destructive and non-destructive tests are carried out upon materials to determine their suitability for use in engineering.

Tensile Test

This test is carried out to ascertain the strength and ductility of a material.

A simple tensile testing machine is shown in Fig. 1.4. The specimen is held in self aligning grips and is subjected to a gradually increasing tensile load, the beam must be maintained in a floating condition by movement of the jockey weight as the oil pressure to the straining cylinder is increased. An extensometer fitted across the specimen gives extension readings as the load is applied. Modern, compact, tensile testing machines using mainly hydraulic means are more complex and difficult to reproduce for examination purposes. For this reason the authors have retained this simple machine. With values of load with respect to extension the nominal stress-strain curve can be drawn, the actual stress-strain curve is drawn for comparison purposes on the same diagram. The difference is due to the fact that the values of stress in the nominal diagram are calculated using the original cross sectional area of the specimen when in actual fact the cross sectioned area of the specimen is reducing as the specimen is extended.

Specimens may be round or rectangular in cross section, the gauge length being formed by reducing the cross section of the centre portion of the specimen. This reduction must be gradual as rapid changes of section can affect the result. The relation, gauge length to cross sectional area of specimen, is important, otherwise varying values of percentage elongation may result for the same material. A formula attempting to standardise this relationship in the U.K. is;

gauge length = 4√ Cross sectional area.

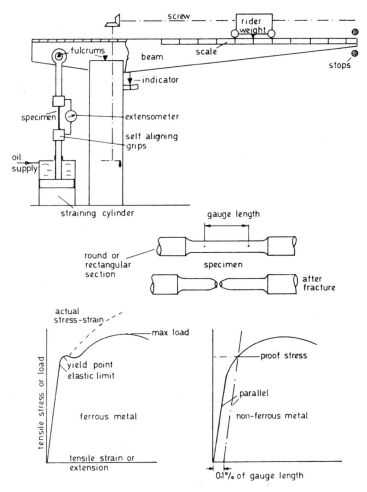

NOMINAL STRESS-STRAIN DIAGRAM
Fig. 1.4

In the tensile test the specimen is broken, after breakage the broken ends are fitted together and the distance between reference marks and the smallest diameter are measured. Maximum load and load at yield are also determined. From these foregoing values the following are calculated:

$$\text{Percentage elongation} = \frac{\text{Final length} - \text{original length}}{\text{Original length}} \times 100$$

$$\text{Percentage contraction of area} = \frac{\text{Original area} - \text{final area}}{\text{Original area}} \times 100$$

$$\text{Ultimate tensile stress (u.t.s.)} = \frac{\text{Maximum load}}{\text{Original cross-sectional area}}$$

$$\text{Yield stress} = \frac{\text{Yield load}}{\text{Original cross-sectional area}}$$

Percentage elongation and percentage contraction of area are measures of a materials ductility. Ultimate tensile stress is a measure of a materials strength. Yield stress gives indication of departure from an approximate linear relationship between stress and strain. It is the stress which will produce some permanent set in the material *e.g.* when tubes are expanded.

Factor of Safety—this is defined as the ratio of working stress allowed to ultimate stress, hence:

$$\text{Factor of Safety} = \frac{\text{u.t.s.}}{\text{Working stress}} \quad \text{and is always greater than unity.}$$

Components which are subjected to fatigue and corrosion fatigue conditions are given higher factors of safety than those subjected to static loading *e.g.* tail end shafts 12 or above, boiler stays about 7 to 8.

Hooke's law states that stress is proportional to strain if the material is stressed within the elastic limit.

$$\therefore \text{Stress } \alpha \text{ Strain}$$
$$\text{or Stress} = \text{Strain} \times \text{a constant}$$

The constant is given the symbol E and is called Young's modulus or the modulus of elasticity.

$$\therefore \frac{\text{Stress}}{\text{Strain}} = E$$

The modulus of elasticity of a material is an indication of stiffness and resilience. As E increases then stiffness increases. By way of a simple explanation, we could consider two identical simply-supported beams, one of cast iron, the other of steel, each carrying a central load W. The deflection of a beam loaded in this way is given by

$$\delta = \frac{WL^3}{48EI}.$$

Where δ = deflection of beam under the load W.
Where L = length of the beam.
Where I = second moment of area of section.
Where E = modulus of elasticity of the material.

Since the beams are identical $\delta \propto \dfrac{1}{E}$

i.e. $\delta \times E$ = a constant.

E for steel is greater than E for cast iron, hence, δ for steel is less than δ for cast iron. Hence, steel is stiffer than cast iron. For this reason as well as strength, less steel is required in a structure than cast iron.

0.1% Proof Stress

For non-ferrous metals and some alloy steels no definite yield point is exhibited in a tensile test (see Fig. 1.4). In this case the 0.1% proof stress may be used for purposes of comparison between metals. With reference to the graph (Fig. 1.4) a point A is determined and a line AB is drawn parallel to the lower portion of the curve. Where this line AB cuts the curve the stress at that point is read from the graph. This stress is called the 0.1% proof stress. *i.e.* the stress required to give a permanent set of approximately 0.1% of the gauge length.

Hardness Test

The hardness of a material determines basically its resistance to wear. There are numerous tests that can be employed to determine hardness, only two will be described.

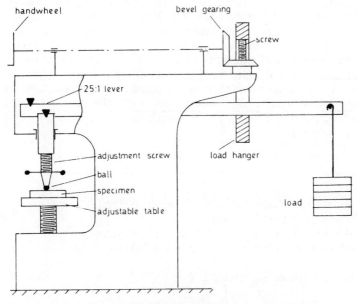

BRINELL HARDNESS TESTING MACHINE
Fig. 1.5

Brinell Test: This test consists of indenting the surface of a metal by means of a 10 mm diameter hardened steel ball under load. The Brinell number is a function of the load applied and the area of indentation, thus:

$$\text{Brinell number} = \frac{\text{Load in newtons}}{\text{Area of indentation in mm}^2}$$

Only the diameter of the indentation is required and this is determined by a low powered microscope with a sliding scale. Tables have been compiled to avoid unnecessary calculations in ascertaining the hardness numeral. Loads normally employed are 30,000 N for steels, 10,000 N for copper and brasses and 5,000 N for aluminium. Duration of application of the load is usually 15 seconds. (Industry is still using the old system of calculating Brinell numbers, *i.e.* load in kilogrammes/area of indentation in mm². Hence, their Brinell numbers will be less by a factor of 10.)

Vickers Pyramid Test: The surface of the metal under test is indented by a diamond square-based pyramid and the Vickers pyramid number (VPN) is determined by dividing the area of indentation into the load applied. This test is also suitable for extremely hard materials, giving accurate results, whereas the Brinell test's reliability is doubtful above 6,000 Brinell. Table 1.2 gives some typical values.

Material	Brinell Number	V.P.N.
Brass	600	600
Mild steel	1300	1300
Grey cast iron	2000	2050
White cast iron	4150	4370

TABLE 1.2

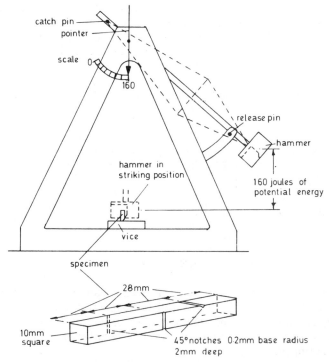

IZOD IMPACT MACHINE

Fig. 1.6

Impact Test

This test is useful for determining differences in materials due to heat treatment, working and casting, that would not be otherwise indicated by the tensile test. It does not give accurately a measure of a material's resistance to impact.

A notched test piece is gripped in a vice and is fractured by means of a swinging hammer (Fig. 1.6). After the specimen is fractured the hammer arm engages with a pointer which is carried for the remainder of the swing of the arm. At the completion of the hammer's swing the pointer is disengaged and the reading indicated by the pointer is the energy given up by the hammer in fracturing the specimen. Usually three such tests are carried out upon the same specimen and the average energy to fracture is the impact value.

By notching the specimen the impact value is to some extend a measure of the material's notch brittleness or ability to retard crack propagation. From the practical standpoint this may be clarified to some extent: Where changes of section occur in loaded materials (*e.g.* shafts, bolts, etc.) stress concentration occurs and the foregoing test measures the materials resistance to failure at these discontinuities.

Table 1.3 gives some typical IZOD values for different materials, considerable variation in IZOD values can be achieved by suitable treatment and alteration in composition.

Material	IZOD Value (Joules)	Uses
18/8 Stainless steel	136	Turbine blades.
0.15C, 0.5 Mn steel	54	General purpose mild steel.
S.G. iron (annealed)	16	Camshafts, gear wheels.
Grey cast iron	up to 3	Cylinders, valves.

TABLE 1.3

Charpy V Notch, using a different hammer and vice arrangement, the IZOD machine can be converted into a Charpy V Notch machine where the specimen is placed horizontally upon two parallel stops between which the hammer swings and breaks the specimen.

The advantage to be gained by this method is that the specimens can be very quickly set up in the machine. Hence impact values for specimens at different temperatures can be accurately obtained.

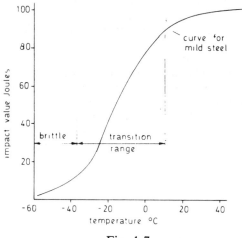

Fig. 1.7

Brittle Fracture, is a fracture in which there is no evidence of plastic deformation prior to failure. It can occur in steels whose temperature has been lowered, the steel undergoes a transition. Fig. 1.7 illustrates the considerable drop in impact value for mild steel as it passes through the transition range of temperature.

Factors which affect the transition temperature are:
1. Elements; carbon, silicon, phosphorus and sulphur raise the temperature. Nickel and manganese lower the temperature.
2. Grain size; the smaller the grain size the lower the transition temperature, hence grain refinement can be beneficial.
3. Work hardening; this appears to increase transition temperature.
4. Notches; possibly occurring during assembly *e.g.* weld defects or machine marks. Notches can increase tendency to brittle fracture.

Obviously transition temperature is an important factor in the choice of materials for the carriage of low temperature cargoes *e.g.* LPG and LNG carriers. A typical stainless steel used for containment would be, 18.5% chrome, 10.7% nickel, 0.03% carbon, 0.75% silicon, 1.2% manganese U.T.S. 560 MN/m², 50% elongation, Charpy V Notch 102 Joules at $-196°C$.

Creep test

Creep may be defined as the slow plastic deformation of a material under a constant stress. A material may fail under creep conditions at a much lower stress and elongation than would be ascertained in a straight tensile test. Hence tests have to be conducted to determine a limiting creep stress with small creep rate.

The creep test consists of applying a fixed load to a test piece which is maintained at a uniform temperature. The test is a long term one and a number of specimens of the same material are subjected to this test simultaneously, all at different stresses but at the same temperature. In this way the creep rate and limiting stress can be determined, these values depend upon how the material is going to be employed. Some permissible values are given in Table 1.4. Creep test results, materials all at working temperature:

Component	Creep rate m/mh	Time of test in hours	Maximum strain
Turbine discs	10^{-9}	10^5	0.0001
Steam pipes, boiler tubes	10^{-7}	10^5	0.003
Superheater tubes	10^{-6}	20×10^3	0.02

TABLE 1.4

Fig. 1.8 shows a typical creep curve for a metal. To obtain the minimum uniform creep rate V (*i.e.* the slope of the line AB) it is

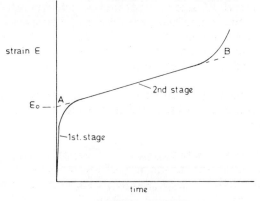

CREEP CURVE
Fig. 1.8

necessary that the test be conducted long enough, in order to reach the second stage of creep. Hence, for a time t greater than that covered by the test, the total creep or plastic strain is given approximately by $\epsilon_p = \epsilon_0 + Vt$.

Where ϵ_p is the plastic strain which would be expected at the end of the first stage, this is important to the designer when considering tolerances, t is the time usually in hours.

Fine grained materials creep more readily than coarse grained because of their greater amorphous metal content, *i.e.* the structureless metal between the grains.

Fatigue Test

Fatigue may be defined as the failure of a material due to a repeatedly applied stress. The stress required to bring about such a failure may be much less than that required to break the material in a tensile test.

In this test a machine that can give a great number of stress reversals in a short duration of time is employed. The test is carried out on similar specimens of the same material at

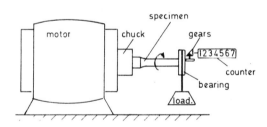

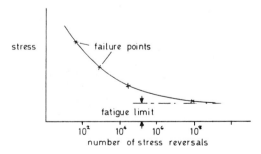

FATIGUE TESTING
Fig. 1.9

different stresses and the number of stress reversals to fracture is noted for each stress, normally 20 million reversals of stress would not be exceeded if failure did not occur. The results are plotted on a graph (Fig. 1.9) from which a limiting fatigue stress (fatigue limit) can be ascertained. It is usual, since the number of stress reversals will be high, to condense the graph by taking logarithms of the stress and number of reversals to give a, log S—log N curve.

Materials have varying fatigue limits. The limit can be increased by suitable treatment, use of alloy steels, etc. It can be reduced due to 'stress raisers'; changes of section, oil holes, fillets, etc. Environment alters the limit, if it is corrosive the limit could be reduced by about a third.

Fig. 1.10 shows the different types of stress that a component could be subjected to in practice:

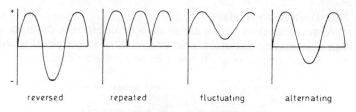

reversed   repeated   fluctuating   alternating

TYPES OF STRESS REVERSAL
Fig. 1.10

Reversed stress: stress range is symmetrical about zero stress line, *e.g.* propeller or centrifugal pump shaft.

Repeated Stress: component is stressed and then completely unloaded. *e.g.* gear teeth, cam.

Fluctuating Stress: component is stressed, either compressive or tensile, but stress range does not pass through zero. *e.g.* tie bolts, bottom end bolts.

Alternating Stress: stress range passes through zero stress line hence it changes from tensile to compressive, but is asymmetrical about the zero stress line. *e.g.* piston rod in double acting engine or pump, crank web in a diesel engine.

What is of greatest importance is undoubtedly the *range* of stress, this governs the life of the component. It has been found that if the range of stress passes through zero this can have the effect of lowering the life span for the same stress range.

A fatigue failure is normally easily recognisable, one portion of the fracture will be discoloured and relatively smooth, whilst the other portion will be clean and also fibrous or crystalline depending upon the material. The former part of the fracture contains the origin point of failure, the latter part of the fracture is caused by sudden failing of the material.

Bend Test

This is a test which is carried out on boiler plate materials and consists of bending a straight specimen of plate through 180 degrees around a former. For the test to be satisfactory, no cracks should occur at the outer surface of the plate (see Fig. 1.11).

Non-Destructive Tests

Apart from tests which are used to determine the dimensions and physical or mechanical characteristics of materials, the main non-destructive tests are those used to locate defects.

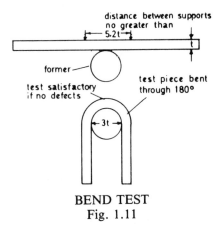

BEND TEST
Fig. 1.11

Methods of Detecting Surface Defects e.g. Cracks.

1. A visual examination, including the use of a microscope or hand lens.

2. Penetrant testing.

Penetrant liquids must have a low viscosity in order to find their way into fine cracks.

a) Oil and whitewash. This is one of the oldest and simplest of

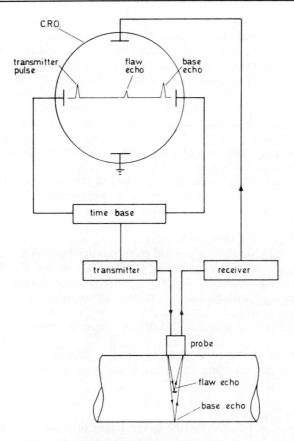

ULTRASONIC TESTING
Fig. 1.12

the penetrant tests, the oil is first applied to the metal and then the metal surface is wiped clean, whitewash or chalk is then painted or dusted over the metal and oil remaining in the cracks will discolour the whitewash or chalk. Paraffin oil is frequently used because of its low viscosity and the component may be alternately stressed and unloaded to assist in bringing oil to the surface.

b) Fluorescent penetrant wiped or sprayed over the metal surface which is then washed, dried, and inspected under near ultra violet light. A developer may be used to act as a blotter to cause re-emergence of the penetrant, so that it can be iridesced at the surface.

c) Red dye penetrant. This is probably the most popular of the penetrant methods because of its convenience. Three aerosol cans are supplied; red dye penetrant, cleaner and developer.

Components must be thoroughly cleaned and degreased, then the red dye is applied by spraying on. Excess dye is removed by hosing with a jet of water, or cleaner is sprayed on and then wiped off with a dry cloth. Finally, a thin coating of white developer is applied and when it is dry the component is examined for defects. The red dye stains the developer almost immediately but further indication of defects can develop after thirty minutes or more.

Precautions that must be observed are (1) use protective gloves (2) use aerosols in well ventilated places (3) no naked lights, the developer is inflammable.

3. Magnetic Crack Detection.

A magnetic field is applied to the component under test, and wherever there is a surface or a subsurface defect, flux leakage will occur. Metallic powder applied to the surface of the component will accumulate at the defect to try and establish continuity of the magnetic field. This will also occur if there is a non-metallic in the metal at or just below the surface.

Methods of Detecting Defects Within a Material.
1. Suspend the component and strike it sharply with a hammer to hear if it rings true.

2. Radiography.

This can be used for the examination of welds, forgings and castings. X-rays or γ-rays, which can penetrate up to 180 mm of steel, pass through the metal and impinge upon a photographic plate or paper to give a negative. Due to the variation in density of the metal, the absorption of the rays is non-uniform hence giving a shadow picture of the material—it is like shining light through a semi-transparent material. X-rays produced in a Coolidge tube give quick results and a clear negative. Radioactive material (*e.g.* Cobalt 60) which emits γ-rays does not give a picture as rapidly as the X-rays, however, to compensate for its slowness, it is a compact and simple system.

3. Ultrasonics.

With ultrasonics we do not have the limitations of metal thickness to consider as we have with radiographic testing, high frequency sound waves reflect from internal interfaces of good metal and defects, these reflected sound waves are then displayed onto the screen of a cathode ray oscilloscope. Size and position of a defect can be ascertained, it can also be used for checking material thicknesses *e.g.* a probe could be passed down a heat exchanger tube (see Fig. 1.12).

A portable, battery operated, hand held, cylindrical detector with cable to a set of headphones can be used to detect leakages *e.g.* vacuum, air lines, superheated steam, air conditioning etc. A recent application of ultrasonics is testing condensers.

A generator placed inside the condenser 'floods' it with ultrasound. By using a head set and probe, tube leakage can be homed in on. Where a pinhole exists sound 'leaks' through and where a tube is thinned it vibrates like a diaphragm transmitting the sound through the tube wall.

TREATMENT OF METALS

Hardening and Tempering

In the process of converting ice into dry saturated steam by supplying heat, two distinct changes of state occur, from solid to liquid and from liquid to dry saturated vapour. When iron is heated up to its melting point two similar arrests occur wherein there is heat absorption. The temperatures at which these arrests occur are called *'critical points'* and these are of great importance. At these critical points considerable changes of internal structure takes place and therefore different physical properties are available if these structures could be trapped.

With steels, these changes in the internal structure of the iron at the critical points affect also the carbon which is present in the form of iron carbide. At the upper critical temperature range 720 to 900°C in the solid state (the range is due to the variable carbon content) the iron structure formed has the ability to dissolve the iron carbide into solution forming a new structure. If at this stage the steel is suddenly quenched in water the iron carbide will remain in solution in the iron, but the iron's structure will have reverted to its original form. This completely new structure which has been brought about by heating and then rapidly cooling the steel is called 'Martensite', a hard needle like structure consisting of iron supersaturated with carbon, and is basically responsible for hardening steels.

If a steel of approximately 0.4% carbon content is heated to a temperature above its upper critical (about 800°C see Fig. 1.13) and was then suddenly cooled by quenching, its Brinell hardness numeral would be increased from approximately 2,000 to 6,000. In this condition the steel would be fully hardened *i.e.* fully martensitic. Choosing a temperature lower than the above but not lower than 720°C (lower critical) and then quenching, will produce a partly hardened steel having a Brinell numeral between 2,000 to 6,000.

Hardening material in this way produces internal stresses and also makes the material brittle. To relieve the stresses and restore ductility without loss of hardness or toughness, the material is tempered.

Tempering consists of heating the material to about 250°C, retaining this temperature for a duration of time (this depends upon the mass and the degree of toughness required) and then quenching or cooling in air.

The combination of hardening and tempering is greatly employed with steels and alloy steels, a wide range of properties is available thereby. Components such as drills, chisels, punches, saws, reamers and other tools are invariably subjected to the above process.

Straight carbon steels whose carbon content is below 0.2% are *not* usually subjected to hardening and tempering processes. The reason could be attributed to the smaller quantity of Martensite which would be produced.

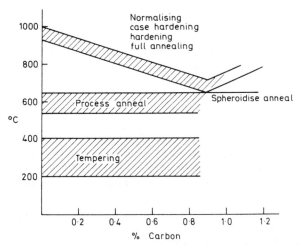

TREATMENT DIAGRAM
Fig. 1.13

Annealing and Normalising

The object of annealing is either to grain refine, induce ductility, stress relieve or a combination of these. Castings, forgings, sheets, wires, and welded materials can be subjected to an annealing process. This process consists of heating the material to a pre-determined temperature, possibly allowing it to soak at this temperature, then cooling it in the furnace at a controlled rate. For full annealing and normalising, the temperature for carbon steels is usually 30° to 40°C above the upper critical temperature. Essentially, the difference between full annealing and normalising is that in the case of the annealing process the material is cooled slowly in the furnace whereas for normalising the material is cooled in still air out of the furnace.

These processes of full annealing and normalising are mainly used on castings since they will usually have a variation in size and shape of grain. The casting is heated to about 40°C above the upper critical temperature and held at this temperature until it is uniform in temperature throughout. Then it is cooled. This produces a uniform grained structure (re-crystallisation temperature about 500°C) with increased ductility, *e.g.* a 0.5% carbon steel casting could have its percentage elongation increased from 18% in the as cast condition to about 35% in the annealed condition.

The more rapid cooling of the casting that occurs with normalising gives a better, closer grained, surface finish.

If steel has been cold worked in manufacture the ferrite grains and the pearlite are distorted. Recrystallisation of the ferrite and increased ductility is brought about by employing an annealing procedure known as process annealing, this is similar in most respects to full annealing except that it is conducted at a temperature between 500 to 650°C which is below the lower critical temperature.

Blackheart Process

For high carbon castings, *e.g.* 2.5% C content, the Blackheart process may be used to produce a softer, ductile and more easily machined component that would be similar mechanically to cast steel.

The castings are placed in air-tight (to prevent burning), heat-resistant metal containers and heated up to 1000°C. They are kept at this annealing temperature for up to 160 h or so depending upon material analysis. The prolonged heating causes breakdown of the cementite to give finely divided 'temper carbon' in a matrix of ferrite, which has a black appearance—hence 'Blackheart'.

Work Hardening

If a metal is cold worked it can develop a surface hardness *e.g.* shot peening is a method of producing surface hardness, this consists of blasting the surface of a component with many hardened steel balls. Expansion and contraction of copper piping, used for steam, etc., can lead to a hardness and brittleness that has to be removed by annealing. Lifting tackle such as shackles, chains, etc., can develop surface hardness and brittleness due to cold working, hence they have to be annealed at regular intervals (as laid down by the factory act).

What actually happens is that the work forces cause dislocations to be set up in the crystal latticework (*i.e.* the geometric arrangement of the metal atoms) of the metal and in order to remove these dislocations considerable force is required, this considerable force is the evidence of work hardening, since it really is the force necessary to dent the surface of the material.

Case Hardening

This is sometimes referred to as 'pack carburising'. The steel component to be case hardened is packed in a box which may be made of fire clay, cast iron, or a heat resisting nickel-iron alloy. Carbon rich material such as charred leather, charcoal, crushed bone and horn or other material containing carbon is the packing medium, which would encompass the component. The box is then placed in a furnace and raised in temperature to above 900°C. The surface of the component will then absorb carbon forming an extremely hard case. Depth of case depends upon two main factors, the length of time and the carbonaceous material employed. Actual case depth with this process may vary between 0.8 mm to 3 mm requiring between two to twelve hours to achieve, for these limits.

Gudgeon pins and other bearing pins are examples of components which may be case hardened. They would possess a hard outer case with good wearing resistance and a relatively soft inner core which retains the ductility and toughness necessary for such components.

Nitriding

In this process the steel component is placed in a gas tight container through which ammonia gas (NH_3) is circulated.

Container and component are then raised in temperature to approximately 500°C. Nitrides are then formed in the material, at, and close to the surface, which increases the surface hardness to a marked degree. A nitride is an element combined with nitrogen, usually nitride promoting elements are present in the steel such as aluminium, chromium, vanadium or molybdenum. Actual depth of hard case is not so great with this process as compared to case hardening, *viz* 0.0125 to 0.05 mm in five to 24 hours for nitriding, compared with 0.8 mm to 3 mm in two to 12 hours for case hardening. An essential difference from case hardening is the more gradual change-over from hardened to unhardened part, thus reducing the risk of exfoliation.

Flame Hardening

This process is used for increasing the surface hardness of cast irons, steels, alloy cast irons and alloy steels. With the increase in surface hardness there is a high improvement in wear resistance.

To flame harden a component (*e.g.* gear teeth), an oxy-acetylene torch is used to preheat the surface of the metal to a temperature between 800° to 850°C. A water spray closely following the oxy-acetylene torch quenches the material thereby inducing hardness. Care in operation of this process is essential, overheating must be prevented.

Induction Hardening

This is a method of surface hardening steels by the use of electrical energy.

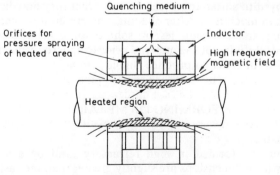

INDUCTION HARDENING
Fig. 1.14

In Fig. 1.14, a high frequency a.c. electromagnetic field is shown heating up the surface of the components to be hardened by hysteresis and eddy currents, after heating the surface is quenched.

Hysteresis loss is heat energy loss caused by the steel molecules behaving like tiny magnets which are reluctant to change their direction or position with each alteration of electrical supply thus creating molecular friction.

Eddy currents are secondary electrical currents caused by the presence of nearby primary current. The resistance of the steel molecules to the passage of eddy currents generates heat.

Important points regarding induction hardening are:

1. Time of application of electrical power, governs depth to which heat will penetrate.
2. Reduces time of surface hardening to seconds—*i.e.* the process is *very fast.*
3. Rapid heating and cooling produces a fine grained martensitic structure.
4. Due to speed of operation no grain growth occurs or surface decarburization.
5. No sharp division between case and core.

Components that are induction hardened include such as gudgeon pins and gear pinions.

Spheroidising Anneal

Spheroidising of steels is accomplished by heating the steel to a temperature between 650° to 700°C (below lower critical line) when the pearlitic cementite will become globular. This process is employed to soften tool steels in order that they may be easily drawn and machined. After shaping, the material is heated for hardening and the globules or spheres of cementite will be dissolved. Refining of the material prior to spheroidising may be resorted to in order to produce smaller *globules.*

FORMING OF METALS

Sand Casting

A mould is formed in high refractory sand by a wooden pattern whose dimensions are slightly greater than the casting to allow for shrinkage. To ensure a sound casting the risers have to be carefully positioned to give good ventilation.

Defects that can occur in castings are:

1. Shrinkage cavities.
2. Blowholes caused by ineffective venting and dissolved gases in steels which have not been killed (*i.e.* de-oxidised).
3. Oxidation.
4. Impurities.

Sand casting is slow and expensive and would only be used if the metal and casting shape are unsuitable for other techniques.

Die Casting
Used mainly for aluminium and zinc base alloys. The molten metal is either poured in under gravity or high pressure—hence gravity and pressure die casting. This process gives a fine-grained uniform structure and the mould can be used over again, whereas for sand casting it has to be removed.

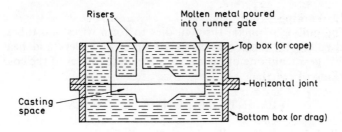

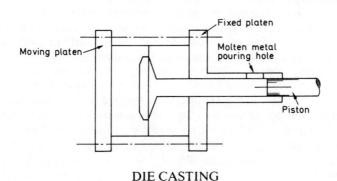

DIE CASTING
FIG. 1.15

Centrifugal Casting

A metal cylindrical mould is rotated at speed about its axis and molten metal is poured in. Centrifugal action throws the molten metal radially out onto the inner surface of the mould to produce a uniform close-grained—due to chilling effect of mould—non-porous cylinder.

Such a casting process can be used for piston rings, the rings being cut from the machined cast cylinder, or for producing cast iron pipes.

Forging

This is the working and shaping of hot metal by mechanical or hand processes with tools called swages. During the process the coarse, as cast, structure of the metal is broken down to form a finer-grained structure with the impurities distributed into a fibrous form.

Items that are forged include connecting rods, crankshafts, upset ends of shafts and boiler stays, etc.

Cold Working

The pulling of metal through dies to form wires and tubes, cold rolling of plate, expansion of tubes in boilers and heat exchangers, caulking of plates, etc., are all examples of the cold working of metals.

ELEMENTS IN IRONS AND STEELS

The following normally occur naturally in the iron ore from which the steels, etc., are originally made.

Manganese

This element which is found in most commercial irons and steels is used as an alloying agent to produce steels with improved mechanical properties. Manganese is partly dissolved in the iron and partly combines with the cementite. Providing the manganese content is high enough, martensite, with its attendant hardness and brittleness will be formed in the steel even if the steel is slow cooled. For this reason the manganese content will not normally exceed 1.8% although one heat treated steel known as Hadfields manganese steel, contains 12 to 14% manganese.

Silicon

Tends to prevent the formation of cementite and produce

graphite. In steels it increases strength and hardness but reduces ductility. As a graphitiser it is useful in cast irons, tending to prevent the formation of white cast iron and form instead graphitic cast iron. The quantity of silicon in an iron or steel may vary between 0.5 to 3.5%.

Sulphur

Reduces strength and increases brittleness. It can cause 'hot shortness', that is, liable to crack when hot. Normally the sulphur content in a finished iron or steel does not exceed 0.1%.

Phosphorus

This also causes brittleness and reduction of strength but it increases fluidity and reduces shrinkage which are important factors when casting steels and irons. It can produce 'cold shortness', that is, liable to crack when cold worked. Normally the phosphorus content does not exceed 0.3%.

EFFECT OF ALLOYING ELEMENTS

Nickel

This element increases strength and erosion resistance. It does not greatly reduce ductility until 8% nickel is reached. A low to medium carbon steel with 3 to 3.75% nickel content is used for connecting rods, piston and pump rods, etc. Nickel forms a finer grained material.

Chromium

Increases grain size, induces hardness, improves resistance to erosion and corrosion. This element is frequently combined with nickel to produce stainless steels and irons which are used for such items as turbine blades, pump rods and valves.

Molybdenum

Used to increase strength, especially employed for increasing strength at high temperatures which is one reason why it is used for superheater tubes, turbine rotors, etc., another reason for its use is its action in removing the possibility of embrittlement occurring in those steels which are prone to embrittlement, *e.g.* Nickel-Chrome steels.

Vanadium

Increases strength and fatigue resistance. Used in conjunction with molybdenum for boiler tube materials.

Other alloying elements include; Tungsten which induces self hardening properties and is used for heat resisting steels, *e.g.* machine tools, copper which improves corrosion resistance, cobalt which is used as a bond in stellite alloys. Manganese and silicon are also employed as alloying agents, these have been previously dealt with.

NON-FERROUS METALS

Copper
This material is used extensively for electrical fittings as it has good electrical conduction properties. It is also used as the basis for many alloys and as an alloying agent. If copper is cold worked its strength and brittleness will increase, but, some restoration of ductility can be achieved by annealing. Hence, in this way, a wide range of physical properties are available.

Brass
Brasses are basically an alloy of copper and zinc, usually with a predominance of copper. When brasses are in contact with corrosive conditions, *e.g.* atmospheric or in salt water, they may dezincify (removal of the zinc phase) leaving a porous spongy mass of copper. To prevent dezincification, an inhibitor is added to the brass. One such inhibitor is arsenic of which a small proportion only is employed. Brasses have numerous uses, decorative and purposeful. Marine uses include: valves, bearings, condenser tubes, etc. Alloying elements such as tin, aluminium and nickel are frequently employed to improve brasses. With these elements the strength and erosion resistance of brasses can be greatly improved.

Bronze
Bronze is basically an alloy of copper and tin, but, the term bronze is frequently used today to indicate a superior type of brass. It resists the corrosive effect of sea water, has considerable resistance to wear, and is used for these reasons for many marine fittings. Wth the addition of other alloying elements its range of uses becomes extensive. Manganese in small amounts increases erosive resistance, forms manganese bronze (propeller brass). Phosphorus, used as a deoxidiser prevents formation of troublesome tin oxides, improves strength and resistance to corrosion, provides an excellent hard glassy bearing surface. Aluminium and zinc give aluminium bronze

and gunmetal respectively, which are suitable materials for casting.

Aluminium

This material is progressively supplanting other materials in use for specific items in the marine industry. It resists atmospheric corrosion and its specific gravity is about one third that of steel. In the pure state its strength is low, but, by alloying and by mechanical and thermal treatment its strength can be raised to equal and even surpass that of steel without great loss of ductility. In this form it is used extensively for structural work.

Copper-Nickel Alloys

Cupro-nickel alloys have considerable strength, resistance to corrosion and erosion. The 80/20 or 70/30 cupro-nickels are used for condenser tubes as they strongly resist the attack of estuarine and sea waters. A well known alloy, monel metal composed of approximately two-thirds nickel, remainder principally copper, is used for turbine blades, pump rods and impellers, scavenge valves and superheated steam valves. Monel metal retains its high strength at high temperatures. With the addition of 2 to 4% aluminium, forming a material known as 'K' monel, it can be temper-hardened thus its strength can be increased still further without detracting from its other properties.

White Metals

White metal bearing alloys may be either tin or lead base materials containing antimony and copper or antimony alone. Tin base white metals are sometimes referred to as 'Babbitt metals', after Sir Isaac Babbitt, who patented them originally, these metals are the most commonly used of the white metals because of (1) their good bearing surface (2) uniform micro-structure.

The use of copper in a white metal ensures uniform distribution of the hard cuboids of the intermetalic compound of antimony and tin within the soft tin rich matrix. Coefficient of friction for a white metalled bearing, when lubricated is approximately 0.002. The melting point of white metal varies with composition but is approximately between 200°C to 300°C. See Table 1.5.

Composition %				Uses
Tin	Antimony	Copper	Lead	
86	8.5	5.5	—	Heavy duty, high temperatures.
78	13	6	3	Normal loading.
—	20	—	80	Normal to low load bearings (Magnolia metal relatively cheap).

TABLE 1.5

Titanium

Ideal where resistance to erosion and impingement-corrosion are the more important requirements. It is virtually completely resistant to corrosion in sea water, only under exceptional conditions of erosion would the protective oxide film be damaged. When alloyed with about 2% copper a moderate increase in strength results. Used in heat exchangers, usually of the plate variety.

NON-METALLIC MATERIALS

Plastics (polymers)

Most are organic materials, synthetic and natural, consisting of combinations of carbon with hydrogen, oxygen, nitrogen and other substances. Dyes and fillers can be added to give colour and alter properties. Some of the fillers used are; glass fibre for strength, asbestos fibre to improve heat resistance, mica for reducing electrical conductivity. Polymers can be plastic, rigid or semi-rigid, or elastomeric (rubber like).

Some of their general properties are (1) good thermal resistance. Most can be blown to give cellular materials of low density which is useful for thermal insulation, also stops the spread of fire (2) good electrical resistance (3) unsuitable for high temperatures. Since they are hydro-carbon they will contribute to fires producing smoke and possibly toxic fumes (P.V.C. releases hydrogen chloride gas) (4) good corrosion resistance.

Some polymers and other materials in common use are:

Nitrile. Used in place of rubber, unaffected by water, paraffin, gas oil and mineral lubricating oil. Can be used for tyres in hydraulic systems (see Pilgrim nut) anti-vibration mountings, jointing etc.

P.T.F.E. Unaffected by dry steam, water, oils and a considerable range of chemicals. Low friction, used for water lubricated bearings, gland rings, jointing tape etc.

Expoxy Resin. Pourable epoxy-resin which cures at room temperature is unaffected by sea water and oils etc. It is extremely tough, solid and durable and is used for chocking engines, winches, pumps etc. Hence no machining of base plates or foundations, simplified alignment retention, reduced time and cost.

Rubber. Attacked by oils and steam, unaffected by water. Used for fresh and salt water pipe joints, water lubricated bearings. In a highly vulcanised state it is called ebonite, which is used for bucket rings in feed pumps.

Asbestos. Unaffected by steam, petrol, paraffin, fuel oils and lubricants. In the presence of water it needs a waterproof binder. Near universal jointing and packing material. Safety hazard (health).

Cotton. Unaffected by water and oils, used as a framework to give strength to rubber and produce rubber insertion jointing, also used in packing.

Silicon Nitride. Used as seals in place of bronze wear rings in sea water pumps. U.T.S. 700 MN/m^2, greatly resistant to erosion, inert chemically and galvanically (latter is important in salt water pumps).

No attempt has been made to cover all the materials used in Marine Engineering as the range is wide and complex, but materials for components discussed elsewhere in the book, not covered in this chapter, will be dealt with as necessary at the appropriate point.

WELDING

Welding processes may be divided into two main groups, pressure welding and non pressure welding.

Any welding process which requires pressure is generally referred to as a forge welding process and these processes do not usually require a filler metal or flux. The parts to be welded however, should be clean and free from grease, etc.

The oldest form of forge welding is blacksmiths forge welding. The process consists of heating the metal components to be welded in a blacksmiths fire until the parts to be united are plastic, then the parts of the components are removed from the

Material	Composition%	Treatment	U.T.S. MN/m²	0.1% P.S. MN/m²	Fatigue Limit MN/m²	% Elongation	Modulus of Elasticity kN/mm²	Brinell Hardness Numeral	Uses
Admiralty Brass	70 Cu 29 Zn 1 Sn	Annealed	340	75		70		650	Condenser tubes and tube plates. Arsenic added to prevent dezincification.
		Cold Worked	590	430		10		1750	
Aluminium	Nearly Pure	Annealed	59		31	60	14	150	As a base metal for many aluminium alloys. Electrical fittings.
Aluminium Brass	76 Cu 22 Zn 2 Al	Annealed	370	105		70	21	650	Condenser tubes and tube plates. Improved resistance to erosion with addition of aluminium.
		Cold Worked	610	460		8		1750	
Brass	70 Cu 30 Zn	Annealed	320	85	114	67.5	20	620	General purpose brass. Bearing liners, etc.
		Cold Worked	460	380	152	19.5			
Cast Iron (Grey)	3.25 C. 2.25 Si 0.65 Mn	Sand Cast	310		138	0	23	2500	Cylinder heads, pistons, etc.
Copper	Nearly Pure	Annealed	217	46	66	60	21	420	As a base metal for many alloys. Electrical fittings.
Cupro-Nickel	70 Cu 30 Ni	Annealed	355	105		45		800	Cooler and condenser tubes where good resistance to erosion and corrosion is required.
		Cold Worked	650	540		5		1750	
Gun Metal	88 Cu 10 Sn 2 Zn	Sand Cast	295	124		16	18.6	850	Pump liners, valves. (Good casting properties).
Monel Metal	68 Ni 29 Cu Fe and Mn	Annealed	540	210		45	36	1200	Pump impellers, valves, turbine blading scavenge pump valves.
		Cold Worked	730	570		20		2200	
Muntz Metal	60 Cu 40 Zn	Hot Rolled	370	105		40	20	750	General purpose brass.
Phosphor Bronze	95 Cu 5 Sn approx. Small amount of P.	Cold Worked	710	640	186	5.5		1880	An excellent bearing alloy. Develops hard glassy surface in use.
Stainless Iron	0.08 C 13.5 Cr 0.15 Ni	Annealed	480			37		1400	Turbine nozzles and blading.
Stainless Steel	18 Cr 8 Ni 0.12 C	Softened	460		260	30		1700	Valves, turbine blading.
Wrought Iron	0.02 C. 0.02 Si 0.05 P 1.0 Slag 0.01 S.	Hot Rolled	310	200	186	30	40	1000	Decorative.

TABLE 1.6

heat source and hammered together to form a union.

Resistance welding is another forge welding process, current and pressure are supplied to the parts being welded but no filler metal or flux is required. The heat which is generated inorder to form the weld depends upon (1) the square of the current supplied (2) the metal to be welded and the contact resistance (3) the time of application of current and pressure. Examples of resistance welding are: studs welded to decks or to boiler tubes in water tube boilers.

Welding processes which do not require any pressure are often referred to as fusion welding processes. Fusion welding processes require a filler metal and often a flux is used. The most popular and most convenient form of fusion welding is the electric arc welding process, sometimes called the metal arc welding process.

Electric Arc Welding

In this process an electric arc is struck between the electrode, which may serve as the filler metal, and the metal to be welded. The heat which is generated causes the electrode to melt and the molten metal is transferred from the electrode to the plate (Fig. 1.16).

If the electrode is bare, the arc tends to wander and is therefore difficult to control. Also, the arc stream is open to contamination from the atmosphere and this results in a porous

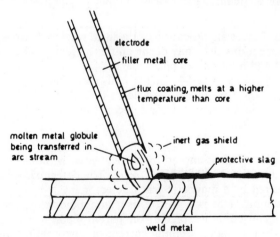

electrode
filler metal core
flux coating, melts at a higher temperature than core
molten metal globule being transferred in arc stream
inert gas shield
protective slag
weld metal

SECTION THROUGH ELECTRIC ARC WELDING
Fig. 1.16

brittle weld. To avoid these defects, flux coated electrodes are generally used.

The flux coating melts at a higher temperature than the electrode metal core thus the coating protrudes beyond the core during welding. This gives better stability, control and concentration of the arc. The coating also shields the arc and the molten metal pool from the atmosphere by means of the inert gases given off as it vaporises.

Silicates, formed from the coating, form a slag upon the surface of the hot metal and this protects the hot metal from the atmosphere as it cools. Also due to the larger contraction of the slag than the metal as cooling is taking place, the slag is easily removed.

Electric arc welding may be done using d.c. or a.c. supply. About 50 open circuit volts are required to strike the arc when d.c. is used, and about 80 volts when a.c. is used.

a.c. supply is usually more popular than d.c. for the following reasons.

(1) More compact plant.
(2) Less plant maintenance required.
(3) Higher efficiency than d.c. plant.
(4) Initial cost is less for similar capacity plants.
    Disadvantages of a.c. supply are:
(1) Higher voltage is used, hence greater shock risk.
(2) More difficult to weld cast iron and non-ferrous metals.

Fig. 1.17 gives an indication of the ideal weld and also some of the imperfections that may occur on the surface or internally to the weld and adjacent metal.

The defects are generally due to mal-operation of the welding equipment and for this reason welders should be tested regularly and their welding examined for defects. Some of the defects with causes are:

(1) Overlap: This is caused by an overflow, without fusion, of weld metal over the parent metal. The defect can usually be detected by a magnetic crack detector.
(2) Undercut: This is a groove or channel along the toe of the weld caused by wastage of the parent metal which could be due to too high a welding current or low welding speed.
(3) Spatter: Globules or particles of metal scattered on or around the weld. This may be caused by too high a current

or voltage making the metal splash or splatter.

(4) Blowhole: This is a large cavity caused by entrapped gas.

(5) Porosity: A group of small gas pockets.

(6) Inclusion: Any slag or other entrapped matter is an inclusion defect. Surface to be welded must be free from foreign matter, *e.g.*, grease, oil, millscale, metal chipping, etc. During welding the slag must not be allowed to get in front of the molten metal or it may become entrapped. Also when welding is interrupted for changing of electrode or when another run is to be laid, the already deposited metal should be allowed to cool, the slag should then be chipped and brushed off.

(7) Incomplete root penetration: Is a gap caused by failure of the weld metal to fill the root. This may be due to a fast welding speed or too low a current.

(8) Lack of Fusion: This could occur between weld metal and parent metal, between different layers of weld metal or between contact surfaces of parent metal. It could be caused by incorrect current or voltage, dirt or grease, etc.

Most of the surface defects that occur in welding can be removed by grinding but internal defects, which can be detected by radiographic or ultrasonic methods, necessitate repeating the operations.

Inspection of welding should be carried out during welding, as well as after, since the defects if discovered early mean a saving in material and labour costs.

During welding by the metal arc process some of the points to be observed are: rate of electrode consumption; penetration; fusion; slag control; length and sound of arc.

Other forms of electric arc welding include the argon arc process. Argon arc welding enables non-ferrous metals such as aluminium, magnesium, copper and ferrous metals such as stainless steel to be welded without using a flux.

In this welding process (called the T.I.G. process, *i.e.* Tungsten inert gas) the arc is struck between a non-consumable tungsten electrode and the parent metal. The arc and molten metal are completely surrounded by argon gas which is supplied to the torch under pressure. Argon is one of the rarer inert atmospheric gases obtained from the atmosphere by liquefaction.

By completely excluding the atmosphere during welding the argon gas prevents oxidation products and nitrides being

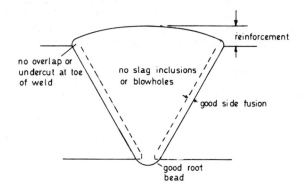

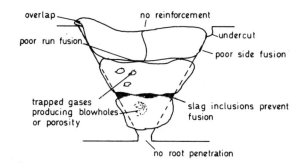

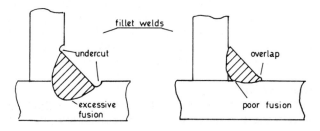

SOUND WELD AND SOME WELD DEFECTS
Fig. 1.17

formed, thus enabling welding to take place without using a flux.

For oxy-acetylene welding, oxygen and acetylene stored in solid drawn steel bottles under pressure is supplied to a torch. Modern torches are often of the combined type, they can be used for either welding or cutting processes and various types and sizes of nozzles are supplied for this purpose.

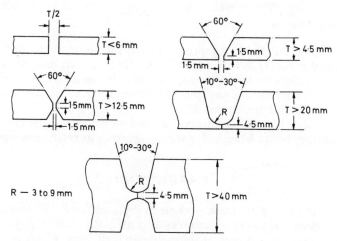

TYPICAL V AND U BUTT PREPARATIONS FOR
WELDING
Fig. 1.18

For welding, a neutral flame is normally required—that is a flame which neither oxidises nor reduces—and a filler metal and flux are used. Oxy-acetylene welding can be used for welding ferrous and non-ferrous metals, *e.g.* stainless steels, cast irons, aluminium, copper, etc. It is also a process that can be used for hard surfacing of materials such as stelliting.

Downhand welding
A preferable terminology is 'flat position welding', it is welding from the upper side of joint where the face of the weld is approximately horizontal.

Heat Affected Zone
In welding or brazing it is that part of the base metal which has had its microstructure and mechanical properties altered but it has not been melted.

Difference between welding, brazing and soldering.

Welding: filler metal used has a melting point at or slightly below that of the base metal.

Brazing: filler used has a melting point above 500°C (approx) but below that of the base metal.

Soldering: filler metal used has a melting point below 500°C (approx).

Brazing and Soldering processes are similar in that the filler metal must (1) wet the parent metal (2) be drawn into the joint by capillary action. Brazing filler metals are alloys of copper, nickel, silver and aluminium. Soldering filler metals are lead & tin or aluminium & zinc alloys.

A flux is used to dissolve or remove oxides, in the case of brazing, borax is used, for soldering; resin in petroleum spirit.

GAS CUTTING

The cutting of irons and steels by means of oxy-acetylene equipment is a very common cutting process that most engineers will have encountered at some time in their lives. Flame cutting or burning as it is sometimes called is convenient, rapid and relatively efficient and inexpensive.

A flame cutting torch is different to a welding torch in that it has a separate, valve controlled, supply of cutting oxygen in addition to the normal oxygen and acetylene supplies (Fig. 1.19).

When cutting, for example steel plate, the plate is first pre-heated by means of the heating flame until it reaches its ignition temperature, this is usually distinguishable by colour (bright red to white). Then the cutting oxygen is supplied and immediately burning commences. The cutting oxygen oxidises the iron to a magnetic oxide of iron (Fe_3O_4) which has a low melting point, this oxide easily melts and is rapidly blown away by the stream of cutting oxygen.

Once the ignition point is reached the cutting process is rapid, since the heat is supplied, in addition to that given by the heating flame, by the oxidation of the iron. It should be noted that the iron or steel is itself not melted but is oxidised or burnt.

Due to the rapid cooling of the plate edge, that takes place once the torch has passed, local hardness generally occurs. Hence dressing of the plate edges by machining or grinding to

remove the hardened material is normally desirable, otherwise
surface cracking may develop.

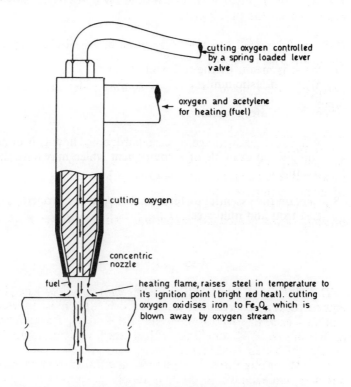

OXY-ACETYLENE GAS CUTTING
(Other gases—Oxy-Hydrogen—Oxy-propane or Oxy-Coal gas)
Fig. 1.19

TEST EXAMPLES 1

Class 3

1. What is meant by the following terms:
   a)   Elastic limit,
   b)   U.T.S.
   c)   Safety factor.

2. What is the advantage of case hardening, how is it done, and give an example of a component which may have this treatment.

3. Explain the essential differences between the properties of cast iron and mild steel.

TEST EXAMPLES 1

Class 2

1. Briefly describe the tests made on a piece of metal to determine its suitability for use in engineering. Explain clearly what is meant by any *four* of the following metallurgical terms:
   (a) Work hardening,
   (b) Case hardening,
   (c) Annealing,
   (d) Normalising,
   (e) Yield point,
   (f) Creep.

2. Sketch graphically, the load—extension diagram for a mild steel test piece. Would you expect a similar diagram if you tested a non-ferrous metal? Explain: yield point, elastic limit, limit of proportionality and proof stress.

3. State the approximate proportions of carbon contained in (a) Cast Iron and (b) Cast Steel and mention the forms in which the carbon may occur therein.
   Compare the physical properties of these two metals and name some of the more important parts of machinery for which these materials are respectively suitable.

4. Explain the difference between "strength" and "stiffness" of steel. Discuss the importance of these properties in shipboard structural members and machinery components.

5. Describe the effects of varying the percentages of the following constituents on the physical properties of steel:
   a) Carbon,
   b) Phosphorus,
   c) Manganese,
   d) Molybdenum.

TEST EXAMPLES 1

Class 1

1. Name four copper alloys associated with Marine Engineering, giving in each case, its constituents, physical properties and a practical example of its use.

2. Explain why a material may fracture when stressed below its yield point. Give examples of components which might fracture in this way if suitable precautions are not taken. Explain how such fractures can be avoided with reference to the materials chosen, careful design and workmanship.

3. Give the approximate composition, and the properties of the following metals:
   (a)   Manganese bronze,
   (b)   Cupro-nickel,
   (c)   Babbitts metal.
   In each case give two examples of the metals in use on board ship, and explain why the metal is chosen for the applications you mention.

4. Give properties, uses and constituents of:
   (a)   Phosphor bronze,
   (b)   Black heart malleable iron,
   (c)   Monel metal.

5. Describe the following:
   (a)   Case hardening,
   (b)   Flame hardening,
   (c)   Nitriding,
   (d)   Induction hardening.

CHAPTER 2

FUEL TECHNOLOGY

LIQUID FUELS

Crude petroleum is first classified broadly into one of three types:

Paraffin Base in which the residue after distillation contains more than 5% paraffin wax.

Asphalt Base in which the residue after distillation contains less than 2% paraffin wax and is mainly composed of asphalt (bitumen).

Mixed Base in which the residue after distillation contains between 2 and 5% paraffin wax mixed intimately with asphalt.

The type obtained depends on the source and also determines the type of refining necessary and nature of the end products produced.

The raw petroleum at the well head is often associated with natural gas, which has a high methane content, this gas can be directly utilised and is piped off for domestic use. Primary separation, by heating and cooling, will allow a yield of well head motor spirit (straight run gasoline). The bulk of the crude is taken to the refinery for processing into a wide range of products depending on the type of crude. Asphalt is mainly found in residual oils and is an indefinite substance, both hard and soft, being mainly combustible although hard asphalt can cause considerable gum deposits in *I.C.* engines.

Composition of Petroleum

Consists in all its forms of hydrocarbons, with small amounts (up to 5%) of nitrogen, oxygen, sulphur, metallic salts, etc., together with water emulsified in the oil and associated with natural gas.

Hydrocarbons

The exact proportions and composition decide the character of the petroleum and hence the refining and processing required. Types of hydrocarbon are made up of at least nine recognisable series, a series being a range of products with the same molecular structure pattern, from $C_n H_{2n+2}$ to $C_n H_{2n-12}$. The four main series are:

Paraffins. $C_n H_{2n+2}$
    for example, methane $(C H_4)$, butane $(C_4 H_{10})$
Napthenes. $_n(C H_2)$
    for example, cyclo—butane $(C_5 H_{10})$
Aromatics. $C_n H_{2n-6}$
    for example, benzene $(C_6 H_6)$
Olefines. $C_n H_{2n}$
    for example, ethylene $(C_2 H_4)$

The first two given are usually classified as *saturated* and the latter two as *unsaturated*. Unsaturated series are rarely found in the crude petroleum but tend to be found by molecular bonding alteration during later processing. Although olefines and naphthenes have the same C/H ratio they are distinguished by an important difference in molecular structure.

The lowest members of any series are gases, graduating to liquids as the molecular structure becomes more complex, thence to semi-solids and to solids. Considering for example the paraffin hydrocarbon series: methane $(C H_4)$ to butane $(C_4 H_{10})$ are gases, pentane $(C_5 H_{12})$ to nonane $(C_9 H_{20})$ are all liquids of decreasing volatility.

By octadecane $(C_{18} H_{38})$ there is a mineral jelly and further up the series gives paraffin wax solid $(C_{21} H_{44})$. With slight deviations from the molecular grouping system millions of different combinations called *isomers* are possible. Composition and characteristics then tend to become chemically complex, this particularly applies to high grade gasoline for aviation and motor vehicle fuels.

Crude oil is first treated for water and dirt removal, natural gas and straight run gasolines being commonly tapped off, and the bulk of the crude is passed to the refinery for distillation. Any refinery must be fairly flexible to cope with reasonable variations of crude type and variation in market demands for the output of distillates.

The Distillation Process

As a first stage the refinery distills the crude petroleum into basic products. This depends on the lightness of the various fractions and their distillation temperatures. A typical primary distillation would be approximately as shown in Fig. 2.1.

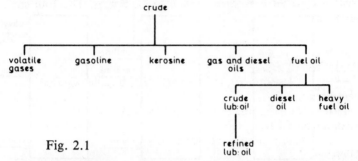

Fig. 2.1

The temperatures for distillation into the various fractions would be approximately as shown in Fig. 2.2.

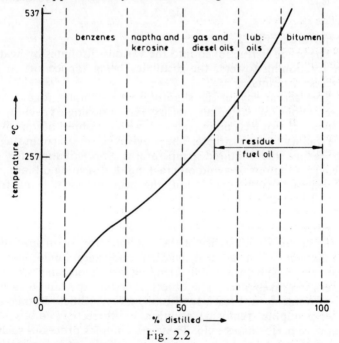

Fig. 2.2

The actual stages as shown may not be so clearly defined, *i.e.* the cut point often has some degree of temperature overlap.

Simple Refinery Layout

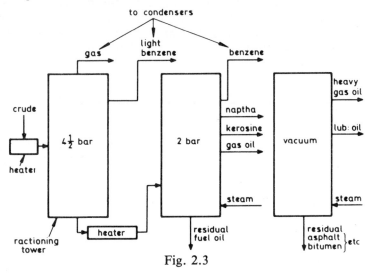

Fig. 2.3

Referring to Fig. 2.3:

The crude is fractioned into the various distillates by heating in fractioning towers, the distillates being tapped off at the necessary points.

The actual layout is slightly more complex due to re-circulation for stripping, reflux for enriching, provision of condensers for gas cooling, etc., all with the object of improving the quality of the distillate. The provision of the vacuum stage is to reduce the required temperatures of distillation for the heavier fractions to avoid oil cracking. Lubricating oils are produced by vacuum distillation, the principal yield being from mixed base crude oil.

Further Processing

To improve the quality of the distillates for use in specialised equipment, such as for aviation and automobile industry requirements, considerable blending and molecular structure alteration takes place. The object in certain specialised cases is improvement in Diesel Ignition Quality, Knock Rating (see later), sulphur removal, addition of corrective additives to improve performance, etc. These are complex processes such as thermal and catalytic cracking, alkylation, cyclisation, dehydrogenation, polymerisation, isomerisation, etc. Olefins and aromatics of widely varying chemical bonding are produced by these processes. The cracking point occurs when dissociation from heavy hydrocarbon molecules to lighter forms takes place. This may be by thermal (high pressure or temperature) or catalytic means. Cracking, caused by extreme operating conditions, must be avoided.

TESTING OF LIQUID FUEL AND OILS

(1) Density (ϱ)

Storage of liquids is often based on volume, some correlation such as density, for the mass to volume relationship, is required. This is important for bunker capacities, choice of heating arrangements, injectors, purifiers, etc.

$$\text{Density } (\varrho) = \frac{\text{Mass } (m)}{\text{Volume } (V)}$$

units usually kg/m^3 (fresh water 1000 kg/m^3).

If the temperature cannot be fixed at 15°C (with for example high viscosity oils) then a correction factor per degree C above 15°C is added to the observed density, or if measured below 15°C, is subtracted from the observed density. Density is taken by hydrometer. The datum temperature is 15°C. Water (fresh) has its maximum density of 1000 kg/m^3 at 4°C.

The reciprocal of density is specific volume (m^3/kg).

(2) Viscosity

May be defined as the resistance of fluids to change of *shape*, being due to the internal molecular friction of molecule with molecule of the fluid producing the frictional drag effect.

Absolute (dynamic) viscosity as used in calculation is difficult to determine, being numerically equal to that force to shear a plane fluid surface of area one square metre, over another plane surface at the rate of one metre per second, when the distance between the two surfaces is one metre. Kinematic viscosity is the ratio of the absolute viscosity to the density at the temperature of viscosity measurement.

$$F = \eta A \frac{dv}{dy}$$

$$\text{Dynamic } (\eta) \ = \ \frac{F \mathrm{d}y}{A \mathrm{d}v} \left[\frac{ML.}{T^2} \ \frac{1.}{L^2} \ \frac{LT}{L} \right] \ = \ \left[\frac{ML.}{T^2} \ \frac{T}{L^2} \right] \ \text{Ns/m}^2$$

$$\text{Kinematic } (v) \ = \ \frac{\eta}{\varrho} \left[\frac{ML^3}{TLM} \right] \ = \ \left[\frac{L^2}{T} \right] \ \text{m}^2/\text{s.}$$

Kinematic methods are increasingly being used, centistokes at 50°C (1 m²/s = 10⁶ c St) is the measurement (sometimes 40°C or 80°C). Kinematic viscosity is measured by capillary flow of a set liquid volume from a fixed head (Poiseuille), a similar method (Ostwald) is much used by the oil industry and a technique using a steel ball falling through the liquid (Stokes) can also be applied.

For practical purposes viscosity is still often measured on a time basis. It is expressed as the number of seconds for the out-flow of a fixed quantity of fluid through a specifically calibrated instrument at a specified temperature.

Considering Fig. 2.4:

The time for 50 ml outflow is taken by stopwatch. Temperature accuracy is vital and a variation of ± 0.1°C is a maximum for temperatures up to 60°C. Water is used as the liquid in the heating bath up to 94°C and oil for higher temperatures. The result is expressed as time in seconds at the quoted temperature, *e.g.* 500 s Redwood No. 1 at 38°C.

Samples and apparatus require to be clean and the appliance must be level.

Viscosity Scales

In British practice the Redwood viscometer was used. Redwood No. 1, the outflow time in seconds of 50 ml of fluid, used up to 2000 s. Redwood No. 2, for oils with outflow times exceeding 2000 s (usually, but not always), designed to give ten times the flow rate of the Redwood No. 1 orifice.

In American practice the Saybolt Universal and Saybolt Furol were used in a similar manner to the above, employing a different orifice size as in the Redwood.

In European practice the Engler viscometer was used, which compares the outflow times of oil and water, results quoted in Engler degrees.

International standardisation has encouraged the development of the kinematic method, units centistokes at 50°C (sometimes 80°C for high viscosity oils).

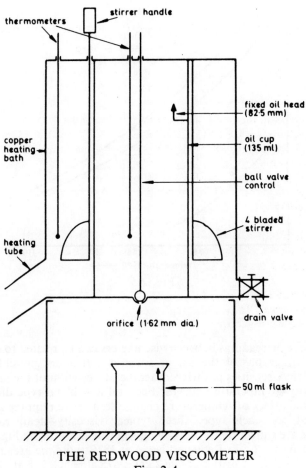

THE REDWOOD VISCOMETER
Fig. 2.4

Temperature

Increase of temperature has a marked effect in reducing fluid viscosity. Temperature and viscosity are closely related in the choice of an oil for a particular duty. For atomisation of fuels it is necessary to heat high viscosity oils so that the viscosity is about 30 cSt at the injector and preferably near 13 cSt for internal combustion engines (the viscosity of Diesel oil being about 7 cSt at 38°C).

It is essential to specify the temperature at which the viscosity is quoted otherwise the value becomes meaningless for correlation.

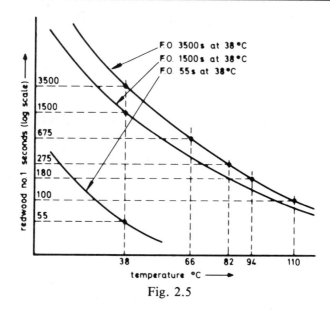

Fig. 2.5

The scale readings between viscometers can be related to each other by graphs or the use of constants. It is not possible to calculate viscosities at different temperatures without the use of viscosity—temperature curves. Each oil and blend type differs with the effect of temperature change so a curve requires to be plotted for each type, three typical viscosity—temperature curves are shown on the diagram given (Fig. 2.5). From Fig. 2.5 it is seen that 3.5 ks Redwood No. 1 at 38°C (note the use in this case of the No. 1 orifice above 2 ks) is 575 at 66°C, 275 at 82°C, 180 s at 94°C and 100 s at 110°C.

Factors influenced by viscosity may be summarised as: frictional drag effects, pipe flow losses, flow through small orifices (atomisation), load capacity between surfaces, fouling factor, spread factor, etc.

Viscosity Index is a numerical value which measures the ability of the oil to resist viscosity change when the temperature changes. A high viscosity index would refer to an oil capable of maintaining a fairly constant viscocity value in spite of wide variation in the temperature. The value of viscosity index is usually determined from a chart based on a knowledge of the viscosity values at different temperatures.

Approximate relationship between the two main scales are:

cSt	30	60	120	180	280	380	500	—at 50°C
R No. 1 secs	200	400	1000	1500	2500	3500	5000	— at 38°C

(3) Flashpoint

This is the minimum temperature at which an oil gives off flammable vapour, which on the application of a flame in a specified apparatus would cause momentary ignition.

The test may be *open* or *closed* depending on whether the apparatus is sealed or not. The closed flashpoint is always *lower* because the lid seal allows accumulation of the volatiles above the liquid surface. The test applied for oils above 45°C, which is the usual marine range, is the Pensky Marten Closed Flashpoint test.

For oils below 45°C the Abel apparatus would be used.

Referring to Fig. 2.6:

When the operating handle is depressed the shutter uncovers the ports (down movement of the handle opens a shutter just below the ports by means of a ratchet, further movement and ratchet travel gives a flame insertion, this detail is omitted on the sketch for simplicity). The flame element is depressed through one port *above* the oil surface. Starting at a temperature 17°C below the judged flashpoint the flame is depressed, left and quickly raised in a period of under 2 s, at 1°C temperature intervals.

Just before the flashpoint is reached a blue halo occurs around the flame, the flash is observed just after, through the two observation ports, stirring being discontinued during flame depression. A fresh sample must be used for every test and care must be taken that no trace of cleaning solvents are present in the oil cup.

Some aspects relating to oils and the use of closed flashpoint may be considered as follows:

Oils with flashpoint below 22°C are classified as *dangerous—highly flammable*, such oils are gasolines, benzenes, etc.

Flashpoints in the range 22°C-66°C would relate to kerosenes and vaporising oils.

Flashpoints above 66°C are classified as *safe* (for marine purposes) and include gas, Diesel and fuel oils. Approximate closed flashpoint values for different oils are:

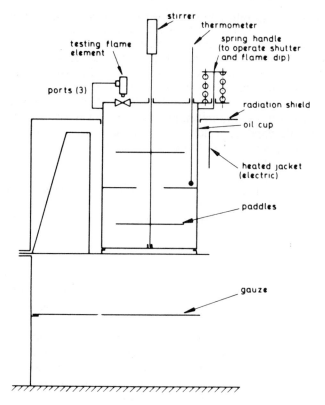

THE PENSKY MARTEN (CLOSED) TEST
Fig. 2.6

Pentane	−49°C	Petrol	−17°C
Carbon	Disulphide		
	−30°C	Paraffin	25°C
Acetone	−18°C	Diesel Oil	95°C
Benzene	−11°C	Heavy Fuel Oil	100°C
Methanol	10°C	Lubricating Oil	230°C

These values are average only, the grade and type cause wide variations, for example, the term petrol could relate to values between −60°C to 25°C.

As flashpoint is indicative of the fire and explosion risk, for storage and transport, it is an important property of the oil. For shipboard requirements it is a rule that the oil for propulsion should have a minimum closed flashpoint of 66°C, also that the oil in storage should not be heated above 52°C.

In special cases where high viscosity oils are used and high degrees of heating are required to produce atomisation, etc., it is allowable to heat the oil to within 20°C of the closed flashpoint. Great care should always be taken regarding the control of heat to heaters situated on the *suction* side of the fuels pumps so as not to cause oil vaporisation and the possibility of explosive vapour formation.

(4) Calorific Value

Is the heating value from the complete combustion of unit mass of fuel, *i.e.* MJ/kg, kJ/kg. etc.

Approximate heat energy values of fuels are:

Coal	34 MJ/kg.
Fuel Oil	42 MJ/kg.
Diesel Oil	45 MJ/kg.
Pure Hydrocarbon	50 MJ/kg (85% C, 15% H_2).

The value quoted is the *higher* calorific value in every case in preference to the lower value. The higher calorific value includes the heat in water vapour formed from water as the products of combustion are cooled, vapours condensed, and hence latent heat becomes re-available for heat utilisation.

The *lower* calorific value is more realistic, from the boiler engineers viewpoint, being the actual heat available for boiler water evaporation, but this does not detract from the fact that this is a fault of utilisation and the higher calorific value is the actual heat available and is therefore the *preferred* value for quotation. Fuels always exhibit a fall of calorific value to some extent during storage.

There are numerous makes of bomb calorimeters but the differences are only slight. The test as conducted is very closely detailed and only a brief synopsis is outlined here. For further close details, if desired, the reader is referred to the relevant *B.S.* specifications. Consider Fig. 2.7:

The oxygen supply is to give an internal pressure of 26 bar and should not be less than $2\frac{1}{2}$ times the theoretical oxygen required. The interior of the bomb must be resistant to condensed acidic vapours from combustion. The thermometer used can be read by means of a lens to 0.002°C, and the temperature of the

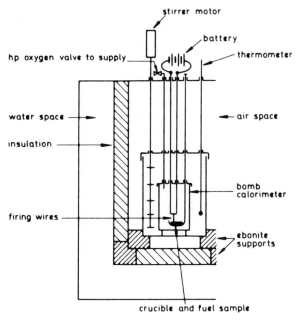

THE BOMB CALORIMETER
Fig. 2.7

enclosing water, of amount 15-20 litres, should be maintained steady up to the test.

A small specimen is fired by electric charge under conditions of pressurised oxygen and the temperature rise of apparatus and coolant is noted. 0.01 kg of distilled water are in the bomb to absorb sulphuric and nitric acid vapours (from sulphur trioxide and nitrogen). Mass of fuel $\times$ hcv $= W.E.$ of apparatus complete $\times$ its temperature rise. The above calculation, using masses in kg and temperatures in °C, gives the hcv of the fuel (MJ/kg or kJ/kg). The water equivalent ($W.E.$) of the apparatus is determined by a test using benzoic acid. This is the calorific value reference fuel, hcv 26.5 MJ/kg, showing relatively no deterioration of calorific value during storage. Correction factors are now applied for acids formed under bomb conditions only, radiation cooling effect, etc. The temperature of test is based on 15°C approx. It should be noted that under the bomb's combustion conditions (high excess air and pressure) sulphuric and nitric acids are formed. Whereas under furnace combustion conditions sulphur is burned mainly to sulphur dioxide, with no acid formation, thereby no trioxide, and nitrogen would pass off in the free state.

(5) Pour Point

This is a determination of the lowest temperature value at which oil will pour or flow under the prescribed test conditions. This value is an important consideration for lubricating oils working under low temperature conditions *e.g.* refrigeration machine lubricants, telemotors, etc.

Referring to Fig. 2.8:

Various mixtures are used in the bath, for very low temperatures solid carbon dioxide and acetone are used. At 11°C above the expected pour point the test begins. At temperature intervals of 3°C the test jar is removed, checked for surface oil tilt and replaced in a time interval of 3 s maximum.

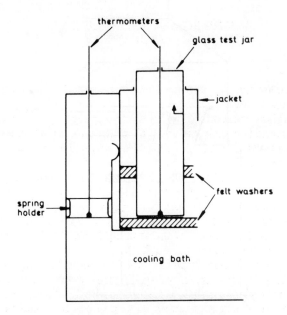

POUR POINT APPARATUS
Fig. 2.8

When surface of oil will not tilt, for a time interval of 5 s, note temperature, add 3°C and this is the pour point. The oil is heated to 46°C before the test and is cooled in progressive stages of about 17°C in different cooling agent baths, in each case the jar must be transferred to another bath when the oil reaches a temperature of 28°C above the bath temperature.

(6) Carbon Residue (Conradson method)
This test indicates the relative carbon forming propensity of an oil. The test is a means of determining the residual carbon, etc., left when an oil is burned under specified conditions. This test has been used much more in recent times in line with the use of high viscosity fuels in *I.C.* engines.

The mass of the sample placed in the silica crucible must not exceed 0.01 kg.

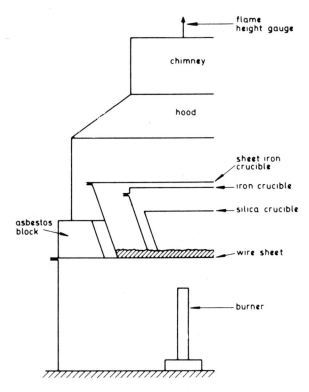

CONRADSON CARBON TEST APPARATUS
Fig. 2.9

Initial heating period 10 minutes ± 1½, vapour burn off period 13 minutes ± 1, further heating for exactly 7 minutes, total heating period 30 minutes ± 2. The covers must be a loose fit to allow vapours to escape.

The heating and test method are closely controlled. After removal of sample and weighing, the result is expressed as 'Carbon Residue (Conradson)' as a percentage of the original sample mass. The test is usually repeated a number of times to obtain a uniformity of results. (see Fig. 2.9).

(7) Water in Oil

A quick test for presence of water in a substance is to add a sample to white copper sulphate ($CuSO_4$) which turns to blue copper sulphate ($CuSO_4\ 5H_2O$) in the presence of water.

The following test is more suitable for oil:

Referring to Fig. 2.10:

The test usually conducted is the *I.P.* standard method. 100 ml of sample is mixed completely with 100 ml of special high grade gasoline having standard properties. Steady heat is applied for about one hour. Water vapours are carried over with the distilled gasoline and are condensed in the condenser and measured in the lower part of the receiver. The result being expressed as say 1% Water, *I.P.* Method.

Note. This sketch is very much simplified. The actual apparatus must be constructed to specific and

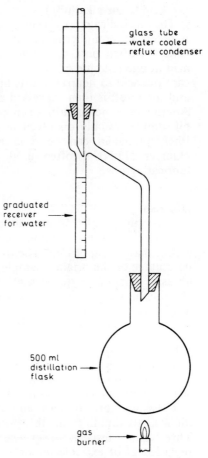

glass tube
water cooled
reflux condenser

graduated
receiver
for water

500 ml
distillation
flask

gas
burner

WATER TEST IP METHOD
Fig. 2.10

exact *B.S.* dimensions which are highly detailed. The test must also be carried out under closely controlled conditions.

(8) Fire Point

This is the temperature at which the volatile vapours given off from a heated oil sample are ignitable by flame application and will burn continuously. The firepoint temperature can be anything up to about 40°C higher than the closed flashpoint temperature for most fuel oils.

(9) Acidity (or alkalinity)

This is indicated by the neutralisation (or saponification) number. This number is the mass, in milligrammes, of an alkali which is often potassium hydroxide, needed to neutralise the acid in one gramme of sample. The oil is often alkaline, in this case the acid to neutralise it is in turn neutralised by the alkali and the result is then expressed as base neutralisation number. Alternatively the quantities can be expressed in ppm for 1 ml of oil sample (usually dissolved in industrial methylated spirits). Phenolphthalein can be used as the indicator. Total Base Number (TBN) is often used for alkalinity indication for lubricating oils.

(10) Ash

A sample of oil (250 ml minimum) is cautiously and slowly evaporated to dryness and ignition continued until all traces of carbon have disappeared. The ash is then expressed as a mass percentage of the original sample. Ash consists usually of hard abrasive mineral particles such as quartz, silicates, iron and aluminium oxides, sand, etc. A residue test (% by volume after heating to 350°C) is sometimes used.

(11) Other Tests

These are numerous, examples being: asphaltenes, sediment, suspended solids, oxidation, emulsion number, cloud point, setting point, precipitation number, etc.

These are more complex laboratory tests whose description is difficult to simplify and therefore are not considered further. Three other tests however, not mentioned previously, are regarded as of extreme importance in *I.C.* engine practice. In view of this these tests namely, octane number, cetane number and crankcase oil dilution, will now be considered.

(12) Octane Number

Is indicative of the knock rating. Knocking or pinking are characteristic of some *I.C.* engine fuels, particularly in spark ignition engines, this can cause pre-ignition, overheat and damage.

Normally on spark initiation the flame front proceeds through the mixture at a speed of about 18 m/s. If, due to engine conditions or type of fuel used, the mixture in front of the flame front has its temperature and pressure raised above the spontaneous ignition point then auto ignition occurs. This means that by the time the last gas charge is reached the flame front speeds can reach 2.2 km/s and detonation, temperature rise and heavy shock waves occur. Knocking tendency is dependent on many variables such as rev/s, compression ratio, turbulence, mixture strength, etc.

Test

Iso-octane ($C_8 H_{16}$) has very good anti knock properties and is taken as upper limit 100. Normal heptane ($C_7 H_{16}$) has very poor anti knock properties and is taken as lower limit zero. Therefore octane number is the percentage by volume of iso-octane in a mixture of iso-octane and normal heptane which has the same knock characteristics as the chosen fuel. The test is conducted under fixed conditions on a standard engine which usually has electronic detonation detection. Modern fuels, for aviation, etc., have octane numbers over 100 and for these the term Performance Number is used. In this case tetraethyl lead (*T.E.L.*) is usually added in specified proportions to the iso-octane, this chemical has a very high anti knock characteristic and is in fact often used as a fuel additive.

(13) Cetane Number

Is an indication of the ignition quality of the fuel. In a compression ignition engine, commonly called Diesel engine, cold starting is required. Also the time interval between fuel injection and firing, called ignition delay, must not be too long otherwise collected fuel will generate high pressures when it does ignite and Diesel knock results. Paraffin hydrocarbons have the best ignition quality and are thus most suitable. Speed and cetane number can be correlated, for high speed engines (above 13.3 rev/s) a cetane number of 48 may be regarded as a minimum, whilst for very slow running engines (below 1.7 rev/s) a cetane number of 15 is a minimum.

A Diesel fuel used in a hot petrol engine would cause detonation, *i.e.* it has a low octane number.

Test

Cetane is a paraffin hydrocarbon, hexadecane ($C_{16} H_{34}$) being its correct designation, of high ignition quality and is taken as the upper limit of 100. Alpha-methyl-napthalene is of low ignition quality and is taken as the lower limit of zero. Thus cetane number is numerically the percentage by volume of cetane in a mixture of cetane and alpha-methyl-napthalene that matches the chosen fuel in ignition quality.

There are a number of tests, one is by measurement of the delay period when running, by use of a cathode ray tube on a standard engine. Another, which is probably the best, is to use a standard engine running under fixed conditions with a variable compression ratio to give a standard delay, and using the compression ratio as an indication of cetane number.

An alternative method called Diesel index can be used but it is not as reliable as cetane number. Density is often indicative of cetane number especially in the middle ranges, *i.e.*, density 850 kg/m³, cetane number about 61, density 950 kg/m³, cetane number about 37. Some success has been achieved by the use of additives such as acetone peroxide.

(14) Crankcase Oil Dilution

Is the percentage of fuel oil contamination of lubricating oil occurring in *I.C.* engines. The lubricating oil sample is mixed with water and heated, fuel volatiles are carried over with the steam vapour formed. By condensation of these vapours and separation, the fuel content can be measured and can be expressed as a percentage of the original lubricating oil sample by mass.

It is also important to check the lubricating oil for water contamination, for this purpose a similar separation test by heating is satisfactory. Severe corrosion of crankshafts has been caused by sulphur products from fuel oil mixing with any water in the lubricating oil to form sulphuric acids which are carried round the lubricating oil system.

Analysis of Fuel Oils (Typical)

It is not practice to assume a trend with one variable will apply to another. As a generalisation the 'heavier' the oil the higher the viscosity and flashpoint and the lower the calorific value. This would indicate extra heating, purification, etc., systems;

Constituent or Property	Petrol	Kerosene	Diesel	Residual
Carbon %	85.5	86.3	86.3	86.1
Hydrogen %	14.4	13.6	12.8	11.8
Sulphur %	0.1	0.1	0.9	2.1
Density, kg/m³	733	739	870	950
Higher calorific value, MJ/kg	47.0	46.7	46.0	44.0
Lower calorific value MJ/kg	43.7	43.6	43.3	41.4
Viscosity, cSt at 50°C	1.5	1.6	5	350
Closed Flashpoint °C	0	50	85	90

TABLE 2.1

reduced storage volume for a given bunkering mass; increased fuel demand for a given power.

Proposed ISO Specification for Marine Fuels

Table 2.2 is a draft specification with the objective of providing an agreed standard internationally.

COMBUSTION OF FUEL

The combustible elements in a fuel are carbon (C). hydrogen (H_2) and sulphur (S). These combustibles when supplied with oxygen (O_2) from atmospheric air combust and liberate heat. *Exothermic* reactions are those involving heat evolution, as are most combustion reactions, but some are *endothermic* and require heat supplied externally.

Combustion of Carbon

$$C + O_2 \rightarrow CO_2$$

Relative Masses $12 + (16 \times 2) \rightarrow 44$

$$1 + 2\tfrac{2}{3} \rightarrow 3\tfrac{2}{3}$$

Thus 1 kg of carbon requires $2\tfrac{2}{3}$ of oxygen and forms $3\tfrac{2}{3}$ kg of carbon dioxide (CO_2). This chemical process liberates about 33.7 MJ/kg of carbon burned. If the carbon is incompletely burned to form carbon monoxide (CO) and that gas leaves the system unburned the following results.

$$2C + O_2 \rightarrow 2CO$$

Relative Masses $(2 \times 12) + (16 \times 2) \rightarrow (2 \times 28)$

$$1 + 1\tfrac{1}{3} \rightarrow 2\tfrac{1}{3}$$

Grade	MA		MB		MC		MD		ME		MF		MG		MH		MI		MJ	
Inspected Parameter	Min	Max	Min	Max	Min	Max	Min	Max	Min	Max	Min	Max	Min	Max	Min	Max	Min	Max	Min	Max
Density at 15°C	—	—	—	0.90	—	0.920	—	0.990	—	0.990	—	0.990	—	0.990	—	0.990	—	0.990	—	—
Viscocity kinematic cSt at 40°C	1.5	5.5	—	11.0	—	14.0	—	—	—	—	—	—	—	—	—	—	—	—	—	—
Viscocity kinematic cSt at 80°C†	—	—	—	—	—	—	—	15	—	25	—	45	—	75	—	100	—	130	—	130
Flash point PM (closed) °C	43	—	60	—	60	—	60	—	60	—	60	—	60	—	60	—	60	—	60	—
Pour point (upper) °C 1 Dec-31 Mar	—	—	—	0	—	0	—	24	—	30	—	30	—	30	—	30	—	30	—	30
Pour point (upper) °C 1 Apr-30 Nov	—	-16	—	6	—	6	—	24	—	30	—	30	—	30	—	30	—	30	—	30
Cloud point °C	—	—	—	—	—	—	—	—	—	—	—	—	—	—	—	—	—	—	—	—
Ramsbottom carbon wt%	—	0.20	—	0.25	—	2.5	—	—	—	—	—	—	—	—	—	—	—	—	—	—
Conradson carbon wt%	—	—	—	—	—	—	—	12.0	—	14.0	—	20.0	—	22.0	—	22.0	—	22.0	—	—
Sulphur wt%	—	1.0	—	2.0	—	2.0	—	3.5	—	4.0	—	5.0	—	5.0	—	5.0	—	5.0	—	5.0
Ash wt%	—	0.01	—	0.01	—	0.05	—	0.10	—	0.10	—	0.15	—	0.20	—	0.20	—	0.20	—	0.20
Sediment by extraction wt%	—	0.01	—	0.02	—	—	—	—	—	—	—	—	—	—	—	—	—	—	—	—
Sediment (total existent)	—	—	—	—	—	*	—	*	—	*	—	*	—	*	—	*	—	*	—	*
Water volume %	—	0.05	—	0.25	—	0.30	—	0.50	—	0.80	—	1.0	—	1.0	—	1.0	—	1.0	—	1.0
Cetane index	45	—	35	—	—	—	—	—	—	—	—	—	—	—	—	—	—	—	—	—
Ignition quality	—	—	—	—	*	—	*	—	*	—	*	—	*	—	*	—	*	—	*	—
Metal contents ppM Vanadium	—	—	—	—	—	100	—	250	—	350	—	500	—	600	—	600	—	600	—	600
Aluminium††	—	—	—	—	—	—	—	30	—	30	—	30	—	30	—	30	—	30	—	—

†An indication of the approximate equivalents in kinematic viscosity at 50°C is given below:
Kinematic viscosity at 80°C 15 25 45 75 100 130
Kinematic viscosity at 50°C 40 80 180 380 500 700

*Considered important but currently no standard test method available.
††An acceptable test method has to be agreed.

TABLE 2.2

Thus 1 kg of carbon requires $1\frac{1}{3}$ kg of oxygen and forms $2\frac{1}{3}$ kg of carbon monoxide. This chemical process liberates about 10.25 MJ/kg of carbon burned. This represents a 70% heat loss with incomplete combustion.

Combustion of Hydrogen

$$2H_2 + O_2 \quad \rightarrow \quad 2H_2O$$

Relative Masses $(2 \times 1 \times 2) + (16 \times 2) \rightarrow (2 \times 18)$

$$1 + 8 \quad \rightarrow \quad 9$$

Thus 1 kg of hydrogen requires 8 kg of oxygen and forms 9 kg of water vapour (steam) (H_2O). This chemical process liberates about 144.4 MJ/kg of hydrogen burned, assuming the products of combustion are cooled and the latent heat is extracted from the water vapour. If the steam escapes from the plant uncondensed, which is usual, it takes the latent heat with it then the net (or lower) heat liberation/kg of hydrogen burned is $144.4 - (9 \times 2.465) = 122.2$ MJ. The 2.465 figure is the specific enthalpy of vaporisation of steam at 15.5°C (the standard temperature).

hcv hydrogen 144.4 MJ/kg,
lcv hydrogen 122.2 MJ/kg.

Combustion of Sulphur

$$S + O_2 \quad \rightarrow \quad SO_2$$

Relative Masses $32 + (16 \times 2) \rightarrow 64$

$$1 + 1 \quad \rightarrow \quad 2$$

Thus 1 kg of sulphur requires 1 kg of oxygen and forms 2 kg of sulphur dioxide (SO_2). This chemical process liberates about 9.32 MJ/kg of sulphur burned. At high temperatures the very small percentage of the sulphur present as sulphates in the fuel is partly expelled as sulphur trioxide (SO_3). The percentage of SO_3 to SO_2 during normal combustion is low, usually of the order of 1%, and the chemical reaction is:

$$2S + 3O_2 \rightarrow 2SO_3$$

This reaction is of negligible importance from a heating viewpoint but is very important from the viewpoint of corrosion. The residual oils in regular use today contain appreciable amounts of sulphur (up to 6%) and so increase the amount of SO_3 in the flue gases. The presence of SO_3 has been shown to raise the acid dewpoint of the gases. This results in the condensation of acid vapours on colder metal surfaces, from the sulphur the formation of sulphurous and sulphuric acids with resulting corrosion. Mild steels are most severely attacked by the dilute acids at temperatures of about 28°C below the dewpoint, for cast irons 50°C.

This is a very relevant problem in air heaters and economisers of boiler plant and cylinder liners of *I.C.* engines.

Chemical reaction:

$SO_3 + H_2O \rightarrow H_2SO_4$ (sulphuric) or $SO_2 + H_2O \rightarrow H_2SO_3$ (sulphurous) then $2H_2SO_4 + O_2 \rightarrow H_2SO_4$

Certain catalysts are known to accelerate the formation of sulphur trioxide, such as vanadium pentoxide which can be present in the fuel, also metallic catalysts such as platinum.

Sulphurous acid is relatively harmless and unstable and in the presence of free oxygen, which invariably exists in flue gases, turns to the more harmful sulphuric acid.

Dilute acids attack the metal continuously but strong acids cause an initial attack which is then stifled by a passive gas layer or skin developed on the metal surface.

Calorific Value

Can be assessed from the approximate empirical formula:

$$hcv = 33.7C + 144.4\left(H_2 - \frac{O_2}{8} \right) + 9.32S$$

$lcv = hcv - 2.465$ (kg H_2O).

Value varies from 32.5 MJ/kg for coal to 44.5 MJ/kg for fuel oils, as discussed previously.

Air for Combustion

Atmospheric air is composed of nitrogen (N_2) and oxygen (O_2) in ratio 77% to 23% by mass, neglecting proportions of other gases as small in comparison.

Nitrogen takes no part in the combustion process merely representing a large but unavoidable heat loss as being inert it is heated and passes up the uptakes to waste. The oxygen required for combustion on a theoretical basis can be determined from the combustion equations.

Theoretical oxygen $\times \dfrac{100}{23}$ = Theoretical air.

In practice complete combustion can only be achieved by supplying excess air. In a boiler plant about 30% excess air (much less in modern practice) is the minimum normally required, *i.e.* about 12 kg of air/kg of fuel. In the *I.C.* engine of the compression ignition type, about 100% plus excess air is normally required, *i.e.* about 40 kg of air/kg of fuel, as complete and rapid combustion are essential. This becomes apparent in that the CO_2 value (% by volume) should be about 18% theoretically whereas 12% and 7%, in the case of the boiler plant and *I.C.* engine respectively, are typical values due to the air dilution of the gases. All the combustion equations given are based on perfect gases measured at the same temperature and pressure. *Standard* temperature and pressure (*stp*) is usually adopted as a basis in combustion work, *i.e.* 760 mm of mercury (1.013 bar) and 15.5°C although *normal* temperature and pressure (*ntp*) is sometimes used, *i.e.* 760 mm of mercury (1.013 bar) and 0°C.

The terms *stp* and *ntp* are not rigid in definition and the assumptions made should be clearly stated. % CO_2 should always be quoted by volume, % CO_2 by mass is higher.

Combustion of Hydrocarbons

Consider as an example methane (CH_4)

$$CH_4 + 2O_2 \quad \rightarrow \quad CO_2 + 2H_2O$$
$$16 + (2 \times 16 \times 2) \rightarrow \quad 44 + (2 \times 18)$$
$$1 + 4 \quad \rightarrow \quad 2\tfrac{3}{4} + 2\tfrac{1}{4}$$

Thus 1 kg of methane requires 4 kg of oxygen for complete combustion and forms $2\tfrac{3}{4}$ kg of carbon dioxide and $2\tfrac{1}{4}$ kg of water vapour.

Other hydrocarbons, for example, acetylene (C_2H_2). hexane (C_6H_{14}), etc., are often considered in the combustion equations. Methane is a gas released in bunker spaces, acetylene is a burning-welding gas and hexane is close to motor spirit gasoline. A series of common gases and their properties in combustion are given in Table 2.3.

The hydrocarbons usually have flammability limits between 1% and 10% but for volatile gases the range is much wider.

All the figures given in Table 2.3 relate to atmospheric pressure and temperature and are average values not to be applied too rigidly.

Temperature increase tends to increase the range of flammability, *e.g.* CH_4 at 15.5°C in the range 6.3 to 12.9% and at 405°C range 4.8 to 16%. Pressure increase is similar but more marked with upper limit increasing and lower limit falling, up to 52 bar. Gas concentration and mixture will also have pronounced effects. Values of spontaneous ignition temperature being lower usually in oxygen and also being affected by pressure, concentration, mixture, and temperature. In the case of other fuels the spontaneous ignition temperatures in common cases are:

cetane 236°C, diesel oil 246°C, gas oil 355°C, gasoline 399°C, steam coal 469°C, coke 555°C (average), etc.

SPONTANEOUS IGNITION TEMPERATURE		
GASES	°C IN AIR	°C IN OXYGEN
HYDROGEN	588	588
CARBON MONOXIDE	649	649
METHANE	700	577
BENZENE	742	731
ACETYLENE	422	416
CYLINDER OIL	420	—
KEROSENE	294	—
LIMITS OF FLAMMABILITY IN AIR		
GASES	% VOL. LOWER	% VOL. UPPER
HYDROGEN	4.0	75.0
CARBON MONOXIDE	12.5	74.0
METHANE	5.0	15.0
BENZENE	1.4	7.4
PETROL	1.4	6.0
COAL GAS	5.3	31.3

TABLE 2.3

Flame Temperature

This varies mainly with the fuel type, typical figures for gaseous fuels would be: methane 1872°C, hydrogen 2037°C, carbon monoxide 1957°C.

The values quoted are theoretical calculated values as the actual values are very difficult to measure, variables such as gas mixtures, radiation and dissociation, etc., are allowed for by the use of charts, in every case these effects serve to reduce temperature. Theoretical values are based on cold gas with theoretical cold air supplied, excess air decreases the flame temperature and air preheat together with rapid combustion increases the value. Hydrogen would give 6297°C by itself with theoretical oxygen, 2307°C with theoretical air and 1397°C with 100% excess air. An average furnace gas temperature may be taken as 1200°C. Flame temperature, radiation, luminosity, particle size, etc., are complex considerations still being subject to much research.

Oil Fuel Additives

Fused slag products, which give corrosive attack, are formed from the vanadium and sulphur content of the fuel oil. A particular type of additive gives the following reactions:

For sulphur dioxide:

$SO_3 + CaCO_3 = CaSO_4 + CO_2.$

For vanadium pentoxide:

$V_2O_5 + CaCO_3 = Ca(VO_3)_2 + CO_2.$

There is an increase in CO_2 content due to more complete combustion of the carbon. It is also usual to find an increase in flue gas temperature indicating better furnace or cylinder combustion.

Similar reactions to the above can be obtained using Barium Carbonate ($BaCO_3$) in place of the Calcium Carbonate ($CaCO_3$) above. The sulphate compounds formed have a higher ash melting point and there is little risk of fused deposits. Removal of Vanadium Pentoxide removes one of the catalysts that assist the formation of sulphur trioxide.

Additives are usually added directly to the empty oil fuel bunker tank before bunkering in quantity about 0.03% of the fuel (for 100 ppm of V or Sr compounds). The additives are usually claimed to give less carbon and soot deposits in furnaces and less gum and general deposits in $I.C.$ engines.

It is unwise to ballast oil fuel tanks with salt water as this accelerates the deposit of V_2O_5, Na_2SO_4 and Fe_2SO_4 as the salt water compounds act as a flux as well as providing slag products directly. For really elevated boiler conditions Calcium Hydroxide or Zinc Oxide additives can be used:

$V_2O_5 + Ca(OH)_2 = Ca(VO_3)_2 + H_2O.$
$V_2O_5 + ZnO = Zn(VO_3)_2.$

Oxides of Barium, Calcium, Zinc, etc., have been used as fuel additives for some years to try and combat sulphur acid attack to air heaters.

ANALYSIS OF FLUE GASES

Various types of apparatus are available. The Orsat apparatus is suitable for a detailed analysis, and three types of CO_2 recorder in fairly common use, are now described. It is suggested that for *examination* purposes the student should be familiar with the Orsat apparatus and any *one* type of CO_2 recorder.

The Orsat Apparatus

The enclosed volume of the apparatus is 100 ml. Pipette A contains a solution of potassium hydroxide in distilled water which absorbs carbon dioxide. Pipette B contains a solution of potassium hydroxide and pyrogallic acid in distilled water which absorbs oxygen. Pipette C contains a solution of cuprous chloride in hydrochloric acid (or ammonia). Pipettes *must* be used in sequence A, B then C. Aspirator bottle water is mixed with sulphuric acid or made salty to stop absorption and methyl orange or other acids or alkalis are commonly used as colouring fluids (see Fig. 2.11).

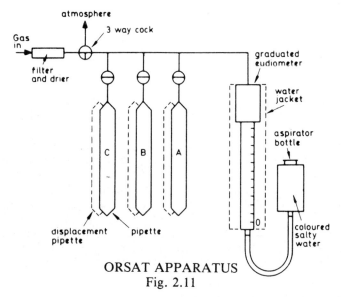

ORSAT APPARATUS
Fig. 2.11

By using the aspirator, *i.e.* raising and lowering to act as a pump the sample is first drawn in, passed through each pipette in turn, measured, and then discharged. The reduction in volume at each stage, always taking readings with water levels in eudiometer and aspirator coincident to ensure equal pressure, is the percentage volume of that gas. Gaseous SO_2 will be registered in any hot gas analysis as CO_2 unless previously gas washed out by, for example, a solution of manganese sulphate.

Typical results:

2.4 ml	12.6 ml	13 ml	13.1 ml
$100 - 2.4$ $= 97.6$ ml gas	$12.6 - 2.4$ $= 10.2$ ml CO_2	$13 - 12.6$ $= 0.4$ ml O_2	0.1 ml CO

$$\%CO_2 = \frac{1020}{97.6} = 10.45$$

$$\%O_2 = \frac{40}{97.6} = 0.41$$

$$\%CO = \frac{10}{97.6} = 0.126$$

$$\%N_2 = 100 - 10.986 = 89.014.$$

Always a dry flue gas analysis (*i.e.* water vapour removed). This is a volumetric analysis, which is the usual method. The hot gases of exhaust containing water vapour and sulphur dioxide are quickly cooled in transit to the apparatus. Water vapour condenses and sulphur dioxide is very readily absorbed by the water so that the Orsat apparatus measures CO_2, CO, O_2 and N_2 by difference quite correctly as no water vapour or SO_2 (to affect the CO_2 reading) are present in the dry sample entering the apparatus. If the gas sample were led directly to say a CO_2 recorder by a fan so that the sample was hot then any gaseous sulphur dioxide would register as carbon dioxide unless the manganese sulphate chemical had been used to absorb the gas.

Chemical Absorption Type CO₂ Recorder

Referring to Fig. 2.12, the CO_2 in the sample diffuses through a porous pot and is absorbed. This causes a reduction in volume which creates a vacuum. The pressure difference can be read off on the H_2O gauge calibrated directly as % CO_2.

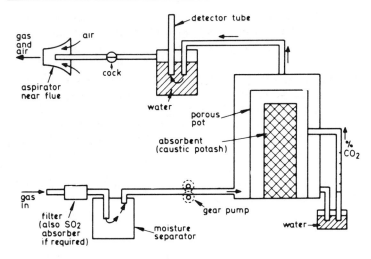

CHEMICAL ABSORPTION TYPE CO_2 RECORDER
Fig. 2.12

Thermal Conductivity Type CO_2 Recorder

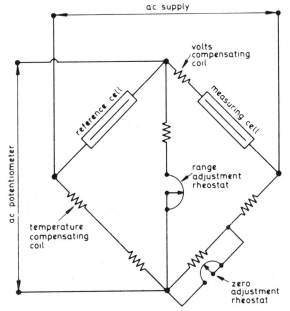

THERMAL CONDUCTIVITY TYPE CO_2 RECORDER
Fig. 2.13

Referring to Fig. 2.13:
Approximate thermal conductivities are in proportion:

$$CO_2 = 1, \ H_2O = 1, \ CO = 4, \ O_2 = 2, \ N_2 = 2.$$

The sample enters via a filter and drier, water vapour must be removed as same conductivity as CO_2. The wire cell resistance is proportional to heat dissipation, proportional to thermal conductivity of gas in cell, proportional therefore to CO_2 content. Air is used in reference cell. Thus the only difference between gas sample and air, from the thermal conductivity viewpoint is CO_2 (as H_2O removed and O_2 and N_2 same value). This assumes no CO or H_2, if these are present (normally only very small proportions) they will be registered as CO_2 unless the sample is first passed over a burner and these two gases burned off before the reading.

Bridge electrical unbalance is dependent on CO_2 content and the unbalance current is measured by the potentiometer.

Mechanical Type CO_2 Recorder

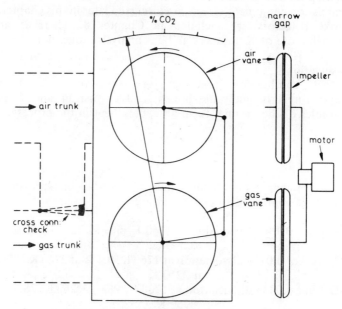

MECHANICAL TYPE CO_2 RECORDER
Fig. 2.14

Referring to Fig. 2.14:

Density of flue gas is proportional to CO_2 content. Couple (torque) of impeller to vane is proportional to density of the medium in the narrow gap. The torques if both in air would balance. Therefore the CO_2 content increases the density, hence torque, the torque unbalance which is directly proportional to the CO_2 content is conveyed through the link mechanisms to the recorder scale or pen. Gas and air are arranged to be at equal total pressure, temperature and saturation. Stainless steel components are used and bearings are of the ball race type with spring loaded adjustments.

Clean Air Act

It is an offence to discharge smoke into the atmosphere, however in marine practice allowance is made for soot blowing, lighting up and breakdown. Emissions from a forced draught oil fired boiler furnace or an oil engine must not be longer than 10 minutes with dark smoke in the aggregate in any period of 2 hours and not more than 4 minutes continuous dark smoke except when soot blowing a water tube boiler.

The practical applications of smoke colour indications and combustion equipment effects are discussed later in this chapter. Smoke detectors are included in Chapter 8. There is an increasing use of R numbers and gas analysis indicators.

Dissociation

Most combustion reactions are reversible. At high temperatures the molecule bonds tend to disrupt and form molecules of the original form absorbing heat in the process.

$$2H_2O \rightleftarrows 2H_2 + O_2$$
$$2CO_2 \rightleftarrows 2CO + O_2$$

There is an increase in volume which is resisted by high pressures so as pressure rises dissociation reduces.

CO_2 1 bar 0.1% dissociation at 1760 K, 6% at 2260 K, 55% at 3250 K.

CO_2 102 bar 0.01% dissociation at 1760 K, 0.1% at 2260 K, 17% at 3250 K.

H_2O 1 bar 0.04% dissociation at 1760 K, 2% at 2260 K, 28% at 3250 K.

H_2O 102 bar 0.004% dissociation at 1760 K, 0.3% at 2260 K, 3% at 3250 K

These figures only relate to the gas or vapour by itself. Gas mixtures and rich oxygen contents tend to reduce dissociation considerably.

Once the temperature falls the molecules reform (re-combustion) and heat is again evolved. Thermal decomposition is non reversible split up under heat, thermal dissociation is reversible split up under heat.

In an *I.C.* engine dissociation causes reduction of maximum combustion temperatures and heat re-appearance during expansion occurs, which tends to raise the curve above the adiabatic.

In a fire there is a danger that the use of superheated steam as an extinguishing agent (say sootblowers on an air heater fire) could in fact *feed* the fire and accelerate the growth. For example the *displacement* which occurs about 707°C

$$\text{Heat} + \text{Hot } 3\ Fe + 12\ H_2O \rightleftharpoons 3\ FeO_3 + 12H_2\uparrow$$

goes to completion giving liberation of volatile hydrogen and makes the combustion more rapid. Such fires are sometimes called '*Rusting*' fires. Although the total displacement reaction is reversible the main factor is *decomposition* of steam vapour and dissociation of steam vapour plays a relatively minor part, however as dissociation is regarded chemically as reversible decomposition then the process is often regarded by engineers as dissociation.

The Boiler Combustion Heat Balance

A typical analysis of the heat utilisation in an oil fired boiler would be as in Table 2.4.

ITEM	% HEAT
IN FUEL (*hcv*)	100
IN STEAM IN EXCESS AIR IN DRY GASES IN WET VAPOURS IN UNBURNED GASES IN RADIATION	80 $3\frac{1}{2}$ 8 3 $\frac{1}{2}$ 5
	100

TABLE 2.4

It can be seen that dry combustion gases, excess air and wet vapours are losses. Minimum excess air and lowest practical flue gas temperature (bearing in mind complete combustion and corrosion in uptakes, etc.) reduce these losses together with close attention to CO_2 content, *i.e.* to reduce unburned combustion gas loss.

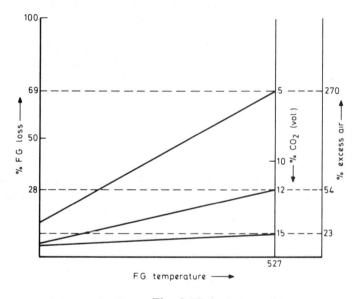

Fig. 2.15

The % flue gas (*F.G.*) loss can be seen to increase with flue gas temperature increase, increase with excess air increase and increase with fall in gas CO_2 content (see Fig. 2.15).

The condition of the gases leaving the funnel is often the best indication of combustion conditions. Black smoke due to insufficient air (among other things), white smoke due to too much air, blue smoke due to burning of lubricating oils (in *I.C.* engines), yellow smoke indicative of high sulphur bearing fuels, etc.

However CO_2 content is often required to give the efficiency of combustion for a particular plant. Each plant however will have its own optimum figure and this may vary for boilers between 10 and 14% depending on many variables.

COMBUSTION EQUIPMENT

Good combustion is essential for the efficient running of the boiler, it gives the best possible heat release and the minimum amount of deposits upon the heating surfaces. To ascertain if the combustion is good, measure the % CO_2 content (and in some installations the % O_2 content) and observe the appearance of the gases.

If the % CO_2 content is correct (or the % O_2 content low) and the gases are in a non smoky condition then the combustion of the fuel is correct. With correct %CO_2 content the % excess air required for combustion will be low and this results in improved boiler efficiency since less heat is taken from the burning fuel by the small amount of excess air. If the excess air supply is increased then the % CO_2 content of the gases will fall.

Condition of burners, oil condition, pressure and temperature, condition of air registers, air supply pressure and temperature are all factors which can influence combustion.

Burners. If these are dirty or the sprayer plates are damaged then atomisation of the fuel will be affected. Types include pressure jet, in various forms, rotary cup, steam jet and ultrasonic.

Oil. If the oil is dirty it can foul up the burners. (Filters are provided in the oil supply lines to remove most of the dirt particles but filters can get damaged. Ideally the mesh in the last filter should be smaller than the holes in the burner sprayer plate).

Water in the oil can affect combustion, it could lead to the burners being extinguished and a dangerous situation arising. It could also produce panting which can result in structural defects.

If the oil temperature is too low oil does not readily atomise since its viscosity will be high, this could cause flame impingement, overheating, tube and refractory failure. If the oil temperature is too high the burner tip becomes too hot and excessive carbon deposits can then be formed on the tip causing spray defects, these could again lead to flame impingement on adjacent refractory and damage could also occur to the air swirlers.

Oil pressure is also important since it affects atomisation and lengths of spray jets.

Air registers. Good mixing of the fuel particles with the air is essential, hence the condition of the air registers and their swirling devices are important, if they are damaged mechanically or by corrosion then the air flow will be affected. Pressure drops over the venturi of 25 mm water gauge give air speeds of about 20 m/s. Modern swirler type stabiliser designs give more efficient mixing with pressure drops up to 300 mm water gauge and air speeds up to 70 m/s.

Air: The excess air supply is governed mainly by the air pressure and if this is incorrect combustion will be incorrect.

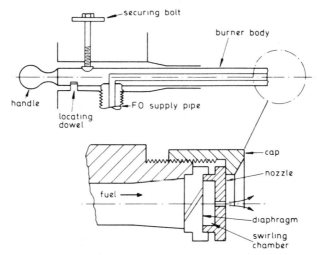

O.F. BURNER (WALLSEND-HOWDEN)
Fig. 2.16

Fig. 2.16 shows a simple pressure jet burner arrangement for a boiler (Wallsend-Howden). Preheated pressurised fuel is supplied to the burner tip which produces a cone of finely divided fuel particles that mix with the air supplied around the steel burner body into the furnace. A safety point of some importance is the oil fuel valve arrangement. It is *impossible* to remove the burner from the supporting tube unless the oil fuel is shut off, this greatly reduces risk of oil spillage in the region of the boiler front.

Fig. 2.17 shows the boiler front air register (top sketch) and tip (middle sketch) for the Y-jet steam atomising oil burner

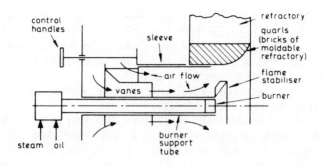

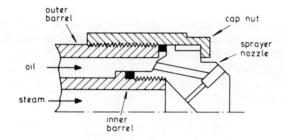

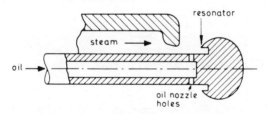

STEAM ATOMISING EQUIPMENT
Fig. 2.17

which is finding increased favour for use with water tube boilers, for the following reasons:

1. Deposits are greatly reduced, hence soot blowing and water washing of the gas surfaces need not be carried out as frequently as before (18 months or more between cleaning is possible).

2. Atomisation and combustion are greatly improved, and lower dew point gives reduced acid formation.

3. $\% CO_2$ reading is increased ($\% O_2$ reading has been lowered

to 1% or below) hence the boiler efficiency is greatly improved (excess air lowered from 15% to under 5%).

4. Atomisation is excellent over a wide range of loads and the turndown ratio is as high as 20:1 (turn down ratio compares maximum and minimum flow rates).

5. With improved combustion, and turndown ratio, refractory problems are reduced.

The major disadvantage of this type of burner is that it uses steam—which means water and fuel—but the steam consumption in the latest type of steam atomiser is extremely small, less than 1% of the oil consumption at peak loads. Maximum oil pressure is 22 bar and steam is supplied at 12 bar, a steam control valve may be fitted to reduce the steam pressure at low loads.

The ultrasonic atomiser (bottom sketch of Fig. 2.17) consists of an annular steam nozzle, a resonator and nozzle with holes. It gives high turn down ratio and low excess air. Ultrasonic energy wave vibration, 5-10 kHz, produced by high speed steam or air flow against the resonator edge ahead of the oil holes gives atomisation with very minute oil droplets.

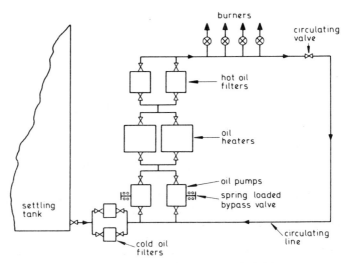

BOILER O.F. SUPPLY SYSTEM
Fig. 2.18

Fig. 2.18 illustrates a simple boiler O.F. supply system.

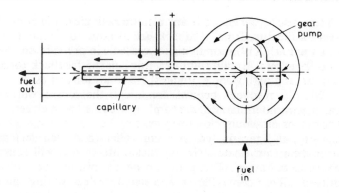

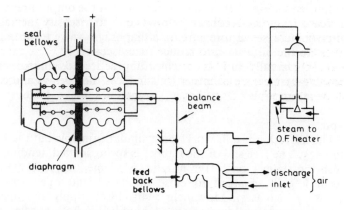

VISCOMETER AND DP CELL TRANSMITTER
Fig. 2.19

Viscosity Control

Consider the viscometer (Fig. 2.19). A gear pump is driven by a constant speed electric motor through a reduction gear. A small constant quantity of oil (fuel in this case) is passed through the fine capillary tube. As the flow is arranged to be streamline (laminar), as distinct from turbulent, the differential pressure across the capillary tube is directly proportional to the viscosity of the oil. This differential pressure in two tappings, shown + and − , is led from the viscometer to a differential pressure transmitter (*D.P.* cell).

Differential pressure from the viscometer is applied across the diaphragm of the transmitter. Increased differential pressure, caused by increased viscosity, causes the diaphragm and balance beam to move to the left. The air inlet nozzle is closed in and air pressure builds up in the feedback bellows due to a relay (not shown on Fig. 2.19), supplying increased air pressure to the feedback bellows. Equilibrium occurs when the feedback force equals the originating force, under these conditions air escape is minimal. The feedback bellows pressure is the control output signal. Transmitter diaphragm chambers are filled with glycerine or silicone as oil would clog the parts.

The output signal is fed to a controller (and recorder) to control the steam flow to the oil fuel heater which will cause viscosity adjustment. The actuator has a piston and valve positioner. The controller has desired value setting and incorporates a reset (integral) action. This detail has been simplified on Fig. 2.19, lower sketch, so that the output pressure increase from the feedback bellows (due to viscosity increase) *directly* increases air pressure on a diaphragm valve to open up steam to the oil heater, to reduce fuel viscosity.

It is generally not good control practice to control one variable by means of another (this induces time delays and can cause appreciable offset) but it is sometimes unavoidable.

Note.

The Viscotherm unit works on a similar principle but there is no relay. The free end of the flapper is spring loaded, tending to push the flapper on to the nozzles. Movement of the balance beam left is arranged to close discharge and open supply (pressure increases). Movement right closes supply and opens discharge (pressure decreases). At equilibrium both nozzles are almost closed which minimises air wastage.

GASEOUS FUELS

There has been a steady increase in the number of 'parcel' tankers which carry a wide range of chemicals. Such vessels are expected to comply with DTp recommendations before an IMO 'Certificate of Fitness for the Carriage of Dangerous Chemicals in Bulk' is issued. Reactions with air, with water, between incompatible chemicals, and with self reactive chemicals can arise and the United States Coast Guard publish 'Bulk Liquid Chemicals; Guide to the Compatibility of Chemicals' — see Table 2.5. These vessels have special requirements relating to construction, materials, pumping systems, tank coatings, safety, etc. It is only proposed here to outline fuel technology aspects.

Chemicals Not on Chart.

The following chemicals form an unsafe combination with each reactivity group shown:

Carbon bisulfide: 1, 4, 19, 20, and epichlorohydrin.

Diphenyl methane diisocyanate, polymethylene polyphenyl isocyanate and tolyene diisocyanate: 1, 2, 3, 4, 5, 6, 7, 8, 13, 14, 15, 16, 17, 19, 20, 22, 23, 24, and carbon bisulfide.

Motor Fuel antiknock compounds: 1, 4, 5, 6, 7, 15, 19, and 20.

Nitropropane: 1, 2, 3, 4, 19, and 24.

Group	1	2	3	4	5	6	7	8	9	10	11	12	13	14	15	16	17	18	19	20	21	22	23	24
1 Inorganic Acids	**1**																							
2 Organic Acids	×	**2**																						
3 Caustics	×	×	**3**																					
4 Amines & Alkanolamines	×	×		**4**																				
5 Halogenated Compounds	×		×		**5**																			
6 Alcohols, Glycols & Glycol Ethers	×					**6**																		
7 Aldehydes	×		×	×	×		**7**																	
8 Ketones	×		×		×			**8**																
9 Saturated Hydrocarbons									**9**															
10 Aromatic Hydrocarbons										**10**														
11 Olefins	×										**11**													
12 Petroleum Oils												**12**												
13 Esters	×	×	×	×									**13**											
14 Monomers & Polymerizable Esters	×	×	×	×										**14**										
15 Phenols	×		×												**15**									
16 Alkylene Oxides	×	×	×	×	×	×	×						×	×	×	**16**								
17 Cyanohydrins	×	×	×	×	×	×	×						×	×			**17**							
18 Nitriles	×																	**18**						
19 Ammonia	×																		**19**					
20 Halogens			×						×	×	×								×	**20**				
21 Ethers	×																				**21**			
22 Phosphorus, Elemental																				×		**22**		
23 Sulphur, Molten																				×		×	**23**	
24 Acid Anydrides	×		×	×		×													×					**24**

COMPATIBILITY CHART
TABLE 2.5.

*Unsafe combinations are indicated by ×. Obtain the group for the chemical and then read chart, first from left to right, then down.

LNG (liquefied natural gas) is a cryogenic, clear, colourless liquid with methane as its main constituent (about 87% by volume), ethane (about 9%), propane (about 3%) and traces of butanes and pentanes. Boiling point is about $-162°C$ and heating value of the gas is about 10 MJ/m³. Heat flow through insultation causes gradual evaporation which maintains pressure above atmospheric and prevents ingress of air.

LPG (liquid petroleum gas) includes such as propane, butane and ammonia. Boiling points are lower than for LNG.

Combustion Equipment

Vaporisation of the liquid (boil off about 0.2% per day) due to heat entry can be utilised as boiler or engine fuel, re-liquefied by suitable vapour pumps and compressors, or the adoption of both is possible. Utilisation as a dual fuel requires sophisticated instrumentation on the gas side and safety interlocks between the two fuel systems. The supply gas can vary appreciably in composition during the voyage and close monitoring of composition, dryness, etc. are necessary with facility for pressure variation, variable heat input etc. Complexities also arise due to differing air requirements, flame speeds, etc. but suitable plant is readily available and the gaseous fuel gives rapid, efficient and clean combustion.

Explosive and Toxic Vapour Concentration

Vessels should be equipped with duplicate combination instruments, one at least of which to be portable, and if instruments for one detection function only are provided then duplicates of each are necessary. Oxygen analysers, to indicate alarm when oxygen content falls below 18% (by volume) in a space, should also be provided.

Toxic Vapours

A number of chemicals have toxic limits well below their combustible gas/air concentration ratio and it is unsafe to enter spaces even if the gas concentration is below the Lower Explosive Limit (LEL). The Threshold Limit Value (TLV) gives the concentration of a substance in air in ppm which must not be exceeded if daily eight hour exposure over extended time periods is intended. Typical TLV values are Anilene (5), Carbon Tetrachloride (10), Benzene (25), Methanol (200) but the value can be very low, under 0.02, for certain chemicals. Detection apparatus utilises input via a bellows for a given volume, colour reaction on selected chemicals is compared colourmetrically.

Explosive Vapours

With low flash point products the danger may exist that the atmosphere lies between the LEL and the HEL therefore creating the risk of explosion. Typical flash points are Pentane $-49°C$, Hexane $-23°C$, Heptane $-4°C$ (Aliphatic hydrocarbons), Benzene $-11°C$ (Aromatic hydrocarbon), Acetone $-18°C$ (Ketone), Methanol $10°C$ (Alcohol), Carbon Disulphide $-30°C$. Vapour pressure is that constant pressure during isothermal isobaric evaporation (or condensation), when liquid and vapour are in equilibrium (quality defined by dryness fraction). LEL and HEL are affected by variations in vapour pressure (see also Chapter 8).

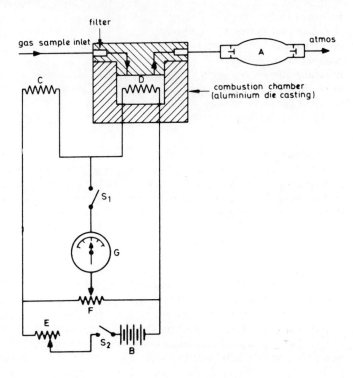

GAS EXPLOSION DETECTOR METER
Fig. 2.20

Gas Explosion—Detector Meter (Fig. 2.20)

The instrument is first charged with fresh air from the atmosphere using the rubber aspirator bulb (A). On-off switch (S_2) is closed together with check switch (S_1) and the compensatory filament (C) and detector filament (D) allowed to reach steady state working temperature. The zero adjustment rheostat (F) can now be adjusted so that galvanometer (G) reads zero. Voltage is adjustable from battery (B) by the rheostat (E). Switch S_2 is now opened.

The instrument is now charged from the suspect gas space and while operating the bulb, the switch S_2 is again closed. If a flammable or explosive gas is present it will cause the detector filament to increase in temperature. This disturbs the bridge balance and a current flows. Galvanometer (G) can be calibrated so that the scale is marked to read '% of Lower Limit of Explosive Concentration of Gas'.

TEST EXAMPLES 2

Class 3

1. What is meant by the term calorific value and how does the calorific value of fuel oil compare with that of coal?

2. Why is the flash point an important criteria with regard to lubricating oil, state how it is determined, and give one reason why the flash point of a lubricating oil sample from an engine might be lower than expected.

3. When referring to fuel oil Cetane Number and Conradson Number are often used. Explain these two terms.

4. Complete the following combustion equations:
   (i) $C + O_2 \rightarrow$
   (ii) $C + \frac{1}{2}O_2 \rightarrow$
   (iii) $H_2 + \frac{1}{2}O_2 \rightarrow$

TEST EXAMPLES 2

Class 2

1. Sketch the apparatus used and describe the test to determine the following properties of oil:
   (a)   viscosity,
   (b)   calorific value.

2. (i)   Suggest, with reasons, which of the following data is relevant and significant to the quality of fuel oil:
   viscosity,   conradson number,
   pour point,   total base number,
   closed flash point,   octane number,
   open flash point,   specific gravity.

   (ii)   Define the significance of lower and higher calorific value in assessing the standard of liquid fuel.

3. (a)   Specify, with reasons, where test samples should be drawn from a main lubricating oil system.

   Describe shipboard tests to determine:
   (b)   water content,
   (c)   acidity,
   (d)   suspended solids.

4. (a)   Describe, with sketches, an instrument for indicating the carbon dioxide content of the gases in the uptake.
   (b)   Explain the meaning and importance of the readings obtained.

TEST EXAMPLES 2

Class 1

1. With reference to fire or explosion explain the significance of the following properties of a flammable gas:
   (a)   vapour pressure,
   (b)   explosive limits,
   (c)   flash point,
   (d)   density,
   (e)   fire point.

2. Define each of the following terms in relation to lubricating oil:
   (a)   pour point,
   (b)   cracking point,
   (c)   flash point,
   (d)   auto-ignition point.
   State, with reasons, when will each of these characteristics be of primary importance.

3. Explain the effects of differences in chemical composition, calorific value and viscosity of the fuel on engine performance.
   Describe how engine operation and maintenance may need changing in order to burn heavy distillate instead of light distillate fuel.

4. For a carbon dioxide recorder explain:
   (a)   the principle of operation,
   (b)   the action to be taken if the reading is unacceptably low,
   (c)   the normal maintenance required,
   (d)   How the accuracy of the recorder is checked and adjusted.

CHAPTER 3

BOILERS AND ANCILLARIES

SAFETY VALVES

At least two safety valves have to be fitted to any one boiler. They may both be in the same valve chest, which must be separate from any other valve chest. The chest may be connected to the boiler with only one connecting neck.

The safety valves must never be less than 38 mm in diameter and the area of the valves can be calculated from the following formula:

$$C \times A \times P = 9.81 \times H \times E \tag{1}$$

Where H = Total heating surface in m^2.

,, E = Evaporative rate in kg of steam per m^2 of heating surface per hour.

,, P = Working pressure of safety valves in MN/m^2 absolute.

,, A = Aggregate area through the seating of the valves in mm^2.

C is a discharge coefficient whose value depends upon the type of valve.

C = 4.8 for ordinary spring loaded safety valves.
C = 7.2 for high lift spring loaded safety valves.
C = 9.6 for improved high lift spring loaded safety valves.
C = 19.2 for full lift safety valves.
C = 30 for full bore relay operated safety valves.

If we consider a boiler operating under fixed conditions of discharge rate (*i.e.* $H \times E$), pressure P then, from (1):

$$A \times C = \frac{9.81 \times H \times E}{P} = \text{a constant}$$

also $\frac{A}{2} = \frac{\pi D^2}{4}$ approximately. Where D is the diameter of the seating of one valve, in mm.

$$\therefore \frac{\pi D^2}{2} \times C = \text{a constant}$$

i.e. $D^2 C = \text{a constant.}$

Hence if C is increased, D must be reduced. But if D is reduced the lift of the valve must be increased in order to avoid any accumulation of pressure. This is accomplished by improving the type of valve fitted to the boiler.

Typical valve lifts are as follows:

When $C = 4.8$ lift $= D/24$ approximately
  ,, $C = 7.2$ and 9.6 ,, $= D_2/12$,,
  ,, $C = 19.2$ and 30 ,, $= D_3/4$,,

Where $D_1 > D_2 > D_3$ and D_1. D_2 and D_3 are the diameters of the seating of the valves in mm.

Improved High Lift Type

For low pressure water tube boilers and fire tube boilers of the Scotch and other varieties, the safety valve generally employed is Cockburns *improved* high lift type. The operative parts of this valve are shown in Fig. 3.1.

This valve has generally superseded the ordinary and high lift types of safety valve. The essential differences between these three safety valves are as given in Table 3.1.

Ordinary	High Lift	Improved High Lift
Winged valve No waste steam piston	Winged valve Waste steam piston No floating ring	Wingless valve Waste steam piston Floating ring

TABLE 3.1

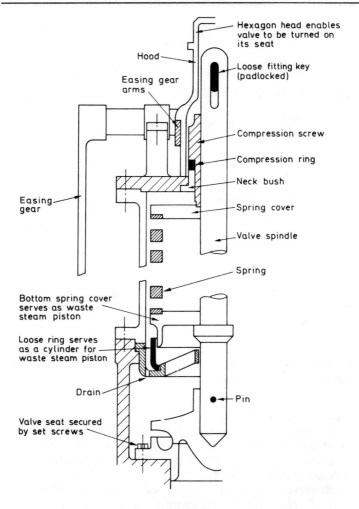

IMPROVED HIGH LIFT SAFETY VALVE
Fig. 3.1

Hence the *improvements* to the high lift safety valve are (1) Removal of valve wings, this improves waste steam flow and reduces risk of seizure (2) Floating ring or cylinder which reduces risk of seizure.

The three spring loaded safety valves, ordinary, high lift and improved high lift, all make use of a special shaped valve seat and a lip on the valve which gives increased valve lift against the increasing downward force of the spring. The action can be seen in Fig. 3.2.

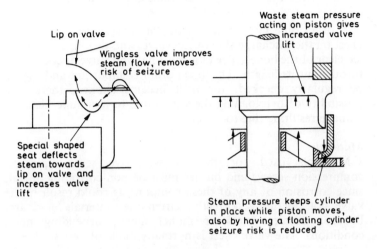

Lip on valve

Wingless valve improves steam flow, removes risk of seizure

Special shaped seat deflects steam towards lip on valve and increases valve lift

Waste steam pressure acting on piston gives increased valve lift

Steam pressure keeps cylinder in place while piston moves, also by having a floating cylinder seizure risk is reduced

Fig. 3.2

For superheated steam the aggregate area through the seating of the valves is increased, the formula is:

$$A_s = A(1 + T_s/555)$$

Where A_s = aggregate area through the seating of the valves in mm² for superheated steam.

,, A = aggregate area through the seating of the valves in mm² for saturated steam.

,, T_s = degrees of superheat in °C.

A_s is obviously greater than A, the reason being that the specific volume of the steam has increased with the increase of temperature at constant pressure and more escape area is required to avoid accumulation of pressure (specific volume is volume per unit mass).

The area of the valve chest connecting neck to the boiler must be at least equal in cross sectional area to one half of the aggregate area A, determined from equation (1). The waste steam pipe and steam passage from the valves must have a cross sectional area of at least:

1.1 × A for Ordinary, High lift and Improved high lift safety valves,

2 × A for Full lift safety valves,

3 × A for Full bore relay operated safety valves.

A drain pipe must be fitted to the lowest part of the valve chest on the discharge side of the valves and this pipe should be led clear of the boiler. The pipe must have no valve or cock fitted throughout its length. This open drain is important and should be regularly checked, for if it became choked, there is a possibility of overloading the valves due to hydraulic head, or damage resulting due to water hammer.

Materials

Materials used for the valves, valve seats, spindles, compression screws and bushes must be non-corrodible metal, since corrosion of any of these components could result in the valve not operating correctly. Often the materials used are: Bronze, stainless steel or monel metal, depending upon conditions. The valve chest is normally made of cast steel.

Maintenance and Adjustment

The makers figures relating to lip clearances, seating widths and wing clearances, etc., must be adhered to. All working parts should be sound, in alignment and able to function correctly.

When overhauling safety valves, care must be taken to ensure the parts are put back in their correct order. When dismantled, the parts are hung by a cord and sounded by gently tapping with a hammer. If they do not ring true, examine for faults. Check drains and easing gear.

Adjustment or setting of safety valves of the direct spring loaded type: With compression rings removed, screw down compression screws, raise boiler pressure to the required blow off pressure. Screw back compression screw until valve blows, then screw down the compression screw carefully, tapping the valve spindle downwards very lightly whilst doing so, until the valve returns to its seat and remains closed.

When set, split compression rings have to be fitted, then hoods, keys, padlocks and easing gear. Finally check and operate easing gear to ensure it is in good working order.

For a multi-boilered installation, raise all the boiler pressures to the required blow off pressure, make sure the boilers are connected up, then proceed as described above, setting each valve in turn.

Accumulation of Pressure Test

Classification societies require that when initially fitted to boilers safety valves must be subjected to an accumulation of pressure test to ensure the valves are of the correct discharge capacity for the boiler. To conduct such a test, all feed inlets and steam outlets to and from the boiler respectively, must be closed, and maximum firing rate arranged. Accumulation of pressure must then not exceed 10 per cent of the working pressure. Duration of test (water permitting) is not to exceed 15 minutes for cylindrical boilers and 7 minutes for water tube boilers. In the case of water tube boilers the test may be waived if damage to superheaters or economisers could result from the test.

Full Lift Safety Valve

The full lift safety valve shown in Fig. 3.3 does not incorporate a waste steam piston, instead the valve itself operating inside the guide acts as a piston in a cylinder.

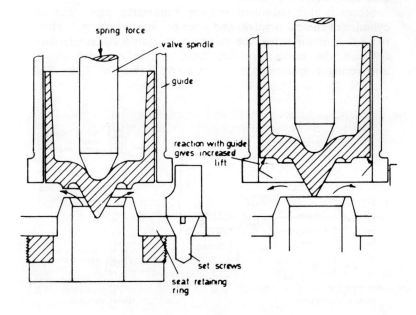

FULL LIFT SAFETY VALVE
(for pressures up to 63 bar)
Fig. 3.3

Details of spring, compression nut, easing gear and valve chest etc., have been omitted for convenience since they are somewhat similar to that for the improved high lift valve.

The operation of the valve is as follows: When the valve has lifted a small amount the escaping steam pressure can then act upon the full area of the valve, this increases the lift until the lower edge of the valve just enters the guide. At this point the reaction pressure generated by the escaping steam with the guide causes the valve to lift further until it is fully open. When the valve is fully open the escape area is said to be equal to the area of supply through the seating.

Full Bore Safety Valve

Fig. 3.4 is a diagrammatic arrangement of a full bore relay operated safety valve suitable for water tube boilers whose working pressure is in excess of 21 bar [2.1 MN/m²].

The operation of the valve is as follows: When the boiler pressure reaches the desired blow off pressure the relay valve lifts, blanking as it does so a series of ports leading to the atmosphere (see Fig. 3.4a).

Steam is then admitted via the connecting pipe, into the cylinder of the main valve, and since the area of piston is about twice that of the valve, the valve opens against boiler pressure.

When the boiler pressure falls, the relay valve closes, uncovering as it does so the ports above it (see Fig. 3.4b). This

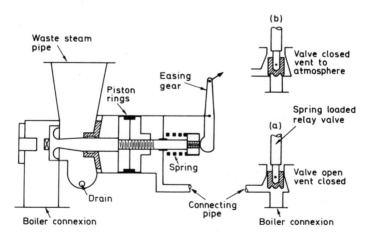

FULL BORE RELAY OPERATED SAFETY VALVE
Fig. 3.4

communicates the cylinder of the main valve with the atmosphere and the boiler pressure then causes the main valve to close rapidly.

This type of valve is suitable for high pressure boilers, since the greater the boiler pressure the more rapid will the valve close, and hence the greater the saving in steam.

The main valve spring assists closing of the valve and also ensures that the valve will be closed when the boiler is cold.

If the valve is to be used for the saturated steam drum of a water tube boiler the main valve and relay valve connexion are sometimes made common to the drum. If however the valve is to be used for superheated steam then the relay valve connexion is taken separately from the main valve connexion to the saturated steam drum, this arrangement subjects the relay valve and main valve piston and cylinder to lower temperature operation.

DIRECT WATER LEVEL INDICATORS

Consider Fig. 3.5

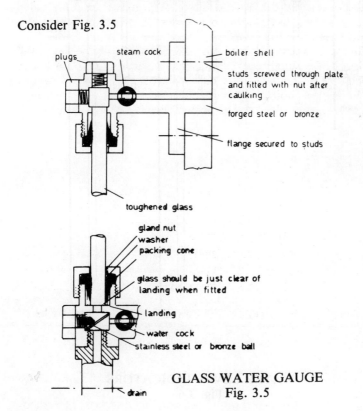

GLASS WATER GAUGE
Fig. 3.5

This glass water gauge is fitted directly to the boiler shell and is suitable for boilers whose working pressure does not exceed 34.5 bar [3.45 MN/m²].

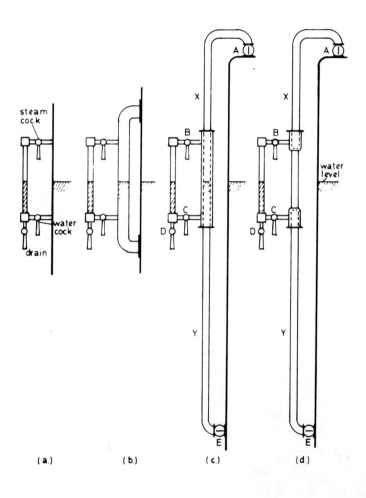

WATER LEVEL INDICATORS
Fig. 3.6

Fig. 3.6a
Blowing Procedure
(1) Close steam and water cocks then open the drain. Nothing should then blow out of the gauge if the steam and water cocks are not leaking.
(2) Open and close water cock to check that the water cock connexion to the boiler is clear.
(3) Open and close steam cock to check that the steam cock connexion to the boiler is clear.
(4) Close the drain.
(5) Open the water cock. Water should then gradually rise up to the top of the gauge glass.
(6) Open the steam cock and the water in the glass should fall to the level of the water in the boiler.

If when (5) is reached the water cock is opened and water does not flow up the gauge glass, the water level in the boiler is below the water cock connexion to the boiler and it is unsafe to put feed water into the boiler.

If when the water clock has been opened the water flows to the top of the gauge glass and then when the steam cock is opened the water flows down and out of the glass, the water level is between the water cock connexion to the boiler and the bottom of the gauge glass. In this case it is safe to put feed water into the boiler.

If after (5) when the glass is full of water, the steam cock is opened and the water in the glass does not descend in the glass, the water level is above the steam cock connexion to the boiler and there is a danger of priming the boiler if any additional feed is put into it.

Fig. 3.6b
This glass water gauge arrangement is similar to Fig. 3.6a except that the gauge is connected to a large bore pipe fitted to the boiler. The pipe has plugs fitted, two at the top and two at the bottom, which can be removed during boiler cleaning in order to clean out the pipe.

The blowing procedure for this fitting is the same as for 3.6a.

Fig. 3.6c
These fittings 3.6c and 3.6d of the hollow and solid column types respectively, are convenience fittings. They bring the water gauge glass clear of other boiler fittings such as gas uptakes, etc., so that the gauge glass can be easily seen by the boiler room

personnel. In addition, by shutting off the terminal cocks on the boiler they should enable the water gauge steam and water cocks to be overhauled whilst the boiler is steaming.

To determine whether the pipes and terminal cocks are clear a blowing procedure sometimes referred to as cross blowing is adopted. With reference to Fig. 3.6c: Cocks A, C and D open, cocks B and E closed, this checks that A, pipe X and the column are clear.

Then with cocks E, B and D open, cocks A and C closed, checks that E and pipe Y are clear.

Next blow the water gauge glass as described for 3.6a with A and E open.

Fig. 3.6d

In this case there is no direct communication between the pipes X and Y hence to check whether the pipes and cocks are clear the blowing procedure employed for 3.6a should be used.

With reference to Figs 3.6c and d. If either of the steam cocks A and B are choked then water will gradually fill the gauge glass due to the steam above the water condensing.

If either of the water cocks are choked water will again fill the glass due to the steam condensing in the upper connexions.

When a water gauge of the types 3.6c and d are blown through and all connexions are clear and all cocks are in operative order the water level in the glass will be the water level in boiler. However, after a period of time (which depends upon conditions *e.g.* ventilation arrangements, etc.) it will normally be found that the water level in the glass will have fallen. This is due to (1) The cooling of the water in the pipe Y, thereby increasing its density. (2) The reduction of condensation of steam in the pipe X, which is caused by an accumulation of air in the upper connexions due to steam condensing.

Hence when blowing through a water gauge of either of the types 3.6c and d check the water level in the glass before blowing with the water level in the glass immediately after blowing, and the difference in levels must then be taken into account whilst operating the boiler.

When any gauge glass fitting is in operation the cock handles should be vertical. If they were arranged horizontally and the gauge is in operation, vibration effects may cause the cock handle to gradually tend to take up a vertical position thereby closing the cock in the case of steam and water cocks, and opening in the case of the drain. (The steam and water cocks for 3.6d *cannot* be used as test cocks).

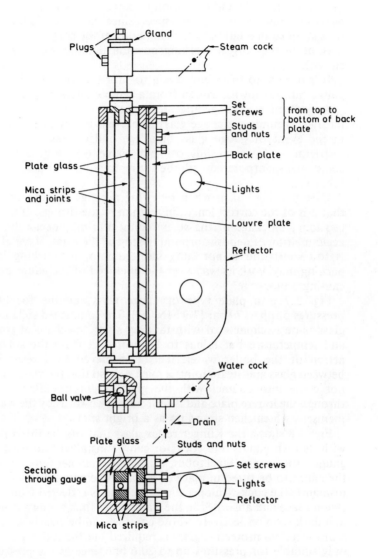

PLATE TYPE OF WATER GAUGE
Fig. 3.7

The relation of handle position to correct working position is also important from another aspect, since if the handle became over strained in relation to the plug body of the cock, the handle may be in the correct working position but the cock may be closed.

It is normal to fit extended controls for the cocks so that the gauge can be blown through from a remote and safe position.

A protective glass arrangement should be provided which partly surrounds the gauge glass to prevent injury to personnel in the event of gauge glass breakage under steam. A steam restrictor and water shut off ball valve (see Fig. 3.5) are sometimes incorporated with the fitting to reduce the severity of breakage.

Care must be taken when renewing a gauge glass to ensure that it is of the correct length in relation to the fittings. If it was too long, blockage of the steam connexion may occur due to accumulation of deposits around the top of the glass. If the glass is too short and is not fully inserted into the packing, the packing may work its way over the open end of the gauge glass causing a blockage.

Fig. 3.7 is a plate type of gauge glass suitable for high pressures of up to 79 bar [7.9 MN/m^2]. The toughened soda lime glass plate is capable of withstanding severe mechanical stress and temperature but it has to be protected from the solvent action of the boiler water. This is achieved by interposing between glass and steam joint, a mica strip so that the water does not come into contact with the glass. Light is deflected up through the louvre plate and is reflected downwards by the water meniscus which then shows up as a bright spot.

Fig. 3.8 shows the Klinger reflex glass that can be fitted new with its own glands and cocks or can be installed into existing gauge cock fittings. Steel tubes, which have spanner flats, enable the gauge to be fitted in place of a glass tube without having to dismantle the cocks. In operation, the light is reflected from the steam space and absorbed in the water space thus giving a bright and dark strip respectively whose contrast can be clearly seen at a distance. No protective glass is required but the reflex glass is only suitable for pressures up to 20.6 bar since as the pressure and temperature increases the solvent action of the water increases.

Remote Water Level Indicators

There are various types of remote water level indicators. Their

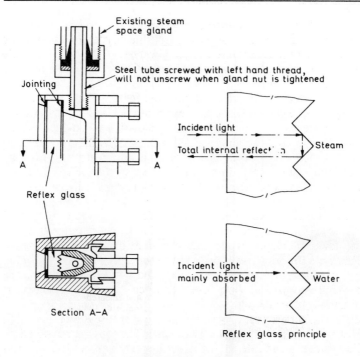

KLINGER REFLEX GLASS
(for steam pressures up to 20.6 bar)
Fig. 3.8

purpose is to bring the water level reading to some convenient position in the engine or boiler room where it can be distinctly seen. These indicators when fitted are normally in addition to the normal statutory requirements for water gauge fittings for boilers.

Fig. 3.9 is a diagrammatic arrangement of the 'Igema' remote water level indicator. The lower portion of the 'U' tube contains a red coloured indicating fluid which does not mix with water and has a density greater than that of water.

The equilibrium condition for the gauge is $H = h + \varrho x$ where ϱ is the density of the indicating fluid. H, h and x are variables.

If the water level in the boiler falls, h will be reduced, x will be increased and H must therefore be increased. The level of the water in the condenser reservoir being maintained by condensing steam.

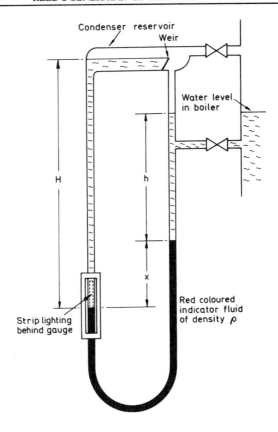

REMOTE WATER LEVEL INDICATOR
Fig. 3.9

If the water level in the boiler rises, *h* will be increased, *x* will be reduced and *H* must therefore be reduced. Water will therefore flow over the weir in the condenser reservoir in order to maintain the level constant.

A strip light is fitted behind the gauge which increases the brightness of the red indicating fluid, which enables the operator to observe at a glance from a considerable distance whether the gauge is full or empty.

Fig. 3.10 is another type of remote water level indicator. In this case the operating fluid is the boiler water itself. The operation of the gauge is as follows:

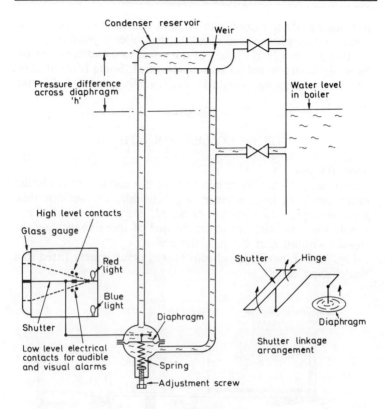

Fig. 3.10

If we consider a falling water level in the boiler, the pressure difference across the diaphragm 'h' will increase, causing the diaphragm to deflect downwards. This motion of the diaphragm is transmitted by means of a linkage arrangement (see insert) to the shutter which in turn moves down pivoting about its hinge, causing an increase in the amount of red colour and a decrease in the amount of blue colour seen at the glass gauge.

It will be clearly understood that if the water level now rises then the red will be reduced and the blue increased.

Separating the blue and red colours, which are distinctive and can clearly be seen from a considerable distance, is a loose fitting black band which moves with the shutter, giving a distinct separation of the two colours.

An adjustment screw and spring are provided to enable the difference in diaphragm load to be adjusted. Hence correct positioning of the shutter and band in relation to the reading of a glass water gauge fitted direct to the boiler is possible.

High and low level alarms of the visual and audible types can be easily incorporated with the instrument. Some form of make and break electrical contacts are usually provided for this purpose.

OTHER BOILER MOUNTINGS

Soot Blowers

Between periodic boiler cleaning the gas surfaces of the boiler tubes should be kept as clean as practicable. To facilitate this, soot blowers, steam or air operated, are often fitted. They enable the tube surfaces to be cleaned of loose sooty deposits rapidly without shut down of the boiler.

Fig. 3.11 shows a typical soot blower arrangement fitted to a Scotch type boiler.

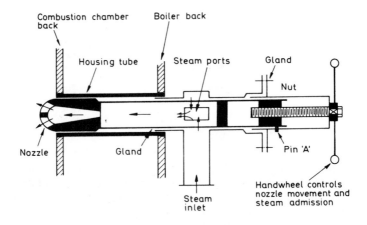

SOOT BLOWER
Fig. 3.11

With steam supplied to the blower and the steam supply line thoroughly drained. Rotation of the blower hand wheel causes the supply tube and nozzle to move towards the combustion chamber. Nozzle and tube are rotated as they move inwards by means of a scroll cut in the nut and a stationary pin A in the body assembly that runs in the scroll. Ports in the tube communicate the steam supply line with the nozzle.

The arrangement enables rotating, fine, high pressure jets of steam to be discharged to the tube plate over a considerable area.

When not in use, the retractable nozzle of the blower is well within the housing tube and is therefore protected from overheating, which could cause burning and distortion of the nozzle.

Too frequent use of the blower should be avoided as this could cause wastage of the tube plate. It is advisable to operate the blower regularly even if the boiler tubes are clean (in this case without steam supply to the blower) to ensure the blower unit is free and in operable order.

Feed Check Valves

Feed check valves for main and auxiliary purposes are normally of the double shut off variety. This is shown diagrammatically in Fig. 3.12.

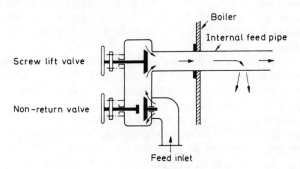

DIAGRAMMATIC ARRANGEMENT OF FEED CHECK
VALVES
Fig. 3.12

The double shut off arrangement does enable the non-return feed check valve to be overhauled whilst the boiler is steaming, since if the screw down valve is shut the non-return valve is then isolated from the boiler. But overhaul of these valves is best done when the boiler is opened up for examination.

The non-return valve is necessary, since if a feed line fractures or a joint in the line blows, then the boiler contents will not be discharged out of the feed line. Also, double shut off reduces risk of leakage into the feed line whilst it is under repair and the boiler is steaming.

BOILERS

Waste Heat Boilers

With Diesel machinery the amount of heat carried away by the exhaust gases varies betwen 20 to 25 per cent of the total heat energy supplied to the engine. Recovery of some of this heat loss to the extent of 30 to 50 per cent is possible by means of an exhaust gas boiler or water heater.

The amount of heat recovered from the exhaust gases depends upon various factors, some of which are: Steam pressure, temperature, evaporative rate required, exhaust gas inlet temperature, mass flow of exhaust gas, condition of heat exchange surfaces, etc.

Composite boilers are often used in conjunction with Diesel machinery, since if the exhaust gas from the engine is low in temperature due to slow running of the engine and reduced power output, the pressure of the steam can be maintained by means of an oil fired furnace. Steam supply can also be maintained with this type of boiler when the engines are not in operation.

It is not proposed to deal with all the various types and makes of waste heat boilers in detail, since for DTp (E.K. General) written examination requirements, only a brief outline of the basic principles involved is generally required.

The Cochran boiler whose working pressure is normally of the order of 7 bar (0.7 MN/m^2) is available in various types and arrangements, some of which are:

Single pass composite, *i.e.* one pass of the exhaust gases and two uptakes, one for the oil fired system and one for exhaust system. Double pass composite, *i.e.* two passes for the exhaust gases and two uptakes, one for the oil fired system and one for the exhaust system. Double pass exhaust gas, no oil fired furnace and a single uptake. Double pass alternatively fired, *i.e.* two passes from the furnace for either exhaust gases or oil fired system with one common uptake.

The material used is good quality low carbon boiler steel plate. The furnace is pressed out of a single plate and is seamless.

Connecting the bottom of the furnace to the boiler shell plating is a seamless 'Ogee' ring. This ring is pressed out of thicker plating than the furnace, the greater thickness is necessary since circulation in its vicinity is not as good as elsewhere in the boiler and deposits can accumulate between it and the boiler shell plating.

Hand hole cleaning doors are provided around the circumference of the boiler in the region of the 'Ogee' ring.

The tube plates are supported by means of the tubes and by

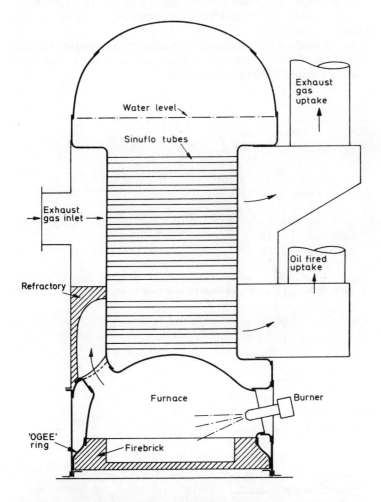

DIAGRAMMATIC ARRANGEMENT OF A SINGLE PASS COMPOSITE COCHRAN BOILER
Fig. 3.13

gusset stays, the gusset stays supporting the flat top of the tube plating.

Tubes fitted, are usually of special design (Sinuflo), being smoothly sinuous in order to increase heat transfer by baffling the gases. The wave formation of the tubes lies in a horizontal plane when the tubes are fitted, thus ensures that no troughs are available for the collection of dirt or moisture. This wave formation does not in any way affect cleaning or fitting of the tubes.

Fig. 3.14 shows the method of attachment of the furnace and 'Ogee' ring for Cochran and Clarkson welded boilers, welded to Class 1 Fusion Welding Regulations.

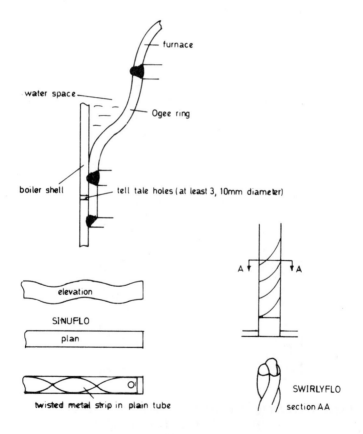

Fig. 3.14

'Tell tale' holes drilled at equal circumferential intervals in the boiler shell enable leakage between the 'Ogee' ring and boiler shell to be detected.

Also in Fig. 3.14 are shown different methods of tube manufacture and arrangement. All, enabling gas path, gas velocity and turbulence to be increased with better heat transfer, more heat extracted and tubes maintained in a cleaner condition.

The Sinuflo tube is fitted to Cochran boilers, the Swirlyflo to Spanner boilers and the plain tube with the twisted metal retarder is common to a wide range of auxiliary and in some cases main tank type boilers.

Cochran Boiler (Spheroid)

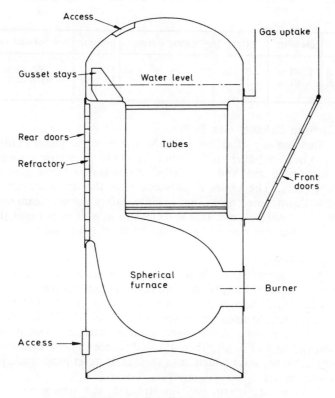

COCHRAN SPHEROID BOILER
Fig. 3.15

This auxiliary boiler has an all welded shell, a seamless spherically shaped furnace and small bore tubes. The advantages of this boiler compared to older designs are:

1. Increased steam output for the same size, mass and cost of earlier designs.
2. Increased radiant heating surface.
3. Efficient and robust ($\eta \cup 80\%$).
4. Easy to maintain.
5. No furnace brickwork required—apart from burner quarls.
6. With small tubes, fitted with retarders, gas velocity and turbulence are increased. This gives cleaner tubes and better heat transfer.

The boiler can be supplied in various sizes ranging from:

	diameter	height	heating surface	pressure	evaporative rate
1.	1.448 m	3.734 m	26 m^2	17.2 bar	995 kg/h
2.	2.591 m	6.325 m	120.8 m^2	10.3 bar	4550 kg/h

Cochran Exhaust Gas Boiler

This consists of all welded tube and wrapper plates made of good quality boiler steel. Tubes are made of electric resistance welded mild steel and are swelled at one end and expanded into tube plate. The boiler is provided with the usual mountings: blow down, feed checks, gauge glass, safety valves, steam outlet and feed control, etc. If it is to be run as a drowned unit (Fig. 3.16a) then the mountings would be modified to suit.

Scotch Boiler

A number of Scotch boilers are still in use today as main and auxiliary units. Few, if any, are being manufactured.

Plain low carbon boiler steel of good quality having an ultimate tensile strength between 430 to 540 MN/m^2 is used for the construction. All flanged plating must be heated after flanging to 600°C and then allowed to cool slowly in order to stress relieve, stays which have their ends upset must undergo a similar process.

Furnaces are corrugated for strength, the arrangement also gives increased heating surface area as compared to a plain furnace of similar dimensions. Various types of corrugation are available, but the suspension bulb type is to be preferred since for a given working pressure and furnace diameter the material thickness can be less than for any other form of corrugation, hence heat transfer will be improved.

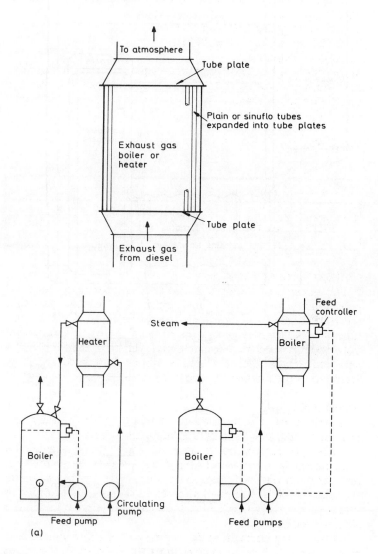

Fig. 3.16

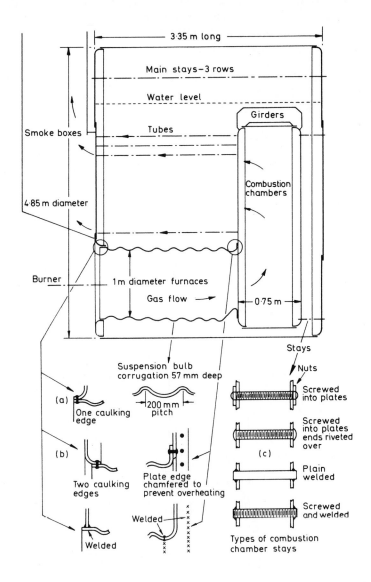

SCOTCH BOILER
Fig. 3.17

Furnace front attachments for riveted or welded construction could be any of those shown in Fig. 3.17. Fig. 3.17a is an arrangement, which compared to Fig. 3.17b, simplifies furnace renewal but has only one caulking edge. Fig. 3.17b, simplifies furnace renewal but has only one caulking edge. Fig. 3.17b is obviously a more water tight arrangement than (a) because of the two caulking edges, but re-riveting of a furnace replacement is more difficult in this case.

The furnaces must be so arranged and fitted as to ensure that furnace renewal can be carried out with minimum possible inconvenience. With this object in mind riveted furnaces have their flange, which is connected to the combustion chamber tube plate, so designed that by suitable manipulation the flange can pass through the opening in the boiler front plating.

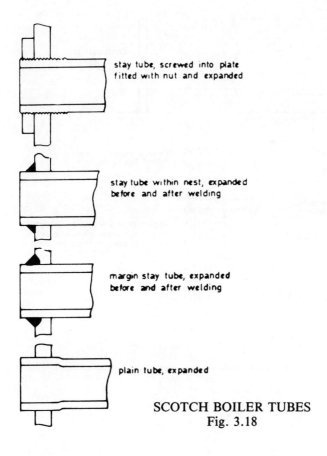

stay tube, screwed into plate
fitted with nut and expanded

stay tube within nest, expanded
before and after welding

margin stay tube, expanded
before and after welding

plain tube, expanded

SCOTCH BOILER TUBES
Fig. 3.18

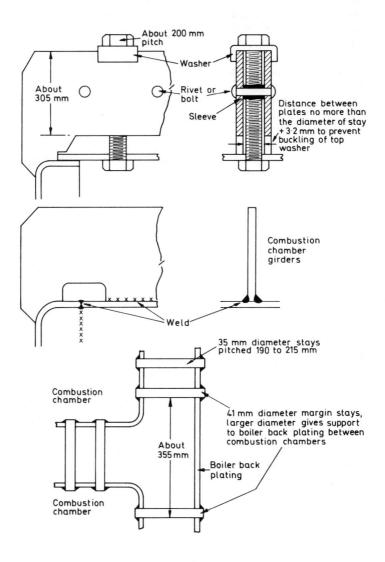

SCOTCH BOILER
Fig. 3.19

All flat plating and nearly flat plating used in the construction of the combustion chambers and boiler shell has to be given adequate support. Tubes, stays and girders are fitted for this purpose. (Figs. 3.18 and 3.19).

Boiler tubes, in addition to carrying the gases from combustion chamber to boiler uptake, support the boiler front tube plate and combustion chamber front plate.

Plain tubes are expanded into the tube plating, and when new the tubes usually extend about 13 mm into the smoke box end which facilitates driving back and re-expanding if the occasion demands.

Stay tubes, within the tube nest are thicker, having the same outside diameter as plain tubes for the boiler. Margin stay tubes are thicker again with the same outside diameter as plain tubes for the boiler.

Stays for combustion chamber back and side plating and for boiler end plates are shown in Fig. 3.17c. The main stays are also to be found at the bottom of the boiler between the furnaces giving support to the boiler end plates, these main stays at top and bottom of the boiler are pitched about 405 mm and are about 66 mm diameter.

Combustion chamber girders which support the top of the combustion chamber may be of the built up or welded types both of which are shown in Fig. 3.19.

Boiler end plating may be arranged in three parts at either end as shown in Fig. 3.17 or in two parts, the upper plate being thicker than the lower. Either riveted or welded construction being used.

The longitudinal seams of the shell plates are generally treble riveted double strap butt joints of strong design. If the longitudinal seams are welded, as in the case of all welded Scotch boilers, certain classification society requirements have to be fulfilled, these include radiographic examination, annealing, tensile, bend and impact tests, micrographic and macrographic examination. The end plating may be riveted or welded to the shell plating.

Manholes cut into the shell and or end plating must be compensated by means of a compensating ring, these being riveted or welded in place.

Reference has been made throughout the foregoing brief description of the Scotch boiler to riveted or welded construction. There are riveted types of Scotch boiler in use today, but this type has been superseded by the part and all welded types.

SOME DEFECTS, CAUSES AND REPAIRS FOR
AUXILIARY BOILERS

Furnaces

Defects that could occur to a furnace are: deformation, wastage and cracking.

Deformation

With cylindrical furnaces, this can be determined by sighting along the furnace or by use of a lath swept around the furnace or by furnace gaugings.

The causes of deformation are: scale, oil, sludge or poor circulation, resulting in overheating of the furnace and subsequent distortion.

Local deformations could be repaired by cutting through the bulge, heating and pressing back the material into the original shape, and then welding. By cutting through the bulge prior to heating and pressing facilitates flow of metal during pressing. Alternatively, the defective portion could be cut out completely and a patch welded in its place.

If the furnace is badly distorted then the only repair possible may be renewal.

A weakened furnace may be repaired temporarily by pressing back the deformation and welding plate stiffeners circumferentially around the furnace on the water side.

Wastage

The causes of wastage are corrosion and erosion. If it is great in extent then renewal of the furnace may be the only solution. Localised corrosion could be dealt with by cutting out the defective portion of furnace and welding in a new piece of material.

Cracks

Circumferentially around the lower part of the connecting necks cracks may be found. These cracks are caused by mechanical straining of the furnace and the defect is generally referred to as grooving.

If the groove is shallow compared to plate thickness (depth can be ascertained by drilling or by ultrasonic detection) it is usual to cut out the groove and weld. However, if the grooving is deep the material is cut right through and welded from both sides.

Cracks, due to overheating, may be found where deformation has occurred, these must be made good in the manner described above.

Combustion Chamber

The defects which can occur to a combustion chamber are similar to those that can occur to a furnace.

Deformation

In addition to the causes of deformation listed for a furnace must be added that of water shortage. The combustion chamber top would be the first place to suffer overheating and subsequent distortion due to water shortage.

Local deformations can be repaired by cutting out the defective portion of plate, generally through the line of stays or tubes, and welding in a new piece of plate. By cutting the plating through the centre of stay or tube holes avoids a continuous weld and reduces the risk of defects that could occur due to contraction stresses.

Slight distortion of combustion chamber and smoke box plating could occur due to the boiler being operated in a dirty condition, this defect is common, and if there is no leakage past the stays or tubes no repair would be necessary, but it would be essential to keep the surfaces of the plating clean to prevent further distortion.

Badly distorted combustion chamber plating is best renewed.

Another cause of combustion chamber plates bulging could be corrosion of stays or tubes leading to a reduction in the support for the plating. The remedy in this case would be renewal of stays or tubes.

Wastage

Leakages past tubes, stays and through riveted seams could cause wastage. If the wastage is not extensive then the defective portion of plate can be built up by welding and the tubes or stays renewed where required. If extensive, then the defective portion of plating should be cut out and a new portion welded in, and stays or tubes where required should be renewed.

Cracks

These can develop due to overheating and mechanical straining.

Likely places are, the landing edges of combustion chamber seams on the fire side due to doubling of plate thickness (riveted only), and impairing of heat transfer, and around tubes and stays due to straining of the boiler and or scale build up around the necks of the tubes or stays.

If the cracks in the seams are not extensive and they are dry they may be left. However, if they are extensive they should be cut out, filled in by welding, and have their rivets renewed.

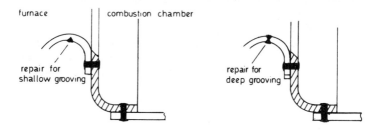

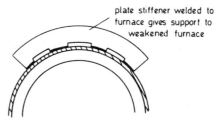

Fig. 3.20

Radial grooving of the plating around stays and or tubes if not extensive can be repaired by cutting out the crack and filling in with welding. If the grooving is extensive the defective portion of plate should be cut out and a new portion welded in its place.

Shell and End Plates

The principal defects to which the shell and end plating may be subjected arc wastage and cracking.

Wastage

This generally occurs at places of leakages, such as riveted seams and boiler mountings.

Leakages at seams and between boiler mountings and shell in the water region of the boiler lead to salt deposition due to water flashing off to steam, leaving behind as it does so some of the salts it contained. These deposits of salts must be thoroughly cleaned away and the plating is then available for inspection for wastage and cracking.

The cracking that could occur may be due to caustic embrittlement, this is dealt with in Chapter 4.

Repairs for wastage may be built up by welding if the wastage is not excessive, or renewal of the defective portion of plate if the wastage tends to be excessive.

If seam leakage is slight and discovered early, and upon examination the material is found to be sound then the only repair necessary may be re-caulking of the seam. Care must be taken however, to ensure overcaulking does not take place as this can lead to lifting of the plates, one from the other, and deposits could accumulate between the plates.

Cracking

In addition to the cracking that may occur due to caustic embrittlement, grooving of flanged end plating may occur, especially where the furnace front plating is flanged inwards to take the furnace.

Repairs for grooving are of the nature previously described for furnaces.

Repairs for cracks due to embrittlement generally necessitate renewal of the affected portion of plate. If caustic cracking of the main seam of a boiler is extensive then the only repair may be as drastic as boiler renewal.

BOILER TESTING ETC

Hydraulic Test

When repairs have been carried out to a boiler it is customary to subject the boiler to a hydraulic test.

Before testing, the boiler must be prepared. All equipment and foreign matter must be removed from the water space of the boiler and the repairs should be carefully examined.

Any welded repair should be struck repeatedly with a hammer to see if any faults develop, the sudden shock increases the stresses that may be in the weld and faults may then show up in the form of cracks.

The boiler safety valves have to be gagged and all boiler mountings, apart from the feed check and air cock, closed. The boiler can then be filled with clean fresh water and purged of air.

Using a hydraulic pump unit connected by a small bore pipe to the boiler direct or to the feed line, pressure can be gradually applied. The testing pressure is normally $1\frac{1}{2}$ times the working pressure, applied for at least 30 minutes.

With the boiler under pressure it can now be examined for leakages and faults. Weld repairs should again be given repeated blows with a hammer to see if they are sound.

Blowing Down and Opening Up a Boiler

If repairs or an examination of the boiler have to be carried out it will have to be emptied. It would always be better, if time

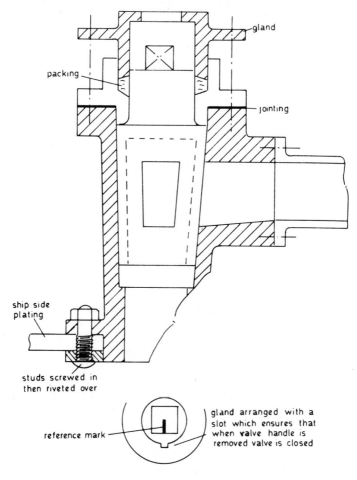

SHIP SIDE BLOW DOWN VALVE
Fig. 3.21

is available, to allow the boiler to cool down in its own time after shut down, then pump the water out. In this way the relatively sudden shock cooling due to complete blow down would be avoided.

If the boiler has to be blown down to the sea, allow as much time as possible after shut down before commencing. The ships side blow down cock must be opened first then the blown down valve on the boiler can be *gradually* opened up. In this way the operator has some measure of control over the situation, if for example the external blow down pipe between boiler and ships side was in a corroded condition, then if the operator opened up the boiler blow down valve first, this could lead to rupturing of the blow down pipe and a possible accident resulting whilst he is engaged in opening up the ships side cock. Fig. 3.21 shows the arrangement of a ships side blow down cock. When the handle is removed the cock must be in the closed position, this is a safety measure to ensure that the cock is not accidently left open.

Our senses tell us when the blow down process is coming to a close, the noise level falls and the pressure will be observed to be low. Care must be taken to ensure that no cold sea water gets into the boiler, the boiler when empty of water would still contain steam which could condense and cause a vacuum condition, this in turn could assist the entry of cold sea water. To help prevent sea water entry, the boiler blow down is usually non-return (on some water tube boilers a double shut off is provided) but even with a non-return valve it is strongly advisable to start closing the boiler blow down valve when the pressure is low enough, and when it is down to the desired value, the valve must be closed down tightly and the ships side cock closed.

At this stage allow as much time as possible for the boiler to cool down and lose all its pressure, and when the pressure is atmospheric open up the air cock and gauge glass drains to *ensure* pressure inside boiler is atmospheric.

Either boiler door can be knocked in at this stage, top or bottom, but not both, provided sufficient care is taken. If it is the top door, secure a rope to the eyebolt normally provided and make the other end of the rope fast. Slacken back but *do not remove* the dog retaining nuts, take a relatively long plank of wood stand well back and knock the door down. The door is now open and the dogs can be completely removed, do not immediately open up the bottom door since if the boiler is hot this would lead to a current of relatively cool air passing through the boiler and subsequent thermal shock.

It it is the bottom door, slacken back on the dog retaining nuts by a very small amount, use a large plank of wood and break the door joint from a safe distance so that if there is any hot water remaining in the boiler no injury will occur to anyone. Again, do not immediately open up the top door of the boiler.

PACKAGED AUXILIARY BOILER

Fig. 3.22 shows in a simplified diagrammatic form a coiled-tube boiler of the Stone-Vapor type. It is compact, space saving, designed for u.m.s. operation, and is supplied ready for connecting to the ships services.

A power supply, depicted here by a motor, is required for the feed pump, fuel pump (if fitted), fan and controls.

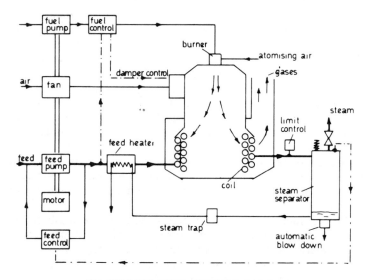

PACKAGE COIL TYPE BOILER
Fig. 3.22

Feed water is force circulated through the generation coil wherein about 90% is evaporated. The un-evaporated water travelling at high velocity carries sludge and scale into the separator, which can be blown out at intervals manually or automatically. Steam at about 99% dry is taken from the separator for shipboard use.

The boiler is completely automatic in operation. If, for example, the steam demand is increased, the pressure drop in the separator is sensed and a signal, transmitted to the feed controller, demands increased feed, which in turn increases air and fuel supply.

With such a small water content explosion due to coil failure is virtually impossible and a steam temperature limit control protects the coil against abnormally high temperatures. In addition the servo-fuel control protects the boiler in the event of failure of water supply.

Performance of a typical unit could be:

Steam pressure	10 bar.
Evaporation	3000 kg/h
Thermal efficiency	80%

Full steam output in about 3 to 4 mins.

Note. Atomising air for the fuel may be required at a pressure of about 5 bar.

REDUCING VALVE

Fig. 3.23 illustrates diagrammatically a reducing valve that can be used for the reduction of steam or air pressure. As steam passes through the valve no work is done since the reduction process is one of throttling, hence the total heat before and after pressure reduction is nearly the same. When air is passed through the valve its pressure is reduced, but as no work is done by the air, or on the air, its temperature will remain nearly constant.

The reducing valve shown would have a body of cast steel or iron. A valve, valve seat and spindle of steel or bronze. Choice of materials depends upon operating conditions.

Fitted on the discharge side of the valve is a pressure gauge to record the reduced pressure and a relief valve to prevent damage to the low pressure side of the system in the event of the reducing valve failing.

Since the valve must be in a state of equilibrium under the action of the forces which act upon it we have:

Downward forces = Upward forces

$$P_1 \times A = (P_1 - P_2) \times a + F$$

If P_1, A and a are constant we have;

P_2 varies directly as F

i.e. $P_2 \alpha F$

Hence if the supply pressure is kept constant the discharge pressure can be reduced or increased at will by rotating the adjustment screw.

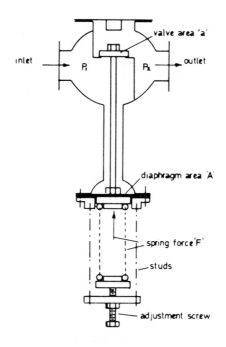

REDUCING VALVE
Fig. 3.23

EVAPORATORS

Fresh water production from sea water for domestic and boiler feed purposes has become an essential requirement aboard most vessels. The stowage space that would have been used for fresh water can now be utilised for fuel or extra space made available for cargo when a fresh water making plant is utilised, for even the simplest plant can produce about 10 tonnes of water for every tonne of fuel used.

Various types of evaporating plant are available but the principal types used on board are the 'single effect plants' and 'double effect plants'.

Single effect means that evaporation takes place at one pressure only. A single effect plant may have more than one evaporator and in this case the evaporators are arranged in parallel.

Double effect means that evaporation takes place at two different pressures and the evaporators would be arranged in series.

The essential requirement of any evaporating plant is that it should produce fresh water as economically as possible and a measure of a plant's economy is its performance ratio. Performance ratio is the kg of vapour produced per kg of steam supplied. For single effect plants this may be as high as 1.1, for double effect 1.9, and for two stage flash 1.5.

Although performance ratio is a good yardstick with which to compare various plants it does not give a complete picture, as the steam which is supplied to the evaporator may be either 'live' or 'waste', *i.e.*, it may or may not have performed some useful work before arrival at the evaporator. In addition, the boiler which produces the steam may be employing heat which it is obtaining from the exhaust gases of a diesel engine thus providing an extra economy. Also it would be difficult to affix some form of performance ratio to evaporators using the waste heat in diesel engine cooling water.

The performance of any evaporating plant is adversely affected by scale formation and frequency of blowing down. If scale formation is rapid, heat transfer is reduced and the performance ratio falls. The evaporator would then be blown down and the heating element or coils subjected to cold shocking in order to facilitate scale removal. Every blow down means heat loss of evaporator contents, hence the more infrequent these interruptions the higher will be the overall economy of the plant.

If scale could be completely eliminated approximately 20 per cent more water could be produced, water treatment is available for evaporators but naturally its cost must be added to the cost of water production. Three scales which are principally found in evaporators are:

Calcium carbonate ($CaCO_3$)
Magnesium hydroxide ($Mg(OH)_2$)
Calcium sulphate ($CaSO_4$)

Calcium carbonate and magnesium hydroxide scale formation depends principally upon the temperature of operation. Calcium sulphate scale formation is principally dependent upon the density of the evaporator contents. The reactions which take place when sea water is heated are:

$$Ca(HCO_3)_2 = Ca + 2HCO_3$$
$$\text{then} \quad 2HCO_3 = CO_3 + H_2O + CO_2$$

If heated up to approximately 80°C:
$$CO_3 + Ca = CaCO_3$$

If heated above 80°C:
$$CO_3 + H_2O = HCO_3 + OH$$
$$\text{then} \quad Mg + 2OH = Mg(OH)_2$$

Hence if the sea water in the evaporator is heated to a temperature below 80°C calcium carbonate scale predominates. If it is heated above 80°C magnesium hydroxide scale is deposited.

If the density of the evaporator contents is in excess of 96,000 p.p.m. (3/32) calcium sulphate scale can be formed but evaporator density is normally 80,000 p.p.m. ($2\frac{1}{2}$/32) and less, hence scale formation due to calcium sulphate should be no problem.

METHODS OF CONTROLLING AND MINIMISING SCALE (EVAPORATORS)

1. Use low Pressure Evaporation Plant *i.e.* operating at a temperature below 80°C so that calcium carbonate scale predominates—that is a soft scale which is easily removed and not such a poor conductor of heat as other scales.

2. Use Magnetic Treatment: a unit consisting of permanent magnets, preceded by a filter, is installed in the evaporator feed line. The water passes through a strong magnetic field which alters the charge on the salts so that amalgamation of the salt crystals, formed during precipitation in the evaporator, is prevented and the salt then goes out with the brine.

3. Use flexing elements: a heating element made of thin gauge monel metal built like a concertina may be used. The advantage of such an element is that when pressure, and hence temperature, vary slightly the element flexes considerably thereby cracking off scale effectively and permitting longer running periods of the evaporator between shut downs.

However, when such an element is used care must be taken to ensure it is not subjected to high pressures otherwise failure can occur.

A safeguard consisting of an air operated trip valve in the steam line, controlled by a solenoid pilot valve actuated by a differential pressure gauge, which registers pressure differential across the element (maximum 0.9 bar pressure difference), may be fitted.

4. Use Continuous Chemical Treatment:

(a) *Organic polyelectrolyte combined with anti-foam.*

This minimises scale formation and foaming, it can be used in evaporators producing water for drinking purposes (DTp). It would be continuously fed into the feed line by a metering pump (to ensure overdosing does not take place) at one to eight p.p.m. of evaporator feed, the rate depends upon evaporator density and output.

The compound is alkaline and should be treated in the same way as caustic soda, it should not be taken internally.

(b) *Polyphosphate compounds with anti-foam.*

These prevent the formation of calcium carbonate scale and minimise possibility of foaming. The compound is a non toxic, non acidic, relatively cheap and safe to handle powder. The DTp allow it to be used in evaporators producing water for drinking purposes if the dosage rate is two to four p.p.m. of evaporator feed.

It is suitable only for low pressure plants, at temperatures around 100°C it forms a sticky grey sludge. It should only be used at temperatures below 90°C.

(c) *Ferric Chloride (FeCl)*, is a stable, non explosive hygroscopic, non toxic, and when dry non acidic chemical compound supplied in sealed drums. When it is mixed with water it becomes acidic, for this reason protective clothing should be worn by personnel handling the chemical.

It completely prevents the formation of calcium carbonate and magnesium hydroxide scales when used correctly. The concentrated solution is injected into the evaporator feed system through plastic injection equipment. This is necessary since the concentrate is intensively corrosive, when it is in the system it is very dilute and quite safe.

Note. High vacuum plant operating at a boiling plant of about 45°C, using diesel engine cooling water as the heating medium, has relatively low tube surface temperature and may not require any feed treatment. Steam heated plant, due to higher tube surface temperature, usually does require water treatment.

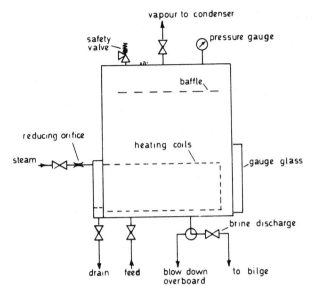

DIAGRAMMATIC ARRANGEMENT OF A SIMPLE
VERTICAL EVAPORATOR
Fig. 3.24

Cleaning

Heat exchange surfaces are usually cleaned by circulating a
10% hydrochloric acid solution. A pump is connected to the
feed inlet to the evaporator and solution return is by gravity via
the brine discharge into an open acid tank from which the pump
draws the solution.

The single effect vertical evaporator shown in Fig. 3.24 is still
in common use. It operates with a vapour pressure between 1.34
to 1.48 bar and steam for the heating coils is supplied direct
from the boiler. The initial cost for such an evaporator is
relatively low, it is also compact and thereby space saving. The
shell and dome of the evaporator is made of good quality close
grained cast iron and the heating coils are made of solid drawn
copper. Mountings provided are: vapour outlet valve, steam
inlet, coil drain valve, feed check valve, blow down valve, brine
ejector, safety valve, gauge glass with fittings, salinometer cock
and a compound pressure gauge. In the diagram, a reducing
orifice fitting is shown on the steam inlet. Its purpose is to
reduce the pressure of steam entering an evaporator shell in the
event of failure of a heating coil.

Statutory requirements:

(1) If the main body is a single casting it may have a working pressure not exceeding 2 bar.

(2) Cast iron should not be used above 3 bar working pressure.

(3) Cast iron, bronze or gunmetal are acceptable if the temperature does not exceed 220°C.

(4) Stress on studs for covers should not exceed 62 MN/m² if the studs are 22 mm diameter or over.

(5) Studs should be at least 22 mm diameter for covers which are to be frequently removed.

(6) Where a reducing orifice is necessary it should be of non-corrodible metal and should be parallel for a length of at least 6.3 mm.

(7) An accumulation of pressure test should be conducted and the accumulation of pressure should not exceed 10 per cent of the working pressure.

LOW PRESSURE EVAPORATING AND DISTILLING PLANTS

This type of single effect plant is designed to give better economy than the older single effect vertical evaporator shown in Fig. 3.24.

Low pressure (*i.e.* operating under vacuum conditions) evaporation plant are widely used because of:

1. Control over type of scale formed, *i.e.* mainly calcium carbonate which is soft and easy to remove.
2. Heating medium supplied can be at a relatively low temperature *e.g.* diesel cooling water or waste steam.
3. Improved heat transfer across the heating element. This is due to higher temperature differences for lower pressures than higher pressures.

Materials For Low Pressure Plant

The shell is usually fabricated steel (or non-ferrous metal like the more expensive cupro-nickels) which has been shot blasted then coated with some form of protective. One type of coating is sheet rubber which is rolled and bonded to the plate then hardened afterwards by heat treatment. The important points about protective coatings are:

(1) They must be inert and prevent corrosion.

(2) They must resist the effects of acid cleaning and water treatment chemicals.

(3) They must have a good bond with the metal.

Heat exchangers use aluminium brass in tube or plate form and with the type of fresh water generator shown in Fig. 3.25 the condenser plates are usually made of titanium, an expensive and virtually corrosion/erosion resistant material.

A knitted monel metal wire demister which scrubs the vapour of sea water droplets is a standard internal fitting.

Heat from diesel engine cooling water is used to evaporate a small fraction of the sea water feed in the plate type evaporator. Unevaporated water is discharged as brine and that which is evaporated passes through the demister to the plate type vapour condenser, where, after condensation it is discharged to the fresh water storage tank by the fresh water pump.

In the event of the salinity of the fresh water density exceeding a pre-determined value (maximum usually four p.p.m.) the solenoid controlled dump valve diverts the flow to the bilge, preventing contamination of the made water. Excess salinity could be caused by sea water leakage at the condenser or the evaporator priming, the former is the most likely.

Feed supply rate to the evaporator is fixed by the orifice plate and sufficient water goes to the ejectors to ensure a high vacuum condition in the shell at all times and that all brine is easily dealt with.

This type of relatively simple, compact, space saving unit is easily accessible for cleaning. Capacity can be altered by altering the number of plates in the heat exchangers and adjusting the orifice size. It can be easily arranged for u.m.s. remote operation if required.

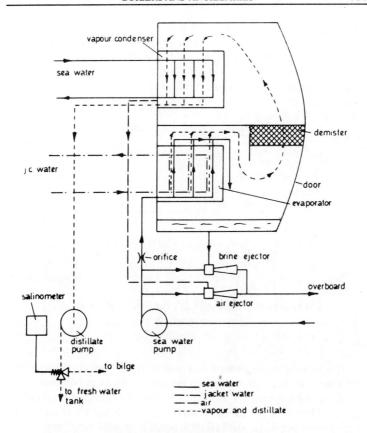

FRESH WATER GENERATOR (ALFA-LAVAL)
Fig. 3.25

TWO STAGE FLASH EVAPORATOR

A double effect flash evaporation plant is shown in Fig. 3.26.

It consists of two identical shells made of fabricated mild steel with protective internal coating, demister screens of knitted monel metal wire and vapour condensers made up of aluminium brass U tubes expanded into rolled naval brass tube plates.

Sea water is pumped through the control valve A to the second, then the first stage, vapour condensers wherein it increases in temperature before final heating to 80°C in the steam supplied heat exchanger.

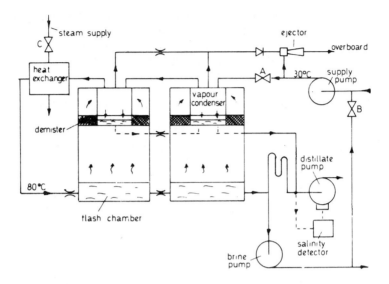

TWO STAGE FLASH EVAPORATION PLANT
Fig. 3.26

The pressurised, heated sea water flows through an orifice into the first flash chamber whose low pressure corresponds to a saturation temperature less than that of the incoming heated sea water. Hence some of the water must be evaporated, in order that its temperature can fall to around that which corresponds to the pressure in the chamber.

Unevaporated water flows through an orifice—which maintains pressure difference—into the second chamber where more water is evaporated since the pressure is lower than in the first chamber.

A brine pump extracts low density unevaporated water and discharges the bulk overboard. Some however may return to the suction side of the supply pump through the auto-valve B to maintain the feed inlet temperature at about 30°C irrespective of how low the sea water temperature may be.

The vapour and non-condensible gases in each of the chambers pass through the demisters then over and down through the vapour condensers. Distillate flows from the first stage to the second through an orifice then it is extracted by the distillate pump and delivered to the storage tank. A salinity detector controls the distillate pump, if the density is too high the pump stops and the distillate passes over the double loop seal to the brine pump suction to be discharged overboard.

Non-condensible gases are extracted by the ejector which maintains the high vacuum condition in the chambers.

For complete automatic operation in u.m.s. vessels,

1. The steam inlet valve C would be thermostatically controlled to maintain sea water feed temperature into the first chamber at 80°C.
2. Valve A, in addition to being controlled thermostatically would also be controlled by two high level float switches in the first chamber.
3. The valve B and the distillate pump would be controlled as outlined above.

Output from such an evaporator could be from 13 to 250 tonnes/day depending upon the size.

Drinking water

Drinking water made from sea water in the foregoing distillation plants will be safe to drink:
1. If it is boiled at temperatures above 75°C— most of the low pressure plants operate at temperatures ranging from 40°C to 60°C.
2. Additives to diesel engine cooling water are not harmful. Those not allowed for health reasons are the chromates. However, sodium nitrite—even though it is considered dangerous to health—is used in some plant.
3. Inhibitors which are sometimes added to sea water systems to prevent fouling by the growth of marine organisms must not be used if the sea water is used in part for supplying the evaporator.
4. The evaporator is not used within the limits from the coastline to about 20 to 50 miles from it.

TEST EXAMPLES 3

Class 3

1. With the aid of a simple sketch, explain how a watergauge fitted directly to a boiler is tested for accuracy when the boiler is steaming.

2. Describe the start up sequence of an automatic auxiliary boiler.

3. Describe how fire tubes are attached to the tube plate of a fire tube boiler.

TEST EXAMPLES 3

Class 2

1. Describe the essential steps in the structural examination of an auxiliary boiler. State with reasons where wastage is likely to be found. Explain why it is equally important to examine the fire side as the water side.

2. With reference to auxiliary boiler safety valves state:
   (a)   with reasons what clearances need checking when lapping in valves and seats.
   b)   why the drain must be kept clear.
   c)   how setting is done under steam.
   d)   why opening gear should be kept in good working order at all times.

3. Sketch and describe a sea water evaporation plant using engine coolant as the heating medium. State how the distillate is rendered fit for drinking.

4. Describe how to 'blow down' and 'open up' an auxiliary boiler for inspection. Identify with reasons those parts which normally require especially close examination during internal inspection.

5. Sketch and fully describe the operation and construction of a remote boiler water level indicator. To what defects is the instrument liable to and how you would remedy these defects?

TEST EXAMPLES 3

Class 1

1. Assess the value of regular systematic inspection of auxiliary boilers and ancillary equipment. With particular reference to a vertical, smoke tube, hemispherical furnace boiler, identify three common faults on the water side and two common faults on the fire side. Describe the remedial action in each case to retard development.

2. With reference to main safety valves for handling steam at 60 bar, 500°C explain:
   a)   why precise, rapid and ample valve movement is essential during opening and closing.
   b)   how the characteristics in (a) are achieved in practice.

3. Discuss the merits of fitting a low pressure exhaust gas boiler into the uptakes of a Diesel engined installation. Sketch a boiler suitable for this purpose.

4. What are the essential differences between an ordinary single spring loaded safety valve and an improved high lift safety valve? How would you set the safety valves for a multi-boilered installation? What is meant by accumulation of pressure and how would you conduct a test to determine if the safety valves are of correct capacity?

5. Sketch and describe two types of remote boiler water level indicator. To what defects are the indicators of your choice liable and how would you remedy these defects?

CHAPTER 4

CORROSION, WATER TREATMENT AND TESTS

CORROSION

The corrosion of metals may be considered as the material returning to its original form of a metal oxide. Some metals corrode more rapidly than others in the same environment. Iron ore for example is an oxide of iron that is converted into the steels and irons used in engineering. If conditions are correct for corrosion; moisture, acids, salts, etc., the tendency is for the material to revert to oxide of iron by combination with oxygen. (An oxide is an element combined with oxygen, hence oxygen must be present for the transformation). Some metals, provide by reaction with the atmosphere, an oxide film upon their surface which is by nature passive, and this can prevent any further corrosion. If this film is broken or destroyed it can in the case of certain metals be very rapidly replaced. Chromium, which is used in stainless steels, can form a microscopic film of chromium oxide upon the surface of the steel which prevents further corrosion. Aluminium, which corrodes very rapidly, is quickly rendered non-corrosive owing to the passive oxide film which forms.

Corrosion is a complex subject not fully understood and research into its mechanisms will continue into the foreseeable future. Various theories have been put forward over the years, some have been adopted only to be discarded as further progress has been made. Formation of galvanic cells is probably the main cause of corrosion and these can be formed in near pure boiler water, sea water or other electrolyte. The galvanic elements could be provided by dissimilar metals or mill-scale, scale, oxide film on the surface of a metal. Or differences in surface structure, inclusion, composition of the metal, or salts, bacteria, oil degradation products in the electrolyte coming into contact with the metal surface.

CORROSION OF METALS IN SEA WATER

Sea water is circulated, heated and stored within a vessel. It is a strongly corrosive medium because it is a good electrolyte.

With dissimilar metals in sea water, galvanic action results and the more anodic metal corrodes. Table 4.1 is an extract from the galvanic series of materials in sea water, any material in the table is anodic to those above it.

Titanium	Noble end of table.
Graphite	
Monel metal	
Stainless steel (with oxide film)	
Inconel	
Nickel	
l70/30 Cupro-Nickel	
Gunmetal	
Aluminium bronze	
Copper	
Admiralty brass	
Manganese steel (without oxide film)	
Cast iron	
Mild steel	
Zinc	
Aluminium	
Mangnesium	Base end of table.

TABLE 4.1

Hence, steel is anodic to bronze in sea water, therefore, it will corrode—we may say that the steel has given 'cathodic protection' to the bronze.

Sacrificial anodes are sometimes used deliberately to give cathodic protection to more expensive material, *e.g.*, iron anodes give protection to brass tubes and plates in condensers, magnesium anodes give protection to steel plates in tanks.

Practical points and methods of minimising galvanic effect.

1. Choose materials close to each other in the series.

2. Make the key component of a more noble metal, *i.e.*, the metal to be protected.

3. Provide a large area of the less noble metal, although its corrosion is increased, it is spread over a larger area.

4. Do not use graphite grease in the presence of sea water, severe corrosion of the bronzes and steels in contact with it may result.

Graphitisation of Cast Iron

Cast iron contains up to 3.5% carbon, which is mainly in the form of graphite flakes (or spheroids) embedded in a metal matrix. In sea water the metal matrix corrodes—graphite being the more noble material—and the graphite is exposed. This graphitisation of cast iron may stimulate corrosion of metals one would expect cast iron to protect, *e.g.*, bronzes and brasses etc. since the graphite is higher in the series.

Velocity of Sea Water

If the velocity of the sea water relative to the material increases the corrosion rate increases—probably up to some limiting value. The reason for this is twofold: (1) increased supply of oxygen; (2) erosion of protective oxide films formed by corrosion.

Stress Corrosion

A metal consists of crystals, or grains, whose atomic arrangement is regular together with amorphous (structureless) metal surrounding them. Corrosion of the weaker amorphous metal, due to galvanic action, in sea water can take place. If stresses are 'locked up' within the metal they can be partly relieved by the corrosion, this can expose more amorphous metal to corrosive attack and the process progresses until possible failure.

Stress corrosion is most commonly found in brasses, but it has occurred in aluminium alloys and stainless steels. Caustic embrittlement—to be discussed later—is another form of stress corrosion.

De-zincification

Brass is an alloy of copper and zinc, in sea water the zinc is anodic to the copper and it corrodes leaving a porous spongy mass of copper, hence de-zincification. This should not occur to brasses in which arsenic has been added and whose zinc content is less than 37%.

A similar attack can occur to aluminium bronzes called de-aluminification, 4% to 5% nickel added to the bronze can avoid this problem but trouble may still take place at welds.

OTHER CORROSION TOPICS

Fretting Corrosion

Can occur where two surfaces in contact with each other undergo slight oscillatory motion, of a microscopic nature, relative to one another. Components to which this may occur are those which have been shrunk, hydraulically pressed or mechanically tightened one to the other.

The small relative motion causes removal of metal and metal oxide films. The removed metal may combine with oxygen to form a metal oxide powder that will, in the case of ferrous metal, be harder than the metal itself thus increasing the wear. Removed metal oxide film would be repeatedly replaced increasing the damage. Factors affecting the damage caused by fretting corrosion:

1. Damage increases with amplitude and frequency of movement.

2. Damage increases with load carried by the surfaces.

3. Damage is reduced if oxygen level is low and moisture is present.

4. Hardness of the metal affects the attack, with ferrous metals the damage decreases as the hardness of the metal increases.

Pitting Corrosion

Corrosion may be over a large area *i.e.* plate type of corrosion or it may be localised *i.e.* pitting corrosion.

Pitting corrosion is caused when there is, relatively, a large cathodic area and a small anodic area. Hence the intensity of attack at the anode is high. Large area differences could be caused by mill scale, oxide films, acid pockets of water, scale from salts, pores or crevices, oils, gases and ingress of metals into the boiler. It is a very dangerous form of corrosion, its rate is generally increased with temperature increase hence where metal surfaces are hottest failure may take place earlier. It should be prevented.

Corrosion Fatigue

If a metal is in a corrosive environment and is also subjected to a cyclic stress it will fail at a much lower stress concentration than that normally required for fatigue failure. This is probably due to the progressive weakening effect of amorphous metal corrosion and stress relief. In boilers, microscopic examination would probably reveal the cracks to be trans-crystalline, rather than inter-crystalline which occurs with caustic cracking. The cyclic stresses may be due to the tubes vibrating or fluctuations in thermal conditions, *i.e.* thermal pulsing.

BOILER CORROSION

To help the reader understand, in part, the mechanism of electro-chemical corrosion it is necessary to first understand some ionic and atomic theory and to appreciate the meaning of the pH value which is an indication of acidity, neutrality or alkalinity.

Atoms and Ions

An atom is composed of a nucleus with an electron or electrons in orbit around it. The nucleus is basically composed of protons and neutrons. Protons have a positive electrical charge and the neutrons are uncharged, as their name would indicate. Electrons however are negatively charged. For the atom, the number of protons present is equal to the number of electrons, hence the resultant electrical charge will be zero, in other words the atom will be electrically balanced. If however an atom gains or loses an electron or electrons there will be an excess of either positive or negative electrical charge. It is then referred to as an ion (Greek wanderer).

Water is basically composed of hydrogen and oxygen atoms but it does also contain ions.

Hydrogen Ion

A hydrogen ion is an atom of hydrogen which has lost its electron. It would normally be written H^+ indicating an excess of positive electrical charge, or $H - \epsilon$ indicating the loss of the electron ϵ.

Hydroxyl Ion

A hydroxyl ion is a compound of oxygen and hydrogen which has gained an electron. It would normally be written OH^- indicating an excess of negative electrical charge, or $OH + \epsilon$ indicating a gain of an electron.

pH Values

Water contains the previously defined hydrogen and hydroxyl ions, the relative concentration of these ions is important. The product of the hydrogen and hydroxyl ion concentration in water at approx. 25°C must always equal 10^{-14} gm ion/litre of solution. If the hydrogen ion concentration exceeds the hydroxyl concentration the water is acidic. If the concentrations are equal the water is neutral. When the hydroxyl ion concentration is greater than the hydrogen, the water is alkaline.

example: $10^{-5}(H^+) \times 10^{-9}\ (OH^-)$ solution Acid
$10^{-7}(H^+) \times 10^{-7}\ (OH^-)$,,   Neutral
$10^{-9}(H^+) \times 10^{-5}\ (OH^-)$,,   Alkaline

Note the product of the concentrations is always 10^{-14} and the powers 5, 7 and 9 for the hydrogen ion concentration serve to indicate the degree of acidity or alkalinity of the solution. Hence the pH values now becomes apparent, p (for power), H (for hydrogen ion). Therefore the pH *value is, the logarithm of the reciprocal of the hydrogen ion concentration.*

e.g. $10^{-5} = \dfrac{1}{10^5}$, reciprocal $= 10^5$, logarithm $= 5$.

pH values range from 0 to 14 *i.e.* from very acidic to very alkaline.

If the water temperature is increased, the hydrogen ion concentration increases and hence there is an increase in acidity or a decrease in alkalinity. Chemicals when added to water alter the hydrogen ion concentration and hence the pH value. Acids lower the pH value, alkalis increase the pH value.

In electro chemical corrosion of metals the pH value is very important for it governs the degree of corrosion.

Electro Chemical Corrosion

When iron is in contact with water which contains hydrogen ions, corrosion may result. The hydrogen ions in contact with the metal surface become hydrogen atoms by taking an electron from the metal. The resultant metal ion (caused through loss of electrons) combines with the hydroxyl ions in contact with the metal surface and so form a metallic hydroxide, which is soluble in the water depending upon the pH value, hence the metal is corroded. This action is similar to a battery action wherein current is caused to flow from anodic to cathodic regions, the

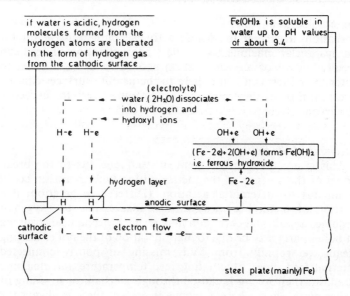

Fig. 4.1

migrating ions in the electrolyte (water) and the electrons in the metal form the circuit.

Hydrogen, which has formed on the surface of the metal due to the combination of the hydrogen ion and metal electron may form a polarising layer upon the metals surface. This will prevent further corrosion. If however, dissolved oxygen is present in the water, it will combine with the hydrogen to form water and no polarisation will occur and corrosion will continue. Also, if the water is acidic enough, the hydrogen can leave the surface of the metal in the form of hydrogen gas, again preventing polarisation and continuing corrosion. Hence the need for boiler water to be alkaline and with little or no dissolved oxygen content.

Some causes of boiler corrosion

Oils

Lubricating oils may contaminate the feed system and find their way into the boiler, this could be caused due to over lubrication of machinery and inefficient filtering of the feed. Oils such as animal and vegetable oils can decompose in the boiler liberating their fatty acids, these acids can cause corrosion. Hence it is advisable to use pure mineral oil for lubrication of machine parts where contamination of feed can result, but oil of any description should never be allowed to enter the boiler as it can adhere to the heating surfaces causing overheating. It can also cause priming due to excessive ebullition.

Mechanical Straining

This is not a corrosive agent in itself but due to the break down of the surface of the metal, pitting type corrosion could result due to differential aeration. (Differential aeration: if a portion of metal becomes partially inaccessible to oxygen it becomes anodic and corrosion may result.) Mechanical straining of boiler parts may be due to mal-operation of the boiler, raising steam too rapidly from cold, missing or poorly connected internal feed pipes, fluctuating feed temperature and steaming conditions. Grooving is caused through mechanical straining of boiler plates, and where a groove is present there is always the danger of corrosion resulting in the groove.

Galvanic Action

When two dissimilar metals are present in a saline solution galvanic action may ensue, resulting in the corrosion of the more base metal. Zinc for example would serve as an anode to iron and iron would serve as an anode to copper. Sacrificial anodes are frequently used to give cathodic protection. In Scotch boilers zinc plates are sometimes secured to furnaces and suspended between tube nests, these act as sacrificial anodes giving cathodic protection to the steel plating, etc., of the boiler.

Corrosion of non-ferrous metals in steam and condensate systems may result in deposits of copper on boiler tube surfaces (known as 'copper pick up'), which due to galvanic action can lead to boiler corrosion.

Caustic Embrittlement

The phenomena of caustic embrittlement (or intercrystalline fracture) is believed to be caused by high concentrations of caustic soda (Sodium hydroxide $NaOH$) and the material under stress. The stress corrosion cracks follow the grain or crystal boundaries of the material and failure of the affected part could result. Concentrations of sodium hydroxide required for embrittlement to occur vary with operating conditions, roughly about 6,000 grains/gallon at 300°C is a guide to the amount of concentration required. Normally such concentrations would never be found in a boiler, but, leakages at rivet heads, seams and boiler mountings, etc., whereby water is flashed off to steam, leaving behind the solids locally, can cause the high concentrations required.

Sodium hydroxide depresses the solubility of sodium sulphate, and sodium sulphate can therefore be made to precipitate. Use is made of this fact to give protection against caustic embrittlement. When concentrations of sodium hydroxide are high and sodium sulphate is present, the sodium sulphate can precipitate and form a protection for the material. Ratios of sodium sulphate to caustic soda for given pressures are the engineers safeguard, from the practical viewpoint. It is recommended that the ratio of sodium sulphate to caustic soda should not fall below 2.5 at all times. Other substances that have been used as inhibitors against caustic embrittlement are, quebracho tannin and sodium nitrate.

Caustic corrosion in *high pressure boilers* is usually indicated by gouging of the tubes and is caused by excess sodium hydroxide and a concentrating mechanism. This phenomenon results in the destruction of the protective magnetic oxide of iron film (Fe_3O_4) and the base metal is then attacked by the concentrated sodium hydroxide.

Effects of Salts and Gases in Feed Water

Feed water employed for marine boilers is usually, unevaporated fresh, evaporated fresh or evaporated salt water. The first and last of these three are normally employed as feed for low pressure boilers, such as the Scotch boiler. Evaporated fresh water is principally employed, along with evaporated salt water for water tube boilers. All of these waters can contain salts which could be harmful to the boiler from the point of view of scale formation and corrosion. Obviously the evaporated fresh and salt waters should be low in solids content and therefore less harmful. However, feed systems can become contaminated with salt water, leaking condenser or an evaporator priming could be the causes.

Salt Water

Average sea water contains approximately 32,000 ppm of total dissolved solids. These solids are made up as follows:

ANALYSIS OF SEA WATER

Salt	Chemical Symbol	Approximate % of Total Dissolved Solids	p.p.m.
Sodium Chloride	$NaCl$	79	25,000
Magnesium Chloride	$MgCl_2$	10	3,000
Magnesium Sulphate	$MgSO_4$	6	2,000
Calcium Sulphate	$CaSO_4$	4	1,200
Calcium Bicarbonate	$Ca(HCO_3)_2$	Less than 1	200

TABLE 4.2

Each of these salts will now be considered in detail, with regard to their effect under boiler conditions.

Sodium Chloride (NaCl)

This is common salt. Heavy concentrations of this salt can cause foaming and priming. Under boiler conditions, the density at which sodium chloride will come out of solution increases as the pressure and temperature increases. In other words its solubility is a variable. Each salt present in the boiler water will in general have varying solubility with temperature variation, and solubility curves for individual salts alone in water can also be affected by the presence of other salts or compounds. In the case of chlorides their solubility is very high and therefore they should normally not come out of solution under normal boiler conditions. Sodium chloride could in conjunction with magnesium sulphate form sodium sulphate and magnesium chloride.

i.e. Sodium   + Magnesium $\rightleftarrows$ Magnesium + Sodium
    Chloride   Sulphate   Chloride   Sulphate

$$2NaCl + MgSO_4 \rightleftarrows MgCl_2 + Na_2SO_4.$$

In a chemical equation of the foregoing nature the number of atoms on either side of the equation must be the same.

Magnesium Chloride (MgCl₂)

Is soluble under normal boiler conditions, but it can to some extent be broken down forming hydrochloric acid and magnesium hydroxides.

Magnesium chloride + Water ⇌ Magnesium hydroxide
                                          + Hydrochloric acid

$$MgCl_2 + 2H_2O \rightleftharpoons Mg(OH)_2 + 2HCl.$$

Magnesium hydroxide has a low solubility and it is also the most common magnesium compound found in a boiler. Due to its low solubility it can deposit and form scale but with suitable treatment it can be precipitated into the form of a non adherent sludge which can be blown out of the boiler. Hydrochloric acid can cause corrosion according to the following reaction.

Hydrochloric acid + Ferrite → Ferrous chloride + Hydrogen
$$2HCl + Fe \rightarrow Fe\ Cl_2 + H_2$$

then Ferrous chloride + Water → Iron hydroxide +
                                          Hydrochloric acid
$$FeCl_2 + 2H_2O \rightarrow Fe(OH)_2 + 2HCl.$$

From the reaction it can clearly be seen that the result of the attack of the acid upon the iron is to produce a chloride of iron which breaks down to form an iron hydroxide with regeneration of the hydrochloric acid, hence the corrosive cycle can continue. With suitable treatment this corrosion can be prevented.

Magnesium Sulphate ($MgSO_4$)
Is soluble under normal boiler conditions, but if too high a density is carried it may deposit and form scale. This salt could to some extent combine with sodium chloride, forming magnesium chloride and sodium sulphate (see NaCl).

Calcium Sulphate ($CaSO_4$)
This salt is possibly the most dangerous scale former present in the boiler water. It can deposit and form a hard tenacious scale which greatly affects the rate of heat transfer, this could cause overheating and subsequent failure of the heating surface. The mechanism of scale formation is complex, in its simplest form it could be described as follows. When a steam bubble is formed upon a heating surface, the plate, under the bubble, becomes overheated, as it is insulated momentarily from the water. The water, containing salts in solution, in contact with the plate around the periphery of the bubble, also becomes overheated. If the salts are those whose solubility decreases with increase of temperature (Calcium sulphate is one) then they will

be deposited in the form of a crystal ring, this is because the water has become supersaturated locally with these salts. Further, when the bubble bursts, the water coming into contact with the overheated plate will again be overheated locally, causing more salt deposition. It would follow therefore that a general statement could be made regarding salts and scale formation due to same, *i.e.* salts whose solubility decreases with increase in temperature are those which form scale upon heating surfaces and sludge upon cooling surfaces. Salts whose solubility increases with increase in temperature do not normally form scale upon heating surfaces but a sludge may be formed if their saturation point is reached.

Calcium Bicarbonate ($Ca[H\,CO_3]_2$)

This salt is decomposed when heated, liberating carbon dioxide and permitting the precipitation of calcium carbonate.

Calcium bicarbonate → Calcium carbonate + Carbon
dioxide + water

$$Ca(HCO_3)_2 \rightarrow CaCo_3 + CO_2 + H_2O$$

Calcium carbonate has a low solubility and this solubility decreases with increase in temperature, it can therefore form scale. The scale so formed is soft and porous in nature and is not such a poor conductor of heat as calcium sulphate scale.

Fresh Water

Unevaporated fresh water is often used as make up feed for boilers, it can contain some or all of the salts present in salt water and other salts besides, but usually in small proportions. Whether a water is classified as salt or fresh, basically depends upon whether it is potable or not. An average sample of fresh water is a practical impossibility, only samples of fresh water can be given.

ANALYSIS OF A FRESH WATER SAMPLE

Salt	Symbol	p.p.m.
Sodium Chloride	$NaCl$	50
Sodium Nitrate	$NaNO_3$	35
Magnesium Sulphate	$MgSO_4$	30
Calcium sulphate	$CaSO_4$	90
Calcium carbonate	$CaCO_3$	200

TABLE 4.3

Hardness Salts

Alkaline hardness salts are the hydroxides, carbonates and bicarbonates of calcium and magnesium. The bicarbonates of calcium and magnesium are called temporary hardness salts since they will be decomposed by heating or boiling the water, liberating carbon dioxide and leaving carbonates.

Non alkaline or permanent hardness salts are the chlorides, sulphates, nitrates and silicates of calcium and magnesium. Hardness due to these salts is not removed by boiling or heating the water. But chemical treatment can remove this hardness.

Total hardness therefore, is the sum of the alkaline and non-alkaline hardness salts present in the water and since these are the scale producing solids a knowledge of the feed water's total hardness is essential.

Silicates

Silica is found in most waters and is also present in the plant, especially when new, from casting sand used for pipe bending and welds.

In low pressure boilers silica combines with calcium and magnesium to form calcium and magnesium silicates which can precipitate and form a hard scale.

In high pressure boilers silica may combine with other elements to form complex silica scales which are glassy, extremely hard and difficult to remove. If the silica content of the boiler water is in excess of about 20 p.p.m. (amount decreases as boiler pressure increases) it is likely that it will volatilize and deposit on turbine blades.

Carbon Dioxide

If the water contains dissolved carbon dioxide, carbonic acid may be formed, which can cause corrosion.

The carbon dioxide may have been absorbed into the feed water due to contact with the atmosphere, it can also be formed due to breakdown of bicarbonates and carbonates present in the feed.

Carbonic acid partially dissociates into hydrogen ions and bicarbonate ions, hence the hydrogen ion content of the water is increased. The bicarbonate ions can combine with the ferrous metal to form ferrous bicarbonate which dissociates into ferrous carbonate and carbonic acid, which is redissolved into the water. If there is a supply of dissolved oxygen in the water the ferrous carbonate is converted into ferric hydroxide with regeneration of the carbon dioxide. Thus the process may be a continuous one providing there is a continuous supply of dissolved oxygen in the water. This reaction due to carbon dioxide is represented below in a simplified form.

Carbon dioxide + water $\rightleftarrows$ Carbonic acid

$$CO_2 + H_2O \rightleftarrows H_2CO_3$$

then

Iron + Carbonic acid $\rightarrow$ Iron carbonate + Hydrogen

$$Fe + H_2CO_3 \rightarrow FeCO_3 + H_2$$

then

Iron carbonate + Oxygen + Water $\rightarrow$
Iron hydroxide + Carbon dioxide
$$4FeCO_3 + O_2 + 6H_2O \rightarrow 4Fe(OH)_3 + 4CO_2$$

Iron hydroxide (ferric hydroxide $Fe(OH)_3$) may break down further to form ferric oxide with loss of water
hence $4Fe(OH)_3 \rightarrow 2Fe_2O_3 + 6H_2O$

Hydrogen

When acid corrosion is rapid *e.g.* when the acid is concentrated under a deposit, damage due to newly formed (nascent) hydrogen molecules at the cathode can result. These hydrogen molecules penetrate the boiler tube metal and react with carbon $C + 4H \rightarrow CH_4$ to produce methane. This carbon loss weakens the metal and the methane gas exerts a pressure which separates the grains of steel. Hydrogen damage can also occur when hydrogen is released by caustic corrosion.

External Corrosion

It must not be forgotten that corrosion of a boiler can occur externally. Causes of corrosion in this case could be, sooty deposits in the uptakes in the presence of moisture which could form sulphuric acid which can corrode, a standing boiler (*i.e.* not under steam) with damp lagging and acidulated bilge vapours.

BOILER WATER TREATMENT

The principal objects of boiler feed water treatment should be:

(i) Prevention of scale formation in the boiler and feed system by (a) using distilled water or (b) precipitating all scale forming salts into the form of a non-adherent sludge.

(ii) Prevention of corrosion in the boiler and feed system by maintaining the boiler water in an alkaline condition and free from dissolved gases.

(iii) Control of the sludge formation and prevention of carry over with the steam.

(iv) Prevention of entry into the boiler of foreign matter such as oil, waste, mill-scale, iron oxides, copper particles, sand, weld spatter, etc. By careful use of oil heating arrangements (close watch on steam drains), effective pre-commission cleaning and maintaining the steam and condensate systems in a non-corrosive condition.

Lime and Soda Treatment (low pressure boilers)

Lime (calcium hydroxide $Ca(OH)_2$ and soda ash (sodium carbonate Na_2CO_3) are used to deal with the calcium and magnesium compounds in the boiler water.

LIME & SODA TREATMENT

Calcium hydroxide [lime, $Ca(OH)_2$] reacts with temporary hardness salts and magnesium compounds as follows:

$Ca(HCO_3)_2$ Calcium bicarbonate	+ $Ca(OH)_2$ + Calcium hydroxide	→ $2CaCO_3$ → Calcium carbonate	+ $2H_2O$ + water			
$Mg(HCO_3)$ Magnesium bicarbonate	+ $2Ca(OH)$ + Calcium hydroxide	→ $Mg(OH)_2$ → Magnesium hydroxide	+ $2CaCO_3$ + Calcium carbonate	+ +	$2H_2O$ water	
$MgSO_4$ Magnesium sulphate	+ $Ca(OH)_2$ + Calcium hydroxide	→ $Mg(OH)_2$ → Magnesium hydroxide	+ $CaSO_4$ + Calcium sulphate			
$Mg(NO_3)_2$ Magnesium nitrate	+ $Ca(OH)_2$ + Calcium hydroxide	→ $Mg(OH)_2$ → Magnesium hydroxide	+ $Ca(NO_3)_2$ + Calcium nitrate			
$MgCl_2$ Magnesium chloride	+ $Ca(OH)_2$ + Calcium hydroxide	→ $Mg(OH)_2$ → Magnesium hydroxide	+ $CaCl_2$ + Calcium chloride			

TABLE 4.4

Sodium carbonate [soda ash, Na_2CO_3] reacts with the calcium compounds originally in the water and those found through using Calcium hydroxide as follows

$CaSO_4$	+	Na_2CO_3	→	$CaCO_3$	+	Na_2SO_4
Calcium	+	Sodium	→	Calcium	+	Sodium
sulphate		carbonate		carbonate		sulphate
$CaCl_2$	+	Na_2CO_3	→	$CaCO_3$	+	$2NaCl$
Calcium	+	Sodium	→	Calcium	+	Sodium
chloride		carbonate		carbonate		chloride
$Ca(NO_3)_2$	+	Na_2CO_3	→	$CaCO_3$	+	$2Na(NO_3)$
Calcium	+	Sodium	→	Calcium	+	Sodium
nitrate		carbonate		carbonate		nitrate

TABLE 4.5

Calcium hydroxide is used to react with magnesium compounds and alkaline hardness salts. Sodium carbonate is used to react with the calcium compounds in the boiler feed including those formed through employing calcium hydroxide. This combination of lime and soda, gives zero hardness and alkaline feed water.

Unevaporated fresh water used as make up feed would contain alkaline hardness salts, which would precipitate and form a soft sludge or scale when the water is heated in the feed heater, economiser or boiler. Hence the water should be treated with lime and soda prior to its entry into the system. Tables 4.4 and 4.5 indicate the reactions which occur when lime and soda are used.

Caustic Soda Treatment

This could be used in place of the soda and lime treatment. Caustic soda (sodium hydroxide, $NaOH$) reacts with the alkaline and non-alkaline magnesium compounds, the alkaline calcium compounds, and it also forms sodium carbonate which can react with the non-alkaline calcium compounds. Table 4.6 indicates the reactions which occur when sodium hydroxide is used.

The sodium carbonate which is formed by employing sodium hydroxide should be in sufficient quantity to deal effectively with the non-alkaline calcium compounds. If however, this is not the case, sodium carbonate will have to be used in conjunction with sodium hydroxide.

Care must be exercised when handling caustic soda as heavy

CAUSTIC SODA (Sodium Hydroxide *NaOH*) TREATMENT

$Ca(HCO_3)_2$	+ $2NaOH$	→	$CaCO_3$	+ Na_2CO_3	+	$2H_2O$
Calcium	+ Sodium	→	Calcium	+ Sodium	+	water
bicarbonate	hydroxide		carbonate	carbonate		
$Mg(HCO_3)_2$	+ $4NaOH$	→	$Mg(OH)_2$	+ $2Na_2CO_3$	+	$2H_2O$
Magnesium	+ Sodium	→	Magnesium	+ Sodium	+	water
bicarbonate	hydroxide		hydroxide	carbonate		
$MgCl_2$	+ $2NaOH$	→	$Mg(OH)_2$	+ $2NaCl$		
Magnesium	+ Sodium	→	Magnesium	+ Sodium		
chloride	hydroxide		hydroxide	chloride		
$MgSO_4$	+ $2NaOH$	→	$Mg(OH)_2$	+ Na_2SO_4		
Magnesium	+ Sodium	→	Magnesium	+ Sodium		
sulphate	hydroxide		hydroxide	sulphate		
$Mg(NO_3)_2$	+ $2NaOH$	→	$Mg(OH)_2$	+ $2NaNO_3$		
Magnesium	+ Sodium	→	Magnesium	+ Sodium		
nitrate	hydroxide		hydroxide	nitrate		

TABLE 4.6

concentrations can cause skin burns.

The foregoing treatments, Lime and Soda, Caustic Soda have declined considerably in use. They have been retained for completeness, interest and instruction as they could prove useful in emergency conditions.

Table 4.7 lists the water treatment recommendations for boilers, the action of the chemicals listed will now be examined.

For the precipitation of scale forming salts into a sludge and to give alkalinity, phosphates are used. Phosphates will combine with the calcium in the boiler water forming tricalcium phosphate $[Ca_3(PO_4)_2)]$, which will precipitate as its solubility is low in the form a sludge or porous scale (scale prevention can be achieved by using coagulants). Phosphates will also combine with the magnesium compounds forming magnesium phosphate $[Mg_3(PO_4)_2]$ which also precipitates into the form of a sludge.

Through using phosphates instead of sodium carbonate for conditioning high concentrations of caustic soda are avoided, since at high temperatures sodium carbonate can break down as follows:

Sodium Carbonate + Water $\rightleftarrows$ Sodium hydroxide +

Carbon dioxide

$$Na_2CO_3 + H_2O \rightleftarrows 2NaOH + CO_2$$

WATER TREATMENT RECOMMENDATION (BS 1170 1983)

Purpose	Chemical	Type of boiler
To prevent scale	Sodium Phosphates	All, up to 84 bar W.P.
To give alkalinity and minimise corrosion	Sodium Hydroxide or Sodium Carbonate	All, up to 84 bar W.P. All, up to 60 bar W.P.
To condition sludge	Polyelectrolytes or Starch or Tannins or Sodium Aluminate	all, up to 84 bar W.P. All, up to 84 bar W.P. All, up to 84 bar W.P. All, up to 31.5 bar W.P.
To remove traces of oxygen	Sodium Sulphite or Hydrazine	All, up to 42 bar from 31.5 to 84 bar
To reduce risk of caustic cracking	Sodium Sulphate or Sodium Nitrate	All, up to 31.5 bar All, up to 31.5 bar
To reduce risk of carry over of foam	Antifoams	Al, up to 84 bar
To protect feed and condensate systems from corrosion	Filming amines or Neutralising amines	All, up to 60 bar 17.5 to 84 bar.

TABLE 4.7

PHOSPHATE TREATMENT

$3CaCO_3$	$+$	$2Na_3PO_4$	$\rightarrow$ $Ca_3(PO_4)_2$	$+$	Na_2CO_3
Calcium carbonate	$+$	Sodium phosphate	$\rightarrow$ Calcium phosphate	$+$	Sodium carbonate
$3CaSO_4$	$+$	$2Na_3PO_4$	$\rightarrow$ $Ca_3(PO_4)_2$	$+$	$3Na_2SO_4$
Calcium sulphate	$+$	Sodium phosphate	$\rightarrow$ Calcium phosphate	$+$	Sodium sulphate
$3CaCl_2$	$+$	$2Na_3PO_4$	$\rightarrow$ $Ca_3(PO_4)_2$	$+$	$6NaCl$
Calcium chloride	$+$	Sodium phosphate	$\rightarrow$ Calcium phosphate	$+$	Sodium chloride
$MgSO_4$	$+$	$2Na_3PO_4$	$\rightarrow$ $Mg(PO_4)_2$	$+$	$3Na_2SO_4$
Magnesium sulphate	$+$	Sodium phosphate	$\rightarrow$ Magnesium phosphate	$+$	Sodium sulphate

TABLE 4.8

It will be noted that the foregoing reaction is reversible, but, in the case of high pressures and temperatures there is a greater tendency to the right than to the left of the equation. Therefore the caustic soda content of the boiler water would increase.

From the reactions shown in the above table it can be seen that through using trisodium phosphate, sodium carbonate is formed. The sodium hydroxide eventually formed due to the breakdown of the sodium carbonate should not normally be excessive, it should give the requisite hydroxyl ions (OH^-) necessary to maintain a moderate alkalinity.

Phosphates normally used are, sodium hexametaphosphate, sodium metaphosphate, disodium phosphate and trisodium phosphate. The metaphosphates are normally put into the feed system as they are slower to react and therefore should not produce scale or sludge in the feed system (feed heaters, etc). Disodium and trisodium phosphate are usually pumped directly into the boiler since they are quicker to react and could possibly form sludge or scale in the feed system.

In the presence of sodium hydroxide in the boiler water, metaphosphate, monosodium and disodium phosphate are converted into trisodium phosphate. Hence depending upon the requisite alkalinity, we can select the necessary phosphate. Due to calcium removal by the phosphates, the tendency for the silicates present in the water to form scale is greatly reduced. They tend instead to remain in solution in the boiler water.

Coagulants

The use of coagulants in the boiler water is to condition the precipitates, rendering them into the form of a sludge which is non-adherent and can be easily blown out of the boiler. Calcium phosphate, magnesium hydroxide and calcium carbonate can form scale, by using coagulants they can be rendered relatively harmless, into a non-adherent sludge. Coagulants used for this purpose are, polyelectrolytes (these are synthetic organic polymers of high molecular weight eg, Sodium polycrylate which may be present in boiler chemical mixtures), sodium aluminate, starch, tannin, gels and casein, etc. Sodium aluminate can also be used with the lime and soda treatment, it can break down and form aluminium hydroxide which combines with the magnesium hydroxide in a flocculent form. Other precipitates can combine with the freely flowing floc and thus be blown out of the boiler. The floc can also combine with any traces of oil which may be present, rendering them harmless.

Note: Coagulants form colloidal suspensions in the boiler water.

Colloids generally consist of sub-microscopic particles (clusters of atoms or molecules) with like electrical charge, that repel each other and prevent the formation of larger particles. They combine with precipitates of opposite electrical charge to produce a floc.

Deaeration

It has been stated that for corrosion to take place oxygen must be present to accomplish the formation of metal oxides. Hence deaeration of the feed water is essential.

Deaeration can be accomplished either mechanically or chemically, or a combination of both. It is usual to carry a reserve of chemicals in the boiler water in order to deal with any ingress of dissolved oxygen that may result due to mal-operation of the deaerating equipment, or some other circumstances. The oxygen scavenging chemicals used for deaerating the water are usually sodium sulphite or hydrazine. Sodium sulphite reacts as follows:

Sodium sulphite + Oxygen → Sodium sulphate

$$2Na_2SO_3 + O_2 \rightarrow 2Na_2SO_4$$

Sodium sulphate, which is formed through using sodium sulphite to deaerate, remains in solution in the boiler water under normal conditions.

Hydrazine solution (60% Hydrazine 40% water approximately) is finding increasing popularity for oxygen scavenging, it reacts under boiler conditions with the oxygen to form water, reactions:

Hydrazine + Oxygen → Water + Nitrogen
$$N_2H_4 + O_2 \rightarrow 2H_2O + N_2$$

thus having the advantage of not increasing the boiler water density.

Initially it was thought that excessive dosage of hydrazine could lead to steam and condensate line corrosion due to ammonia being produced as the excess hydrazine decomposed:

(Hydrazine → Ammonia + Nitrogen)

However, a *controlled* excess is beneficial to the steam and condensate system as it counteracts the effect of carbon dioxide corrosion.

There may be a delay in the build up of a reserve of hydrazine in the boiler water since it reacts with any metal oxides (apart from Fe_3SO_4) that may be present.

Hydrazine should be stored in a cool, well ventilated place since it is a fire hazard. When handling, protective clothing should be worn—treat in the same way as caustic soda. Hydrazine should be injected into de-aerated feed.

Sodium sulphite may still be used as an oxygen scavenger, if that is the case then the following points regarding it are important:—(a) pH value is important to reaction rate with the oxygen, at about 7 pH it is a maximum hence the sodium sulphite should be injected into the system before any alkaline ingredients (b) In high pressure boilers the sulphite can break down to give hydrogen sulphide (H_2S) and possibly sulphur dioxide (SO_2) which can attack steel, brass and coper. (c) It increases dissolved solids content.

Condensate Line Treatment

Where the steam is wet, and also in the condensate system, corrosion can occur due to the presence of carbon dioxide carried over with steam. To ensure alkalinity in this section of the system a volatile alkaliser may be injected into the steam line. These alkalisers are generally ammonia or cyclo-hexylamine, they combine with the steam as it condenses to form carbonates and bicarbonates which decompose in the boiler to give back the CO_2 and the alkaliser, some of which then returns to the steam system.

If the pH value of the condensate is maintained at about 9 this should ensure no corrosion in the low temperature steam and condensate sections of the plant.

Filming amines: the most common is octadecylamine, it is insoluble in water at room temperature but volatile in steam. Filming amines prevent corrosion by forming a protective adsorbed layer on metal surfaces.

Neutralising amines: colourless, volatile liquids that can burn and whose fumes are toxic.

Monocyclohexylamines or morpholine in solution is supplied in sealed containers and should be stored in a cool place.

Antifoams: these are complex organic compounds of high molecular weight. They are used to control the foam in the boiler drum and thus prevent carryover. They will generally be included in boiler chemical mixtures.

Prevention of Caustic Embrittlement

Sodium sulphate is used for the prevention of caustic embrittlement and the ratio of sodium sulphate to caustic soda should be kept at or above the recommended value of 2.5.

Alternatively sodium nitrate may be used, the ratio of sodium nitrate to caustic soda should not fall below 0.4 to 1 at all times.

BOILERS NOT IN SERVICE

When boilers are taken out of service for short or long periods of time they must be protected from corrosion.

In the case of water tube boilers out of service for a short period of time (*e.g.* two days) the boiler can be fired at intervals to keep the boiler pressure above about 3.5 bar and the boiler water must be maintained in composition as required for the boiler when under normal steaming conditions. Alternatively the boiler could be filled whilst hot, with hot deaerated alkaline feed water and about 0.5 kg of anhydrous sodium sulphite added for each tonne of water in the boiler. In this latter case, the boiler must be topped up periodically and any air in the system must be got rid of.

With fire tube boilers out of service for short periods the only action that need be taken is to ensure that the alkalinity to phenolphthalein is not less than the recommended value, or completely fill the boiler with alkaline water.

If the boiler is to be taken out of service for long periods it should be drained completely, then dried out by means of heater units. Then trays of quicklime should be placed internally in suitable positions throughout the boiler before it is sealed up. Blanks should be fitted to the pipe connections in the event of steam being maintained in other boilers and the blow down should be blanked in any case. The lime shold be renewed at least once every two months.

CLEANING OF NEW BOILERS

The purpose of pre-commission chemical cleaning is mainly to remove surface rust and mill scale which occur during boiler erection and manufacture and also dirt and traces of oil.

A comprehensive example of the treatment which would be carried out by a firm of specialists in boiler treatment could be, in order:

1. Boil out the boiler at atomspheric pressure with an alkaline solution to remove traces of oil and dirt.

2. Wash out boiler with a heated acid solution to remove rust and mill scale.

3. Rinse boiler with a weak acid solution.

4. Flush the boiler out repeatedly to remove debris.

5. Subject the boiler to a passivation process, this would be carried out under pressure with hydrazine. The feed system would be subjected to a similar process but the alkaline boil out would obviously be omitted and the passivation would be done at atmospheric pressure with hydrazine.

BOILER WATER TESTS

Boiler water should be regularly tested and the treatment of the boiler water should be conducted according to the results obtained from the tests.

For low pressure boilers such as the multitubular Scotch, vertical Cochran or thimble tube, salinometer and litmus papers are still frequently used as testing equipment.

Salinometer

The range of the scale is normally from 0 to $\frac{4}{32}$ and when the salinometer is floating in pure water at 93°C which has a relative density at that temperature of unity, the salinometer reading is zero. When the salinometer is floating in solutions of common salt at 93°C the salinometer reading is $\frac{1}{32}$ (approx. 32,000 p.p.m.) when the relative density of the solution is 1.025. (The relative density of salt water at 93°C is approximately 1.025 or $\frac{1}{32}$ on the salinometer.)

If sea water is used as make up feed for low pressure boilers it is recommended that the boiler density should be maintained as close as possible to $\frac{4}{32}$ (approx. 125,000 p.p.m.). This would be attained by resorting to blow down. The use of sea water as make up feed for boilers should be avoided as far as possible, but if it has to be used a certain amount of protection for the boiler can be provided by using soda ash.

Litmus Papers

These are used to ascertain the degree of acidity or alkalinity of the water. A litmus paper when inserted into a sample of boiler water may change colour, turning blue if the water is alkaline, or red if the water is acidic. The degree of colouration is a very rough indication of the pH value of the boiler water.

FREQUENCY OF TEST		DAILY	DAILY	WEEKLY	DAILY	DAILY	DAILY	DAILY	DAILY
BOILER WATER TEST		Alkalinity to Phenolphthalien	Chlorides (Max)	Caustic Alkalinity	Dissolved Solids Conductivity at 25°C (Max)	EDTA Hardness (Max)	Sulphite Excess	Phosphate Reserve	Hydrazine Reserve
RESULTS EXPRESSED		p.p.m. as $CaCO_3$	p.p.m. as NaCl	p.p.m. as $CaCO_3$	$\mu s/cm$	p.p.m. as $CaCO_3$	p.p.m. as Na_2SO_3	p.p.m. as PO_4	p.p.m. as N_2H_4
BOILER									
PRESSURE(bar)	TYPE								
UP TO 17.5	SCOTCH	300-700	3000	150-500	10000	5	50-100	30-70	-
UP TO 17.5	VERTICAL	300-500	1200	150-400	4500	5	50-100	30-70	-
UP TO 17.5	PACKAGE OR STM/STM.GEN	150-300	350	75-250	3000	5	50-100	30-70	-
UP TO 17.5	WATERTUBE	150-300	350	75-200	2250	5	50-100	30-70	-
17.5-31	WATERTUBE	150-300	150	100-250	1500	5	50-100	30-70	-
31-42	WATERTUBE	100-150	100	50-100	750	1	20-50	30-50	0.1-1.0
42-60	WATERTUBE	50-100	50	40-60	600	1	-	30-50	0.1-1.0
60-80	WATERTUBE	50-80	30	40-60	450	1	-	20-30	0.1-1.0

TABLE 4.9

For accurate testing of the boiler water, the foregoing salinometer and litmus paper methods are inadequate. Table 4.9 gives recommended values for low and high pressure boilers, to ascertain whether these values are being maintained, more refined testing methods are used.

Alkalinity

Tests for alkalinity are as follows:

(1) *Alkalinity to Phenolphthalein*
Take 100 ml sample of boiler water,
add 1ml (10 drops) of Phenolphthalein,
add N/50 sulphuric acid to clear the sample.
Calculation: ml of N/50 acid used × 10 = p.p.m. $CaCO_3$

Phenolphthalein is less alkaline than hydroxides or carbonates, and when it is added to a sample containing hydroxides and or carbonates it will turn pink in colour. The acid used after this colouration will first neutralise the hydroxides, forming salts, it will then react with the carbonate molecules present forming bicarbonate molecules. Bicarbonate molecules are less alkaline than phenolphthalein, hence, the pink colouration will disapear once all the hydroxides and carbonates have been dealt with by the acid. One bicarbonate molecule is formed from two carbonate molecules, hence in the test the quantity of acid used is a measure of the alkalinity due to the hydroxides (caustic) present and half the carbonates.

(2) *Total Alkalinity*
Take alkalinity to phenolphthalein sample,
add 10 drops of methyl-orange, result yellow colouration,
add N/50 sulphuric acid until pink
Calculation: ml of N/50 acid used for both tests × 10
= p.p.m. $CaCO_3$.

Methyl-orange indicator is less alkaline than phenolphthalein and bicarbonates. It can be used initially in place of phenolphthalein or as is more usual, as a continuation after the alkalinity to phenolphthalein test. If no yellow colouration results when the methyl-orange is added to the alkalinity to phenolphthalein sample no bicarbonates are present. Hence no carbonates are present. Therefore, the alkalinity as determined in the alkalinity to phenolphthalein test has been due to hydroxides alone. Note: Hydroxides and carbonates can co-exist together in a solution but hydroxides and bi-carbonates cannot.

(3) *Caustic Alkalinity*
    Take 100 ml sample of boiler water,
    add 10 ml of barium chloride,
    add 10 drops of phenolphthalein, result pink colouration,
    add N/50 sulphuric acid to clear the sample.
    Calculation: ml of N/50 acid used $\times$ 10 = p.p.m. $CaCO_3$

In this test barium chloride is first added to the boiler water sample in order to precipitate all the carbonates which are present. The test is then carried out as for the alkalinity to phenolphthalein test but in this case only the hydroxides (caustic) will be measured.

Chloride Test
    Take alkalinity to phenolphthalein sample,
    add 2 ml of sulphuric acid,
    add 20 drops of potassium chromate indicator,
    add N/35.5 silver nitrate solution until a brown colouration results.
    Calculation: ml of N/35.5 solution used $\times$ 10 = p.p.m. Cl or ml of N/50 silver nitrate solution used $\times$ 10 = p.p.m. $CaCO_3$.

Chlorides may be present in the boiler water sample and it is essential that they be measured as they would be an indication of salt water leakage into the feed system, either a leaky condenser or a primed evaporator, etc. The alkalinity to phenolphthalein sample taken, has had the hydroxides and carbonates dealt with and they will play no further part in the test now conducted for chlorides. The sample is made definitely acidic by the addition of a further small quantity of acid, this is to speed up the chemical reactions which next take place. Silver nitrate has an affinity for potassium chromate and chlorides, its principal preference however is for the chlorides. When it has neutralised the chlorides present in the sample it is then free to react with the potassium chromate, in doing so it produces a reddish brown colouration. It is therefore apparent that the amount of silver nitrate solution used is a direct measure of the chloride content of the boiler water sample. Note: As the drops of silver nitrate strike the sample, a reddish brown local colouration results which quickly disappears if chlorides are present. This should be ignored.

Sulphite Test

Take 100 ml of boiler water sample,
add 2 ml of sulphuric acid,
add 1 ml of starch solution
add potassium iodide-iodate solution until sample is blue in colour
Calculation: ml of iodide-iodate solution used $\times$ 12.5 = p.p.m. Na_2SO_3.

The boiler water sample is made slightly acidic to speed up the chemical reactions which are to take place. Potassium iodide-iodate produces a blue colouration through reaction with starch, but it has a preferential chemical reaction with sulphite if it is present in the sample. Hence when the potassium iodide-iodate solution has dealt with all the sulphite present, it is then free to react with the starch present in the sample, producing a blue colouration. It is therefore apparent that the amount of potassium iodide-iodate solution used is a direct measure of the sulphite content of the boiler water sample. As far as is possible the atmosphere should be excluded in this test otherwise an incorrect result may occur. If the test indicates that an adequate reserve of sodium sulphite is present in the boiler water there is no need to conduct a test for dissolved oxygen.

Phosphate Test

Take 25 ml of filtered boiler water sample,
add 25 ml vanadomolybdate reagent,
fill comparator tube with this solution and place in right hand compartment of comparator.

In left hand compartment place a blank prepared by mixing equal volumes of vanadomolybdate reagent and de-ionised water. Allow colour to develop for at least three minutes and then compare with disc.
Calculation: phosphate reserve in p.p.m. (mg/l) from the disc reading.

Hardness Test

Take 100 ml of filtered boiler water sample,
add 2 ml (20 drops) of ammonia buffer solution,
add 0.2g of mordant black 11 indicator and stir until dissolved.

If hardness salts are present the solution turns wine-red. Titrate with EDTA solution until colour changes to purple and then blue (with some waters a greyish coloured end point is reached).

Calculation: ml of EDTA solution used × 10 = p.p.m. $CaCO_3$

pH Value

A boiler water's pH value can be obtained by three basic methods.

      (1) Litmus papers.
      (2) Colourimetrically.
      (3) Electrolytically.

The litmus paper method has already been described but the test does not give a very accurate pH result, indicating merely if the water is acidic or alkaline. Tests (2) and (3) however give a reasonably accurate pH value.

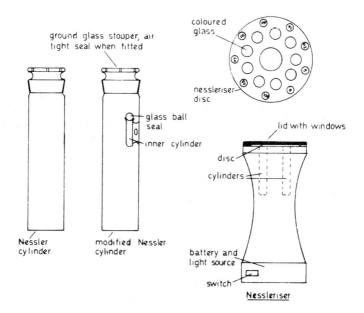

Fig. 4.2

Colourimetric Method (see Fig. 4.2)
    Take sample of boiler water.
    Place one thymol blue tablet in a 50 ml Nessler cylinder.
    Add 50 ml of sample to Nessler cylinder and ensure tablet is
    dissolved.   (1)
    Put 50 ml of sample into the other Nessler cylinder.   (2)
    Place (1) in right hand compartment of the Nessleriser.
    Place (2) in left hand compartment of the Nessleriser.
    Place appropriate disc in Nessleriser and match the colours,
    then read the pH value from the right hand window.

Electrolytic Method
    An electric cell, using the boiler water as an electrolyte and
two special electrodes, both made of glass, is used. The potential
difference between the electrodes is directly dependent upon the
hydrogen ion content of the electrolyte (boiler water). This
potential difference is measured by a sensitive voltmeter
connected into the external circuit of the cell and calibrated to
read p*H* values.

Dissolved Oxygen Test
    Take 500 ml of boiler water sample,
    add 0.3 ml of manganese chloride,
    add 0.3 ml of potassium hydroxide,
    add 1 ml of hydrochloric acid,
    add 2 ml of ortho-tolidine.

    In this test it is essential that the atmosphere be excluded from
the sample being tested. To arrange for this a specially designed
sampling flask is used. After the addition of the various
chemicals to the boiler water sample, the resulting solution is
compared colourimetrically with a colour chart, or a series of
indicator solutions whose dissolved oxygen content is known.
Where colours of sample and indicator coincide, the dissolved
oxygen content of the boiler water sample is read from the
indicator.

Alternative test
    To 8 ml of prepared stock reagent, made up of indigo carmine
glucose tablet dissolved in glycerol, 2 ml of potassium hydroxide
solution is added to make Leuco reagent.
    Some of the Leuco reagent (which must be used within 15
hours) is used to fill the inner tube of a modified Nessler
cylinder.

A glass ball is then placed on to the inner cylinder sealing in the reagent — no air must be trapped below the ball. Boiler water sample is run into the Nessler cylinder for at least 2 minutes to obtain a good sample and exclude all air, the cylinder stopper is quickly fitted and then by inverting the cylinder the glass ball will fall from the inner cylinder and the reagent will mix with the sample. When the two are thoroughly mixed the cylinder is placed into one compartment of a Nessleriser and a cylinder containing boiler water sample only is placed in the opposite compartment. An appropriate Nessleriser disc is then fitted and rotated until the colours match, when this occurs a reading in ml/litre is obtained in the small window.

If the dissolved oxygen content is high (above 0.2 ml/litre) it is recommended that no attempt should be made to reduce it by means of sodium sulphite (Na_2SO_3), otherwise considerable quantities of this chemical would have to be used increasing the total dissolved solids content of the boiler water.

When dissolved oxygen content is high, it could be due to a leakage into that part of the system which operates at a pressure below atmospheric, faulty deaeration equipment, air ejectors, etc., the matter should be corrected as early as possible to reduce risk of corrosion.

Total Dissolved Solids

These are ascertained by use of a hydrometer or electrical conductivity meter.

Hydrometer: Usually graduated in grains per imperial gallon (to convert grains per imperial gallon to p.p.m. multiply by 14.3). Care must be taken when using the hydrometer to account for the water meniscus and to ascertain accurately the temperature of the sample. Temperature correction tables for the hydrometer are usually supplied with it.

Conductivity Meter: A portable, battery operated, electrical conductivity meter is used in this test. The removable conductivity cell is washed out and filled with a treated boiler water sample (treatment consists of cooling to 15 to 20°C, adding phenolphthalein and removing pink colouration with acid). The filled cell is plugged into the meter, its temperature checked and the temperature control set to correspond. A range switch is set to approximate range of reading expected, then a central control is operated until 'null' balance of the electrical bridge circuit (the cell forms one resistance) is achieved. Position of the central control indicates the total dissolved solids in the water usually in p.p.m. but it may be conductivity in micromhos (to convert; p.p.m. total dissolved solids = conductivity in micromhos × 0.7).

Hydrazine Test

Take 250 ml of boiler water sample, exclude air and cool to 16 to 25°C. Add 15 ml of 0.5N hydrochloric acid to each of two Nessler cylinders. Add 25 ml of boiler water sample and 10 ml of 4-dimethylaminobenzaldehyde to one cylinder   (1)
Add 35 ml of boiler water sample to other cylinder   (2)
Place (1) in right hand compartment of the Nessleriser.
Place (2) in left hand compartment of the Nessleriser.
Match samples against disc colours.

Calculations: $\dfrac{\text{disc reading}}{25}$ = p.p.m. hydrazine.

The hydrazine reserve in the boiler water should be between 0.1 to 1 p.p.m.

TEST EXAMPLES 4

Class 3

1. Why is oil in boiler water considered dangerous, where does it usually come from and how can it be removed?
2. Water for boilers is usually kept as pure as reasonably possible. Give reasons why this is so.
3. Briefly describe why boiler water needs to be tested periodically and state two of the tests.

TEST EXAMPLES 4

Class 2

1. Give an analysis of the dissolved solids in an average sample of:
   (a)   Sea water,
   (b)   Fresh water.
      Which of these solids can form scale and which can cause corrosion?

2. Discuss the contamination of boiler feed water. What action should be taken in the event of such contamination to prevent damage to boilers and machinery? What tests are made?

3. What are the causes of corrosion in boilers? What precautions would you take to prevent corrosion
   (a)   when boiler is steaming?
   (b)   when boiler is idle?
      How would you test the boiler water for acidity and alkalinity?

4. Suggest with reasons which four of the following impurities in the feed water of a 'package' boiler operating at 7 bar, dry saturated are likely to contribute most to scale formation:
   a)   silica,
   b)   iron compounds,
   c)   sodium chloride,
   d)   magnesium bi-carbonate,
   e)   calcium bi-carbonate,
   f)   calcium sulphate,
   g)   sodium sulphate,
   h)   magnesium chloride.

5. Give a reason why sodium phosphate, sodium hydroxide and hydrazine are each used in boiler water treatment. Describe any three of the analytical tests normally applied to boiler water. Explain how the results influence further treatment. State two precautions to be observed when storing and handling these chemicals.

TEST EXAMPLES 4

Class 1

1. Describe how you would make a quantitative test of boiler water for:
   (a)   alkalinity,
   (b)   chlorinity,
   (c)   hardness.
   State the values obtained from the above tests that you would consider suitable for a water tube boiler. Describe in each case the action you would take if a test gave an unsatisfactory result.

2. Why is it necessary to keep oxygen out of the boiler? Describe how this is done mechanically and chemically. State the procedure for laying up a boiler:
   (a)   for a considerable period,
   (b)   a few days.

3. Enumerate the scale forming solids in fresh and sea water respectively. How would you steam a boiler on contaminated feed? Give reasons for your action.

4. Describe the boiler water tests carried out for boilers, and the results expected from:
   (a)   low pressure boilers,
   (b)   high pressure boilers,

5. Specify, with reasons, those parts requiring particularly close scrutiny during internal and external examination of independently fired auxiliary boilers. With reference to those examinations distinguish between metal fatigue due to caustic embrittlement, corrosion fatigue, overheating (plastic flow) and direct overpressure.

CHAPTER 5

STEERING GEARS

This chapter will include Telemeter (Transducer) Systems, Power (Amplifier) Units, Actuator (Servo) Mechanisms and conclude with a short account of related principles as utilised with ship stabilisers.

TELEMETER (TRANSDUCER) SYSTEMS

The steering gears to be described, electro-hydraulic and electrical, when operated by auto-pilot illustrate fundamental closed loop control principles. The telemotor itself employs a 'master and slave' principle. The transmitter is situated on the bridge and the receiver at the steering gear unit. Mechanical movement is transduced hydraulically or electrically for distance telemetering and then transduced back again. The steering wheel may be retained as an ornament.

Hydraulic Transmitter (Fig. 5.1)

As the bridge steering wheel is moved to starboard the rotating pinion causes the right hand ram to move down, pushing oil out to the receiver unit along the right hand pipe. The left hand ram moves up, so allowing a space for oil to come from the receiver unit. The fluid is virtually incompressible, hence any down movement of the right hand ram produces an identical movement at the receiver unit. This in turn displaces the same quantity of fluid which is taken up in the extra space created by the left hand ram moving up. The fluid in the replenishing tank acts as an oil reservoir.

The casing is usually gunmetal, with bronze rams, and copper pipes are led in by drilled leads in the casting. Some device is required in the system to allow for variations in oil volume due to temperature changes and also to allow for equilibrium between both sides of the system.

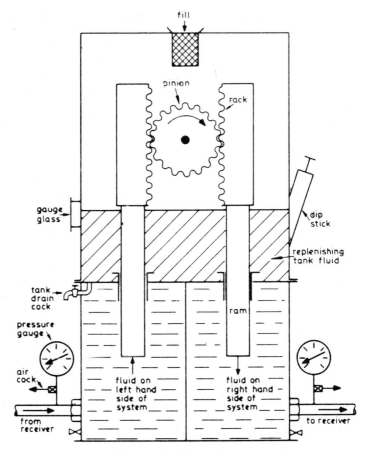

HYDRAULIC TRANSMITTER
Fig. 5.1

The device is called the bypass valve, which has the additional functions of topping up the system in the case of leakages and acting as a relief valve in case of pressure rise.

The Bypass Valve

Referring to Fig. 5.2:
Operation can only be carried out when the wheel is in the mid

position. This is achieved by having the operating rod butting against a circular disc, in mid position of the wheel the slot in the driven revolving disc allows the operating rod to be depressed through it. With some types the operating rod is depressed by hand whilst with other types the rod is automatically depressed by a cam each time the wheel passes mid position. In the case of the former the rod is operated at regular intervals and *must* be operated when either pressure gauge registers above 4.5 bar, with the wheel *at mid position*. When the rod is depressed both sides of the system are connected so giving pressure balance. The connection to the replenishing tank is also joined to both sides of the system, so that any expansion or contraction of the oil can be corrected. In some types a relief valve is fitted in the line to the replenishing tank, set about 18 bar, and a replenishing valve, working in the opposite direction is also provided, which is loaded (about 2.5N). Other types employ direct piping to the replenishing tank with no valves.

To test most gears for tightness the wheel can be lashed over, first one side then the other, at a pressure of *about* 42 bar (which

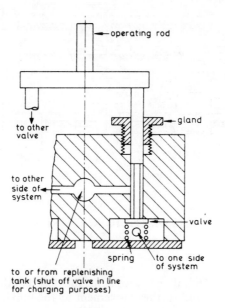

BYPASS VALVE ($\frac{1}{2}$ VIEW)
Fig. 5.2

should hold for a considerable time). Leakage at either side means that all pipe joints and glands must be examined. To test the bypass valve the above procedure is repeated but with the liquid saving (or circuit valves) on the receiver telemotor shut, this loads each of the valves on the bypass unit in turn.

Hydraulic Receiver (Fig. 5.3)

Considering the starboard (*clockwise*) movement of the bridge wheel (as mentioned for the steering telemotor). The depressed right hand ram pressurises the right hand side of the system. The pressure force acts on the central web of the moving cylinder until the movement caused corresponds to the movement of the ram in the steering telemotor. Oil is pushed back on the left hand side of the moving cylinder central web to the steering unit.

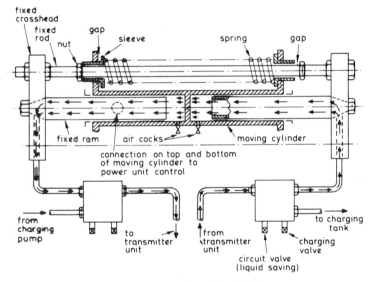

HYDRAULIC RECEIVER
Fig. 5.3

After a small initial movement the left hand sleeve butts against the nut and further movement by the moving cylinder to the left compresses the springs. When the steering wheel is returned mid-ships the springs, which are under initial compression, return the moving cylinder to mid position.

For a port wheel rotation the left hand ram of the steering unit moves down and the receiver moving cylinder goes in the opposite direction *i.e.* in the given case left to right. Together with the bypass valve the springs form the adjusting, centralising, device.

The moving cylinder is connected by a linkage to the control unit of the steering engine. Thus any movement of the bridge telemotor unit by wheel rotation is almost directly opening the control device which causes rotation of the steering engine and rudder movement.

Electro-Hydraulic Type

Utilises control signals from an auto-helmsman order synchro amplified to operate solenoid valves controlling the direction of flow from a small oil pump to one side or the other of a ram connected to the actuator control rod (with feedback synchro).

Telemotor Fluid

Good quality mineral lubricating oil is used with the following properties:
(1) Low pour point (2) non sludge forming (3) non corrosive (4) good lubricating properties (5) high flash point (6) low viscosity, to reduce frictional drag, but not too thin to make gland sealing difficult. Typical properties would be: density 880 kg/m^3 (at 15.5°C), viscosity 12 cSt (at 50°C), closed flash point 150°C, pour point—30°C.

Charging System (Fig. 5.4)

First consider the *cleaning* of the system. The charging and replenishing tanks are first drained and washed through with clean oil until perfectly clean. The lower part of the steering telemotor is similarly drained and cleaned via inspection doors and finally washed through with clean oil. The system oil will have been drained off at the lowest point. The connections for charging at the steering telemotor, *A* and *B*, are joined with a spare gear pipe and the pipes at the charging valves, *C* and *D*, are disconnected. Clean oil is now added to the charging tank and a head must be maintained here at all times.

Using the pump, oil is pumped until a clear discharge occurs at *C*, the pipe connection at *C* can now be replaced, open charging valves *C* and *D* and the circuit valves *E* and *F*. Continue pumping until the oil passes right through the circuit to discharge at *D*, when clear, close the pipe connection joint at

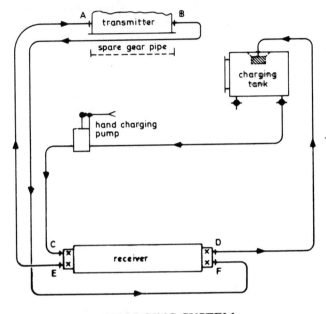

CHARGING SYSTEM
Fig. 5.4

D, remove spare gear pipe and couple up pipes to steering telemotor.

Considering now the *charging*. Open all air cocks. A constant head must at all times be maintained in the charging tank otherwise air can be admitted to the system. A spring loaded valve is provided, normally in the return line, to the charging tank to prevent oil backflow from the highest point (steering telemotor) when charging, and giving air entry and vacuum problems.

The steering wheel is put to mid position, bypass valve open, charging shut off valve open. Pump until replenishing tank is full and all air clear at steering telemotor, close shut off valve and air cocks.

Repeat the procedure for the receiver telemotor until all air is clear and oil returns to the charging tank. Close charging valves, close bypass valve, open charging shut off valve.

The gear is now ready for testing (a) for leaks (b) that movement at each receiver corresponds in direction and amount (c) that there is definitely no air in the system.

Air in System

Air in any hydraulic system must always be avoided and the telemotor system is no exception.

Air being compressible gives incorrect balance between units, time lags and irregular operation, which can be dangerous. Its presence in the system is indicated by defective steering, jerky operation and perhaps 'jumping at the pressure gauges'. Air can usually be kept out with a tight system after proper charging but should air get into the system it may be removed by purging at the air cocks. Should a large quantity of air gain access giving faulty steering then probably the only course is to totally empty and recharge. Water and dirt should also be avoided in the system.

Emergency Operation

In the event of a total failure of the telemotor system it is a requirement that the ship can be steered directly from a position aft. This is usually carried out by a direct gear from the aft steering wheel station to the power unit control. Both the receiver unit and hand gear unit linkage can each operate the control unit through a sliding rod. When the telemotor pin is fitted to the *receiver linkage hole* the receiver motion is given to the control unit, the hand gear merely sliding in the sleeve. If the pin is removed and put into the *hand gear sliding linkage hole* this operates the control unit and the telemotor connection merely slides in the sleeve. Only one telemotor pin is provided to be used in the required position, in port the pin should be in the hand position and both the main and emergency steering wheels lashed amidships.

Pin detail can be seen in Fig. 5.9.

Electrical Telemotor

Bridge remote control is either electric, hydraulic or gyro pilot. The system of Fig. 5.9 has been reduced in size and grouped into an oil bath box as shown in Fig. 5.5 in which the principle is almost identical but the input is electric in this case.

A bridge lever moves rheostat B and unbalance current flows to rotate the control torque motor and hunt rheostat A back to equilibrium when the motor will stop (see details given later of Ward Leonard System electrical steering gear).

Electrical input is most common in modern practice and motor drive via a flexible coupling (or electromagnetic clutch) rotates the screw shaft in the control box. This causes the screw block to move and, through the floating lever, causes movement of the actuator control rod. This electrical-mechanical transducer also has limit switches and may utilise synchros and gear trains.

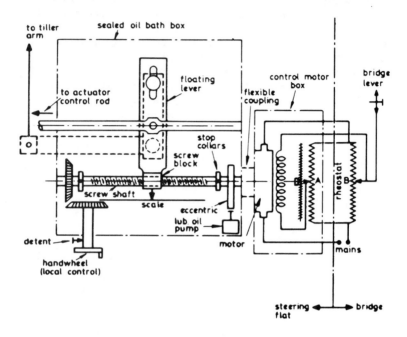

ELECTRICAL TELEMOTOR
Fig. 5.5

To change to local mechanical input control the electrical control is switched off and the spring detent on the handwheel lifted whilst the handwheel shaft is pushed home so that the spur gear engages when the detent is released to lock the shaft (electrical remote input, mechanical local input).

Control Terminology

It is useful to consider control aspects. The *deviation* signal on the control rod is the result of a *proportional* movement of the screw block from the helm (*desired value*) and the *feedback* signal from the tiller arm rod—shown under as dotted—acting on the floating lever.

POWER (AMPLIFIER) UNITS

The function of the power unit is to amplify (and possibly transduce) the receiver output signal, in the correct direction, for transmission to the final controlling actuator operating the rudder.

Electrical

A separately excited generator system is usually used and a description is given under Electrical Steering Gears later in the chapter.

Hydraulic

A variable delivery oil pressure pump is used and two designs will now be considered.

The Hele-Shaw Pump

Considering Fig. 5.6:

The shaft is stationary and the cylinder body forming the cylinders rotates around the shaft, being driven by a constant speed and direction electric motor (or steam engine). The plungers are connected to slippers which run in annular grooves inside two circular rings on each side of the plungers. When the centre of the rings coincide with the shaft centre (O) the pump travel is at mid position. At this position the plungers rotate at a fixed radius distance from the shaft centre (distance OC), this means there is no *relative* motion between the plungers and the shaft and no pumping action takes place.

If now the circular slipper rings are moved to the right by the operating rod, through the casing from the telemotor rod, then the centre of rotation of the slippers and plungers is at B which is eccentric to the centre of the shaft. O. This means the *greatest* distance the plunger gudgeons are from O is OG and the *shortest* distance is OF. With the direction of rotation as shown, in travelling round from G to F the plungers are moving *in* relative to the fixed central shaft and ports hence the top port T acts as a *discharge*. In completing the circular route from F back to G the plungers are moving *out* relative to the central shaft and ports and the bottom port B acts as a *suction*. The path is shown on the sketch dotted, likewise the relative plunger movement at four positions.

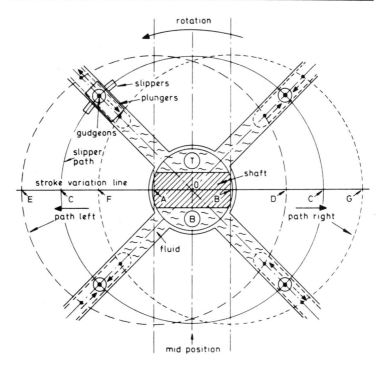

HELE-SHAW PRINCIPLE
Fig. 5.6

If the circular slipper rings are moved left so the centre of plunger rotation is at *A* then the *shortest* distance is *OD* and the *greatest* distance is *OE*, *i.e.* plungers are moving *out* in top half of rotation and *T* is a *suction* and *in* during bottom half of rotation and *B* is a *discharge*. The path and plunger movement are shown here as dashed line.

As the stroke of the plungers depends on the movement of the slipper path *horizontally* and hence the eccentricity, so the pump is of the variable delivery type. Also direction of flow depends on movement left or right of central position so that for uni-directional rotation the direction of flow is reversible.

A simplified construction sketch is as shown (Fig. 5.7).

The drive for the cylinder body can be seen rotating in roller bearings outside the fixed central shaft with the oil block fastened to the casing. Plunger and gudgeon pin connection to slippers can be seen with the slipper running in the annular

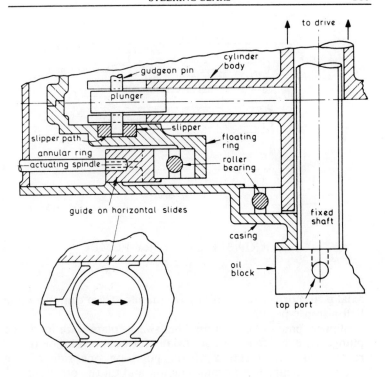

HELE-SHAW PUMP DETAIL (¼ PLAN)
Fig. 5.7

groove of the circular ring. The circular rings are not rigidly
fixed but are free to rotate as floating rings on roller bearings,
this reduces oil churning and friction losses.

The control or actuating spindle passes through the casing and
moves the floating ring *horizontally* left or right by means of the
floating ring guide on horizontal slides.

In practice the pump is usually provided with an odd number
of cylinders, usually seven or nine, which produces more even
hydraulic flow and better pump balance.

Variable Delivery Pump—Alternative Design

This type of pump has been used with ship stabiliser units (see
later). Consider Fig. 5.8.

This utilises a similar principle to the Hele-Shaw but has axial
piston drive from a tilting swash plate. Similar designs utilise

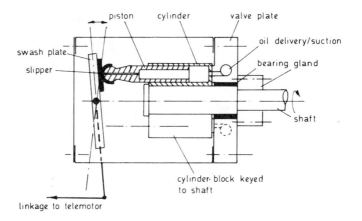

VARIABLE DELIVERY PUMP
Fig. 5.8

axial piston drive from a tilting trunnion or from cam faces (see ball piston type, Fig. 5.17).

Slipper pads bear against the swash plate face and the plungers are driven in and out axially for each revolution of the rotor. For one direction of tilt ports on one side of the horizontal centre line become suction and on the other side of this centre line become discharge. For the opposite direction of tilt the direction of flow is reversed. The quantity of discharge depends on the angle of tilt. In mid position no relative movement exists between piston and end plate and no pumping action takes place.

ACTUATOR (SERVO) MECHANISMS

There are two main types of steering 'engine' now in use namely electro-hydraulic and all electric. For each type two designs are given:

Electro-Hydraulic: Ram, Rotary Vane.
All Electric: Ward Leonard, Single Motor.

Electro-Hydraulic Ram Steering Gear

The pump unit delivers to rams which are virtually directly coupled to the rudder stock forming the actuator mechanism.

Referring first to the diagrammatic plan view of the electro hydraulic steering gear given in Fig. 5.9. Consider a movement

of the wheel to starboard and hence ship's head to starboard, the
rudder movement will be to starboard so that the rams will move
starboard to port (right to left).

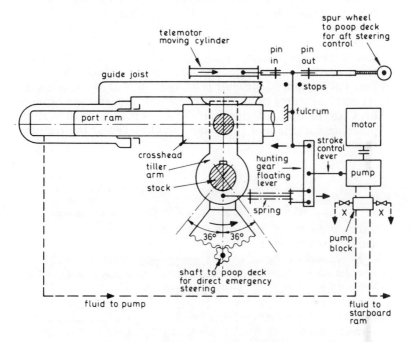

ELECTRO-HYDRAULIC STEERING GEAR
Fig. 5.9

The steering telemotor moves from right to left (as considered
previously) but is mounted on the joist bracket through 180
degrees so that the movement on Fig. 5.9 is left to right. The
receiver motion is given to a lever which is fixed at the centre
(fulcrum) so that the other end moves right to left. There is a
hand gear control, two positions for the telemotor pin, and
movement stops. The movement right to left of the lever draws
out the pump stroke control lever, to which is connected the
actuating lever for the stroke variation and control for the
pressure pump. The pump driven by an electric shunt-motor at
constant speed now *delivers* oil to the starboard ram and *draws*
from the port ram. The rams therefore move right to left along
the guide joists. Stops are provided, on the joist, to limit travel.

As the rams slide across they push on the ram crossheads moving the tiller arm to port, the arm sliding through the swivel bearing. The crosshead detail is shown in Fig. 5.10. A wear down rudder allowance of 19 mm is provided so as not to induce bending stresses on the ram. With the tiller arm going to port the rudder moves to starboard. The rotating stock movement is led back by a spring link to the pump control floating lever. This constitutes the hunting gear (feed back) in that when the telemotor movement stops, the floating lever stops going to the left. The bottom of the lever is being pushed to the right and so the stroke control of the pump is almost immediately brought back to pump mid position. This means the pump stops pumping and the unit is virtually fluid locked at the required rudder position.

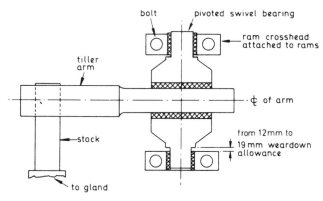

CROSSHEAD ARRANGEMENT
Fig. 5.10

The tiller-rudderhead bearing and carrier usually have the main casting of cast steel, with a large machined base for fitting to the deck. A bronze thrust ring is on top of this casting and the tiller boss has a machined ring face to go against this thrust face. The thrust ring is in halves and dowelled against rotation and lubrication is provided. The main gland bush, in halves, is usually of gunmetal and is grease lubricated.

Fabricated assemblies are common in modern practice.

Rudder, stock and other parts have weight transmission to the tiller by means of a steel support plate and eyebolt on top of the rudder stock.

At the pump block are non return valves and connections leading to the sump or replenishing tank to act as suction and replenishing leads (*XX*). The ram pipes to and from the pump to the rams are also led into the pump block. The oil used in the system is well filtered pure lubricating oil. The gear is filled by coupling up to the hand steering and rotating port and starboard with the motor running, having previously filled suction sump or replenishing tank and ram cylinders, replenishing valves and bypass valves open. The bypass valves are then shut and the gear fully rotated port and starboard whilst the air is purged from the ram cylinders, etc., at the air cocks. The bypass valves are two fold units in the block, consisting of bypass and isolating valves. Two other valves, of the *spring loaded* type act as double shock relief valves. Each valve connects both sides of the system when the pressure in either ram cylinder reaches 80 to 190 bar (depending on the design) the valve lifts, so letting the rudder give way when subject to severe sea action. When giving way the pump actuating spindle is moved and the pump acts to return the rudder to the previous position when the loading reduces. The relief valves, when operating, are effectively providing feedback (with increased offset between set and desired values in the short term which will be reduced as soon as normal conditions prevail when relief valves close).

The relief valves lifting pressure setting therefore fixes the maximum loading on the rams. This in turn limits the maximum torque that is exerted on the rudder stock and the maximum torsional stress is so limited to about 34.5 MN/m^2. The gear works on the well known principle of the 'Rapson Slide' and knowing the maximum lifting pressure of the relief valves then the ram load is fixed, applying the leverage for distance to stock gives the torque exerted, which allows size calculations for the stock diameter, and horse power and sizes for the motor and pump. Higher pressure systems have relief valves acting at about 190 bar. For a detail of the pump block see Fig. 5.11.

Emergency Operation

In many installations four rams are provided, two on each side of a double tiller arm, together with twin motor and pump units. All connections are normally open with one pump unit in service, the other is a stand by which can be quickly switched on if the service motor fails. See also Fig. 5.11, 5.13 and P.195.

During manoeuvring in dangerous waters both pump units are often used together. Such installations are usually arranged to operate from emergency essential service battery *and/or* generator circuits in the event of a main power failure. The above considerations satisfy the most onerous required regulations.

For *less* onerous rule requirements a hand pinion drive (as shown in Fig. 5.9) or hand pumping may be acceptable. In the extreme case of emergency a block and hawser arrangement could be rigged up.

A complete armature and field coil would normally be carried as part of the spare gear.

Control Valve Block

Refer to Fig. 5.11 which illustrates a system which is acceptable, but by no means standard, for electro-hydraulic type gears.

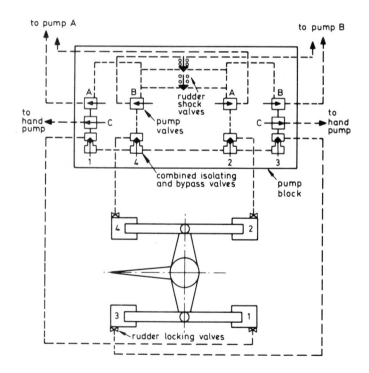

CONTROL VALVE BLOCK
Fig. 5.11

Rudder locking valves on all cylnders are open except in cases of emergency.

The main valve block contains three groups of valves (1) Two rudder shock (relief) valves (2) Four pump isolating valves (two valves for each pump A and B) (3) Four combined ram cylinder isolating and bypass valves connecting to each cylinder.

When a pump is not in use it is prevented from motoring and relieved of a starting load by a spring loaded discharge valve. This valve is kept in a bypass position until the pump is started up and its discharge pressure is sufficient to move the valve. The bypass connection is then automatically closed and the isolating connection opened, by valve movement, so connecting the pump hydraulically to the steering gear. This detail is *not* shown on Fig. 5.11. An alternative is to use a centrifugal coupling, between motor and pump, whose pawls open out when running but when stopped the pawls engage a ratchet so locking against rotation.

Under *normal* conditions either pump with four rams is in use and to bring in the other pump only requires the operation of the starter. The four pump valves marked ABAB are open and the two hand pump valves marked CC, are closed.

For *emergency* conditions with pumps shut down the four pump valves are closed and the two hand pump valves opened.

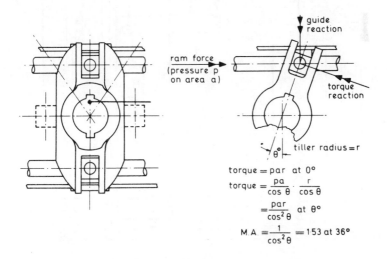

torque = par at $0°$

torque = $\dfrac{pa}{\cos \theta} \cdot \dfrac{r}{\cos \theta}$

$= \dfrac{par}{\cos^2 \theta}$ at $\theta°$

M.A. $= \dfrac{1}{\cos^2 \theta} = 1·53$ at $36°$

RAPSON SLIDE FORK TYPE TILLER
Fig. 5.12

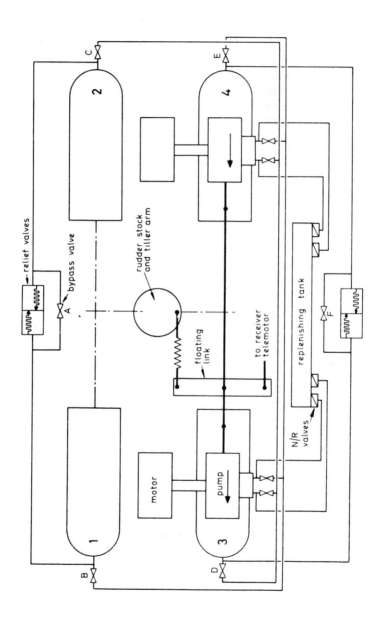

FOUR RAM STEERING GEAR
Fig. 5.13

Five combinations of rams are usually possible *i.e.* all four, two port, two starboard, two aft, two forward. A diagonal arrangement is not usually possible. As sketched the combined valves are all open on the isolating connection and closed on the bypass connection. To operate with rams 1 and 2, valves 1 and 2 are open, and valves 3 and 4 shut. To operate with rams 2 and 4, valves 2 and 4 are open, and valves 1 and 3 are shut. Similar procedure applies for the other two combinations. A valve is classed as open if the isolating connection is shut (bypass connection is obviously open when the isolating connection is closed, and vice versa).

Fork Type Tiller (Fig. 5.12)
This is a more recent design in which the rams as a single forging act upon a codpiece which slides in slots which are machined into upper and lower jaw pieces of the tiller.

Rapson Slide (Fig. 5.12)
This illustrates the increasing with angle mechanical advantage (frictionless) of this well known mechanism.
The mechanical advantage (frictionless) for pinned actuators increases with angle and is 1.53 at 36° (for rotary vane type the mechanical advantage is unity for all angles).

Four Ram Steering Gear
Fig. 5.13 illustrates diagrammatically the well known Hastie type of four ram gear with a valve arrangement differing from the previous example. In this case only three combinations are possible (1) all four cylinders in operation (2) with valves B, C and F open, A, D and E closed as cylinders 1 and 2 operational (3) with valves A, D and E open B, C and F closed cylinders 3 and 4 are operational.
The hunting gear arrangement is similar to the two ram system and two pumps are normally employed.

Electro-Hydraulic Rotary Vane Steering Gear
Details are as sketched in Fig. 5.14. Rotation depends on which side of the vane is connected to the pump pressure feed, this should be clear from the plan view as sketched. The rotary vane unit is normally designed for a maximum pressure of about 90 bar as distortion and leakage are liable to occur at higher pressures. The design is simple and effective and has proved popular in practice. In fact the apparent space and weight saving is not as great as may be imagined due to the higher pressures

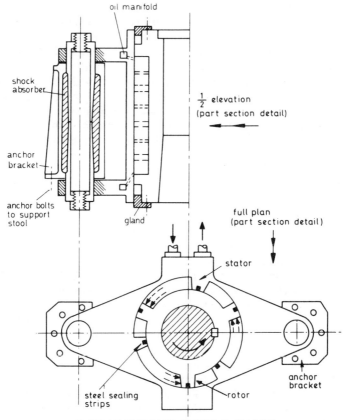

ROTARY VANE UNIT (3 VANE)
Fig. 5.14

and integrated construction utilised in modern hydraulic ram designs. There is however, a definite space saving but the first cost is usually higher. Absorption and transmission of torque relief is essential to avoid excess radial loading of vanes. Support has resilient shock absorber mountings which also allows for small misalignment—where spade type rudders are used axial and radial thrust bearings are provided. The three vane type is used for rudder angles of 70° and for larger angles a two vane unit would be used. Vanes, of SG iron, are secured to the rotor or stator by dowels and keyed (full length). The vanes themselves act as rudder stops. Steel sealing strips backed by synthetic rubber are fitted into grooves along the working faces of rotor and stator vanes.

Comparison of Units

Torque is dependent (for one actuator) on pressure, area and effective leverage. The ram design is more adaptable to increase of these variables—pressure is certainly limited on the vane type to about half that on rams (due to sealing difficulties). Up to a certain torque the vane unit may well be smaller and lighter. However, integral design produces problems of construction, weight and size when the variables are increased. Provided alternative hydraulic pressure sources are available emergency operation is readily achieved with either type although the ram type is more flexible to alternative mechanical leverage. Rudder support, and shock loadings, require more careful consideration with vane units because of the very close and direct connection between rudder and actuator.

Automatic Fail Safe System

Donkin utilise the bedplate oil tank, with control division plate up to two thirds height, so each side is connected to its own pump. Each pump is associated with a pair of rams (optionally mounted one above the other to save deck space) so that two complete half power steering gears are formed (giving up to 20° rudder movement at maximum ship speed or full manoeuvring at two thirds maximum ship speed). In normal operation (at full tank) the two systems are joined by two common lines each fitted with a solenoid operated spool valve (normally open) so allowing a free balanced flow of oil between the circuits.

If leakage of oil does occur, the first stop of the oil tank float switch closes, which isolates one of the pump motors and simultaneously closes its associated valve on the line between the two systems, putting the ram cylinders of the suspect circuit into the bypass condition. Operation is instantaneous with no interruption to steering; audible and visual alarms are fitted on the bridge.

As the choice of circuit isolated is preset, if the incorrect circuit has been chosen, the oil level in the tank will continue to fall and eventually close the second stage of the float switch. This at once changes over the pump motors and their corresponding isolating valves so leaving, by process of elimination, the correct circuit in use. After the operation of the second stage of the float switch, two thirds of the tank contents still remain thus ensuring an adequate supply of oil for continued working of the rudder actuator. As the defective circuit is now completely isolated, any repairs that are necessary can be carried out without interruption to steering.

Two or four ram units have been fitted to vessels up to 90,000 g.r.t.

The Ward Leonard Electrical Steering Gear

In this case telemotor, power and actuator units are considered in one. A brief and simplified description of the electrical principles involved, sufficient only for examination purposes, is given.

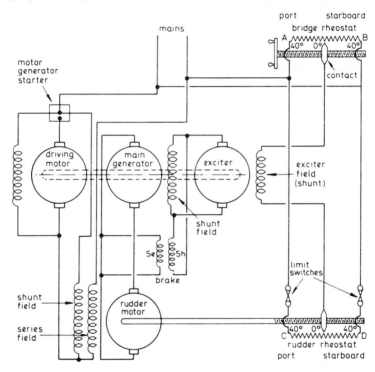

ELECTRICAL STEERING GEAR (WARD LEONARD)
Fig. 5.15

There are four electrical facts that are important in the system:

(1) If a direct current generator is driven at constant speed and direction then the magnitude and direction of the voltage is dependent on the magnitude and direction of the current through the field windings.

(2) The magnitude and direction of the armature current to a direct current motor having constant field excitation in one direction decides the magnitude and direction of the output torque.

(3) When a steady current flows in a uniform conductor there is a steady voltage drop along the length of the conductor.

(4) If a voltage is applied to the ends of two uniform conductors joined in parallel then a current between zero and maximum can flow in either direction by connecting suitable points on the conductors.

Considering Fig. 5.15, the control gear employs two rheostats connected up as a 'Wheatstone bridge' circuit connected to the mains supply. With the two contacts in the same positions (*equal* electrical voltage) *i.e.* correspondence of rheostat position on the conductor or rheostat of bridge and rudder, then no current flows between them.

If the wheel is moved say from amidships to starboard the contact moves on the screw towards *B* and alters its position on the bridge rheostat. This means the two contacts are at *different* voltages (Fact 3). Current therefore flows between the contacts in a fixed direction, if the wheel had been moved to port *i.e.* towards *A*, current would have flowed in the reverse direction, the magnitude of the current depending on the amount of movement of the steering wheel contact along its rheostat (which gives the necessary voltage difference between the contacts). Thus a variable magnitude *and* direction current can be made to flow in the exciter shunt field (Fact 4).

The main motor drives the main generator and exciter, the motor taking current from mains supply. With the contacts in equivalent positions no current flows in the exciter field and no current is induced in its armature even though it is rotated, similarly for the main generator, hence it produces no voltage and no current is supplied to the rudder motor armature. The rudder motor is field excited from the ship's mains but this will not produce torque without armature current so the motor is stationary.

With the bridge contact moved to starboard, current flows in *one* direction through the exciter field, and the armature now produces volts which sends a current through the generator field. A current now flows through the rudder motor armature and the rudder motor rotates the rudder. The hunting gear now functions so that the rudder movement moves the contact on the rudder rheostat to follow the bridge rheostat *i.e. towards D.* When the bridge wheel is stopped, the hunting gear brings the two contacts into equivalent voltage again to cause no current to flow through the exciter and subsequent circuits and so stop the rudder motor in the correct position.

If the wheel is moved to port, current flows in the reverse direction so that the generator produces *reverse* direction current (Fact 1). This current will produce *opposite* direction of rotation for the rudder motor (Fact 2) and the contact of the rudder rheostat is hunted *towards C* until equilibrium again exists. The exciter is really a current amplifier to reduce the current required at the rheostat contacts whilst giving sufficient current through the generator field. The series field of the rudder motor automatically gets a boost current when the driving motor comes on extra power with the generator and exciter producing current, and this boost serves to overcome the inertia of the rudder gear. Limit switches are fitted on the contacts to cut off current at about 36° positon before the mechanical stops are reached. The brake is kept on whilst no current flows in the rudder motor armature and when current flows another resistance comes into parallel so *reducing* the total resistance and allowing rotation of the rudder. The brake functions to slip at a predetermined load so producing current, and this boost serves to overcome the inertia of the movement and is usually transmitted by a pinion, wheel and spur gear or by worm and wheel to a rudder quadrant.

To stop excessive hunting a damping coil in the exciter circuit is provided which is wound in opposition to the exciter field winding.

Emergency Operation

Many installations are provided with completely separate twin electrical equipments on to one quadrant. A changeover switch allows independent operation and either equipment can be directly operated from a rheostat aft for hand emergency steering. The electric circuit will be on the essential services emergency circuit, being battery operated or battery and emergency generator operated. In addition a spur gearing from poop to quadrant teeth can be provided. The above conditions would serve to satisfy the most onerous rules applicable. Suitable spare gear for all essential parts would require to be supplied.

Electric Single Motor Steering Gear.

Consider Fig. 5.16.

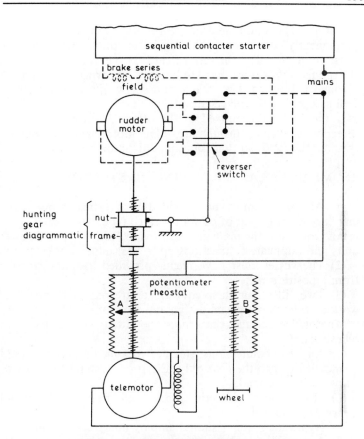

**ELECTRICAL STEERING GEAR
(SINGLE MOTOR)
Fig. 5.16**

The armature of the telemotor is fed directly from the mains and so is the potentiometer rheostat. If B is moved, say down, by the wheel then current flows due to the difference of potential between A and B. The telemotor field is now excited and the telemotor rotates so as to bring A into line again and restore equilibrium.

Through a screw nut, frame and fulcrum arrangement the reverser switch is moved up and so closed. Mains current then flows through the brake field (to release the brake), through the rudder motor series field and through the rudder motor armature. The shunt field of the rudder motor (not shown) is permanently connected to the mains but this is insufficient to cause rotation unless the series field is also excited. Rotation of the rudder motor is arranged to hunt back the rheostat contact A through a floating lever frame and screw nut arrangement as well as opening the reverser switch.

If the reverser is moved in the other direction the current direction is reversed through the rudder motor armature, but not through the field, so that rotational direction changes.

SOME RULES APPERTAINING TO STEERING GEARS

(1) All vessels must be provided with efficient main and auxiliary steering gear of power operated type. An auxiliary gear is not required if the main gear is provided with duplicate power units and duplicate connections up to the rudder stock.

(2) The vessel must have means provided to allow steering from a position aft.

(3) Two tillers, or their equivalent, are required unless the working tiller is of special design and strength.

(4) Power operated gears must be fitted with a device to relieve shock.

(5) Any lead connections, steam, hydraulic or electric should be independent to the gear only. Electric leads and fuses are to allow 100% overload.

(6) Moving parts of steering gears should be guarded to avoid injury to personnel.

(7) Hydraulic systems should employ non freezing fluid.

(8) A clear view from the steering position is required and the wheel, tell tale indicators, and rudder movement must correspond in the correct amount and in the correct direction for the ship's head.

(9) Operating trials should be carried out on steering gears to ascertain degree of action, time of operation, angle of heel at speeds, etc.

It should be noted that the steering gear should have a *reasonably* quick action, as an indication 'full port' to 'full starboard' rudder movement should take place in about 30 s with vessel at speed.

In view of serious accidents the IMO regulations relating to duplication of rudder actuators should be noted (also see automatic 'fail-safe' system, earlier): Every oil tanker, chemical tanker or gas carrier of 10,000 tons gross tonnage and upwards shall comply with the following:

(i) The main steering gear shall be so arranged that in the event of loss of steering capability due to a single failure in any part of one of the power actuating systems of the main steering gear, excluding the tiller, quadrant or components serving the same purpose, or seizure of the rudder actuators, steering capability shall be regained in not more than 45 seconds after the loss of one power actuating system.

(ii) The main steering gear shall comprise either:

(1) two independent and separate power actuating systems, each capable of meeting the requirements; or

(2) at least two identical power actuating systems which, acting simultaneously in normal operation, shall be capable of meeting the requirements. Where necessary to comply with this requirement, inter-connection of hydraulic power actuating systems shall be provided. Loss of hydraulic fluid from one system shall be capable of being detected and the defective system automatically isolated so that the other actuating system or systems shall remain fully operational.

(iii) Steering gears other than of the hydraulic type shall achieve equivalent standards.

For oil tankers, chemical tankers or gas carriers) of 10,000 tons gross tonnage and upwards, but of less than 100,000 tons deadweight, other solutions to an equivalent standard may be acceptable. Such regulations may well extend to all vessels.

THE SHIP STABILISER

As the operating principle of this equipment is very similar to that of an electro-hydraulic steering gear it is advisable to have a working knowledge of stabilisers.

The electric circuits and hydraulic relays involved are numerous and a detailed consideration on the equipment is not necessary. A simplified presentation is therefore given with the system considered in three parts, namely electrical control, hydraulic operation and gear, and the fin detail.

A knowledge of the operating principle from the aspect of the fin action of the ship rolling, with an understanding of the control system (using the analogy of the electro-hydraulic steering gear, avoiding the rather complex electrical, oil pump, and motor descriptions) is adequate.

Note. Development in the stabiliser field has been very rapid. Even the type of gear described may be regarded as obsolete in a few years. Modern designs are available to reduce the large space athwartships required for the design given. This is achieved by types in which the fin gear is retracted by swinging round on trunnions into the ship's hull. The fin itself rotates on the fin shaft, being rotated by an oil motor. Hydraulic systems have also been simplified.

Electrical Control

A selection switch on the bridge gives settings related to hand control, normal stabilising or automatically controlled rolling, together with an output control switch for beam sea, following sea, etc., conditions. The electrical control is identical with the hydraulic telemotor principle but functions with electrical relays. This means that a transmitted signal produces a corresponding movement at the stabiliser station, through a hunting gear, which is converted to a mechanical movement with hydraulic amplification to operate the fin operating gear.

There are two gyroscopes. One is a *vertical keeping* gyroscope whose signal goes through two selective transmitter magslips to a follow through magslip which is similarly operated by a rolling velocity gyroscope. The combined selected signal is transmitted to the hunter magslip of the oil motor and pump. The mechanical movement of a gyroscope alters the rotor position of the transmitter magslip and the current flow moves the rotor of the hunter magslip to a corresponding positon (just as transmitter and receiver telemotors). The rotor movement of the hunter magslip operates to allow oil to be pumped from the pump to the oil motor which rotates. The pump is driven at constant speed and direction by a small motor. The oil motor can rotate in either direction from neutral depending on the direction of movement of the hunter magslip rotor. As the motor rotates, a mechanically driven resetting transmitter magslip serves as a hunting gear and tends to fetch the hunter magslip back to the neutral position and stop rotation of the oil motor.

Hydraulic Operation

This has two distinct functions, the first is to *extend* or house the fins and the second, which is under gyroscope control, is to *tilt* the fins.

Oil is supplied from the storage tank to the servo pump which is driven at constant speed and direction by a motor. The pump is of the variable delivery tilting box (or swashplate) type but there is no reversal of suction and discharge lines.

The pump supplies oil in two pressure ranges, low pressure (29 bar maximum) to tilting control and high pressure (77 bar maximum) for fin housing, selection by change over valve and control by control cylinder. When extending the fins the oil is supplied to the housing piston rod and flows *through* an inner tube into the fin shaft which it pushes out to the extreme position. Oil behind the piston flows through a port and along the *outside* of the central tube back to the pump suction, surplus oil due to volume of piston rod is accommodated in the storage tank, during the housing operation when the flow of oil is reversed. Control valves for this operation are located in a central control box.

Consider now the fin tilting operation: With the fins extended the tilting operation is controlled by the gyroscope signal which is transmitted to the hunter magslip and functions to decide the amount *and* direction of movement of the oil motor. The output shaft of the oil motor is connected by gearing to the reset magslip rotor which serves to hunt the gear back to neutral position and stop motor rotation at the required position.

The oil pump and motor are in line. The electric motor *continuously* drives the pump shaft on which is splined the rotor, running in a liner and casing. Usually seven pump cylinders are formed by *axial* bores in the rotor and each cylinder contains two balls separated by springs, and the ball faces as they rotate run on the faces of control cams (see Fig. 5.17).

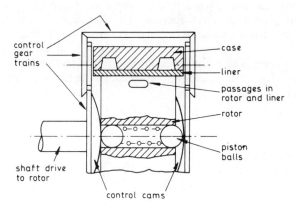

OIL PUMP (PART VIEW)
Fig. 5.17

In the sketch shown the balls have no *relative* velocity to each other and this is the non pumping position. The cams are rotatable in opposite directions by use of the gear trains. In the *maximum* pumping position the two cam peaks both face each other so that during rotation the balls approach and leave each other. This produces a discharge (at about 7 bar pressure) and a suction during each revolution, a port at mid length of each cylinder leads out from the rotor. Four equidistant radial ports in the liner lead oil to wells, two suction and two discharge, in the casing, which lead oil to the suction and discharge ports which are located at opposite sides of the pump. Thus a variable delivery pump is supplying oil to the oil motor. The oil motor is similar in construction to the pump but the cams are *fixed*. Oil pressure supplied between the balls from the pump causes rotor rotation when the balls are *descending* the cams, on the return stroke oil is discharged to exhaust. By movement of the main valve, rotation is reversed in that pressure oil is now led to the port previously acting as exhaust and exhaust occurs through the port previously acting for pressure. The pump supplies oil to a pressure controller which functions to maintain a constant pressure under all outputs. The pump discharge to the control valve is then directed to the motor, whose rotational direction is dependent on the rotation of the hunter magslip rotor. With the main control valve shut the pump merely idles and the gear is then in the neutral position.

The final servo operated stage is now almost identical in operation to that of the electro-hydraulic steering gear. The movement from the cam operates the tilting control valve. This allows oil from the servo pump to move the tilting control cylinder in the required direction which in turn causes the fin tilting pumps, which are *continuously* driven by the main power unit electric motor, to deliver oil to move the rams in the tilting cylinders across.

The tilting control cylinder is virtually acting as a receiver telemotor, with similar hunting gear arrangement. The rams instead of rotating a tiller serve to tilt the ram by means of the toothed quadrant (see Fig. 5.18).

The variable delivery pump for the fin tilting and servo unit has been described previously (see Fig. 5.8).

Fin Detail

The principle of operation is to impose on the hull a rolling motion *equal* and *opposite* to that caused by the wave motion, this is achieved by utilising the forward velocity of the ship through the water. On the ship rolling to starboard the starboard fin is set by the gyroscope signal so that its *leading* edge is *above*

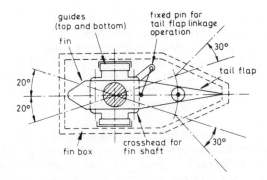

DETAIL OF FINS AND FLAPS

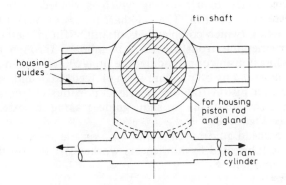

DETAIL OF QUADRANT FOR TILT
Fig. 5.18

the axis of tilt so causing an *upward* thrust. The port fin is set to the opposite tilt *i.e.* with its *leading* edge *below* the axis of tilt so giving a *downward* thrust.

Two rectangular fins, one at each side of the ship located directly opposite if space is available, are of aerofoil section. To the trailing edge of each is a hinged tail flap which is moved automatically by a simple linkage when the main fin shaft is rotated. This flap gives a very much more pronounced restoring torque action of the fin that would a plain large fin of similar area. The fins are mounted on stainless steel shafts, the fin being fitted on to a taper and is bolted up internally, the fin plating being welded over the built up internal structure. The main fin can be tilted 20° each side of the neutral horizontal position. The tail flap is inclined at 30° to the main flap when this flap is at its maximum 20° position and in the *same* direction, both being in line horizontally in neutral position (see Fig. 5.18).

Fins and shafts are placed athwartships, near amidships, near the turn of the bilge, and the axes of fins and shafts are inclined downwards to the outboard ends at about 15° to the horizontal plane. The 20° of tilt is suitable at about 15 knots but this maximum is reduced to about 11° at 24 knots to keep reasonable fin loading.

The fin is supported near the load applicaton by a fin shaft crosshead which moves on top and bottom guides during housing or fin extending operations. Guides and shaft are inside the fin box, of fabricated construction, which is flanged at the outboard end and welded to stools at the inboard end. The flanging is bolted to a trunking which is welded to the hull adjacent to the tank top. The fin shaft passes through the fin box and trunk (which completely contain the fin in the housed position) emerging from the fin box inboard through a sea gland. When housing or extending, the fin is centralised and as it is drawn in or out by oil pressure from oil feed led in and out via the yoke and piston rod (as described previously), the guide shoes on each side of the fin shaft guide it along the extension guides (see Fig. 5.18).

The crosshead guides, sea gland, etc., on the sea side are oil and grease lubricated by lubricators worked off the fin tilting shaft ram motion.

AUTO CONTROL

Both the ship steering gear (on auto pilot) and the ship stabiliser utilise classic control principles best illustrated by block diagrams.

Fig. 5.19 shows a block diagram for auto steering. The controller will be three term with adjustment for beam sea (or wind) and dead band operation to reduce response to small random signals. Both rudder and ship are acted upon by external forces.

Fig. 5.20 shows a block diagram for stabilisation. The controller is usually two term and feedback from the measure unit has roll angle and velocity components from gyroscopes. Every input utilises the forward velocity of the ship and the usual 'hunting action' feedback applies between amplifier (hydraulic oil pumps) and actuator (fin tilt). The ship is acted on by external forces, selector switches allow for variation in sea conditions.

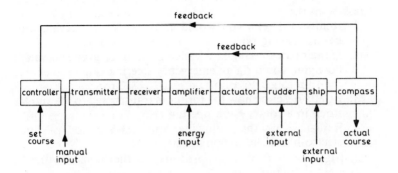

BLOCK DIAGRAM (AUTO STEERING)
Fig. 5.19

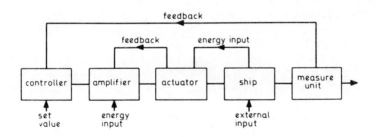

BLOCK DIAGRAM (STABILISERS)
Fig. 5.20

TEST EXAMPLES 5

Class 3

1. Itemise the tests you would carry out on a steering gear before leaving port.
2. If the main steering gear failed on a small coaster describe how you would rig an emergency steering system to enable the ship to get to a port.
3. Briefly describe how the torque is transmitted to the rudder stock in a rotary vane steering gear.
4. Explain how the following are achieved for a ship's electro-hydraulic steering gear:
    (i)   relief of over pressure in the rams' hydraulic circuit,
    (ii)   replenishment of hydraulic oil to make good losses caused by minor leakages from glands.

TEST EXAMPLES 5

Class 2

1. (a) Sketch a hunting gear as fitted to a hydraulic steering gear labelling the principal items.
   (b) Explain the purpose of the hunting gear.
   (c) State how worn pins in the hunting gear effect steering gear operation.

2. With reference to hydraulic steering gears explain why:
   (a) relief valves are provided as well as shock valves,
   (b) the pump is of constant speed, variable stroke,
   (c) the ram glands are filled with soft or simple moulded packing.

3. Describe a simple test to ensure that steering gear hydraulic telemotor systems are 'air free'.
   (a) Define two ways whereby air enters such systems.
   (b) Give reasons why it is essential that such systems be 'air free'.

4. With reference to electro hydraulic steering gears explain how the ship can be steered in each of the following circumstances:
   (a) destruction by fire of primary supply cables,
   (b) destruction by fire of telemotor lines,
   (c) bearing failure in running pump.

TEST EXAMPLES 5

Class 1
1. With reference to stabiliser fins which either fold or retract into hull apertures:
    (a)   make a simplified sketch of the essential features of the activating gear for both fin extension and altitude,
    (b)   explain how it operates.
2. With reference to steering gears explain why:
    (a)   multi-piston variable stroke pumps are used rather than rotary positive displacement pumps with controlled recirculation or delivery,
    (b)   independent, widely separated power supplies to the electrically driven pumps are provided together with duplication of pumps in many instances, yet the hydraulic telemotor system has usually only one run of double piping from the bridge to the receiver,
    (c)   pump, piston and cylinder wear is of considerable consequence.
3. State effects of the following faults in steering gear telemotor systems:
    (a)   low liquid level in replenishment tanks,
    (b)   weak receiver springs,
    (c)   worn cup leathers or rings in transmitters or receivers,
    (d)   leaking pump connections,
    (e)   specify with reasons the nature and properties of the fluid generally used in such systems.
4. With reference to steering gears, explain:
    (a)   why four rams are commonly employed on large vessels,
    (b)   how the steering function is maintained despite loss of hydraulic fluid from the telemotor system.

CHAPTER 6

SHAFTING

ALIGNMENT

The method of alignment and the amount of flexure varies considerably with the type of vessel and propelling machinery. Midship installations with long, and thus fairly flexible shafting, require a different approach to aft end installations with short rigid shafting. Similarly, long reciprocating engine crankshafts present different problems to geared turbine machinery, and the flexibility of welded vessels gives different results to more rigid riveted types.

As a main basis the alignment for an all welded, midship engined vessel, having a long reciprocating engine crankshaft, for example say a four cylinder *IC* engine, will be described in detail after some introductory general remarks. This description, to give a complete picture, must include shafting alignment in ship, crankshaft and bedplate alignment in shops, and lastly engine to shafting as one integral unit in ship.

Then the amendments necessary for turbine engined vessels and aft end installations will be described briefly.

General Considerations

Hog and sag effects due to state of loading and draught, effects of waves, etc, can quite easily be as much as 1 mm per 1 m of ship length and even more.

The effect of waves and sea action is mainly indeterminate and over the bedplate length of say 16 m is ignored. However this indeterminate influence gives a realisation of how difficult it is to put a heavy engine and shafting length, in perfect alignment, on a flexible beam form of a ship under the action of sea influences, such realisation must show that some amount of reasonable flexing and allowances for same must always be accepted.

Stiffening of tank tops and engine seating supports, together with the use of rigid bedplates, can reduce central deflection to a maximum of about 13 mm over the engine room length and less, and to about 2 mm maximum over the bedplate from the no load to the full load condition. Invariably the bedplate has a *sag* form when light ship of say 1 mm and a *hog* form when fully loaded of say 1 mm. The average ship is rarely sagged as can be shown by drawing load and buoyancy curves for average conditions. An engine crankshaft set true at light ship *could* when hogged 2 mm introduce static bending stresses of say 90 MN/m². Most engine builders have their own records and experiences for dealing with this problem (see Fig. 6.4).

It is often suggested that the engine main bearings in the above case should be lined down in a deflection curve, of 1 mm maximum in the *centre* of length, for the new engine. This means the shafting is true at $\frac{1}{2}$ load and maximum static bending stresses are on each side of this, *i.e.* 45 MN/m² instead of true at light ship giving all bending on one side, *i.e.* 90 MN/m².

The figures quoted are intended for illustration only, using high values, in many cases lining in a curve may only require a deliberate offset of about one tenth of the quoted figures, *i.e.* 0.1 mm. The degree of offset depends on the type of ship and engine, stiffness, variations due to loading, etc. These factors can only be established correctly by experience before the builder can decide on the best method of lining up to suit the requirements of these variables. In the following alignment description this offset will not be considered (but see Fig. 6.4).

Older alignment methods used piano wires and micrometers, feelers between coupling faces, etc., whereas modern methods utilise optical telescopes and targets giving accuracies of $\pm$ 2μm per 1 m length. To fully describe the methods it will be assumed that the shafting and engine are first lined up by the older method, being checked at each stage by the modern method, although in practice such duplication may not be considered due to time factors, that is not to say that it would not be advisable. Increased power, size and cost of modern vessels and engines make it essential to ensure correct initial alignment so as to avoid continuous trouble later.

Shafting Alignment in Ship

Reference datums here are the height of the shaft above the keel aft, and the height of the crankshaft centre above the keel extended to the forward machinery space bulkhead (also centre athwartships) forward. These two datums are taken from the ship drawings.

The rough bore of the stern frame is fitted with a plate flange, this flange has a small hole (say 1 mm) drilled at the correct height above the keel. With this centre the reference circle can be drawn for the setting up of the exact boring of the frame. Similarly at the engine room forward bulkhead a small flangé in the bulkhead has the small hole drilled at the correct engine height above the keel and at the midship point athwartships.

An electric light is sighted behind the hole in the forward machinery space bulkhead and by looking from outside the stern frame this light can be seen through the two sight holes. Now at the aft peak bulkhead and the aft machinery space bulkhead and any water-tight bulkhead through which the shaft passes, sighting plates are used. At these points the horizontal plate is moved vertically up until the light line of sight is masked, a horizontal reference mark is now made across the bulkhead. The plate is moved vertically down until the light is masked and another horizontal reference mark made, bisection of these two lines gives the *horizontal* centre (see Fig. 6.1).

sight holes say 800 µm max. error 1·6 mm i.e. 1mm per say 40m length

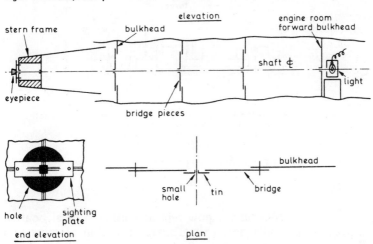

SIGHTING BY LIGHT
Fig. 6.1

readings in mm, all journal diameters equal.

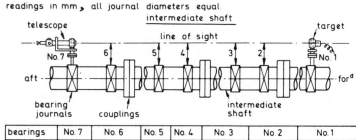

bearings	No. 7	No. 6	No. 5	No. 4	No. 3	No. 2	No. 1
scale	500·0	501·8	499·2	498·0	497·9	499·1	500·0
difference	0	+1·8	−0·8	−2·0	−2·1	−0·9	0

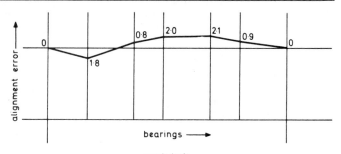

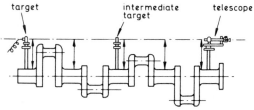

telescope micrometers allow variation of ±1·00 mm on perpendicular crosslines but the radial markings on the telescope which are graduated up to 25 mm diameter allow much greater misalignment to be read directly from target without using micrometers at all

SIGHTING BY OPTICAL TELESCOPE
Fig. 6.2

The same procedure is now repeated using vertical boards, moved horizontally port to starboard, bisection of these two lines gives the *vertical* centre. Rough bores are now bridged, the centre is fixed temporarily with a tin plate and a small hole is centred. Now from aft to forward a continuous light should be visible through all bulkheads, the reference circles can now be drawn for exact boring. The exact borings are now made and the ship is ready for the optical telescope checking (see Fig. 6.2).

The optical telescope with eyepiece and cross lines, focus, vertical-horizontal micrometer adjustments, etc., is set up in a spherical mounting on a base with adjustment bracket (magnification about 30 times). The assembly is mounted on a spigoted plate and bolted into the aft end of the stern frame, being an exact fit. The target which has circular, vertical and horizontal markings is fitted into an adjustable spherical mounting with a light. This assembly is fitted to a flange bracket and set at the correct height and athwartships position on the forward machinery space bulkhead.

The telescope is now adjusted vertically and horizontally until the target is perfectly centred, this is now the line of sight. Targets are now fitted into adaptor plates and placed with a tight fit into all intermediate bores. The telescope is focused on each in turn so giving any vertical or horizontal error, the telescope should be refocused on to the line of sight datum after each intermediate bore checking. Mirror targets can be used if it is thought desirable to check squareness. Now a check is available on the initial lining up which should indicate a close degree of accuracy.

At this stage the sterntube, tail end shaft and propeller would be fitted and the ship launched and taken to the fitting out berth, or the stern frame may be blanked and these fittings made after the launching. The intermediate shaft is now fitted right up to the engine by using feelers at four points between the coupling faces and chocking the tunnel bearings with hard wood blocks on to the stools. The intermediate shaft is now ready for checking with the telescope.

The line of sight for telescope and target is fixed at the extreme ends, positioned at equal distances from the two journal diameters by cups mounted on matched stands which are in blocks strapped to the shaft. The target is usually mounted on the first bearing in the tunnel and the telescope on the last bearing before the tail end shaft, and so the line of sight is established. Readings can now be taken for all intermediate bearings by focusing on a lighted graduated scale held vertically on each bearing in turn. A graph can now be plotted of any misalignment and the chocking adjusted until a true line is effected. It is also advisable to check all journal diameters for equality and also to take a horizontal alignment to ensure correct port and starboard line. All tunnel bearings are now permanently chocked and bolted down, coupling bolts fitted and thrust block (if separate) fitted and bolted to place. The ship is now ready for the engine fitting.

Crankshaft and Bedplate Alignment in Shops

The bedplate is first levelled up on the shop floor, usually being in two parts, the whole assembly having been surface planed and the main bearing gaps machined. The bedplate is now lined up and rough chocked by the use of spirit levels. Piano wires are mounted along the full length of the bedplate, one port and one starboard, passing over end pulleys and loaded. Micrometer readings between wire and the machined top edge of bedplate are taken at say 1 m intervals, standard allowance being made for the wire sag, and the bedplate chocked up until a true horizontal reading is achieved. The bedplate is now ready for optical checking.

The telescope is mounted vertically, standing on adjustable tripod feet, the reference plane being obtained by mounting a pentagonal prism under the telescope (with a micrometer adjustment) and rotating it about an axis concentric with the telescope, this prism deviates the line of sight by 90°. The flat plane, being independent of gravity, is adjusted to pass through three definite height targets on the surface and a travelling target enables all other points on the surface to be adjusted to bring the whole area into that common plane. The bedplate lining up is completed by a set of readings through the bearing bores by piano wire or light method, being checked by optical telescope in a similar manner to the method previously described prior to fitting sterntube and tail end shaft (see Fig. 6.2).

A dummy shaft is now used to bed into the lower halves of the main bearing bushes, after which the crankshaft is bedded to place. A set of readings would be taken on the shaft, as described for the intermediate shaft, by optical telescope, the engine would then be assembled, crankshaft deflections taken and the test bed trial carried out. Before the engine is dismantled a set of piano wire readings, port and starboard, would be taken from the bedplate together with a recheck of crankshaft deflections. If the telescope was used then optical readings along the bedplate, port and starboard, would replace piano wire readings and in addition a set of readings on the crankshaft through the running gear would be taken, using the oil holes through the bearing caps for the scales. The engine is now dismantled to an extent whereby it can be easily transported and lifted into place on board ship.

The description given is somewhat elaborate, due mainly to the two method description given, but it should be remembered that if the engine setting in the shops is correct and a reference is taken, then ship alignment is much simplified by simply setting back to this correct reference alignment.

Engine to Shafting in Ship

The aft engine coupling is lined up to the forward thrust shaft face coupling with feelers. Screw jacks to place and temporary chocking between bedplate and tank top right the engine into position. The engine is now chocked to the final test bed readings taken before dismantling and the crankshaft deflections taken. The holding down bolts or studs are either fitted from a template set to the forward thrust block face or fitted with the bedplate in place. As a complete check on the whole integral setting of crankshaft and intermediate shaft the use of the optical telescope is most advantageous. This also allows a spot check on alignment without disturbing the shafting at any time.

Unfortunately a complete sight from tailend shaft to forward end of the crankshaft is usually impossible due to the ship construction, as the height of sight required above the crankshaft causes the line to foul the tunnel roof a few feet aft of the aft engine room bulkhead.

Therefore the two lines of sight (l.o.s.), intermediate shaft and crankshaft sights respectively, have to be used. These lines of sight are extended to give as much overlap as possible. The measurement differences at No. 1 bearing and at thrust journal should be identical, indicating parallel lines. Divergence from each other indicates a gradient, *i.e.* mm/m length. To give maximum overlap a tube may be welded into the hold above the tunnel roof with a down tube to a bearing further along the intermediate shafting. Fouling of lines of sight may occur at the turning wheel, this can be overcome by slackening the halves and reclining the wheel over whilst still exerting its load on shaft.

This completes ship and engine alignment. A typical set of readings would be as plotted in Fig. 6.3 (opposed piston four cylinder oil engine and shafting).

Aft End Installations

Such engined vessels do not suffer the same misalignment effects due to the short rigid shaft length. There should be no need to line the engine down for load variations, the engine being lined exactly true, light ship, in the standard way. The

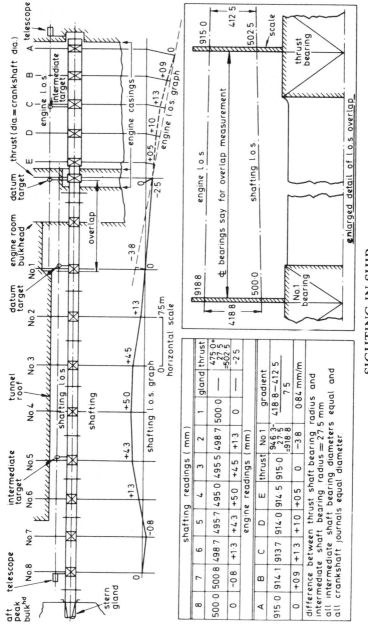

SIGHTING IN SHIP
Fig. 6.3

main problem with these vessels is that the large tailshaft weardowns allowed (8 mm plus) in say a 5 m shaft connection to the engine, throws a heavy load on the aft end of the crankshaft. These vessels are somewhat more prone to tail shaft and aft end crankshaft failure. Very great care is advised in investigating torsional vibration characteristics. To offset the weardown load it is advisable to fit the tunnel and thrust bearings with fitted top halves and it would be advantageous to limit weardown very strictly. The alignment method is a more simple form of that described (due to shorter shafting) but it should be mentioned that even though the shaft length is small, alignment errors have caused serious trouble in such a short rigid length. Slew effects as much as 6 mm aft (crankshaft) to 18 mm forward (crankshaft) with an engine hogged vertically 3 mm have occurred in the past. Optical telescopes here allow a continuous sight forward to aft over extreme ends which is most advantageous.

Turbine Engined Vessels

The alignment of shafting is as described but the problem here, from the engine aspect, is virtually one of two or three turbine wheel shafts through pinions lined on to a large gear wheel thence to the thrust block. In the past, alignment errors have commonly reflected back through the gearing to cause excessive pitting, scuffing, heavy wear, etc., on the second reduction pinions. The turbine-gearing alignment was somewhat complex involving long inside micrometers, much cross siting to turbine stools and later to turbine wheel shafts, which with piano wires and light methods made the process highly detailed. In modern practice use of the optical telescope, together with the pentagonal prism for line of sight deviation, allows cross siting from a fixed standard flat reference plane (say horizontal gearcase-turbine joint) to any number of points including height checks of all bearings, making the gearwheel-turbines alignment much easier. The gearwheel will have been lined to the thrust block face having previously checked by telescope through main wheel bearings. The following points are worthy of consideration:

(1) The lift of the shafts due to the oil film should be taken into account.

(2) Due to the high rotational speeds of the turbines there are precessional torque effects.

(3) The flexible coupling copes with a considerable degree of misalignment.

(4) Turbine troubles, when they do occur, seem to persist and invariably stem from initial mis-alignment or vibration characteristic errors.

Pilgrim Wire Method

Reference has already been made to the use of taut (piano) wires and some elaboration of this method is relevant. This technique produces fairly accurate results especially in a vibration free situation. For crankshaft aligment with five cylinder engines and above, using telescope or wire methods, it is usually necessary to remove one connecting rod to allow the sight (or wire) to pass over the full shaft length. The alternative is to take readings with an overlap across two central main bearings, possibly at two different heights, and then adjust to a common datum. Allowance for wire sag varies with wire diameter and tension, an empirical formula is generally used. For a wire of 0.5 mm diameter, tension 200 N, an approximate expression is $\text{sag} = L^2/29.25$ where sag is in mm and L (half length of wire) is in m. Interpretation of readings, and variation with ship loading conditions, are as described for telescope methods (Fig. 6.3).

A light method can be used in calibration. One pole of battery is earthed and the other, in series with an indicator lamp, is connected to dial indicator touch stylus. As wire is earthed the slightest touch of stylus on wire causes indicator lamp to light.

CRANKSHAFT DEFLECTIONS

Excessive deflection of this form, in main or auxiliary reciprocating machinery, *i.e.* *variation* of distance between crankwebs during a full engine turn, causes dangerous bending stresses in web and fillet between crankpin and web. This deflection is indicative of true deflection, *i.e.* vertical hog or sag measurement, thus the value of these deflections can be assumed to be then dependent on two main factors *for a given mass per unit length* (conn. rods, pistons, etc.).

(1) Distance between supports of shaft (*i.e.* main bearing inner faces), as the further apart the supports the greater the sag effect.

(2) Distance out from shaft centre line the measurement is taken. This is usually close to the extreme edge of the web. For a sawcut in a shaft the further one moves from the shaft centre the greater the gap. The web's extreme distance and size of section is usually proportional to the engine stroke.

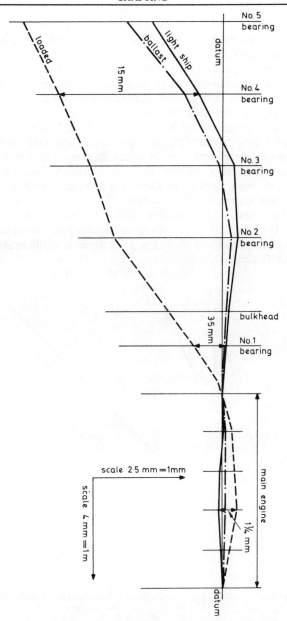

SHAFTING ALIGNMENT VARIATION FOR DIFFERENT
SHIP LOAD CONDITIONS
Fig. 6.4

Note:

Vertical deflection = 5 $mgl^4/384$ EI for a simply supported uniformly distributed loaded beam.

Thus as a *generalisation* it may be said that crankshaft deflection is proportional to total engine stroke and distance between main bearing faces. On this assumption Fig. 6.5 has been prepared. To illustrate its use:

Consider an engine of 1.5 m stroke and 1.5 m between main bearing faces. From Fig. 6.5 allowable test bed deflections (maximum) based on 1 m between bearing faces is 167 μm, therefore for this engine (1.5 m between bearing faces) maximum initial deflection allowed is 250 μm. Based on Fig. 6.5 as a rough approximation: Correct 70 μm/1 m stroke/1 m face distance (max. 118). Realign 240μm/1 m stroke/1 m face distance (max. 330). A set of typical figures for a six cylinder IC engine and the method of taking deflections is as illustrated (Fig. 6.6 and Table 6.1).

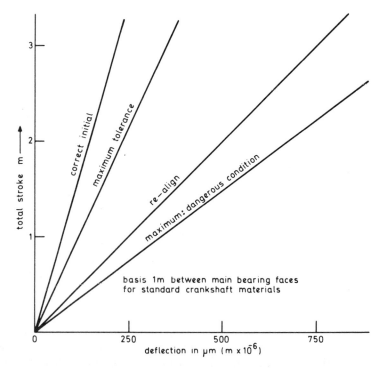

CRANKWEB ALLOWABLE DEFLECTIONS
Fig. 6.5

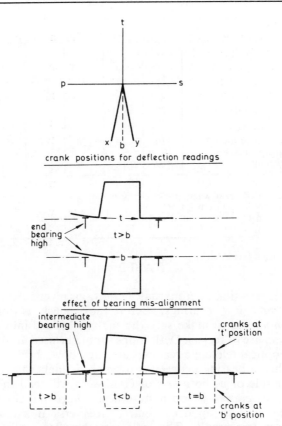

crank positions for deflection readings

effect of bearing mis-alignment

DEFLECTION READINGS AND BEARING HEIGHTS
Fig. 6.6

Stresses caused by static deflection are difficult to assess but as a rough guide, each μm crankweb deflection (which *may* be somewhere about 1 μm central vertical deflection) *could* cause a bending stress of about 33 kN/m². ` `

It must be pointed out that specific figures must *always* be treated with extreme caution and are only used for a general picture and guidance. Some engine manufacturers fix maximum deflection difference at 10C μm (smaller single acting types) but opposed piston designs generally cannot fix anything like such close limits. A scale ratio for the latter is over 3:1.

Crank position	Cylinder Number					
	1	2	3	4	5	6
x	0	0	0	0	0	0
p	50	20	60	−80	−30	10
t	100	30	120	−140	−80	40
s	50	30	60	−80	−60	30
y	−20	20	−20	0	0	−20
b = (x + y)/2	−10	10	−10	0	0	−10
Vertical plane misalignment (t–b)	110	20	130	−140	−80	50
Horizontal plane misalignment (p–s)	0	−10	0	0	30	−20

Positive deflection when crankwebs open out.
Gauge readings in μm (mm/1000).
High bearings—No. 1 (end) and between Nos. 3 and 4 cylinders.

TABLE 6.1

Interpretation of crankshaft deflections gives an indication of high and low bearings. Before any check is made it is advantageous to make sure the shaft is bedded into the lower half *i.e.* use of feelers. Deflections should be used in conjunction with optical telescope readings and weardown bridge gauges.

When a bearing between two cranks is higher than those on either side of it, both sets of crankwebs will tend to open out when the cranks are on bottom dead centre and close in when cranks are on top dead centre, vice versa if a low bearing between two cranks. The scale ratio between vertical bearing heights compared with crankshaft deflections is often taken as 2:1 *i.e.* 0.1 mm change in bearing height produces 0.05 mm change in crankshaft deflections).

SHAFTING STRESSES

Ratio of strengths of solid and hollow shafting; Consider a solid shaft, diameter D_1, compared to a hollow shaft, diameter outside D_2 diameter inside d_2.

$$\frac{\text{Strength solid}}{\text{Strength hollow}} = \frac{\text{Torque Solid } (T_1)}{\text{Torque hollow } (T_2)} = \frac{q_1 J_1 r_2}{q_2 J_2 r_1}$$

where r is shaft radius

as $\dfrac{T}{J} = \dfrac{q}{r}$,, q is working shear stress maximum
,, J is polar second moment of area

thus for the same working stress:

$$\frac{\text{Strength solid}}{\text{Strength hollow}} = \frac{J_1 D_2}{J_2 D_1} = \frac{\pi D_1^4}{32 \times D_1} \times \frac{32 D_2}{\pi(D_2^4 - d_2^4)}$$

$$\frac{\text{Strength solid}}{\text{Strength hollow}} = \frac{D_1^3 D_2}{(D_2^4 - d_2^4)}$$

Consider a solid 360 mm dia. shaft of mass 5×10^3 kg and compare this to a hollow 380 mm × 250 mm dia. shaft of the same length, this has a mass of 3×10^3 kg.

$$\frac{\text{Strength solid}}{\text{Strength hollow}} = \frac{360^3 \times 380}{(380^4 - 250^4)} = \frac{1.76}{1.66}$$

i.e. approximately the same.

∴ Approx. 40% weight reduction for the *same* length. Hollow shafting is however more expensive. Consider next the case of a 300 mm dia. shaft with a flaw detected 25 mm deep. Now shaft power is proportional to torque:

$$\frac{T}{J} = \frac{q}{r} \text{ and therefore } T = \frac{2Jq}{D}$$

$$\therefore T = \frac{2 \times \pi D^4 \times q}{D \times 32} \qquad \therefore T = \frac{\pi D^3 q}{16}$$

Thus power ℓ torque ℓ diameter^3

Thus power reduction for 25 mm flaw:

$$\text{Reduction ratio} = \frac{250^3}{300^3} = \frac{1.56}{2.70}$$

i.e. power reduction to about 58% of the original power.

Before considering the regulations appertaining to shafting sizes for the various types of shafting it would be as well to first build up a set of simple calculations for the various different shafting lengths in turn. Only the broad aspects will be considered, *much simplification* and *many assumptions* being necessary in order to clarify and present the results as a reasonably simple picture.

Intermediate Shafting

This is usually involved in the first part of the calculation. The shaft is subject to torsion, based on the required horse power and taking a safe stress the diameter can be arrived at. The couplings and coupling bolt dimensions can also be calculated. The fundamental torsion equation $T/J = q/r = G\theta/l$ being the basis for most calculation.

End thrust, from the propeller, is small in comparison with other stresses and it acts on all the shafting. A thrust ahead of about 500×10^3N would only induce a compressive stress of about 1.73 kN/m², this can normally be ignored except where such thrust is transmitted to the hull, *i.e.* at the base of the thrust collar.

Bending stresses could really only arise from the ship movements and alignment variation and the effects should not be large.

Summarising then, one could say that the intermediate shaft is subject to a torsional shear stress which influences the factor of safety and hence resultant working stress, a slight compensation would be allowed for end thrust (reversed), bending and possible variations of torque due to propeller racing.

Thrust Shaft

Calculation is almost the same as for the intermediate shaft but virtually no misalignment bending would occur in such a short shaft length over a stiffened tank top. The thrust action on the collar would require a thicker diameter at the collar root but once clear of say the thrust pads the shaft could be tapered down to the intermediate shaft diameter.

Propeller Shaft

The shaft is subject to torque and end thrust, as is the intermediate shaft, but torque variations due to propeller racing would be somewhat more fluctuating. In addition the shaft is subject to a bending stress due to the propeller net weight in still water. Assuming the propeller immersed in still water and taking the loading as existing in Fig. 6.7. The weight, after allowing for upthrust of water is say 45 kN, and treating as a simply supported cantilever beam then the bending moment is $mgl = Wl$ *i.e.* $45 \times \frac{3}{4} \approx 33$ kN m on the shaft where it enters the hull.

This is fairly appreciable but when the propeller rises out of the water due to racing in heavy seas this value is increased considerably, so it must be assessed as a heavy, fluctuating, largely indeterminate, bending moment.

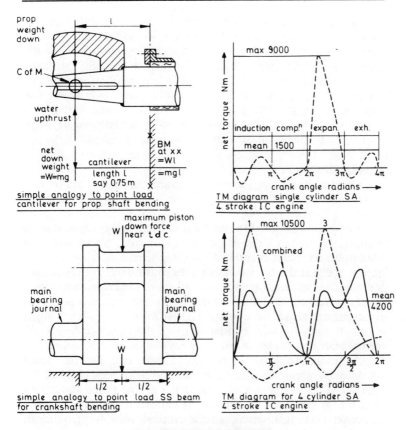

SHAFTING STRESSES
Fig. 6.7

Coupled with the above it should be borne in mind that the shaft is worked in a corrosive medium and there is a *possibility* of direct contact between shaft and sea water, in spite of precautions taken to exclude this possibility. Some authorities consider that the fatigue strength of elements in sea water is 25% of that for the same parts in air.

Summarising for this shaft, there is fluctuating, combined bending and twisting, with a degree of uncertainty of magnitude, together with end thrust and the possibility of corrosive attack.

With these facts in mind the factor of safety employed is high, usually over 12. The tail shaft may always be looked on as probably the weakest link in the machinery. Various types of material have been used here, such as nickel and chrome additions to mild steel, but the preferred material after much experience is often still mild steel because of ductility, strength factors and fatigue resistance. Tensile strength not normally to exceed 540 MN/m². Propeller shafts are withdrawn for examination every two years (five years for those fitted with continuous liners or oil type with special stress reduced keyways or keyless or most c.p. designs).

Crankshafts

Consider the turning moment diagrams illustrated in Fig. 6.7:

The maximum to mean torque ratio for the single cylinder *IC* engine is 9.0:1.5, *i.e.* 6:1.

Two facts emerge: (1) the torsional shearing stress due to turning moments of the engine is fluctuating, (2) variation of maximum to mean torque ratio is high with *IC* engines. The *mean* torque is the power transmitted to the drive per revolution but the shafting sizes must be based on the *maximum* torque.

Next referring to the combined torque diagram it is seen that for cranks at π rad, firing order 1, 3, 4, 2 the ratio is 2.5:1 which is much improved in comparison to the single cylinder *IC* engine. On this diagram only one revolution is considered and the induction, exhaust, compression effects, etc., for Nos. 2 and 4 cylinders, occurring during this 2π rad have been omitted for simplicity, although the combined curve has taken them into account. It can be seen that the addition of cylinders gives a smoother turning moment and a reduced maximum to mean torque ratio. However the main two facts are apparent in that there is still torque fluctuation and the torque ratio is high for *IC* engines. This analysis gives some idea of the torsional stresses involved and the next factor to consider is bending.

It should be noted that the net or output available torque is the summation of applied gas torque and inertia torque required to accelerate or retard the moving parts, being a numerical addition, due account taken of positive and negative torque signs at any crank angle.

Mass of parts also needs consideration.

Referring to Fig. 6.7 we may consider the case for simplicity as a simply supported beam with a central point load, this load having a maximum value near tdc.

Consider an *IC* engine with 762 mm dia. cylinders and maximum firing pressure of 5.5 MN/m² then maximum firing force is:

$$W = \pi/4 \times 0.762^2 \times 5.5 = 2.5 \text{ MN}$$

Assuming the simply supported beam case:

Bending moment $= \dfrac{mgl}{4} = \dfrac{Wl}{4} = \dfrac{2.5 \times 1\frac{1}{3}}{4}$

$= 0.833 \text{ MN m } [833 \text{ kN m}]$

assuming distance between main bearing faces as $1\frac{1}{3}$ m, *i.e. l.*

The conclusions are: (1) a crankshaft is subject to heavy bending loads, (2) the loading is very rapidly applied in the *IC* engine, being a form of impact.

There will be some slight end thrust on the crankshaft but in comparison with bending and torsional stresses it is negligible.

After consideration of simple applications of stress to the main shaft lengths a reasonable picture of the stress factors involved should now be available and the necessary shafting regulations or rules can now be considered.

SOME SHAFTING RULES
(Class I passenger vessels, minimum requirements)

Ingot steel for shafts and coupling bolts should have a *u.t.s.* of 430-500 MN/m², the couplings should be forged in with the shaft or have the shaft ends hydraulically upset, separate couplings may be ingot steel or steel castings.

Crankwebs for built up crankshafts should be ingot steel or cast steel and shaft liners should be of bronze. All materials should be subject to the required tests and treatment.

Intermediate Shaft (diameter *d*)
To comply with empirical formula based on theoretical principles and practical experience. There is a separate formula for each and every engine type, *e.g.* steam turbine, turbine-electric drive, motor machinery (with all variations of number of cylinders, firing intervals, type of cycle, etc.).

Crankshafts and Turbine Wheel Shafts
As above.

Crankwebs (built up shafts)
Thickness parallel to shaft $0.625 \times$ crankshaft diameter,

thickness radialy around crankpin 0.438 × crankshaft diameter.

Webs should be securely shrunk on to pins, shrinkage allowance about diameter/625, dowels may be fitted.

Thrust Shaft

At collar root diameter to be $1.15d$.

Outside collar root may be tapered down to d.

Sterntube Shaft

1.14d.

If any part of the shaft is in contact with sea water these sizes are to be increased $2\frac{1}{2}\%$.

Note: this is the case of a shaft passing through sterntubes, which does not support the propeller weight (*i.e.* twin screw bracket support).

(Clearance will be dependent on bearing type, lubrication method, sealing design, hammering, etc.).

Propeller Shaft

This is the case of the shaft which supports the weight of the propeller.

$$\text{diameter} = (d \times c) + P/K$$

$c = 1.14$

$P =$ propeller diameter in mm

$K = 144$ if i. a continuous liner is fitted, ii. the shaft is oil lubricated and sea water is excluded and iii. where the shaft material is resistant to corrosion by the water in which it will operate.

$K = 100$ for all other shafts.

At the coupling, the flange may be tapered down to $1.05d$.

Stern bush

Of required thickness and of length four times the shaft diameter inside bush (traditional types — less for modern designs).

Liners

Thickness from prescribed formula and shrunk or hydraulically pressed on, without dowels. Shaft and liner joint at all points must exclude entry of sea water and any cavity, *i.e.* non fitting strip should be filled with a suitable composition.

Couplings and Coupling Bolts

Coupling bolt, diameter from prescribed formula. Flanges of thickness at least equal to bolt diameter (propeller shaft coupling at least $0.27d$). Fillet radii on shafts at diameter $\times$ 0.08.

Note: in all cases, shafting, couplings and bolts must provide resistance to astern pull.

THE PROPELLER SHAFT AND STERNTUBE

Water Lubricated Type

A design for a 6 MW shaft output is detailed in Fig. 6.8 which should be self-explanatory. The maximum weardown is best set at 8 mm with the continuous liner to be examined every three years. For twin screw vessels it may be regarded as advantageous if the propeller shaft could be withdrawn quickly sternways; a coupling with this in mind is also shown in Fig. 6.8, it is more costly and adds complexity. Some patent types utilise rubber bearing surfaces but are not generally used for the larger shaft sizes. Impregnated plastic resin compounds on plastic type bases have been used successfully in place of lignum-vitae. One such type is called Tufnol.

This is a thermo-setting laminate produced from cotton fabric and phenolic resin as the main constituents. The fabric is impregnated with the resin and the layers of this impregnated material are pressurised under heat until the fabric laminations are bonded into one sheet. This material gives uniform density, hardness and swelling together with good wettability and low coefficient of friction plus an ultimate compressive strength (flatwise) approximately twice that of lignum-vitae. A coefficient of friction of 0.005 when water lubricated can be achieved and short length-diameter ratios with a greater continuous bearing surface could be designed at very high loadings with this material. A water supply to the inboard end of the bearing is essential and grease and oils should never be used.

The best method of fitting the staves and the most preferred water grooves (*UV* type) are as shown in Fig. 6.9. The swelling expansion due to water absorption is greatest in the direction normal to the laminate and will not normally exceed 1 mm in 40 mm thickness. Diametric clearance is about 2 mm for 500 mm shaft.

This material can be used for many other duties such as general bearings, gears, resilient mountings, flexible couplings, etc. Physical properties of a type suitable for tailshaft bearings would be:

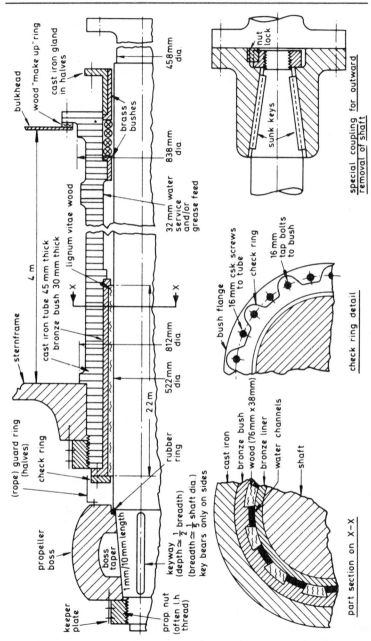

PROPELLER SHAFT AND STERNTUBE (WATER)
Fig. 6.8

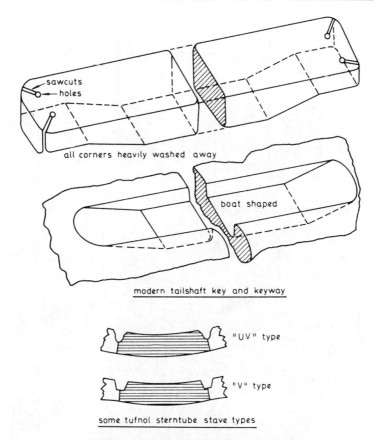

sawcuts
holes

all corners heavily washed away

boat shaped

modern tailshaft key and keyway

"UV" type

"V" type

some tufnol sterntube stave types

ALTERNATIVE KEYS AND STAVES
Fig. 6.9

u.t.s.	62 MN/m²
Compressive stress (ultimate, flatwise)	290 MN/m²
Shear strength (ultimate, flatwise)	100 MN/m²
Youngs modulus	7 GN/m²
Impact value	1.08 mN

(Note the more modern type key shown in Fig. 6.9).

Oil Lubricated Type

This sterntube has been in use for many years. Various designs are available but the same principle is apparent—seal the ends of the tube with a gland and supply oil under pressure. Water should be regularly drained off and in port the tube should be

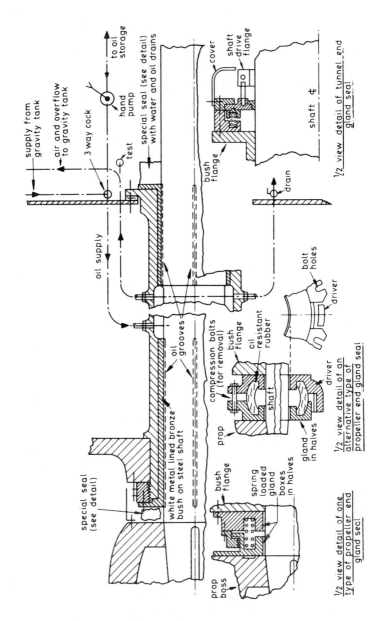

PROPELLER SHAFT AND STERNTUBE (OIL)
Fig. 6.10

emptied and drained. A typical oil tube is as sketched in Fig.
6.10. Weardown for the white metal should not normally exceed
2 mm to avoid hammering out and the period between
inspections is about six years. A highly resilient reinforced
plastic material is often used in place of white metal. It is
claimed to have superior load carrying capacity, high resistance
to fatigue and shock loading, with good lubrication properties.
Stern tube seals, with oil lubrication, have also tended to use
rubber rings increasingly. Fluoric rubber (Viton) with additives
has been shown to be more effective than nitrile butadiene
rubber for seal rings. In these designs four seal rings are usually
located in the support housing aft with oil pressure supply to the
middle chamber. Two similar ring seals, with oil feed between,
are arranged in a floating housing at the forward end. Ceramic
coated liners can also be used.

Withdrawable Stern Gear System
    The advantage of this arrangement is that inspection, re-
alignment or repair can be carried out quickly with the ship
afloat and without the need to disturb the propeller or uncouple
the shaft. It can be used with fixed or controllable pitch
propellers, flange or cone mounted, and with most types of seal.
With the bearing (split in halves) withdrawn the propeller and
shafting weight is supported on a ring permanently secured to
the sternframe. The overall layout is similar to Fig. 6.10 but
there is an integral tube-bearing, split in halves, which is fitted
(or removed) from inboard—see Fig. 6.11.
    The whole unit, including the outer seal, can be moved along
the shaft inboard for inspection. Note also the more modern
practice of hydraulic floating a keyless fit (taper 1:30) with
advantages of simplicity and reduced stress factors. Closure is
with a hydraulically tightened nut. The unit is generally more
costly than the conventional design. Short, large diameter (1300
mm) spherical SKF roller bearing units are available capable of
inward withdrawal. Connection between intermediate and
propeller shaft is by SKF oil injection coupling and standard
inner and outer seals are used, clearance would be about 0.8
mm.

Alternative Stern Gear
    The tendency to fit increasing diameter and weight propellers
(in excess of 70 tonnes), so as to drive very large vessels with low
revolutions to give higher performance, has made increased
shaft flexibility and reduced bending moments very desirable

features. This has been achieved in the design illustrated in Fig. 6.12.

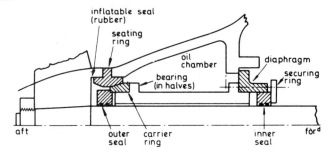

WITHDRAWABLE STERN GEAR
Fig. 6.11

The propeller has its own self contained bearing and the drive torque shaft is more flexible. Hollow helical (spiral spring) roller bearings are used giving differential radial expansion allowance and flexibility to shock loading—plain outer races allow shaft axial movement. Note the flanged connection to the propeller boss—this is simple and trouble free but it requires a special (muff) coupling at the inboard end to allow withdrawal aft. Such a coupling is shown in Fig. 6.9—astern thrust resistance is increased with an inner nut. A similar design to Fig. 6.12 is available utilising a plain bearing inside the propeller boss in place of roller bearings. If shaft withdrawal inboard is essential a cone and taper, with nut arrangement can be used to secure a flanged coupling for bolting to the propeller boss (to replace the flange detail as sketched in Fig. 6.12).

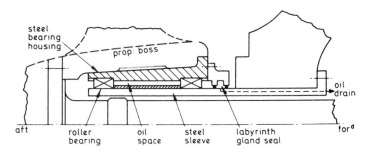

ALTERNATIVE STERN GEAR
Fig. 6.12

Propeller

Consideration deserves special attention and this is best achieved by reference to a work on naval architecture for propeller design, pitch theory, etc. However, the increased use of controllable pitch propellers requires some knowledge of the principles involved.

Controllable Pitch Propeller

Use of these propellers has increased with the greater use of unidirectional gas turbine and multi-diesel drives and bridge control. Engine room (or bridge) signal is fed to a torque-speed selector which fixes engine speed and propeller pitch—feedbacks apply from each. Consider Fig. 6.13:

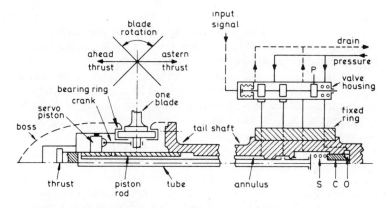

CONTROLLABLE PITCH PROPELLER
Fig. 6.13

The input fluid signal acts on the diaphragm in the valve housing and directs pressure oil via one piston valve through the tube to one side (left) of the servo piston or via the other piston valve outside the tube (in the annulus) to the other side (right) of the servo piston. Movement of the servo piston, through a crank pin ring and sliding blocks rotates blades and varies pitch.

The feedback restoring signal, to restore piston valves to the neutral position at correct pitch position, is dependent on spring(s) force (*i.e.* servo piston position) which acts to vary the orifice (o) by control piston (c) so fixing feedback pressure loading on the pilot valve (p) in the valve housing. The central part of the tailshaft includes a shaft coupling and pitch lock device (not shown). Emergency local pitch control, communication/alarm systems and fail-safe (navigable ahead pitch) are required.

SHAFTING ANCILLARIES

In case of engine breakdowns it is usually advisable to fit a shaft friction brake at the first coupling from the propeller shaft so as to allow engine examination with safety. In case of towing, after breakdown, a trailing collar working on a tunnel bearing face is often fitted to allow shaft disconnection and reduce propeller resistance by allowing idling. Under normal conditions the collar is set about 18 mm clear.

The Torsionmeter

The first requirement is the determination of the shaft power (shaft kW or shaft MW) constant from a shaft calibration, a typical calculation would be as follows:

A shaft of 300 mm dia. and 6.5 m long is rigidly clamped at one end and the free end has a clamp and lever, applied to which loads can be added at a radius of 3 m. A load force of 222 kN produces an angle of twist of 1 degree.

shaft kW $= 2\pi NT$ if T in kN m
$= 6.284 \times N \times 222 \times 3$ in *this* example,

shaft kW for 1° twist $= 6.284 \times N \times 666$ in *this* example,
shaft kW for θ° twist $= 6.284 \times N \times 666 \times \theta$ for *any* case,
$= 4180 \times N \times \theta$

shaft MW $= 4.18 \times N \times \theta$

∴ the meter or shaft constant $= 4.18$

Thus knowing the angle of twist in degrees for the given shaft length the shaft MW for the given rev/s can be determined. The requirement then for the torsionmeter is to measure the angle of twist in degrees between two points the correct datum length apart.

There are *four* types of torsionmeter:

(1) Mechanical—gearing set from shaft with a differential screw reading device—this is not popular as wear immediately gives errors.
(2) Acoustical—the pitch of a note from a vibrating wire varies

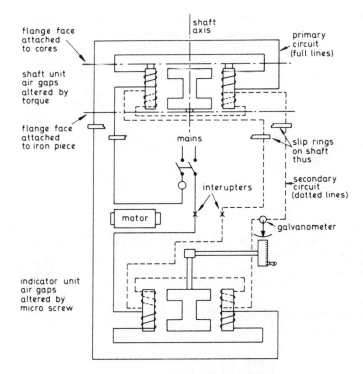

ELECTRICAL TORSION METER
Fig. 6.14

with the torque (tension produced)—not popular at present as difficulty of cyclic variations.

(3) Optical—lag of a light flash is indicative of twist—simple but tends to give average value over a range of revolutions, no indication of cyclic variations.

(4) Electrical—variation of transformer air gap due to twist—possibly most accurate and popular. The electrical type will be briefly considered (Fig. 6.14).

Two sleeves rigidly fixed to shaft having flanges at 180° to the shaft axis, twist causes relative displacement between the flanges. Two cores are attached to one flange and the iron piece to the other so that relative movement between flange faces, due to shaft twist, alters the air gap of the differential transformer.

The primary circuit is wound to give the same polarity and the secondary circuits are in opposition, the provision of a motor driven interrupter to give *ac* supply is required if *dc* mains. With no torque the air gaps are equal and the two secondary circuits are equal and opposite, but when torque is applied air gaps become unequal and a current flows in the secondary circuit which can be read on the galvanometer. An identical unit is fitted in the indicator box and by rotation of the handle the iron

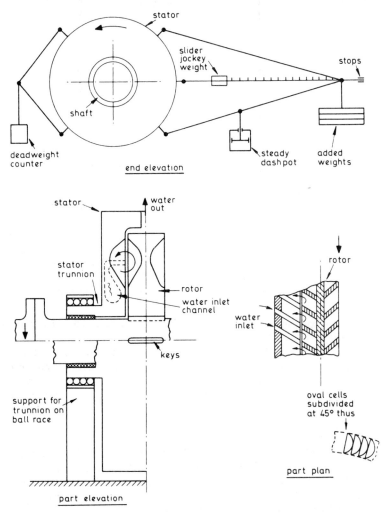

DYNAMOMETER PRINCIPLE
Fig. 6.15

piece can be moved until the air gaps in the indicating unit are identical with those of the shaft unit. This restores the electrical equilibrium in the secondary circuit, as opposed equal currents the galvanometer reads zero, and the amount of movement at the indicating box dial is indicative of the angle of twist restoration required and hence gives the angle of twist for the length of shaft between the two flange faces in the shaft unit.

By application of the meter constant and rev/s the shaft MW is thus determined.

The Dynamometer

Consider the hydraulic type as sketched in Fig. 6.15.

The engine under test drives the shaft to which the rotor is directly coupled. The shaft bearings are inside the casing containing the stator which is free to swivel on trunnion supports.

Each face of the rotor has pockets or cells of semi-elliptical or oval cross section divided from one another by oblique 45° vanes, the stator is similar. Water enters at the stator inlet channel, entering between 45° vanes and passes into rotating rotor. The water is constantly circulated around the cells in a vortex action so the torque is transmitted from rotor to stator via the water. This torque tends to turn the stator, this action being resisted by a load measuring device so that the resisting torque will equal the applied torque and is thus being measured.

$$\text{Shaft power} = \text{Torque applied by weights} \times 2\pi N$$

For testing in both directions of rotation two rotors are provided one used astern, the other ahead.

In modern practice the load measure devices are much simplified by use of levers. In some designs resistance to motion is caused by a measurable electrical field coil resistance which causes variation of eddy current resistance to rotor rotation, in place of the hydraulic resistance.

The Thrust Block

Modern types of work on the Michell principle. The thrust of the collar is transmitted through the oil film and pads to the casing. The white metal surface would be more likely to yield than the oil film at pressures as high as 500 bar (compressive yield of white metal say 560 bar = 56 MN/m²).

The oil scraper bears on the outer periphery of the thrust collar and delivers oil to the reservoir-stop from where it

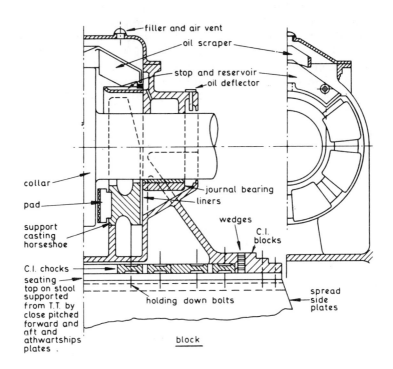

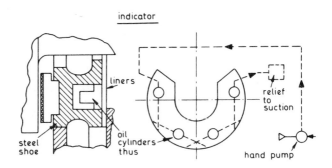

THRUST BLOCK
Fig. 6.16

cascades on to the pads and bearings. The pads fit radially in the inverted horse shoe castings, pads being secured circumferentially by the stop. The castings back on to liners so ensuring location in fore and aft direction and fixing the clearance, which can be adjusted. The radial pivot line on the pad back varies from half to two thirds of the pad width from the leading edge (see also Fig. 6.17).

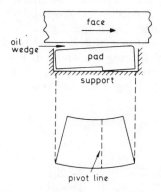

the pivot line should theoretically be nearer the outlet edge to coincide with the point of maximum pressure, in practice a central pivot is often satisfactory.
in place of a pivot line, a pivot hardened stud is commonly used especially on smaller types.

Fig. 6.17

The lower half casting acts as an oil reservoir sump, being provided with oil level gauge glass and a cooling coil. The total oil clearance is approximately 1 mm for say a 500 mm diameter shaft. The wedges at base have a slow taper of about 20 mm/m and act to relieve the holding down bolts of shear. The floors in the double bottom tank below the thrust stool are closely pitched. Clearances are measured using wedges or hydaulic ram movement.

Michell Thrust Indicator

The standard block is modified so that a cast steel shoe is replaced by a forged mild steel one having a number of holes in the back making up interconnected oil cylinders. A hand pump, pressure gauge, piping and relief valve are provided. Under oil pressure from the hand pump the internally formed pistons move forward so transferring gradually the thrust load from the liners to themselves, the thrust shoe now floats on pistons and pressure is read on the gauge. When half the axial clearance has been traversed the relief valve lifts so preventing over pumping. Astern thrust could be measured by a duplicate on the other side of the collar. The piston loading pressure is about 175 bar.

Ball and Roller Bearings

Wherever rolling friction, as with a wheel on a road, is substituted for sliding friction, as with a pin rotating in a journal, the frictional effects are much reduced. Such bearings are expensive, require minimum grease lubrication, must be sealed from dirt entry and grease escape and once overloaded are rapidly destroyed. However they are shorter, allow more accurate shaft centring (negligible diametric clearance), have a virtually constant coefficient of friction of about 0.003 at all speeds (a journal bearing cannot match this figure until high speed film lubrication exists) and can be self aligning. Simple sketches of three types of ball bearing are given in Fig. 6.18, similar types of roller bearings are available, their main advantage being that greater bearing loads are possible for a given diameter.

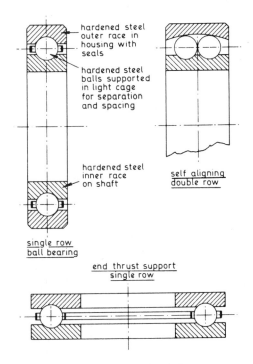

BALL AND ROLLER BEARINGS
Fig. 6.18

SIMPLE BALANCING

This is a complex subject closely related to vibrations. Only some very simple fundamentals are discussed at this stage, these points could be expanded a little further as a motorship problem when considering *IC* engines with reference to firing order, etc.

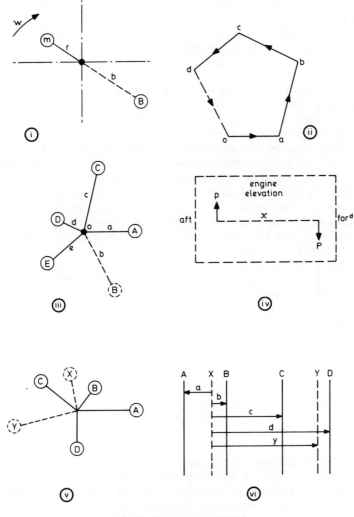

SIMPLE BALANCING
Fig. 6.19

Single Revolving Mass (Fig. 6.19.i)

An unbalanced mass m at radius r, to balance introduce an opposite mass, B at radius b, in the plane of rotation such that:

$$B\omega^2 b = m\omega^2 r$$

i.e. equal centrifugal force effects.

$$Bb = mr$$

Several Revolving Masses in One Plane (Figs. 6.19.ii and 6.19.iii)

Draw a mass moment (actual mass × radius) polygon and closing side give Bb magnitude and direction.

(from od on Fig. 6.19.ii)

Several Revolving Mases in Different Planes (Figs. 6.19.iv, 6.19.v and 6.19.vi)

A couple is a tendency to rock the shaft in its bearings in the form of an end to end turning moment.

Magnitude of the couple shown = Px(see Fig. 6.19.iv)

Proceed as before and draw the mass moment polygon to find the unbalance mass moment as in Fig. 6.19.ii. Assume it is necessary to add say two balance masses, having equivalent mass moment to that found, for convenience at say X and Y, *i.e.* one big mass to a particular point may not be convenient so the mass is split up (see Fig. 6.19.v and 6.19.vi). These two masses are also in different planes.

By using one of the planes, X or Y, as a fixed reference it can be fixed and then ignored, having no moment. Then a couple polygon or a tabulation is drawn for the other position. Thus the masses, radii and location of the planes for balance are determined.

Inertia Force of a Reciprocating Mass

$F = Fp + Fs + \ldots\ldots\ldots\ldots\ldots\ldots\ldots\ldots\ldots\ldots\ldots\ldots\ldots\ldots\ldots\ldots\ldots$

i.e. primiary + secondary + $\ldots\ldots\ldots\ldots\ldots\ldots\ldots\ldots\ldots\ldots\ldots\ldots$

extended to further orders such as 4th, 6th, etc.

$$Fp \simeq ma \cos\theta$$

$$Fs \simeq ma \cos 2\theta/n$$

m refers to the mass of the reciprocating parts, a acceleration of crosshead, n ratio of connecting rod to crank length, and θ the crank inclination to *tdc*. A single revolving mass cannot totally balance a reciprocating mass. However partial primary balance can be attempted with the object of shifting the form of the unbalance to a more acceptable condition.

In Line Engines

The reciprocating masses are often considered as the line of stroke component of equal mass at the crankpins. A force polygon (mass moments) on revolving forces can then be drawn and also a couple polygon, for each of primary, secondary, etc. Where possible, couple balance for some IC engines can often simply be arranged (for an even number of cylinders), by arranging one half of crankshaft as a mirror image of the other, firing order say 1, 3, 4, 2 (4 stroke).

SIMPLE VIBRATION

General Vibration

This subject is a compromise between complex mathematics and practical exprience and only the most bare outline is quoted. There are three modes of vibration, transverse, longitudinal (axial) and torsional.

Every vibration problem reduces to the solution of an equation of forces:

$$\text{Inertia} + \text{Damping} + \text{Spring} + \text{Exciting} = 0$$

Each force may be modified, *i.e.* changing the size to alter inertia, providing oil type dashpots to amend damping, altering shaft stiffness to vary spring force and varying amplitude or frequency of an engine exciting force.

Consider the alternating current electrical analogy. For a R, L, C series circuit at a particular frequency (f) the inductive reactance X_L equals the capacitive reactance X_C. In this case the circuit behaves as a purely resistance circuit, *i.e.* impedance equals resistance and current $I = V/R$ following Ohms law. The condition gives maximum current flow and the circuit at resonance is called an acceptor circuit (for a R, L, C parallel circuit it is rejector at resonance).

In the mechanical system the behaviour is identical with inertia, damping and stiffness terms in place of inductance, resistance and capacitance. Resonance here gives severe vibratory forces and stresses. Resonant frequencies in electrical systems have their equivalents as critical speeds in mechanical engine systems. Variations to amend the four force terms given earlier can cause a critical speed to be moved away from a particular running speed.

Note the electrical resonance curve given in Fig. 6.20.

Transverse Vibration

This occurs in the athwartships direction with large reciprocating engines. It is usually due to cylinder pressure forces and inertia forces giving a resulting couple about the engine crankshaft centre line and through the guide shoe. Propeller torque variations can increase or decrease this couple.

The usual solution is to stay the engine to the hull with lateral stays. Such stays must be connected to the hull by pins that would shear if the hull was distorted in collision. The hull attachment must be rigid, transverse deck beams are best. The stays must provide adequate and even stiffness to raise the resonant frequency above the service rev/s. When dealing with resonant frequencies inside the running range great care is required as minor stiffening can make the vibration worse. Doubling resonant frequency can quadruple exciting forces within the running speed.

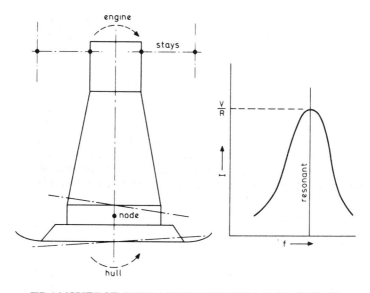

TRANSVERSE VIBRATION RESONANCE CURVE
Fig. 6.20

Such vibration of the order of 1 mm can cause failure to pipes and welded joints as well as being most unpleasant in machinery and accommodation spaces. The rocking tendency can be seen from Fig. 6.20.

Axial Vibration

Some axial movements of amplitude ± 2.5 mm have been noted, a movement of ± 1 mm can quite easily introduce crank bending stresses of 28 MN/m². Invariably these movements are propeller excited occurring as say 4th order vibrations (8 vibrations per second at 2 rev/s of shaft). In this respect a 4 bladed propeller is causing the axial vibration with 2 blades passing the aperture every ¼ rev giving an axial pulse, the introduction of 5 bladed propellers and more rigid thrust seatings have done much to reduce such amplitudes of vibration. Some experiments have been tried to utilise the principle of the Michell thrust indicator to introduce a dashpot damping effect.

Torsional Vibration

A node is a point at which the shaft is undisturbed by vibration, *i.e.* at the node the shaft can be imagined as clamped, the sections at each side vibrating opposite in phase but with the same frequency. One node gives one mode of vibration, two nodes two modes, etc., most shafting systems can be simplified to a one or two mode form, *i.e.* first or second degree of vibration as at least a first assumption. This means for calculation the shaft system is considered as a 3 mass system, engine in one, flywheel and propeller.

Only one serious critical occurs in the running range usually, for aft end installations commonly above the maximum revolutions and for midship installations commonly below, this being a broad generalisation. The two node form is usually the decider in crankshafts, 9th order, 2 mode, at 18 vib/s (2 rev/s) whilst the one node is usually the decider in intermediate shafting 2nd order 4 vib/s and 4th order 8 vib/s, 1 mode.

Detuners and Dampers

The object of the forward flexible flywheel (detuner) sometimes fitted is usually to shift the node to the crankshaft centre and reduce vibration. This flywheel causes a variable stiffness with the torque variation and hence causes a change of natural frequency as load changes. Any tendency to build up torsional vibrations is reduced by frequency change and the amplitude settles down to a value below that of a rigid system. Thus this is really a flexible mass addition to the system which is self adjusting. Referring to Fig. 6.21.B and 6.21.C it is seen that the spring is supported over a long span at full loads and a short span at overloads. The spring connects the drive to the driven mass, which is thus floating.

Torsional vibratory stresses investigated for a motor ship may appear as in Fig. 6.21.D.

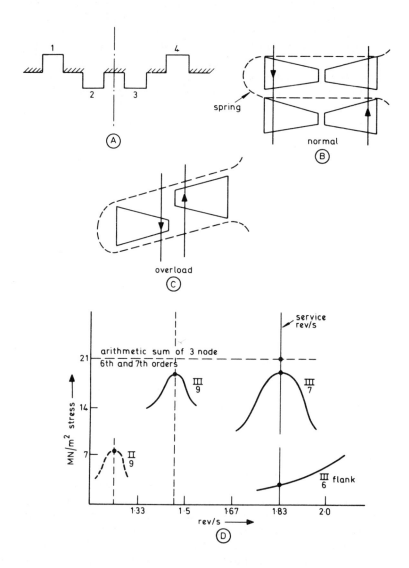

VIBRATION CHARACTERISTICS (TORSIONAL)

Fig. 6.21

Torsional Vibration Damper

A vibration damper will dissipate energy given to the system by exciting forces. This energy would otherwise be absorbed and appear as either strain energy at the nodes or kinetic (velocity) energy at the antinodes. Shown in Fig. 6.22 is the diagrammatic principle of a 'Holset' type of damper in which the damping fluid is between the driven casing and revolving mass. Such a damper may be fitted at an antinode.

Torsional vibration eliminators often utilise damping and detuning, for example in magnetic slip couplings, spring and centrifugal friction coupling or clutch drives, etc.

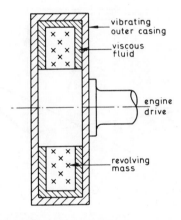

vibrating
outer casing

viscous
fluid

engine
drive

revolving
mass

TORSIONAL VIBRATION DAMPER
Fig. 6.22

Torsional Elastic Curves

Fig. 6.23 illustrates a four cylinder engine flywheel and propeller system which as a first simplification can be reduced to a three rotor torsional system as shown. For known moments of inertia the critical speeds can be evaluated, the elastic line is drawn to represent the amplitude of vibration on a length scale. Intersection of elastic line and shaft axis gives the position of the node or nodes depending on the degree of vibration, *i.e.* a single rotor placed at *N*, or two rotors placed at the two positions shown for *N*. Higher degrees of vibration exist.

Aft Engined Vessels

Modern vessels have higher powers hence giving greater magnitude exciting forces. Welded structures give less damping than riveted structures. Propeller excited forces are usually the result of insufficient hull-propeller clearances and incorrect blade form. To cause hull vibration the excitation force would act on or near the antinode. The main antinode is usually at the aft end so that large aft engined reciprocating units are most prone to vibration effects, *i.e.* large motor tankers.

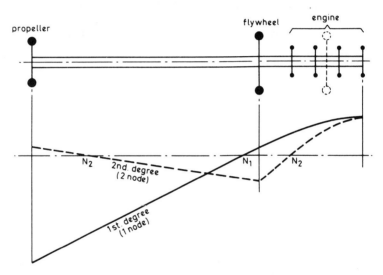

TORSIONAL ELASTIC CURVES
Fig. 6.23

TEST EXAMPLES 6

Class 3

1. How is alignment of a crankshaft checked, does the loaded condition of the ship have any effect on alignment?
2. What are the forces on a diesel engine crankshaft and are these forces uniform along the length of the crankshaft? Give reasons for your opinion.
3. What is the purpose of putting a thrust bearing between the main engine and the propeller? How is the thrust bearing cooled?
4. Explain how a variable pitch propeller operates.

TEST EXAMPLES 6

Class 2

1. With reference to keyless propellers explain:
   - (a) why keys and key ways have been eliminated,
   - (b) how angular slip is avoided,
   - (c) why mounting upon and removal from a propeller shaft requires a different technique than that employed for propellers with keys.

2. (a) Sketch a coupling enabling external withdrawal of propeller shafts.
   - (b) Give a general description of the coupling.
   - (c) Give one advantage and one disadvantage of this coupling compared to the solid flange type.

3. With reference to controllable pitch propellers:
   - (a) explain why the blade attitude, assumed upon control failure is considered safe,
   - (b) describe how the 'fail safe' feature operates,
   - (c) state how the ship can be manoeuvred when the bridge control is out of action.

4. (a) Describe how unequal loading of main transmission shaft bearings may be partially corrected at sea.
   - (b) Suggest, with reasons, what remedial action should be taken upon arrival in port.
   - (c) State the indications whilst at sea, that unequal loading of such bearings exists.

TEST EXAMPLES 6

Class 1

1. Describe how alignment of shafting between engine and propeller shaft is checked with the vessel afloat.

   State how alignment is corrected in the case of appreciable hull deflection.

2. (i)   Make a simplified sketch of the operating mechanism for a controllable pitch propeller.

   (ii) Describe briefly how pitch is altered in accordance with telemotor signal.

   (iii) State what 'fail safe' feature is incorporated into the logic of the mechanism.

3. Identify the defects to which propeller shafts are commonly susceptible.

   Explain how propeller shafts are surveyed in order to detect these defects.

4. (a)   Sketch a 'muff' (flangeless or sleeve) coupling for connecting adjacent lengths of main transmission shafting.

   (b)   Describe the manner in which the coupling is mounted on and transmits torque between the adjacent lengths of shafting.

   (c)   State how astern thrust is accommodated by the coupling.

CHAPTER 7

REFRIGERATION

The field of refrigeration is large and varied, much expansion and development having taken place in recent years.

In view of the introduction of new plants such as air conditioning, completely automated main and domestic units, etc., it has been considered advisable to concentrate on accepted modern practice.

BASIC PRINCIPLES

Ice-Water-Steam Phase Changes

Most refrigerant vapours have similar characteristics and properties to steam except that they have a much lower boiling point. Consider changes that occur when 1 kg of ice at say $-23°C$ is converted into superheated steam at say 1.013 bar, 200°C.

These temperature-heat energy changes are best illustrated graphically (Fig. 7.1).

(1) Heat added to raise the temperature of 1 kg of ice at $-23°C$ to $0°C = 1 \times 2.094 \times 23 = 48.2$ kJ.

(Specific enthalpy, of solid ice is -48.2kJ at $-23°C$ $i.e.$ h_i)

(2) Heat added for fusion of 1 kg of ice at $0°C$ to 1 kg of water at $0°C = 1 \times 333 = 333$ kJ.

(Specific enthalpy of fusion, for ice is -333kJ $i.e.$ h_{if})

(3) Heat added to raise the temperature of 1 kg of water at $0°C$ to saturation temperature (t_s) 419.1 kJ. At 1.013 bar, $t_s = 100°C$ and $h_f = 419.1$ kJ. (Tables).

(This is liquid specific enthalpy, for water).

(4) Heat added for vaporisation of 1 kg of water at 100°C to 1 kg of steam at 100°C ($i.e.$ constant t_s) $= h_{fg} = 2256.7$ kJ (2.257 MJ). (Tables).

(This is specific enthalpy of vaporisation, for steam).

(5) Heat added to superheat 1 kg of steam from 100°C (t_s) to 200°C $(t) = 299.2$ kJ. (Tables).

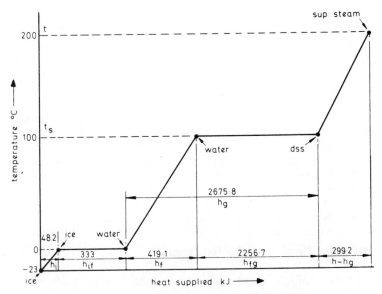

ICE-WATER-STEAM PHASE CHANGES
Fig. 7.1

(This is specific enthalpy to superheat, above dss).
Degree of superheat = $(200 - 100) = 100°C$.

(6) Heat added to change water at 0°C to dry saturated steam (dss) at $100°C = 2675.8$ kJ (2.676 MJ). Also see Tables. (This is specific enthalpy (h_g) for dry saturated steam vapour.)

The given diagram should clarify the use of terms like specific enthalpy of vaporisation, superheat, etc., used at a later stage when considering the refrigerants. Normally if the specific heat capacity (c_p) is constant (with temperature), specific enthalpy with no phase change is given by:

Heat exchange $Q = m\, c_p\, (t_2 - t_1)$, m is the mass.

The datum for water is taken as 0°C (273 K), due to the phase (state) change at that point, but for refrigerants it is often taken at $-40°C$, this having no significance apart from the fact that it reduces the use of negative heats (absolute zero and the Kelvin scale does the same).

Note

The preferred term for heat energy (liquid or vapour) is enthalpy. Heat/kg, as energy, is specific enthalpy (the specific heat capacity of ice is 2.094 kJ/kg and the specific enthalpy of fusion of ice is 333 kJ/kg).

A subcooled or undercooled liquid is a liquid existing at a temperature lower than the saturation temperature for that pressure whilst a liquid exactly at saturation temperature is a saturated liquid, *e.g.*, water at atmospheric pressure is a subcooled liquid at 77°C and a saturated liquid at 100°C.

Wet saturated, dry saturated and superheated vapour refers to the degree of heat saturation, wet vapour has dryness fraction (or quality).

Specific volume is volume occupied by 1 kg of liquid or vapour in m^3 (reciprocal of density).

REFRIGERANTS

Desirable Properties of a Refrigerant

1. Low boiling point (otherwise operation at high vacua becomes a necessity).
2. Low condensing pressure (to avoid heavy machine and plant scantlings and reduce the leakage risk).
3. High specific enthalpy of vaporisation (to reduce the quantity of refrigerant in circulation and lower machine speeds, sizes, etc.).
4. Low specific volume in vapour state (reduces size and increases efficiency).
5. High critical temperature (temperature above which vapour cannot be condensed by isothermal compression).
6. Non corrosive and non solvent (pure or mixed).
7. Stable under working conditions.
8. Non flammable and non explosive (pure or mixed).
9. No action with oil (the fact that most refrigerants are miscible may be advantageous, *i.e.* removal of oil films, lowering pour point, etc., provided separators are fitted).
10. Easy leak detection.
11. Non toxic (non poisonous and non irritating).
12. Cheap, easily stored and obtained.

Refrigerants

Three vapours are:

Freon 12 (CCl_2F_2) (Dichlorodifluoro Methane)
Carbonic Anhydride (CO_2) (termed Carbon Dioxide)
Anhydrous Ammonia (NH_3) (termed Ammonia)

Many other refrigerants are available, the Freon family (halogenated hydrocarbons) being very large.

No refrigerant has all the desirable properties, each one having various advantages and disadvantages. Ammonia and carbon dioxide are not now used; they are included here to illustrate properties so as to allow comparisons to be made.

PROPERTY	CCl_2F_2	CO_2	NH_3
DISCHARGE PRESSURE, bar	7.4	72	11.7
SUCTION PRESSURE, bar	1.8	23	2.4
CRITICAL PRESSURE, bar	40	73.8	113.7
CRITICAL TEMPERATURE, °C	112	31	133
SPECIFIC ENTHALPY OF LIQUID, kJ/kg, AT −15°C	22.3	48.9	112.4
SPECIFIC ENTHALPY OF VAPORISATION, kJ/kg, AT −15°C	158.7	274.7	1314.2
SPECIFIC ENTHALPY OF VAPOUR, kJ/kg, AT −15°C	181.0	323.6	1426.6
SPECIFIC ENTHALPY OF LIQUID, kJ/kg, AT 30°C	64.6	193.8	323.1
SPECIFIC ENTHALPY OF VAPORISATION, kJ/kg, AT 30°C	135.0	63.1	1145.8
SPECIFIC ENTHALPY OF VAPOUR, kJ/kg, AT 30°C	199.6	266.9	1468.9
SPECIFIC VOLUME OF LIQUID, m³/kg	0.0007	0.001	0.0015
BOILING TEMPERATURE, °C, AT 1.013 bar	−30	−78	−33
SPECIFIC VOLUME OF VAPOUR, m³/kg AT −15°C	0.093	0.017	0.51
QUANTITY, kg/s FOR 200 kJ/s ($x\ 10^{-3}$)	31.3	28.8	3.4
VOLUME, m³/s FOR 200 kJ/s ($x\ 10^{-3}$)	2.9	0.5	1.7
THEORETICAL POWER RATIO	1.00	1.63	0.99
LIQUID SPECIFIC HEAT CAPACITY kJ/kgK	0.96	3.23	4.65
CORROSIVE (PURE)	NO[2]	NO	NO[1]
TOXIC	NO	NO	YES
FLAMMABLE	NO[3]	NO	YES
EXPLOSIVE	NO	NO	YES
COST	FAIRLY EXPENSIVE	CHEAP	CHEAP
LEAKAGE TEST	HALLIDE TORCH	SOAP & WATER	WET LITMUS
MISCIBLE WITH OIL	YES	NO	SLIGHTLY

[1]NH_3 VERY STABLE IN WATER, HIGHLY SOLUBLE (1 m³ H_2O ABSORBS 900 m³ NH_3), NH_3 CORROSIVE TO BRASS AND BRONZE IF WATER PRESENT.
[2]CCl_2F_2 ATTACKS RUBBER.
[3]LIBERATES TOXIC PHOSGENE GAS FROM THE FIRE.

TABLE 7.1

Properties of Refrigerants

The properties of the refrigerants are as given in the refrigerant table (Table 7.1) and by careful analysis the advantages and disadvantages can be weighed against each other and a choice made depending on preference, experience, properties, conditions of use, etc. Freon is almost standard use today (see later).

In order to compare refrigerants under various conditions of working, *standard* conditions are adopted. These conditions are defined as pressures coresponding to saturated vapour temperatures of $-15°C$ at compressor intake and $30°C$ at compressor discharge; $5°C$ subcooling and $5°C$ superheating fix the final refrigerant temperatures used at intake to expansion valve and to compressor respectively. For simple conditions $-15°C$ and $30°C$ are used, discounting subcooling and superheating, and the given properties are based on this standard (Table 7.1).

This condition is referred to as *the standard*.

Table 7.1 can be analysed to give advantages and disadvantages of one refrigerant with another, simply to illustrate this consider CO_2:

Advantages are:

Low boiling point, low specific volume (hence low volume flow rate), cheap, non explosive, non flammable, non corrosive, non toxic, etc.

Disadvantages are:

Very high pressures (hence heavy construction and careful joint attention is required), low specific enthalpy of vaporisation (hence high mass flow rate), low critical temperature (reduces plant efficiency at higher sea temperatures), rather low comparable efficiency, etc.

Not all the properties can be fully analysed fromTable 7.1 but quite sufficient properties are given to enable a good comparison between the main refrigerants to be drawn.

Freon Refrigerants

Whilst Freon 12 has been the main Freon refrigerant used in the past there is now an increasing use of Freon 11 (a very low pressure refrigerant; particularly suitable for large air conditioning installations), Freon 22 (very suitable for low temperatures without negative evaporator pressures *i.e.* in vacuum) and Freon 502 (for hermetic *i.e.* integral gas tight motor and compressor). The main advantage claimed is an improved refrigerating effect for a given size of machine. Again it should be noted that there is no ideal choice in the Freon group as there are advantages and disadvantages for R.11 (CCl_3F),

R.12, R.13 ($CClF_3$), R.22, R.113 ($CCl_2F/CClF_2$) and R.502. (R:-refrigerant).

Table 7.2 allows quick comparison between the three main types of Freon refrigerants.

PROPERTY	FREON 12 CCl_2F_2	FREON 22 $CHClF_2$	FREON 502 $CHClF_2/CClF_2CF_3$
DISCHARGE PRESSURE, bar	7.4	12.0	13.1
SUCTION PRESSURE, bar	1.8	3.0	3.5
REFRIGERATING CAPACITY, J/s	318	571	561
POWER, kW	89	170	188
REFRIGERATION EFFECT RATIO	1.0	1.55	1.7
COMPRESSION HEAT RATIO	1.0	1.0	1.43

The above figures relate to standard conditions and are based on an 8-cylinder, W-type machine (178 mm × 140 mm), running at 12.5 rev/s (as described later). The actual refrigeration effect would be about 400 kJ/m^3, and compression heat 66 kJ/kg for Freon 12.

TABLE 7.2

THE VAPOUR COMPRESSION SYSTEM (ONE UNIT)

Operating Cycle

Marine practice would require complete duplication of all units.

Considering Fig. 7.2:

The vapour is discharged from the compressor at 93°C (degree of superheat 63°C) and is condensed in the condenser, condensation temperature 30°C. For good heat energy transference rate a temperature differential of about 8°C between cooling water inlet and condensation temperatures is usual. The condenser gauge registers condensation (saturation) pressure and corresponding saturation temperature (t_s) on a dual scale, for example Freon 12 would be 7.4 bar, 30°C, the actual superheated vapour temperature as read from the thermometer being 93°C.

Some undercooling, which is advantageous, will occur in the condenser, under standard conditions this will be 5°C so the liquid will leave at 25°C. The liquid now passes through the expansion valve where throttling at constant enthalpy to the desired vaporisation pressure will occur. Some flash off of liquid to vapour will occur, the greater the undercooling the less will be the flash off percentage. This represents a loss, as any vapour formed before the evaporator will not now extract its specific enthalpy of vaporisation from the brine, giving a resultant loss of refrigeration effect. Ideally the fluid should be totally wet entering and just dry leaving the evaporator which means full specific enthalpy of vaporisation absorption from brine. In theory superheating is non advantageous but in practice it is advantageous to make the vapour superheated at entry to the compressor, giving a fairly high superheat leaving the compressor.

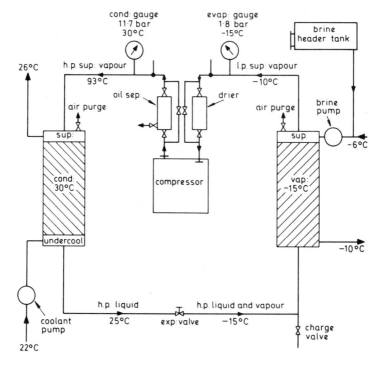

THE VAPOUR COMPRESSION SYSTEM
Fig. 7.2

The vapour now leaves the evaporator under assumed standard conditions having 5°C of superheat. The evaporator gauge registers vaporisation (saturation) pressure and corresponding saturation temperature (t_s) on a dual scale, for example again Freon 12 would be 1.8 bar, −15°C, the actual superheated vapour temperature as read from the thermometer being −10°C. For good heat transference rate a temperature differential of about 5°C between brine outlet and vaporisation temperatures is usual.

The vapour now enters the compressor to start the circuit again. It should be clearly understood that Fig. 7.2 refers to *one definite condition*, *i.e.* a sea temperature of 22°C and a particular expansion valve setting determining that condition. Variations of sea temperature or vaporisation pressure would indicate completely different readings but the basic temperature differentials of 8°C and 5°C should still exist.

Note, using Table 7.1, for comparison purposes, each kg of CO_2 entering totally as liquid and leaving as dry saturated vapour would absorb 275 kJ, being the specific enthalpy of vaporisation, this figure would be 1314 kJ (1.31 MJ) for NH_3 under the same conditions. However 5 kg CO_2, which would extract 1375 kJ (1.38 MJ) has a volume of 0.085 m³ whereas 1 kg of NH_3 has a volume of 0.51 m³, *i.e.* for same refrigeration effect a high mass flow rate for CO_2 but a very high volume (capacity) rate for NH_3, which affects machine sizes. This illustrates the error of strictly referring to one numerical figure when considering advantages. $8\frac{1}{2}$ kg of CCl_2F_2 extracts 1350 kJ/kg (1.35 MJ/kg) and has a volume of 0.79 m³ *i.e.* the specific volume is 0.093 m³/kg and the specific enthalpy of evaporation 158.7 kJ/kg.

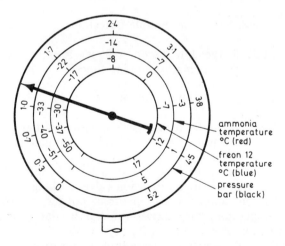

COMPOUND PRESSURE GAUGE
Fig. 7.3

The compound pressure gauge shown in Fig. 7.3 illustrates the dual scale of saturation temperature and pressure. Ammonia is shown for illustrative comparison purposes only, *i.e.*, normally only one refrigerant, pressure and temperature is on the scale. Commonly all readings are taken in temperatures only. Correct differentials are an indication of correct working with sufficient vapour charge.

Under correct running conditions the compressor discharge pipe should be fairly hot to the touch and the suction pipe should be just frosting up near the compressor. The compressor discharge and suction lines are commonly provided with crossover valves in addition to the stop valves. These valves allow the pumping out of the hp side to the lp side for overhauls and allow an easy discharge for starting. Refrigerant is added, with the machine running normally, at the charge cock.

Many of the circuits employ a liquid receiver after the condenser and CO_2 types commonly had intermediate liquid cooling receivers. The capacity of a liquid receiver is usually sufficient to cover the outlet to the liquid line. Methods of control of the flow of refrigerant are: (a) low side float, (b) high side float, (c) hand manual control, (d) capillary, (e) direct expansion with constant pressure, (f) direct expansion with constant superheat, these are discussed later.

The system should always be kept clear of water, air and dirt.

Common Faults and Simple Detection

1. Undercharge: low discharge gauge reading, lack of frost on suction pipe, lengthy running times.
2. Air in system: high discharge gauge reading (assuming sufficient vapour), jumping of gauge pointers, inefficient working.
3. Dirty condenser or insufficient cooling water: high discharge gauge reading and incorrect condenser temperature differentials.
4. Overcharge: unlikely, but gives high discharge gauge reading and very sensitive expansion valve working.
5. Oil on cooling coils: incorrect condenser and evaporator temperature differentials (oil is an insulator), excess frost on suction pipe.
6. Choked expansion valve: caused by dirt or freeze up by water, gives starving of evaporator and rapid condenser pressure rise.

7. Short cycling: condenser coolant restriction causing hp discharge cut outs, choked expansion valve giving 1p suction cut outs, etc.

Thermodynamic Cycles

The circuit appears on the theoretical charts as shown in Figs. 7.4 and 7.5. Entropy being a theoretical property of a fluid that remains constant during frictionless adiabatic operations.

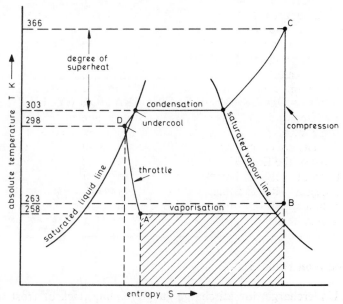

ABSOLUTE TEMPERATURE-ENTROPY
Fig. 7.4

Referring to Fig. 7.4:

Heat energy received from cold chamber = area under AB.
Heat energy rejected in the condenser = area under CD.
Heat energy equivalent
of work done = heat energy rejected—
       heat energy received
= area under CD—area under AB
= area of figure ABCDA
+ area under throttle curve DA.

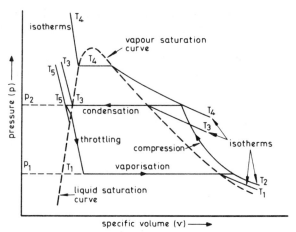

$p \sim v$ DIAGRAM OF REFRIGERATION CYCLE

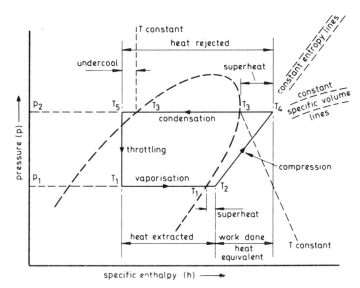

$p \sim h$ DIAGRAM OF REFRIGERATION CYCLE
Fig. 7.5

$$\text{Coefficient of Performance} = \frac{\text{heat energy received}}{\text{heat energy equivalent of work done}}$$

The compression is taken to be isentropic (frictionless adiabatic) for calculation work, this means the compression line is vertical (constant entropy). Unit mass of refrigerant is the usual basis. Coefficient of performance for Freon is approximately 4.7.

It should be noted how undercooling, in moving point A to the left, increases the heat received from the cold chamber thus increasing refrigerant effect.

Refrigeration Cycle p ~ v Diagram (Fig. 7.5)

This diagram is shown to allow comparison of this refrigeration cycle with other more familiar, cycles covered in theoretical work on $p \sim v$ diagrams. In practice the $p \sim v$ diagram is rarely used in refrigeration.

Refrigeration Cycle p ~ h Diagram (Fig. 7.5)

Once basic theory has been established by using $T \sim s$ charts, the emphasis shifts in practice to the $p \sim h$ (Mollier) chart. This diagram has the big advantage that heat extracted, heat rejected and work done heat equivalent can be read off directly from the h axis in kJ/kg.

Intermediate Liquid Cooling

It has been mentioned previously that there is a loss in refrigeration effect due to flash off to vapour when the liquid is being throttled through the expansion valve. Undercooling before the expansion valve reduces flash off after throttle, so lowering quality, and increasing refrigeration effect in the evaporator. (Although this applies to all refrigerants the loss is only taken as *serious* with CO_2 because of its very low liquid specific enthalpy to specific enthalpy of vaporisation ratio). The practical flash off loss is about 20% in terms of refrigeration effect for Freon.

This does not justify the complexity of fitting two expansion valves and an intermediate liquid valve between them.

Critical Temperature

Is that temperature beyond which the gas cannot be liquefied by isothermal compression, *i.e.* as a gas, no amount of compression will liquefy if the temperature remains above the critical temperature for that substance. CO_2 has a low value (31°C) and once the sea temperature (coolant) reached 23°C the critical had been reached (8°C differential) and from this point the efficiency of the CO_2 plant steadily decreases. The critical temperature for most refrigerant vapours is however well above the normal condensing temperatures.

COMPRESSOR

There are four main types: reciprocating, rotary, centrifugal and screw.

Reciprocating compressors are in the majority in marine applications as they are most suited to low specific volume vapours and large pressure differentials, characteristics of all the main refrigerants.

Reciprocating

Almost all modern machines are motor driven, high speed (up to 30 rev/s) single acting types which have adopted many improvements in line with the automobile industry. The only gland seal here is the crankshaft seal where the shaft emerges from the crankcase, such seal being mainly subject to suction pressure (Fig. 7.6).

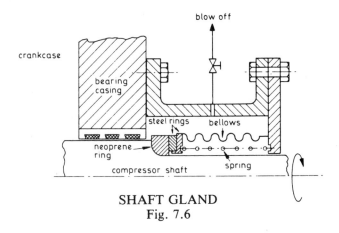

SHAFT GLAND
Fig. 7.6

General

The actual machine itself needs little practical description to the trained engineer as most of the construction is standard reciprocating practice. Multi cylinder in line types are popular but there is an increasing usage of Vee and modified W designs.

Pistons are usually of the trunk type, two or three compression rings and a lower oil seal ring, the suction valve may be located in the head of piston or in the cylinder head, the most modern arrangements have the suction and discharge valves in a valve plate in the cylinder head. Compressor bodies are close grained castings of iron or steel. The crankshaft can be eccentric drive type or more conventional crank and connecting rod, lubrication being either dip and splash or forced, with pump.

Modern valves are of the reed or disc type mounted in the head and are of high grade steel on stainless steel seats with a usual lift of about 2 mm in average sizes. The discharge valve retainer is normally held down to a set position by heavy springs, if oil or liquid is discharged the retainer lifts giving extra valve lift so reducing over pressure, cylinder relief valves and overpressure cut outs are also standard practice fittings.

With valve in piston head types the piston is often long and cut away at the side to the centre so that suction vapour enters here and there is no connection through to the crankcase, which reduces oil pumping effects. Screw type service valves are double seated, full open or full shut, which allows easy gland packing changes. All reciprocating compressors should have the minimum reasonable piston clearance, 1.5 mm as a maximum usually, so as to give maximum efficiency.

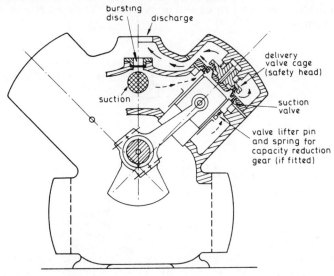

VEEBLOC COMPRESSOR DETAIL
Fig. 7.7

Veebloc

In general there are 4, 6 or 8 cylinders radially round the upper half of the cast iron crankcase with from two to four connecting rods from each of two crank throws (see Fig. 7. 7 for 4-cyinder *V* and Fig. 7.8 for 8-cylinder *W* types).

The aluminium piston is fitted with two compression rings and one scraper ring, piston and gudgeon details are given in Fig. 7.8.

A differential oil pressure switch and overload electrical switch protect the machine from low oil or high vapour pressure. In addition the discharge valve cage is spring-loaded to lift in case of liquid carry-over and there is an over-pressure nickel bursting disc to relieve excess discharge pressure to the suction side of the machine. Connecting rods are aluminium with steel-backed, white metal bearings, the crankshaft is *SG* iron.

Provision is made for reducing the capacity of the machine either manually or automatically. Capacity reduction gear lifts and holds open the alloy steel suction valves of a specified number of cylinders, this is operated by oil pressure on a servo piston in the automatic type. This can also provide total or partial un-loading for easier starting.

The lubrication should be clear from Fig. 7.8. Oil is supplied by a rotor type of pump in which the inner rotor has one less tooth than the outer rotor and oil is induced to flow between the two rotors.

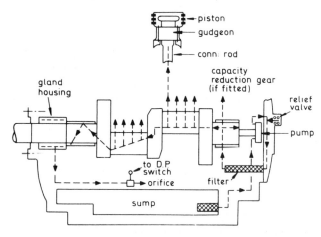

W TYPE COMPRESSOR LUBRICATION
Fig. 7.8

An eight-cylinder machine of 178 mm bore and 140 mm stroke running at about 12.5 rev/s would require a drive of about 90 kW for a refrigerating capacity of about 320 kJ/s with Freon 12 refrigerant.

For low suction temperature operation (say −20°C or lower) and high temperature of discharge (say 30°C or higher) excessive temperatures may be reached in the reciprocating compressor. This is even more liable to occur in the unloaded state than in the loaded state. It is most often found in the fast running smaller bore-stroke size of compressor. In certain cases an oil cooler—operation direct expansion, thermostatic—must be used particularly when automatic unloading is required, and the above conditions apply. Compound compression units must be provided or special change over valves can be fitted so that an 8-cylinder unit will operate in a single-stage down to −20°C and for temperatures below this 6 cylinders can perform the initial compression and the remaining two cylinders perform the final compression.

For suction pressures below atmospheric (with say Freon 12) the risk of air leakage is an important consideration.

Crankcase oil heaters are usually fitted for use with the machine stopped, this prevents formation of liquid refrigerant and oil frothing on starting. Auto compressors should be fitted with solenoid operated liquid stop valves (see magnetic liquid stop valve, Fig. 7.15 later).

Rotary

These types are usually of the form shown in Fig. 7.9.

At the position shown the discharge and suction strokes are half completed, 270°C. At 0° discharging at compression stroke, induction at suction stroke. At 90° start of compression and end of suction. At 180° compression taking place and the suction stroke has just started. Thus the leading flank of the rotor acts as the discharger and the lagging flank acts as the inductor.

Such compressors mainly find application in household and domestic units but modern practice is extending their use to cargo purposes.

A variation on the above is a multiblade type whereby the eccentric rotor contains spring loaded blades (or relies on centrifugal force). When any rotary compressor is not in use the oil film between eccentric rotor and cylinder is broken which

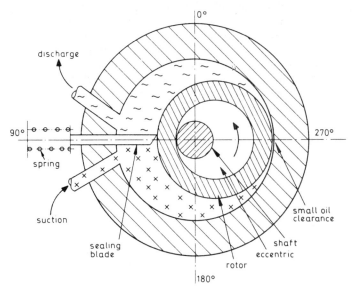

ROTARY COMPRESSOR
Fig. 7.9

means pressure equalisation and easy starting but requires the fitting of a non return valve in the suction line. To reduce sizes these machines are direct drive from the motor.

Centrifugal

These machines work on a similar principle to the centrifugal pump whereby discharge velocity energy is converted to pressure head. For high pressure differentials, as normally exist, a series of impellers are required on a fast running rotor, each impeller feeding to the next in series to build up pressure. These machines are best suited to low differential pressure, high volume capacity work such as air conditioning. Capacity reduction is effected by directional blades at the rotor inlet port. Efficiency is increased if interstage flash vapour formed during liquid expansion is returned to an appropriate stage of the compressor.

Screw

These compressors can be visualised as a development of the gear pump. A male rotor with say four lobes on the shaft, meshes with a female rotor of say six lobes on a parallel shaft. Clearance between lobe screws and casing is kept to a minimum with sealing strips and oil film. As the space between two adjacent lobes of the female rotor passes the inlet port at one end of the compressor a volume of gas is drawn in. With rotation, a lobe of the male rotor progressively fills this space so compressing the vapour and, due to the helical screws, forces it axially to the outlet port at the other end. To reduce capacity sliding sleeves around the barrel can be moved axially to bring the outlet port nearer to the inlet port.

Lubricant

The first essential for such an oil is that it should have a low pour point, *i.e.* must remain fluid with good lubrication properties at low temperatures. Oils which are miscible with the refrigerant can be carried round the circuit and could congeal on the evaporator coils so drastically reducing heat transfer rates. The oil should be free from moisture under all conditions to prevent plant corrosion and freezing at the expansion valve. The viscosity should not be seriously affected at low temperature.

Typical analysis:
Density 900 kg/m³
Flashpoint 235°C
Viscosity 12cSt at 50°C
Pour point—42°C.

A pure mineral oil is advised (Arctic, Seal oil, etc.). The above is suitable for reciprocating compressors.

Compressors should not be run too hot otherwise there is a danger of oil vaporisation and subsequent ignition by the heat of compression.

HEAT EXCHANGERS

Condensers

Condensers used in water cooled marine plants are virtually all of the shell and tube type. The shell is welded construction of mild steel with vapour inlet, purge, drain and liquid outlet connections, on the main body. The vapour condenses on the outside of the tubes and falls to the lower part of the condenser which commonly acts as the liquid receiver. The water flow is multi pass (usually 2, 4 or 8 flow types so keeping inlet and outlet branches at one end) through cast iron end covers. Tube plates are ferrous, of welded mild steel, with steel tubes expanded into place, or non ferrous, of muntz metal with aluminium brass expanded tubes. Galvanic protection blocks (zinc or iron) should be provided and steel tube plates are best treated with chromium for corrosion resistance.

Temperature differences are not high and the little expansion can be taken up by metal resilience. (It should be noted that non ferrous metals are attacked by ammonia refrigerant, this will mean all jointing of lead or soft iron and use of steel tubing.) Air cooled condensers are only used for small domestic units; they usually have finned tubes and air circulation may be fan assisted.

Evaporators

Modern evaporator grid types are only used on small plants and the distance between supply and return headers is very short so giving quick maximum extraction of vapour formed.

Large evaporators are invariably of the shell and tube type almost identical to condensers in design and construction. Brine circulates through the tubes in multi-pass flow and the vapour-liquid mixture enters at the bottom at one end. The evaporated vapour leaves at the top of the other end so that speedy vapour extraction, full heat flow and full evaporation are achieved.

Heat Transfer (Fluids)

The two examples following serve to revise basic theory:

1. A liquid refrigerant evaporates at 3°C and cools water from 11.5 to 6.4°C in a heat exchanger of cooling surface area 360 m² for which the overall heat transfer coefficient is 100 W/m²K. Evaluate the log mean temperature difference and heat transfer rate.

$$\theta = \frac{(11.5 - 3.0) - (6.4 - 3.0)}{\ln(8.5 - 3.4)} = 5.566 \text{ K}$$

$$Q = 100 \times 5.566 \times 360 = 200376 \text{ W}$$

2. Calculate the effectiveness of a heat exchanger which cools air from 25 to 15°C with refrigerant evaporating at 5°C.

$$\eta = \frac{25 - 10}{25 - 5} \times 100 = 75\%$$

Liquid Level Control

Hand operated expansion valves have the disadvantage that they require fairly regular manual adjustments. The float type of

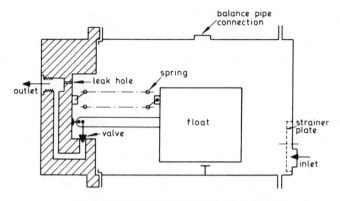

HIGH PRESSURE FLOAT VALVE
Fig. 7.10

valve automatically maintains a controlled liquid level. A diagrammatic part sectional view of such a valve is as shown in Fig. 7.10.

There are two types of float valves fitted, high pressure and low pressure.

The high pressure type as sketched is the more usual and is fitted with the float operating in *hp* liquid after the condenser, with the object of draining the condenser or liquid receiver of liquid to the float level and feeding the liquid to the evaporator. The level is adjustable by altering the spring tension and to prevent gas locking an equalising or balance pipe is usually led to the condenser top.

The low pressure type is to maintain a constant level of liquid in the evaporator. The valve is located with the float operating in *lp* liquid in the evaporator or in a separate float chamber connected to the evaporator by balance pipes. As the liquid evaporates and is drawn off the liquid level falls and more liquid flows in to take its place.

Control by capillary tube is sometimes applied in small hermetically sealed units. The small bore capillary tube, between the cooling unit and receiver, controls the point of pressure drop between the high and low pressure sides by its length. The system is strictly tied to refrigerant quantity and capillary tube bore and length. Thus once fixed for a set loading this cannot be changed without altering the capillary tube, these limitations reduce its application.

Small domestic units are usually of the direct expansion type where the refrigerant coil is in the cold room. Such types work on constant pressure or constant superheat expansion valve control and are described later in detail.

DIRECT EXPANSION UNITS

The control automation required is (1) start, (2) stop, (3) expansion valve, (4) emergency cut out, (5) cooling air or water circulation, (6) oil separation, (7) liquid in suction line, etc. Obviously this is closely related to electrical control. A few of the components have been simplified and are presented here:

Referring to Fig. 7.11:

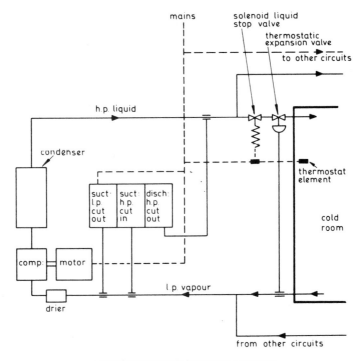

DIRECT EXPANSION UNIT
Fig. 7.11

The compressor is started and stopped by a thermal element pressure switch. An emergency pressure cut out is provided and the expansion valve is of the thermostatic control type. The function of the solenoid liquid stop valve is to isolate different circuits and to shut just before the machine cuts out so that the compressor clears the suction line before it stops. This prevents liquid knock when restarting.

When there are a number of circuits, meat, fish, veg. rooms, ice tanks, ready use chambers, etc., each circuit is a tapping off the main line.

Each circuit has its own thermostatic expansion valve and solenoid stop valve. When one chamber is cooled the thermostat shuts the liquid stop valve and cuts out that chamber only. This happens progressively to all circuits and when all circuits are cut out the rapid drop in suction pressure will cut out the compressor.

Electrical Control Switch (Fig. 7.12)

The capillary tubes are usually filled with a volatile liquid (or the refrigerant itself) so that temperature variations cause

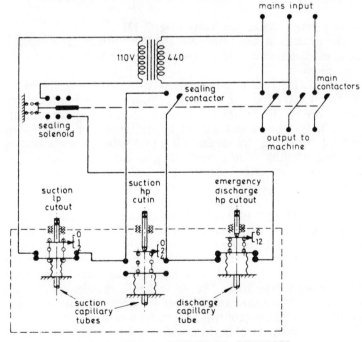

ELECTRICAL CONTROL SWITCH
Fig. 7.12

pressure variations on the flexible metallic bellows. The motion of the bellows operates the trip switches. As the temperature of the suction line *increases*, the bellows pressure *increases* against the spring compression upwards and *closes* the selector switch (*hp* cut in at centre) at say 2 bar, so cutting in the motor. With the compressor running the suction temperature *falls* and hence the bellows pressure *falls*. This action against a tensile spring will eventually *open* the other selector switch (*lp* cut out at left) at say 1 bar so cutting out the motor and compressor. The differential between these two is set for reasonable running.

The emergency *hp* cut out, to operate if cooling failure and pressure build up occurs, works to *open* the switch as for cut out action.

The sealing contactor maintains the electrical circuit when the *hp* suction cut in opens with the machine running.

For manual operation push buttons (start and stop) would replace the two suction bellows.

Electrical protection is by thermal trips operating the main contactors, these have an inherent time delay during heating.

Thermostatic Expansion Valve (Fig. 7.13)

The expansion valve shown is the thermostatic type which is designed usually to give a vapour just superheated leaving the cold room.

Considering Fig. 7.13 in relation to forces: *Down* forces are *hp* liquid valve force, adjustable compression spring force and power bellows force. *Up* forces are evaporator vapour pressure upon body bellows and tension spring force. For given spring settings the spring forces and *hp* liquid valve forces balancing gives equilibrium, then force tending to *close* valve depends on evaporator saturation temperature and force to *open* valve depends on temperature of bulb at location, *i.e.* valve operation is controlled by difference of these two temperatures, *i.e.* superheat. Degree of suction superheat is controlled by the adjusting nut and is usually set at about 5°C. If the room temperature tends to *rise* the superheat *increases*, bellows down force from capillary tube *increases* and the valve *opens* to increase flow of liquid refrigerant until the temperature equilibrium is restored. The valve has a certain equilibrium setting at one pressure and another setting at another pressure, *i.e.* the valve has no control over suction pressure.

The pressure control type expansion valve works to maintain a fixed evaporator coil pressure. This type is similar to the lower part of the valve sketched but is more simple. It consists of the

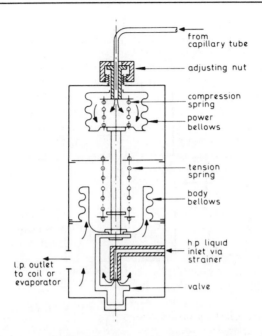

THERMOSTATIC BELLOWS TYPE EXPANSION VALVE
Fig 7.13

liquid valve and body bellows, the body bellows being loaded by an adjustable compression spring. *Up* forces on the bellows (evaporator pressure) balances *hp* liquid valve force *down* for a given setting. Evaporator pressure reduction *opens* valve, pressure increase *closes* valve, and when compressor stops the rising pressure causes closure.

Automatic Water Valve (Fig. 7.14)

When the condenser temperature builds up the capillary bellows pressure increases and the valve opens to permit circulation. This device operates almost immediately after compressor cut in and serves to reduce water usage. The device can easily be modified to operate a starter for fan air circulation.

Magnetic Liquid Stop Valve (Fig. 7.15)

When current flows in the motor circuit the solenoid attracts up the valve and holds it open provided the room thermostat allows the solenoid current to flow, *i.e.* high temperature. When the room cools the current fails and the valve shuts and due to a

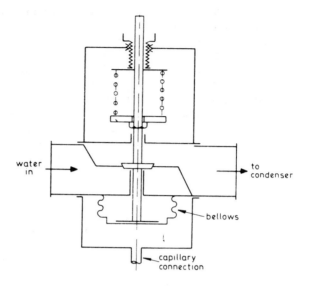

AUTOMATIC WATER VALVE
Fig 7.14

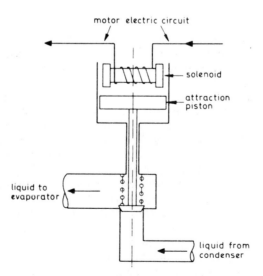

MAGNETIC LIQUID STOP VALVE
Fig. 7.15

time delay the compressor will pump out the room coil and so avoid liquid knock on restarting.

In multiple circuits this valve serves to cut out or cut in the particular chamber to which it is thermostatically connected. Each room has its own stop valve (thermo-electric) and thermal expansion valve as well as a hand isolating valve. The various circuits will cut out *in sequence* as the temperatures fall and the coolest chamber closure will then serve to stop the machine.

The thermostat switch is simply an electrical contact, working with a spring action against the bellows pressure caused by the room temperature and employing a certain temperature differential.

Sight glasses for liquid observation are commonly fitted at various points in the domesic type systems.

Automatic Oil Separator

The oil is retained in the separator until the oil level rises and unbalances a float causing the vapour pressure to blow the oil back to the compressor.

The float is dead loaded so that a considerable blow back is possible before the valve reseats, to avoid fluctuating action.

ABSORPTION TYPE REFRIGERATOR UNIT

This device has no moving parts and is continuous in operation when provided with a heat source, such as a town gas burner or electric element. The total pressure, which is the sum of the partial pressures, is constant through the system. Consider Fig. 7.16:

1. Hydrogen vapour, which is insoluble in water, leaves the absorber and rises until it meets ammonia liquid falling into the entry to the evaporator. Due to the hydrogen pressure causing a lowering of the ammonia pressure (two media exerting the same pressure as previously exerted by only one) this assists in vaporisation of the ammonia. Ammonia and hydrogen vapour are carried down to the absorber where water absorbs and dissolves the ammonia and the hydrogen vapour re-cycles.

2. Ammonia vapour, which is highly soluble in water, rises with the water vapour from the generator to the separator where the water vapour and some ammonia vapour condenses. Ammonia vapour then rises, is liquefied in the condenser, reduced in pressure and vaporised in the evaporator, and falls to be absorbed in the absorber. Ammonia, dissolved in water, falls down into the lower pipe to the generator.

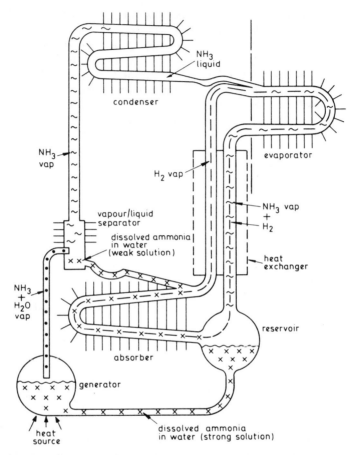

ABSORPTION TYPE REFRIGERATION UNIT
Fig. 7.16

3. Water vapour leaves the generator, is condensed in the separator, falls through the absorber dissolving the ammonia vapour, and returns to the generator.

The unit requires no compressors, or pumps, and is silent and vibrationless. It is fairly often used in domestic units on shore, but rarely on board ship, as correct and steady level is critical for correct working.

Condenser, evaporator and vapour liquid separator, are air-cooled, with fins welded or brazed on to the piping to give extended surface heat transfer.

In many designs the hydrogen vapour rises up through the absorber to the *underside* of the evaporator. It then passes up through the evaporator and carries ammonia vapour down to the reservoir where ammonia and hydrogen separate out, ammonia condensing and hydrogen rising through the absorber.

The precise method adopted depends on the dimensions of the equipment and the thermodynamics and flow pattern of the media in the unit.

BRINE CIRCUITS

Properties of Brine

It is an advantage if the coolant coil through the cold chamber contains a fluid which is virtually non harmful to the contents of the space in the event of leakage.

Small domestic units circulate the coil with the refrigerant (direct expansion) but larger cargo units usually employ an evaporator and a loop of circulation through the evaporator to the cold chambers and back which contains brine. A big advantage is that the brine pipes have a much larger reserve of cold than refrigerant coils when the plant is stopped, also having the advantage that various circuits can easily be arranged, *e.g.* cooling, chilling, defrosting, etc.

The brine as used is a mixture of distilled water (preferably) and calcium chloride ($CaCl_2$). The colder the brine circuit the more dense the brine in circulation has to be to avoid any freeze up. Table 7.3 gives the densities and corresponding freezing points.

Under certain conditions sodium chloride ($NaCl$) could be used with water but an alkali such as caustic soda ($NaOH$) would be required as an addition as about 1% of the solution. The brine should be maintained in an alkaline state under all conditions, this can easily be checked by the use of litmus paper, phenolphthalein, etc. Brine density should also be taken regularly by standard hydrometer test at 15.5°C and a regular check should also be taken for brine leakage at the brine header tank which serves to keep a head on the system.

There is a possibility that the air content of brine rooms could become explosive or inflammable under conditions of hydrogen gas liberation due to corrosive action, it is advisable not to allow naked lights.

The brine circuit consists of a brine room, containing distribution headers, mixing tanks, evaporators, pumps, etc., then the various piping systems to cold storage spaces

FREEZING POINT(°C)	DENSITY AT 15.5°C (kg/m³)
− 3	1050
− 7	1100
−13	1150
−21	1200
−32	1250
−46	1290

TABLE 7.3

maintained under pressure. The piping is usually tested to 7 bar, or $2.5 \times W.P.$, whichever is the greater, pipes commonly of mild steel externally galvanised and painted, about 40 mm bore.

It is usual to regulate the flow of brine by the return valves on the distribution and return headers.

For chilling chambers about 3m³ of chamber would require about 1 m² of pipe cooling surface, increased to 4.5 m³ if air circulated. For freezing chambers the ratio is about 1.5 m³/m² (2.2 m³/m² air circulated).

Normally 1250 kg/m³ density would be satisfactory for most brine circulation with a *pH* value of 8.5.

Non-freezing solutions can also be based on organic fluids; ethylene and propylene glycol are in general use.

Battery System

This system is to blow air across a brine or direct expansion grid and circulate the storage space. It is well suited to higher temperature storage, *e.g.*, shellac, as there is no dripping from overhead grids on to the cargo. Also this system gives some control over the humidity as moisture will be deposited on the cooling coil. The supply of air circulation to any storage room will reduce the brine cooling surface required by as much as 50%. Direct expansion grids employ only about 40% of brine cooled grid pipe surface but do not have the same large reserve of cold.

Ice Making

The ice tank is usually wrought iron and contains lead coated sheet steel ice moulds.

The moulds are immersed in a brine bath and a cooling coil, brine or refrigerant, lowers the bath temperature until the water in the moulds is converted to ice. The tank is insulated and coil supply and return valves are fitted.

A direct expansion coil would be approximately 120 m² of surface area per kg of ice per second.

Hold Ventilation Control

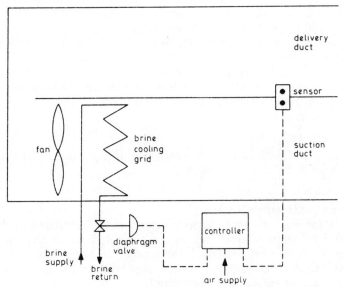

delivery
duct

sensor

fan

brine
cooling
grid

suction
duct

diaphragm
valve

controller

brine
supply

brine
return

air supply

HOLD VENTILATION TEMPERATURE CONTROL
Fig. 7.17

Shown in Fig. 7.17 is a method of air delivery temperature control very suitable for fruit cargoes. The sensor bulb is situated in a bypass pocket in the air trunk and senses air delivery temperature whether fans operate normally or reversed.

The diaphragm operated control valve can be supplied as direct acting (fail in the open position) or reverse acting (fail in the shut position).

For fruit cargo where frost damage could occur, reverse acting valves which would fail in the shut position on air failure are used.

For chilled meat cargo where failure would mean a long period of time would pass before the temperatures could be again reduced to the correct value, direct acting valves are preferred.

Refrigerated containers may each have their own refrigerator or the containers may be connected to the ships' ducts.

BASIC PRINCIPLES OF AIR CONDITIONING

Air conditioning is the control of humidity, temperature, cleanliness and air motion. Winter conditioning relates to increasing temperature and humidity whilst summer conditioning relates to decreasing temperature and humidity. Basically the practical difference is dependent upon whether the air fluid is passed over a hot grid (steam) or cold grid (brine or direct expansion refrigerant). Water can be used instead of brine.

Comfort cooling for accommodation will only briefly be described although the field covers in addition much industrial usage as well as heating applications in both cases.

Specific Humidity

Is the ratio of the mass of water vapour to the mass of dry air in a given volume of mixture.

Per Cent Relative Humidity

Is the mass of water vapour per m³ of air compared to the mass of water vapour per m³ of saturated air at the same temperature. This also equals the ratio of the partial pressure of the actual air compared to the partial pressure of the air if it was saturated at the same temperature *i.e.*

$$\frac{m}{m_g} = \frac{p}{p_g}$$

Partial Pressures, Dalton's Laws

Barometer pressure = partial pressure $N_2 + p.p.$ $O_2 + p.p.$ H_2O, from Dalton's Laws, viz:

1. Pressure exerted by, and the quantity of, the vapour required to saturate a given space (*i.e.* exist as saturated steam) at any given temperature, are the same whether that space is filled by a gas or is a vacuum.
2. The pressure exerted by a mixture of a gas and a vapour, of two vapours, or of two gases, or a number of same, is the sum of the pressure which each would exert if it occupied the same space alone, assuming no interaction of constituents.

Dew Point

When a mixture of dry air and water vapour has a saturation temperature corresponding to the partial pressure of the water vapour it is said to be saturated. Any further reduction of temperature (at constant pressure) will result in some vapour condensing. This temperature is called the dew point, air at dew point contains all the moisture it can hold at that temperature, as the amount of water vapour varies in air then the partial pressure varies, so the dew point varies.

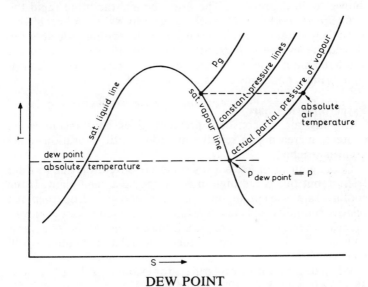

DEW POINT
Fig. 7.18

It can be seen from Fig. 7.18 that cooling at constant pressure brings the low pressure superheated vapour to the dew point after which condensation occurs. It can also be noted that cooling at constant temperature increases the partial pressure until the saturation point is reached thus relative humidity can be found.

$$\% \text{ R.H.} = \frac{m}{m_g} \times 100 = \frac{p}{p_g} \times 100.$$

$$= \frac{p \text{ dew point}}{p_g} \times 100.$$

where *g* refers to the saturation condition. This means dry air contains maximum moisture content (100% *R.H.*) at the saturation condition.

Dry Bulb and Wet Bulb Temperatures

The hygrometer (or psychrometer) consists of an ordinary thermometer which gives the dry bulb temperature and a wet bulb thermometer (wetted gauze cover). The wet bulb reading will be less than the dry bulb reading, the difference is quoted as the wet bulb depression. The drier the air, the more rapid the moisture evaporation from the gauze giving a cooling effect. Thus the greater the difference between the readings the drier the air and the less the % *R.H.* Still air thermometers are inaccurate and hand sling types to secure air motion across the wick until equilibrium conditions exists are preferred.

Psychrometric Chart

Cooling air at constant pressure gives constant moisture content, increasing in relative humidity until saturation (dew) point is reached.

Cooling air in practice gives some pressure drop due to fluid friction but this is not high in a correctly designed plant. If the cooling rate is kept in line with the pressure drop then the relative humidity will stay constant, if the cooling rate is slower the relative humidity will reduce, if the cooling rate is faster (as it will be usually in practice) then the relative humidity will increase.

When dealing with air mixtures, for example, *Z* 17 m³ of air at 35°C *D.B.* and *R.H.* 40% mixed with *X* 83 m³ of air at 27°C *D.B.* and *R.H.* 50%, set off on Fig. 7.19 and proportion *XZ* off so that:

$$\frac{XY}{XZ} = \frac{\text{mass of 17 m}^3}{\text{mass of 83 m}^3}$$

the masses being found from specific volumes (ignoring small water mass) then *Y* is condition of 100 m³ of mixture. (100 m³ 28°C *D.B. R.H.* 48%).

Points *X*, *Y* and *Z* on Fig. 7.19 as shown are merely illustrative. The chart is drawn for a pressure of 1 bar but is sensibly accurate between 0.9 and 1.1 bar.

From wet and dry bulb readings the various properties of the air-vapour mixture can be estimated. Enthalpy is a function of

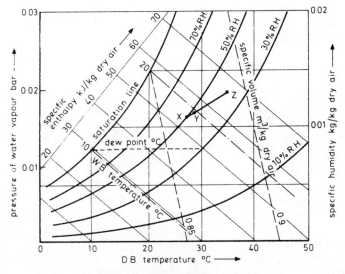

PSYCHROMETRIC CHART
Fig. 7.19

the wet bulb temperature, and moisture content and vapour pressure are functions of dew point. The chart gives a quick performance check on the air entering and leaving the cooling coil, dew point, temperature, humidity, enthalpy, etc.

Comfort under summer conditions is dependent on dry and wet bulb readings and relative humidity as well as air motion. For a given degree of air turbulence (75 mm/s to 127 mm/s), relative humidity between 30% and 70%, average 50%, and thermometer readings 19°C to 25°C, average 22°C, gives the best degree of summer comfort. Air at low temperature and high humidity can be as comfortable as air at high temperature and low humidity.

A differential of about 7°C between inside and outside conditions is usually aimed at but this is variable with the outside conditions, as a coil can extract large amounts of heat from warm dry air, so reducing temperature appreciably, or large amounts of moisture from humid air with little temperature reduction.

Air Conditioning Circuit

A typical circuit is as illustrated in Fig. 7.20.

The average temperature differential is about 11°C between fan discharge and room temperature. The amount of air

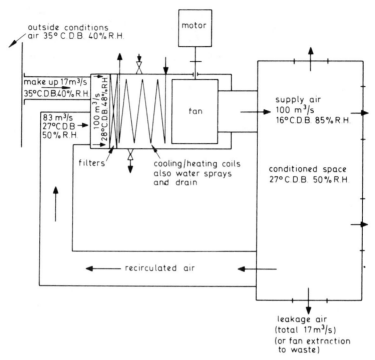

AIR CONDITIONING CIRCUIT
Fig. 7.20

recirculated depends on the installation, space conditions (smoking, etc.), degree of air motion (draughts, etc.) and so number of air changes per day is a balance of quantity and temperature. Thus temperature, humidity and air motion are interrelated and the designer must correlate correctly. About 0.1 m³/m² floor space (accommodation) to 1.33m³/m² floor space (kitchens) may be regarded as typical maximums, air motion about 100 mm/s.

The air conditioning unit (compressor, evaporator, condenser, etc.) will usually be independent from the rest of the refrigerating plant, although located often in the same space. The brine supply will be distributed to the cooling grids incorporated in a unit. The number of units would depend on the number of accommodation circuits necessary, say at least one unit per accommodation deck. Size of the plant would depend on the type of vessel.

Each unit would exist in a similar circuit to that shown in Fig. 7.20. Leakage air must be cut to a minimum by closure of ports and doors. Air circulation would be through the normal louvre system to the various spaces, when heating is required the air would bypass the shut down cooling grid and be passed over heating elements, in this case a controlled water spray controls humidity before leaving the unit.

The temperature and humidity are controlled at the grid, drainage condensation being led away from the unit. Air motion will be determined by the initial design of the fans, ducts and louvres. The flow is usually by centrifugal or propeller type fans and the humidistat or thermostat controller is situated at the unit together with fan controls. Cleanliness and purity depend on the filters. In marine practice viscous type filters are used in which the filter medium (glass wool, fibre, compressed cardboard) is inserted between metal grids (about 50 mm apart) and the assembly mounted as a removable case. The cartridge is immersed in an odourless oil and then dried. Such filters are usually arranged to be cleaned by steam, alkalis, etc.

Other types are available which are in cardboard cases and are destroyed when dirty but they have little marine usage as yet. Similarly dry filters (paper compressed screens) and electric precipitator types are available but also have no great application in marine services as yet.

Simple Heat Pump Circuit

The circuit, in conventional diagrammatic form, as shown in Fig. 7.21 should be clear. It is arranged for warming the accommodation in winter.

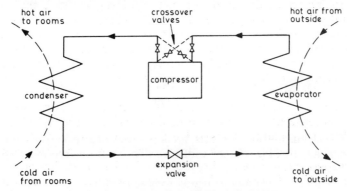

SIMPLE HEAT PUMP CIRCUIT
Fig. 7.21

By reversing the direction of flow, by means of the cross-over valves, the heat pump can cool the accommodation in summer. Coefficient of performance averages about 5.

Dehumidifier (Fig. 7.22)

Moisture is removed from the humid air by passing the air through a fluted rotating drum of asbestos type material surface impregnated with water absorbing salts. A separate stream of heated air passes through the drum over a 1.6 radius sector in the opposite direction to continuously remove the moisture deposited on the salts. The drum is mounted on two rollers covered with a high frictional coefficient material. A motor drive to the rollers causes rotation of the drum in the two air streams.

Heat input of 6.7 W would remove 21.4×10^{-3} kg/s of moisture from humid air at 27°C and 60% *R.H.* and flow rate of 0.77 m³/s.

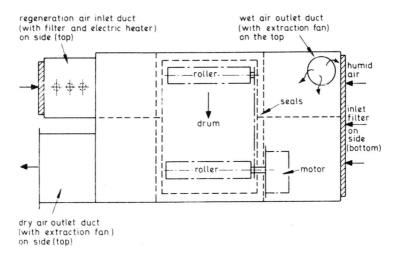

regeneration air inlet duct
(with filter and electric heater)
on side (top)

wet air outlet duct
(with extraction fan)
on the top

dry air outlet duct
(with extraction fan)
on side (top)

DEHUMIDIFIER (DIAGRAMMATIC PLAN VIEW)
Fig. 7.22

The dehumidifier prevents moisture damage to cargo from direct moisture deposit or moisture deposited on internal ship surfaces.

One unit is normally provided for each hold and an electrical control and recording panel is provided on the unit as well as at a centralised station.

The fan units would normally each provide about 70 air changes in one day for the full hold volume and damper units are arranged to give re-circulation or ventilation with outside air.

Two recorders are normally utilised per unit, one recorder with sensors for ship skin moisture *i.e.* weather temperature, weather dew point, sea water temperature and hold dew point and the other for cargo moisture with sensors for weather dew point, cargo temperature and hold dew point. Cargo storage temperatures are given at the end of this chapter (Table 7.5). Fruit and vegetables are mainly stored at high humidity (90—95) but meats generally must be in drier air and modern deep freezing is at lower temperatures ($-18°C$). The atmosphere needs to be monitored, for such as oxygen and carbon dioxide, and controlled.

INSULATION

Shipside insulation is as shown in Fig. 7.23 and Fig. 7.29. An alternative space saving method is to put the granulated cork in the air space so moving the vertical tongued and grooved board with zinc sheathing right up to the insulating paper.

Tank top insulation is as shown although in some cases the lower battens and bottom tongued and grooved board can be omitted. In the case where the insulation extends right across a bilge, with a tank margin plate form of construction, access doors must be provided as shown.

Deckhead insulation is virtually the same as side shell or bulkhead insulation, the fastenings being to the deck beams.

All insulation should be rat and vermin proofed and vapour proofing is also required. Air flow through walls will reach dew point and moisture will form which destroys the insulating value and rots the material. Vapour proof papers are commonly used, and all joints and concrete plaster over wire mesh covers should be coated with odourless asphalt (bitumen), tar or oakum.

Hatch covers, inspection doors etc., are of heavy construction usually of the wedge type, the taper being lined with felt or having ball rubber joint inserts.

Brine rooms etc., are usually concreted on wire mesh on the inside to give a smooth clean appearance. Piping to and from the compressor to the brine or evaporator room should also be effectively insulated. Silicate cotton also sawdust are packed 192 kg/m³ and granulated cork about 128 kg/m³. Plastics which flow easily and form firm hygienic mouldings are now in more general insulation use. Fibre glass and cork slabs are also used. See Table 7.4.

Cargo containment-piping systems for LNG and LPG utilise aluminium-stainless steel with membrane double skin tank construction and perlite insulation (boxed) — alternative polyurethane foam inside and-or outside. Cascade reliquification plants are usually provided.

INSULATING MATERIAL	THERMAL CONDUCTIVITY W/mK AVERAGE VALUES
Polyurethane Foam	0.026
Expanded Polystyrene	0.034
Corkboard	0.043
Fibreglass	0.043
Rockwool	0.036
Kapok	0.035
Ground Cork	0.043
Celotex	0.052
Building Brick	0.346—0.692
Concrete	0.737—1.373

TABLE 7.4

PRODUCT	APPROX: STORAGE TEMPERATURE °C
Chilled Beef	2
Frozen Beef	-4
Chilled Mutton	2
Frozen Mutton	-6
Poultry	-8
Fish	-7
Milk	0
Butter	-11
Cheese	1
Eggs	-1
Chocolate	2
Wines	7
Beer	1
Vegetables	2
Apples and Pears	1
Peaches and Oranges	7

TABLE 7.5

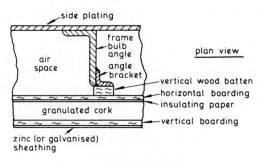

plan view

shipside insulation

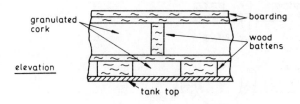

elevation

tank top insulation

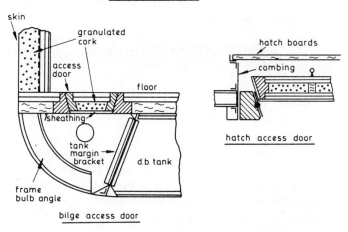

bilge access door

hatch access door

INSULATION DETAILS (1)
Fig. 7.23

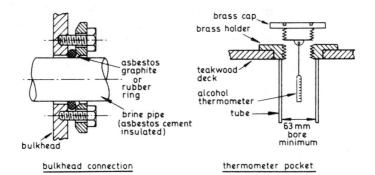

bulkhead connection thermometer pocket

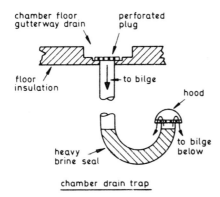

chamber drain trap

INSULATION DETAILS (2)
Fig. 7.24

Heat Transfer (Insulation)

The two examples following serve to revise basic theory:

1. A brick wall, 0.225 m thick with a thermal conductivity of 0.6 W/mK, measures 5 m long and 3 m high, and has a temperature difference of 25 K between inside and outside faces. What is the heat conduction rate?

$$Q = \frac{0.6 \times 5 \times 3 \times 25}{0.225} = 1,000W$$

2. A brick wall 0.24 m thick has a concrete surface facing 0.015 m thick. Thermal conductivities are 0.6 and 1.5

W/mK respectively; surface heat transfer coefficients, inside and out, are 3.333 and 20 W/m²K respectively. Evaluate the overall heat transfer coefficient needed to estimate the heat conduction rate through the wall.

$$R_t = R_i + R_c + R_b + R_o$$

$$\frac{1}{U} = \frac{1}{h_i} + \frac{x_c}{k_c} + \frac{x_b}{k_b} + \frac{1}{h_o}$$

$$= \frac{1}{3.333} + \frac{0.015}{1.5} + \frac{0.24}{0.6} + \frac{1}{20}$$

$$= 0.76$$

$$U = 1.316 \text{ W/m}^2\text{K}$$

TEST EXAMPLES 7

Class 3

1. Sketch a simple refrigerant cycle of the compression type and on the sketch show a position in the cycle where you would expect the refrigerant to be:
   (a)   a liquid,
   (b)   a gas.
2. Describe the basic refrigerant circuit for a compression type plant. What kind of gas is commonly used in this type of plant?
3. State the reasons why Freon 12 is a popular refrigerant gas.
4. Explain why the refrigerant gas in a compression type domestic refrigeration plant is passed through a condenser after being compressed.

TEST EXAMPLES 7

Class 2

1. (a)   Draw a line diagram of a refrigeration system for servicing a large number of insulated containers labelling the principal items and showing the direction of flow in all lines and ducts.

   (b)   Explain how the system works in order to maintain containers at different temperatures.

2. Suggest, with reasons, the most likely cause of the trouble if the suction to a multicylinder refrigerant compressor is subject to considerable icing under the following simultaneously prevailing conditions:

   (a)   compressor in good condition and running at normal speed,

   (b)   throttling regulator valve open more than usual,

   (c)   no detectable loss of refrigerant,

   (d)   brine temperature rising,

3. With reference to refrigeration plants state how:

   (a)   very low evaporator temperatures are achieved,

   (b)   automatic expansion valves in direct expansion plants are adjusted,

   (c)   compressors are protected against appreciable 'carry over' of liquid refrigerant,

   (d)   air in the system is detected,

   (e)   over charge of refrigerant is indicated.

4. Briefly describe how in main refrigeration plants:

   (a)   sea temperature can restrict plant operation,

   (b)   the limitations in (a) are overcome,

   (c)   short cycling occurs,

   (d)   short cycling is avoided.

TEST EXAMPLES 7

Class 1

1. (i)   Draw a line diagram of an accommodation air conditioning plant, labelling the principal components and showing the direction of air flows in all ducts.
   (ii)   Explain why humidity control is essential for comfort.
   (iii)   State how ambient temperature affects humidity control.
   (iv)   Give a reason why compensation for air losses is necessary and how it is accomplished.

2. (i)   Identify, with reasons, those properties of Freon which makes it such an attractive refrigerant.
   Give reasons why each of the following gases has fallen into disfavour as a refrigerant:
   (ii)   carbon dioxide,
   (iii)   ammonia,
   (iv)   methyl chloride,

3. Give a reasoned opinion as to the validity of the following references to accommodation air conditioning:
   (i)   'rule of thumb' method whereby rate of air change is directly related to cubical capacity of the compartment concerned is quite satisfactory for all practical purposes,
   (ii)   mechanical ventilation with air heating is inadequate for comfort in ships operating within a wide range of ambient air temperature and humidity,
   (iii)   humidity control is absolutely essential for long term comfort of personnel.

4. In refrigeration what is meant by:
   (a)   specific heat capacity,
   (b)   specific enthalpy of evaporation,
   (c)   specific volume,
   (d)   critical temperature,
   Give typical values for each of the above for three refrigerants.

CHAPTER 8

FIRE AND SAFETY

One of the most dangerous hazards that seafarers may encounter on shipboard is that of fire. *Prevention is better than cure*, is a well worn axiom that was never more appropriate.

PRINCIPLE OF FIRE

This may be stated in general terms as the chemical combination of combustible elements or compounds with oxygen, resulting in the liberation of heat.

Materials such as coal, wood, paper and any goods which are manufactured from them contain carbon which is a combustible element. Any of these materials if subjected to heat will ignite, in other words, the carbon will combine readily with the oxygen from the atmosphere because conditions are correct, and heat energy will be liberated.

Oils and vapours given off from the oils are basically hydrocarbon *i.e.* they contain the combustible elements hydrogen and carbon which again, if conditions are correct *i.e.* temperature and pressure, will ignite in the presence of oxygen.

FIRE PREVENTION AND PRECAUTIONS

Cleanliness, vigilance and common sense are the principal weapons with which to prevent fire.

Tank tops should be kept clean and well lighted, it is recommended that tank tops be painted *white* so that any oil leakages from drip trays, pipes, joints, filters and valves may be easily spotted and the leakage dealt with promptly before any dangerous accumulation of oil arises.

Bilges must be kept clean and the pumps and strainers for the bilges maintained in good working order.

All fire fighting appliances must be kept in good working order and tested regularly. Emergency pump and fan stops, collapsible bridge oil valves, watertight doors, etc., should all be tested frequently and kept in good operative order. All fire detection devices should be regularly tested and any faults rectified.

All engine room personnel should be fully conversant with the recognised procedure for dealing with a fire aboard ship and should know the whereabouts and method of operating *all* fire fighting equipment.

When coal is carried, as cargo, the compartment or compartments where it is situated should be well ventilated and the coal should, as far as possible, be stacked in such a way so that it presents as large a surface area as possible to the atmosphere. This will reduce risk of an outbreak of fire due to spontaneous combustion of the coal. Personnel should be thoroughly familiar with the problems associated with any special cargo the vessel may be carrying, *e.g.* LPG, LNG and chemical carriers.

TYPES OF FIRES AND METHODS OF EXTINGUISHING

(1) Oil Fires
The vapours given off from the oil can be ignited, causing a rise in temperature of the oil so that more oil vapour is readily given off from the oil to replace that already burnt. The methods of extinguishing oil fires are as follows:

(a) Sand, used for small oil fires, it serves as a blanket so excluding the atmosphere.

(b) Water spray, this must *completely* cover the surface of the burning oil, the water has a cooling effect that will reduce the rate at which vapour is given off from the oil. The water spray also smothers.

(c) Foam, serves as a blanket to smother the fire.

(d) Dry powder, serves as a blanket to smother the fire.

(e) Inert gas, *e.g.* Carbon dioxide, heavier than air hence it displaces the oxygen bearing atmosphere.

(f) Steam, smothers the fire.

(g) Asbestos blanket, used for smothering small fires.

(2) Coal Fires
The methods by which a coal fire is extinguished are principally by cooling. Hence water is generally used. Soda-acid, carbon dioxide and water portable extinguishers may be used to extinguish small coal fires.

(3) Material Fires

Wood, paper, waste, bedding and other similar materials when burning may be extinguished by cooling, principally with water or, again, soda-acid, carbon dioxide and water. Dry powder portable extinguishers may be used.

(4) Electrical Fires

Electrical equipment may take fire due to overheating of some component or components or some other such cause. If it is possible to interrupt the supply of current to the electrical appliance the fire may then be extinguished by using water. If it is *not* possible to interrupt the supply of current the following may be used to extinguish the fire (a) Dry powder, (b) Inert gas *e.g.* CO_2.

FIRE DETECTION METHODS

Fire Patrols

These are not normally carried out on a regular basis upon most vessels but they should be conducted (1) immediately prior to, or upon sailing. A thorough inspection of the vessel being made especially in hold compartments, stores, engine and boiler rooms, etc. (2) when the vessel has been vacated by shipyard personnel whilst the vessel is in port undergoing repair. Someone may have been using oxy-acetylene burning or welding equipment on one side of a bulkhead totally unaware that the beginnings of a fire were being created on the other side of the bulkhead.

The patrol should, in addition to looking for fire, assess and correct any possible dangerous situation, *e.g.* loose oil or paint drums, incorrectly stored chemicals, etc.

Fire Alarm Circuits

These consist of an alarm panel, situated outside of the machinery spaces, which gives indication of the fire zone. Zone circuits, audible alarms and auxiliary power supply (Fig. 8.1).

Circuits

When the contacts in a detector head close (open under normal conditions) they short the circuit and cause operation of the audible fire alarm. The lines in the circuit are continuously monitored through 1 to 2 and 3 to 4, hence any fault which develops, *e.g.* damaged insulation, break in the cable, causes the system failure alarm to sound.

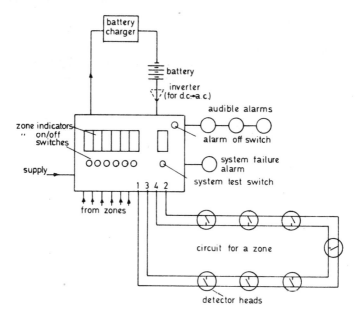

FIRE ALARM CIRCUIT
Fig. 8.1

Power failure

In the event of failure of mains supply power, automatic auxiliary power is supplied from fully charged stand-by batteries for up to 6 hours. Most systems operate on 24V. dc, however, for those operating at mains supply of 220V. ac an inverter converts the 24V. dc to 220V. ac.

Audible Alarms

The fire alarm is usually an intermittent audible signal whereas fault and manual test are normally a continuous audible signal.

Fire Detector Heads

Various types are available for fitting into an alarm circuit, choice is dependent upon fire risk, position, area to be covered, volume and height of compartment, atmosphere in the space, etc. To economise and simplify, standard bases are generally used in the circuit into which different types of detectors can be fitted.

Heat Sensors

These may be fixed temperature detectors, rate of rise detectors or a combination. Rate of rise detectors do not respond and give alarm if the temperature gradually increases, *e.g.* moving into tropical regions or heating switched on.

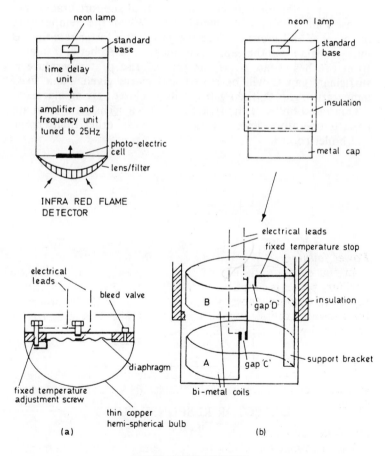

FIRE DETECTORS
Fig. 8.2

Fig. 8.2(a) *Pneumatic Type:*

Increase in temperature increases the air pressure inside the hemi-spherical bulb, if the bleed of air through the two way bleed valve from the inside of the bulb is sufficient the diaphragm will not move up and close the contacts. If however the rate of rise of temperature causes sufficient pressure build up inside the bulb to close the contacts, alarm will be given. In either case a bi-metal unit will at a pre-determined temperature close the contacts on to the fixed temperature adjustment screw, giving alarm.

Fig. 8.2(b) *Bi-metal Coil Type:*

Two bi-metal coils attached to a vertical support bracket are encased in a protective metal cap. When the temperature increases A will move to close the gap C at a faster rate than B moves to maintain the gap, this is due to B being better insulated from the heat than A. If the rate of rise of temperature is sufficient, gap C will be closed and alarm given. At a *fixed* temperature gap D, then gap C will be closed, giving alarm.

Quartzoid bulbs of the type fitted into a sprinkler system are fixed temperature detectors used for spaces other than engine and boiler rooms.

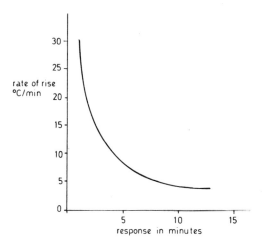

DETECTOR RESPONSE CURVE
Fig. 8.3

Relevant Points

Sensitivity: a typical response curve for a rate of rise detector is shown in Fig. 8.3. The greater the heat release rate from the fire the poorer the ventilation and the more confined the space, the quicker will be the response of the detector and the sooner an alarm sounds.

Fixed temperature setting depends upon whether the detector is in accommodation or machinery spaces and can vary from 55°C to 70°C.

The detector is useful for dusty atmospheres as it is completely sealed but it does not give as early a warning of fire as other types of detectors. It can be tested by a portable electric hot air blower or muff.

Infra Red Flame Detector

Fig. 8.2 also shows in simplified form this type of flame detector. Flame has a characteristic flicker frequency of about 25 Hz and use is made of this fact to trigger an alarm. Flickering radiation from flames reaches the detector lens/filter unit, which only allows infra-red rays to pass and be focused upon the cell. The signal from the cell goes into the selective amplifier, which is tuned to 25 Hz, then into a time delay unit (to minimise incidence of false alarms, fire has to be present for a pre-determined period), trigger and alarm circuits.

Relevant Points

Very early warning of fire is possible, suitable for areas where fire risk is high, *i.e.* machinery spaces—but not in boiler rooms where naked flame torches are to be used for igniting oil. Reflected radiation can be a problem in boiler rooms and from running machinery. Obscuration by smoke renders it inoperative. It can be tested by means of a naked flame.

Photo-electric Cell Smoke Detectors

Three types are in use, those that operate by light scatter, those that operate by light obscuration and a type which combines scatter and obscuration.

Light Scatter Type (Fig. 8.4):

A photo-cell separated by a barrier from a semi-conductor intermittently flashing light source are housed in an enclosure whose containment allows smoke but not light inside. When smoke is present in the container, light is scattered around the barrier on to the photo-cell and an alarm is triggered.

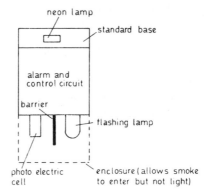

SMOKE DETECTOR. LIGHT SCATTER TYPE
Fig. 8.4

Relevant Points

Smoke may be present without much heat or any flame, hence this detector could give early warning of fire. Photo-cells and light sources are vulnerable to vibration and dirt. Testing can be done with smoke from a cigarette.

The light obscuration type is used in oil mist detectors for diesel engine crank cases and the obscuration/scatter type is to be found in the detecting cabinet of the carbon dioxide flooding system shown in Fig. 8.17.

Standard Bases

The standard bases shown in the figures for the various detector heads have a neon light incorporated which flashes to indicate which detector head has operated. Detector heads can be simply unplugged from the base and tested in a portable test unit which has an adjustable time delay, audible alarm and battery.

Combustion Gas Detector

A circuit diagram of a combustion gas detector is shown in Fig. 8.5. Two ionisation chambers connected in series contain some radioactive material which emits a continuous supply of ionising particles.

The detecting chamber is open, the reference chamber closed and operating at a constant current since it contains air which is being ionised and the applied potential ensures that saturation point is passed. Current strength is dependent upon the applied

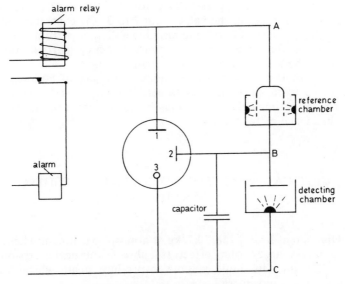

COMBUSTION GAS DETECTOR
Fig. 8.5

potential, since if the potential is low not all the ionised particles reach the electrodes, some will combine with electrons and thus be neutralised.

When the potential reaches a certain value all the ions formed reach the electrodes giving saturation. Beyond this, the current will remain approximately constant irrespective of any further increase in potential. In this way the reference chamber has a constant resistance.

If combustion particles, visible or invisible, pass through the open detecting chamber the current will drop since the combustion products are made of larger and heavier particles than normal gas molecules. When ionised, the particles are less mobile than ionised air particles and because of increased bulk and lack of mobility, can readily combine with particles of opposite charge and hence be neutralised. The effect is to greatly increase the resistance of the detecting chamber, this change in resistance produces a substantial change in the potential at the centre point B.

Normal voltage A to C is 220, A to B 130 Volts, B to C 90 Volts. When voltage shift, due to increasing resistance in the detecting chamber, reaches 110V across BC this is sufficient to trigger a discharge in the valve from 2 to 3, the capacitor then unloads itself across 2 to 3 encouraging a discharge from 1 to 3, by-passing the chambers and causing heavy current flow through the alarm relay and the alarm to sound.

It can be tested by cigarette smoke or the use of butane gas delivered from an aerosol container. It is a very sensitive fire alarm and a time delay circuit may be incorporated to minimise the incidence of false alarms.

CRITICAL ANALYSIS OF FIRE EXTINGUISHING MEDIUMS

Water

High latent heat, 2256.7 kJ/kg at atmospheric pressure hence it has a very large cooling effect. If it absorbs this heat it expands to 1,700 times its liquid volume to produce steam which is a smothering atmosphere.

It is plentiful, non-toxic, safe to use on most fires, can be easily directed over considerable distances.

When used on oil fires all the liquid surface should be covered by the water spray, and surrounding hot metal should be cooled to prevent re-ignition. If water droplets enter the hot oil they will be converted to steam—this rapid expansion from water to steam leads to spluttering and possible spread of the fire. The water droplets should be fine enough (mist or fog) so that they cool by taking heat from the burning vapours, this is especially necessary in the case of oils with low fire points, *e.g.* crude, petrol, etc., direct cooling of these oils is not possible.

Steam

Has a very limited cooling effect, its higher temperature makes the control of smoldering fires somewhat protracted. It is not always available and large quantities are necessary. Steam should not be used in conjunction with carbon dioxide for hold compartments, since to use it after carbon dioxide would be to replace a good fire fighting medium with a relatively poor one. Steam smothering is not recommended.

Foam

Foam, which is used principally for extinguishing oil fires, may be generated chemically or mechanically.

Chemical generation of foam is accomplished by mixing together a solution of sodium bicarbonate and a solution of aluminium sulphate in the presence of a stabiliser (*e.g.* soap or liquorice). The result of the chemical reaction which takes place between these two solutions, is a mass of tough skinned bubbles containing carbon dioxide. An increase in volume also accompanies the reaction, in the proportion of approximately one of solutions to eight of foam.

Mechanical generation of foam is done either by mixing, using a suitable agitator, a dry powdered protein compound of hoof, horn and hydrolised blood with water and air or mixing a synthetic detergent concentrate with water and air.

Chemical foam deteriorates in storage and hence there is a fall off in performance; regular testing and recharging are required.

'Throw capability' depends upon the expansion ratio, *i.e.* the volumetric ratio of the amount of foam to the amount of water used in its formation. Low expansion foam (8:1) has a reasonable throw but medium and high expansion foams (about 150:1 and 1,000:1 respectively) have very little throw capability.

Mechanical foam can be pumped to foam monitors (foam guns at suitable deck stations, *e.g.*) from which it can be thrown considerable distances, depending upon the pumping pressure.

A mechanical low expansion foam (about 12:1) containing a free flowing agent (per fluorinated surfactant) which alters the surface tension and thereby enables the foam to flow rapidly and evenly across large areas, may be used for deck fires on product carriers and chemical tankers. In addition, this AFFF (aqueous, film, forming, foam or light water foam) may have, due to additive, imiscibility with certain cargoes (*e.g.* Methyl alcohol) thus preventing break down of the foam due to water loss.

Foam extinguishes oil fires by providing a heat radiation blanket from the flames burning above the oil and this cuts off the supply of fuel to the fire. The water content of the foam may in part be converted to steam, this produces a cooling and smothering action.

Carbon Dioxide

Relatively low latent heat hence it has a limited cooling effect. When released it expands to some 450 times its liquid volume to produce a heavier than air, cold gas which has a penetrating three dimensional action, displacing the atmosphere, lowering the oxygen level and smothering the fire.

Its vapour pressure is approximately 40 bar at 0°C, hence if it is liquid at ambient temperature its pressure must be greater than

40 bar. Containers (except for bulk systems) are heavy, which limits the size of portable extinguishers.

Carbon dioxide is non-corrosive, toxic, does not deteriorate and does no damage. It is a non-conductor of electricity, clean and relatively inexpensive fire fighting medium suitable for most fires except those that liberate oxygen whilst burning.

Vaporising Fluids

Halogenated hydrocarbons BCF and BTM are accepted for use on shipboard.

$$\text{BCF is known as Halon 1211 } (CV_rClF_2)$$
$$\text{BTM is known as Halon 1301 } (CB_rF_3)$$

Since their characteristics are somewhat similar, and the BCF is slightly preferable, only the BCF will be discussed.

BCF

Higher latent heat than carbon dioxide therefore it has a better cooling effect. It extinguishes fires by breaking the fire chain, *i.e.* it acts as a 'negative catalyst' and extinguishes a flame in milli-seconds.

Its vapour pressure is about 1.2 bar at 0°C hence containers of BCF are only slightly pressurised and therefore light and portable.

BCF is less toxic and 40 per cent more effective by weight than carbon dioxide. This means less storage space and only 5 to 5.5 per cent saturation of a compartment is required.

It has a high electrical resistance, better throw characteristic than carbon dioxide, is expensive, relatively difficult to obtain and its products of pyrolysis are toxic (*i.e.* the gases and vapours given off when BCF contacts flame or burning surfaces).

As previously stated BCF and BTM characteristics are similar, their main difference being vapour pressures, BTM vapour pressure being higher means heavier, stronger storage vessels, less portability, quicker discharge and probable first choice for fixed installations.

Halons are very expensive, the weight required is one third to one half that of carbon-dioxide required, they have to be discharged very quickly (in fixed fire installations about 20s maximum) and they are not suitable for deep seated smouldering fires. Hence for large spaces and holds carbon dioxide will remain the most popular.

FIRE EXTINGUISHERS (FOAM)

Nine Litre Foam Fire Extinguisher
Construction

A 9 litre portable foam fire extinguisher of the inverting type
is shown in Fig. 8.6. The inner and outer containers are made of
lead or zinc coated steel, the outer container being of riveted
construction. Cap and nozzle are made of brass and a loosely
fitting lead valve may be situated at the top of the inner
container to provide a seal. The brass cap has a series of small
radial holes drilled through it which communicate the inside of
the extinguisher with the atmosphere when the cap is being
unscrewed, hence these holes serve as a vent if the nozzle is
blocked.

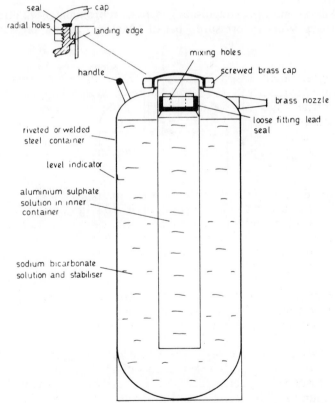

9 LITRE PORTABLE FOAM FIRE EXTINGUISHER
Fig. 8.6

Contents

The inner container is filled with a solution of aluminium sulphate and the annular space formed by the inner and outer containers is filled up to the level indicator with a solution of sodium bicarbonate and foam stabiliser. Proportions of solutions approximately 1:3 inner and outer containers respectively, total solutions 9 litres.

Operation

By inverting the extinguisher the lead seal will fall, clearing the ports in the inner container and the two solutions can then freely mix. As the solutions mix they react, generating foam under pressure which is discharged through the nozzle.

Performance

9 litre foam fire extinguisher generates approximately 72 litres of foam. Working pressure 7 bar (0.7 MN/m²), testing pressure

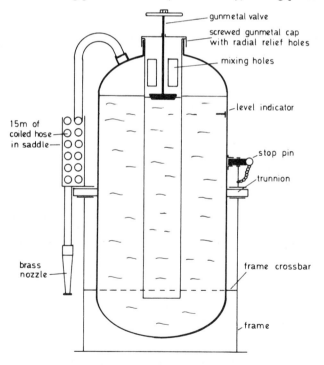

136-LITRE FOAM FIRE EXTINGUISHER
Fig. 8.7

25 bar (2.5 MN/m²), length of jet 7.5 to 9 m, duration of discharge 1½ minutes approximately.

136-litre Foam Fire Extinguisher

This fire extinguisher is similar to the 9 litre type apart from the screw down valve, hose and frame.

To operate, the hose is uncoiled, valve opened, stop pin removed and the extinguisher is pivoted until it rests on the crossbar. This causes the two solutions to mix and generate foam.

The performance figures are: Foam generated 1,000 litres, working pressure 15 bar (1.5 MN/m²), testing pressure 25 bar (2.5 MN/m²), length of jet 18 m, duration of discharge 15 minutes approximately.

Testing

In order to test the extinguisher contents, 5 ml of the acid solution should be mixed with 15 ml of the alkali solution in a graduated vessel and this should produce about 160 ml of foam. Testing should be carried out about every four months with a thorough inspection and test every 12 months.

Nine Litre Portable Mechanical Foam Fire Extinguisher
Construction

The body is made of welded steel, zinc coated, with a solid brass neck ring silver soldered to it. The removable head assembly which incorporates the plunger, is made from a solid brass pressing. When the head assembly is screwed into the neck ring it presses down on to a thick rubber washer and flange on the charge container thus providing a seal and securing the charge container in place.

A nozzle made of aluminium alloy with fin-protected air holes is connected to a reinforced hose one metre in length. The hose is coupled to a brass elbow coupling which is soldered to the stainless steel diptube.

To prevent accidental discharge a swivel safety-guard is provided which also, when in position, holds the spring-loaded plunger valve open which vents the extinguisher thus preventing dribbling from the nozzle.

Contents

The body is filled with 8.25 litres of water and the charge container is made up of (1) 0.85 litre liquid air foam concentrate in a sealed plastic bag (2) a sealed 0.074 kg capsule of CO_2 at a

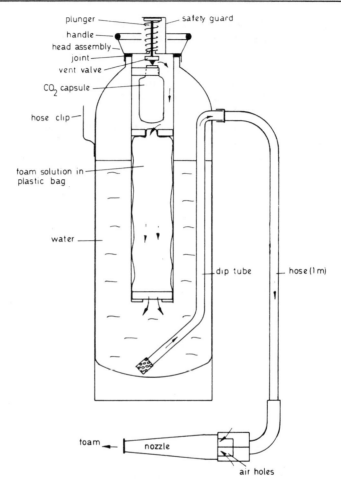

PORTABLE MECHANICAL FOAM FIRE
EXTINGUISHER
Fig. 8.8

pressure of 53 bar, both of which are contained in an aluminium
alloy tube.

Operation

When the plunger is depressed it pierces the thin copper seal
releasing CO_2 which ruptures the plastic bag and forces out the
liquid foam concentrate into the water, where rapid mixing takes

place. The foam solution is then driven up the steel dip tube, through the hose to the nozzle, here it is aerated into good quality fire-smothering air foam.

Performance

The 9 litres of solution produce approximately 72 litres of foam, length of jet approximately 7m. Duration of discharge is about 50 seconds and the body is pressure-tested to 25 bar.

This type of extinguisher can be rapidly reloaded, all that is needed is to fill body with water to the required level, drop in a new charge container and replace head assembly.

FOAM SPREADING INSTALLATIONS

When fitted, permanently piped foam spreading installations, operated external to boiler or machinery space, which supply foam to boiler and/or engine room tank tops must have sufficient capacity to give a depth of foam of at least 152 mm over the whole tank top.

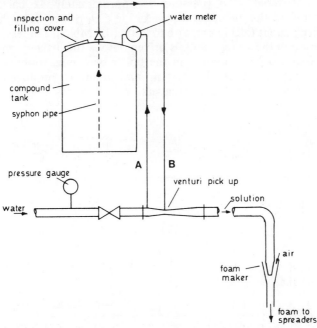

MECHANICAL FOAM INSTALLATION
Fig. 8.9

Water at a pressure of at least 6 bar (0.6 MN/m²), supplied from the ships mains, passes through the water control valve into the venturi fitting. Two small bore pipes are connected to the venturi fitting, pipe A is the high pressure pipe led through a water meter to the top of the foam compound tank, pipe B is the low pressure pipe which permits a controlled quantity of foam compound to be entrained into the venturi fitting. The protein foam compound and water pass along the main delivery pipe to the foam makers situated in the boiler or engine room, as the mixture passes through the foam maker air is entrained which then produces a stable foam which is delivered to the foam spreaders. A diagrammatic representation of a foam maker is included with Fig. 8.9.

Pre-mixed Foam

This type of mechanical foam installation is self contained, *i.e.* does not require motive power from the ships pumps. To put the system in operation it is only necessary to pierce the CO_2 bottle seals by means of the operating gear provided. The CO_2 is then delivered at a pressure of approximately 42 bar (4.2 MN/m²) to the metering valve. As the CO_2 passes through the orifice plate it falls in pressure to 8 bar (0.8 MN/m²) or less. The solution in the storage tank is driven out via the delivery pipe to the foam makers situated in the boiler or engine room space, wherein, air enters the system and foam is produced for distribution to the foam spreaders.

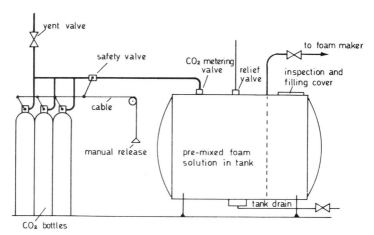

PRE-MIXED FOAM INSTALLATION
Fig. 8.10

For tanker installations the foam may be delivered to the pump room, the engine or boiler room sprayers, or to a hydrant system to which hoses can be connected which have foam making nozzles attached (see Fig. 8.10).

Foam Compound Injection System

Fig. 8.11 shows diagrammatically the compound injection system often found on tankers for deck and machinery spaces. Tank and pumps may be situated wherever it is convenient.

Foam compound is drawn from the sealed tank by the compound pump, air enters the tank through the atmospheric valve (this being linked to the compound valve). Both open simultaneously and delivery is to the automatically regulated injector unit. The injector unit controls the amount of water to compound ratio for a wide range of demand by the foam spreaders etc. A fire pump delivers the foam making solution at sufficient pressure to the deck monitors (multi-directional type foam guns) so that foam can reach any part of the deck, or to the spreaders for machinery spaces.

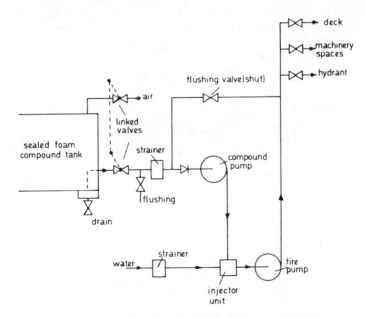

FOAM COMPOUND INJECTION SYSTEM
Fig. 8.11

To bring the system into operation it is only necessary to open the linked air/foam compound valves and start the pumps. After use the system must be thoroughly flushed through and recharged.

In chemical foam installations the principal disadvantages is the deterioration of the chemicals and chemical solutions, hence regular checking is necessary to ensure the system is at all times capable of effective operation. However, with the chemical foam system good quality uniform foam is capable of being produced.

With mechanical foam systems, storage and deterioration of the foam compound presents no difficulty, which is one of the reasons why this particular type of system is generally preferable.

High Expansion Foam System

This recently introduced foam system has been recognised by the DTp as an alternative fire extinguishing medium for boiler and engine room compartments.

The generators are large scale bubble blowers which are connected by large section trunking to the compartments (Fig. 8.12).

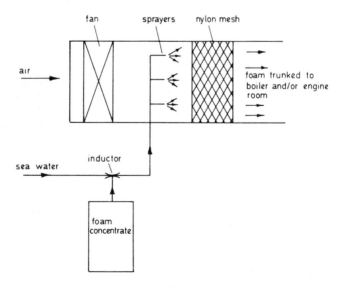

HIGH EXPANSION FOAM SYSTEM
Fig. 8.12

A $1\frac{1}{2}$ m long, 1 m square generator could produce about 150 m³/min of foam which would completely fill the average engine room in about 15 minutes. One litre of synthetic detergent foam concentrate combines with 30 to 60 litres of water (supplied from the sea) to give 30,000 to 60,000 litres of foam.

Advantages:
(1) Economic; (2) Can be rapidly produced; (3) Could be used with existing ventilation system; (4) Personnel can actually walk through the foam with little ill effect.

Disadvantages:
(1) Persistent, could take up to 48 hours to die down in an enclosed compartment; (2) Large trunking required; (3) Should be trunked to bottom of compartment to stop convection currents carrying it away.

FIRE EXTINGUISHERS (CO_2)

CO_2 Portable Fire Extinguisher
Construction
A 4.5 portable CO_2 fire extinguisher is shown in Fig. 8.13. The body is made of solid drawn steel which is hydraulically tested to 227 bar (22.7 MN/m²) and it is coated internally and externally with zinc, the external surface being finally painted.

A solid brass pressing forms the head assembly and this is screwed into the neck of the steel bottle. The head assembly incorporates a lever-operated valve, copper dip tube, bursting disc and a discharge horn made of non-conducting (electrically) material that can be swivelled in one plane only into the desired position.

Contents
The body is charged with 4.5 kg of liquid CO_2 at a pressure of 53 bar (5.3 MN/m²) approximately.

Operation
A safety pin (not shown in sketch) would first be removed and then the valve operating lever would be depressed. The liquid CO_2 would pass into the discharge horn and emerge as a cloud of CO_2.

Performance

Range about 3 to 4 m in still air, duration of discharge about 20 s, about 2.5 m³ of gas is produced.

Note: CO_2 extinguishes a fire by cooling and smothering, the gas has the advantage that it can get into inaccessible places. CO_2 extinguisher contents, can be checked by regular weighing, this should be done about every four months.

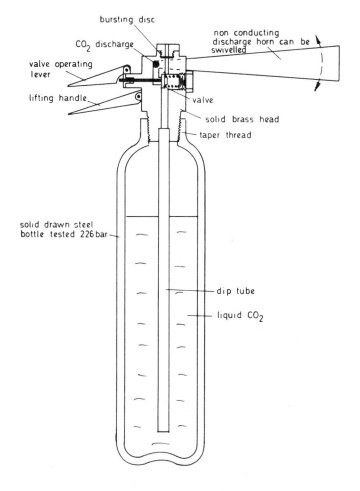

CO₂ FIRE EXTINGUISHER
Fig. 8.13

CO_2 and Water Portable Fire Extinguisher.
Construction (Fig. 8.14)

The body of the extinguisher is of welded steel zinc coated, with the external surface painted. A brass neck ring is silver soldered to the top of the steel body and the brass head assembly, which incorporates plunger, handle and swivel safety guard, is screwed into it and seals on a thick rubber washer. Small radial vent holes are drilled in the head assembly which serve to relieve internal pressure when the head is being unscrewed in the event of the nozzle being blocked.

A brass double purpose nozzle is fitted to the delivery end of the reinforced rubber hose and the nozzle can be operated to give water jet or spray as desired.

When the swivel guard is in the protective position the spring loaded piercer is slightly depressed, this serves to keep the extinguisher vented when not in use and prevents water overflow due to change in atmospheric conditions.

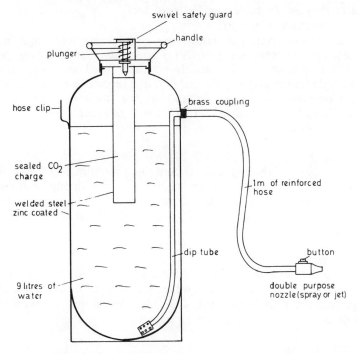

CO_2 AND WATER PORTABLE FIRE EXTINGUISHER
Fig. 8.14

Contents

The body contains 9 litres of fresh water, usually a wetting agent is added to the water which enables the water to spread more readily. The inner container is welded steel, zinc coated, and is charged with 74 mg of CO_2 at a pressure of approximately 36 bar (3.6 MN/m²).

Operation

The hose is first uncoiled from the body and the swivel guard is swung to uncover the plunger. The plunger is then depressed, this releases the CO_2 which then drives the water out of the extinguisher via the dip tube and hose.

Performance

Length of jet 10.6 m approximately, spray 6.06 m with about 36 m² of cover. Duration of discharge approximately 60 seconds. Body tested hydraulically to 25 bar (2.5 MN/m²).

Dry Powder Portable Fire Extinguisher
Construction (Fig. 8.15)

Body is of riveted or welded steel with a brass neck ring. The neck ring incorporates the CO_2 injection tube. Screwed over the neck ring is the head assembly which is fitted with a spring-loaded plunger and has screwed into it, a replaceable CO_2 bottle.

Connected to the outlet end of the discharge tube is a reinforced hose which leads to a brass nozzle that is fitted with a lever-operated control valve.

Contents

The body of the extinguisher contains approximately 4.5 kg of dry powder, this powder charge is principally sodium bicarbonate with some magnesium stearate added to prevent the powder from caking. The CO_2 bottle contains about 60 mg of CO_2.

Operation

The extinguisher is removed from its supporting bracket and the safety cap is removed. When the plunger is depressed it pierces the CO_2 bottle seal, CO_2 then blows out the powder charge.

Performance

Range about 3 to 4 m, duration of discharge about 15 s. Body is tested to 35 bar (3.5 MN/m²).

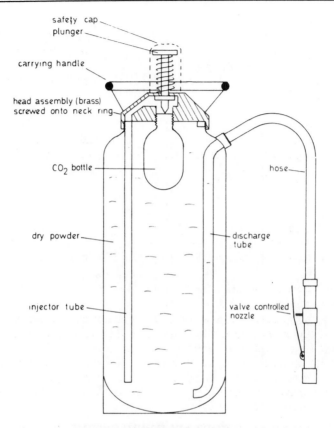

DRY POWDER FIRE EXTINGUISHER
Fig. 8.15

Dry powder acts to smother a fire in a similar way to a blanket. Owing to the great shielding properties of the powder cloud the operator can approach quite close to the fire.

The sodium bicarbonate powder will, due to the heat from the fire, produce CO_2 which should further assist in smothering the fire.

Soda-acid Portable Fire Extinguisher
Construction (Fig. 8.16)
Riveted mild steel, lead coated internally and externally, is used for the body of the extinguisher. A screwed brass neck ring is riveted to the top dome of the mild steel body and the brass

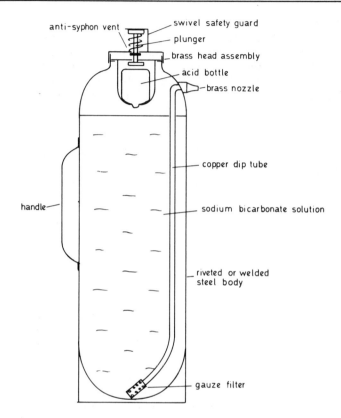

anti-syphon vent

swivel safety guard

plunger

brass head assembly

acid bottle

brass nozzle

copper dip tube

handle

sodium bicarbonate solution

riveted or welded steel body

gauze filter

SODA-ACID PORTABLE FIRE EXTINGUISHER
Fig. 8.16

head assembly, which incorporates plunger and acid bottle carrying cage, is screwed into it. The head assembly joint is either acid resisting rubber or greased leather. The nozzle is made of brass and the delivery tube with loose gauze filter, generally copper.

To ensure that the solution does not leak out of the nozzle due to increase of air pressure in the enclosed space above the solution (due to increase of temperature), a non-return vent valve is usually incorporated in the head assembly.

Contents

A 9 litre sodium bicarbonate solution fills the body to the limit of the level indicator and the glass bottle in the carrying cage contains sulphuric acid.

Operation

When the plunger is depressed the acid bottle is shattered and the acid is released. The sulphuric acid will then react with the surface of the sodium bicarbonate solution and the result of this chemical reaction is CO_2. The CO_2 builds up in pressure and the solution is then driven out of the extinguisher through the dip tube and nozzle.

Performance

Length of jet 9 m approximately, working pressure 2.7 bar to 3 bar, duration of discharge $1\frac{1}{2}$ minutes. Body is tested hydraulically to a pressure of 25 bar (2.5 MN/m²) approximately.

Soda-acid fire extinguishers should *not* be used in machinery spaces for fighting oil fires as the principal substance discharged from such extinguishers is water.

CO₂ FLOODING SYSTEMS

This system (Fig. 8.17) of smoke detection, alarm and CO_2 flooding is frequently used for hold spaces and in some instances may be found as additional fire fighting equipment for engine rooms.

For the detection of smoke, 20 mm diameter sampling pipes are led from the various hold compartments in the vessel to a cabinet on the bridge. Air is drawn continuously through these pipes to the cabinet by suction fans, which deliver the air through a diverting valve into the wheel house.

When a fire breaks out in a compartment, smoke issues from the diverting valve into the wheelhouse, warning bridge personnel of the outbreak. Simultaneously, an electronic smoke detector in the cabinet sets off audible alarms, hence if the bridge is unoccupied (*e.g.* in port) the notice of outbreak of fire is still obtained.

With the cabinet is a dark chamber wherein the sampling pipes terminate in labelled chimneys. Diffused light illuminates strongly any smoke issuing from a chimney, hence the compartment which is affected by fire can easily be identified. Below the dark chamber in the cabinet is a well lighted compartment fitted with a glass window and hinged flap cover. Inside this compartment, 13 mm diameter glass tubes are fitted which are the ends of the sampling pipes, these glass tubes protrude into the metal chimneys in the dark chamber above.

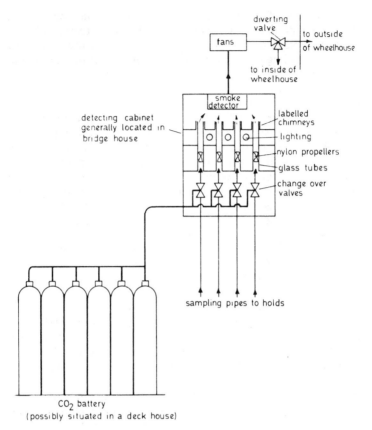

CO₂ FLOODING SYSTEM FOR HOLDS
Fig. 8.17

Small nylon propellers are visible inside the glass tubes in the lighted portion of the cabinet and when the fans are in operation these propellers will be seen to be continuously whirling if the sampling tube is not blocked.

Change over valves are generally situated inside the lower portion of the cabinet, one for each of the sampling pipes. To flood an affected compartment with CO_2 gas, the operator would first operate the appropriate change over valve and secondly release the requisite number of CO_2 cylinders for the compartment. CO_2 gas would then pass through the sampling pipe to the space in which the fire exists.

When a smoke detection system is to be used for the hold

compartments of a refrigerated cargo vessel the lines to the refrigerated holds will be blanked-off in the detector cabinet. These blanks can be removed once per watch as a test (for a few days after loading cargo) and removed altogether when the hold is open and defrosted.

Note:

When an outbreak of fire in a compartment is detected, the fire may be of small proportions and be capable of being extinguished by means other than flooding with the CO_2 equipment provided. In this event it would be necessary for personnel to enter the compartment in order to extinguish the fire. However, after inspection, the fire may be such that CO_2 flooding is necessary. Before this is done, an audible alarm should first be operated warning personnel that CO_2 flooding of the compartment is about to be used.

After the fire has been extinguished, the compartment must be well ventilated before entry for damage inspection, as CO_2 gas is heavier than air and does not support human life.

CO_2 Total Flooding System for Machinery Spaces

For machinery spaces containing diesel propelling machinery, or auxiliary machinery whose total power is 746 kW or more a fixed fire-fighting installation has to be provided. One such system is the CO_2 total flooding system which must give a 40% saturation of the compartment, of which at least 8.5% must be discharged into the compartment in about two minutes.

CO_2 flooding is often used for tanker engine rooms and pump rooms even if the machinery used is steam turbine.

Operation (Fig. 8.18)

First ensure that the compartment is evacuated of personnel and sealed off. This necessitates closing all doors to the engine room, shutting down skylights, closing dampers on vents and stopping ventilation fans. Pumps should also be stopped and collapsible bridge valves closed. In a modern vessel the sealing off can be done by remote control from the fire control station generally using a compressed air or hydraulic system.

The door of the steel control box situated at the fire control station would then be opened, this operates a switch which may have a dual purpose. One is to operate audible and visual alarms in the engine room spaces, the other may be to shut off ventilation fans. The CO_2 direction valve handle would then be pulled and this would be followed by gas release.

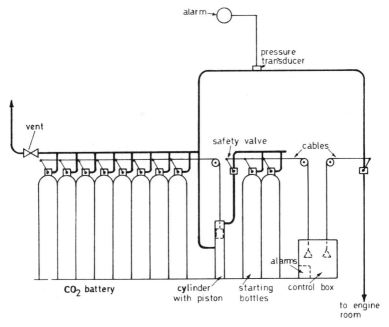

CO₂ TOTAL FLOODING SYSTEM
Fig. 8.18

Maintenance and Testing

Ensure that all moving parts are kept clean, free and well lubricated. Wires must be checked for tightness, toggles and pulleys must be greased. With the use of compressed air the CO_2 distribution pipes could be blown through periodically. CO_2 bottles must be weighed regularly to check contents (an ultrasonic or radioactive isotope unit detector could be used to check liquid level).

Note:

The CO_2 storage bottles have seals which also act as bursting discs, should there be a CO_2 leakage from one or more of the starting bottles this cannot result in CO_2 discharge into the engine room from the battery because of the cable-operated safety valve. When leakage occurs either in the starting section or main battery a pressure switch in the lines will cause alarms to be sounded, vents to atmosphere can then be opened.

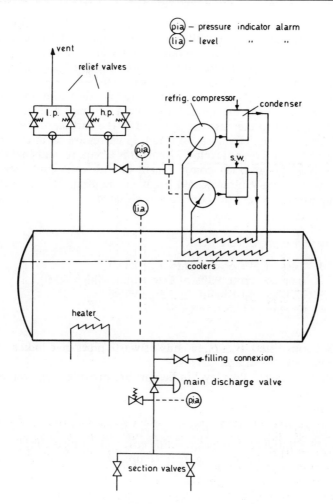

BULK CARBON DIOXIDE SYSTEM
Fig. 8.19

Bulk Carbon Dioxide System

This system was designed to replace the flooding systems for machinery and hold spaces which use a considerable number of carbon dioxide bottles.

It consists of a large, well insulated container (older systems may have two containers) which holds carbon dioxide at a working pressure of about 21 bar, temperature about $-20°C$. In order to maintain this low temperature, duplicated refrigeration units automatically controlled by the pressure of the carbon dioxide are used. One refrigeration unit would be in operation and in the event of failure, the other would cut in automatically and warning would be given (see Fig. 8.19).

Since it is essential that pressure in the container be maintained for fire extinguishing within a set range a heater cuts in if required to increase the pressure of the carbon dioxide.

Two sets of relief valves are fitted, lp valves are set at around 24.5 bar, hp valves at around 27 bar. It is a requirement that the hp valves vent into the compartment in which the container is situated — this venting would occur in the event of fire in the compartment where the container is situated.

Alarms

These are provided for:

1. Loss of 5% of contents (low level).
2. Increase up to 98% of free volume (high level).
3. Leakage past main discharge valve.
4. Opening of section valve.

Balloons fitted over open ends of waste pipes give indication of relief valve leakage.

High pressure. Two level indicators are provided, one remote the other local.

Advantages

Lower initial cost, reduced filling cost and filling is simplified. About a 50% saving in weight compared to a multi-cylinder system.

Disadvantages

Relatively complex system, this reduces reliability. A power supply is required.

Operation

The appropriate section valve is opened (alarm sounds) and the main discharge valve is opened. The main discharge valve is usually fitted with an actuator for remote control, carbon dioxide is then delivered for a specified period (which depends upon the size of the compartment) and the main valve is closed.

Inert Gas Generator (Fig. 8.20)

This was originally developed to supplement CO_2 flooding systems. Since, if a fire occurred on board a ship at sea and the fire was extinguished through using all the CO_2 available and a further outbreak of fire occurred, the situation could be dangerous.

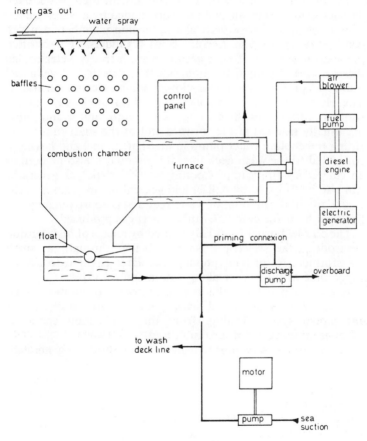

INERT GAS GENERATOR
Fig. 8.20

In a compartment wherein there is an outbreak of fire, the minimum percentage of oxygen in the atmosphere in the compartment which will allow combustion to proceed varies with different materials between 12 to 16 per cent approximately. Hence if the oxygen content of the compartment can be reduced below 12 per cent, insufficient would be present to allow combustion to continue. This reduction in oxygen content can be achieved by employing a generator which will supply inert gas which is heavier than air, so displacing the atmosphere in the compartment.

The generator consists of a horizontally arranged brick lined furnace cylindrically shaped and surrounded by a water jacket. This is connected to a vertical combustion chamber in which water spray units and Lessing rings (cylinders of galvanised metal arranged to baffle the gas flow) are fitted. A water cooled diesel engine, usually fitted alongside the generator, drives a fuel pump, a constant volume air blower and an electric generator. The electric generator supplies current to an electric motor which in turn drives the cooling water pump, motor and pump are usually situated at the forward end of the shaft tunnel. By fitting the cooling water pump in the shaft tunnel and having it connected to the wash deck line, this pump can also be used as an emergency fire pump. Cooling water for the gas generator can also be supplied by ballast and general service pumps in the engine room, the amount of water required is approximately 545 litres per hour for every 27.7 m^3 of inert gas produced.

The oil fuel burner is initially lighted by means of high tension electrodes, the electrical supply being through a small transformer. A constant pressure regulator is fitted to the oil supply line to the burner along with a control valve.

A control panel for the gas generator incorporates a CO_2 recorder, water and oil fuel alarms and pressure gauges. In the gas piping system leading from the combustion chamber, condensate traps and drains are fitted.

The following is an approximate analysis of the gas generated.

Oxygen	0—1 per cent
Carbon monoxide	Nil
Carbon dioxide	14—15 per cent
Nitrogen	85 per cent

Remainder, unburnt hydrocarbons and oxides of nitrogen.

Inert Gas Installation for Tankers

Fig. 8.21 shows diagrammatically a system of inert gas supply for the cargo tanks of an oil tanker. Gas from boiler uptakes passes through two pneumatically operated, remote controlled, high temperature valves. It then passes through a scrubber into

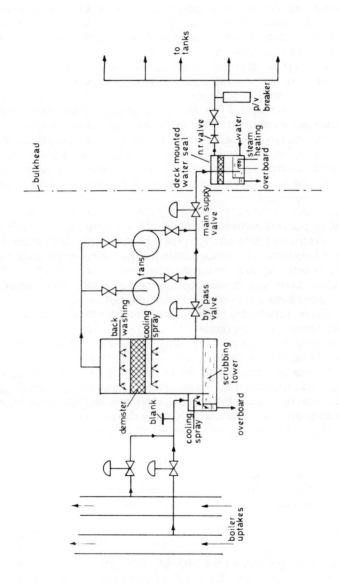

INERT GAS SYSTEM
Fig. 8.21

which sea water is sprayed for cooling the gases to about 3°C above water temperature and scrubbing out soot particles and most of the sulphur oxides.

The gas then passes through a plastic demister which can be cleaned by back flushing.

After the scrubbing the gas analysis would be about 13% carbon dioxide, 4% oxygen, 0.3% sulphur dioxide, remainder nitrogen and water vapour.

Two centrifugal blowers are provided, only one would normally be operated the other being a stand-by unit.

The supply of cleaned dry inert gas at a pressure of 1.2 to 6 kN/m^2 gauge pressure is regulated by the automaticaly controlled bypass valve which is linked to the main supply valve. When the main valve starts to close the bypass begins to open and vice-versa.

Safety features control and alarms:

1. High temperature gas valves: open/shut indication on control room panel, close automatically when soot blowing of the boiler is put into operation.

2. If inert gas temperature gets too high, automatically delivery valves are closed and fans stopped.

3. Low water flow to seals and scrubbers.

4. High gas temperature.

5. Scrubbing tower overflow.

6. High oxygen content in the gas.

The system is suited to boiler installations, gas from diesel engines contains large quantities of excess air. An inert gas generator may be installed for gas delivery to the system in the event of no gas being available from the boilers.

Advantages of the system are:

1. No explosive mixtures can form in the tanks.

2. Reduces corrosion.

3. Voyage cleaning of tanks is unnecessary.

4. Reduces pumping time because of the positive pressure in the tanks at all times.

WATER SPRAY SYSTEMS

Automatic Sprinkler System

The sprinkler system is an automatic fire detecting, alarm and extinguishing system that is constantly 'on guard' to deal quickly and effectively with any outbreak of fire that may occur in accommodation or other spaces.

Briefly the system is composed of a pressurised water tank with water pipes leading to various compartments. In these compartments the water pipes have sprinkler heads fitted which come into operation when there is an outbreak of fire.

Fig. 8.22 is a diagrammatic arrangement of the system. The pressure tank is half filled with fresh water through the fresh water supply line. Compressed air delivered from the electrically driven air compressor raises the pressure in the tank to a predetermined level, this should be such that the pressure at the highest sprinkler head in the system is not less than 4.8 bar (0.48 MN/m²).

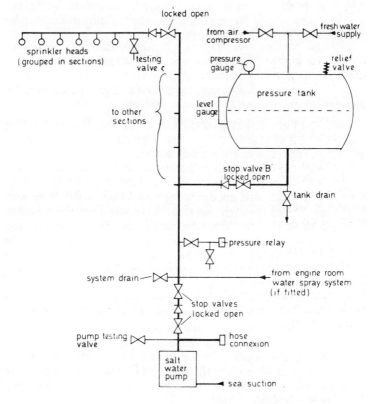

AUTOMATIC SPRINKLER SYSTEM
Fig. 8.22

Sprinkler heads are grouped into sections with not more than 150 heads per section and each section has an alarm system. Each sprinkler head is made up of a steel cage fitted with a water deflector. A quartzoid bulb, which contains a highly expansible liquid, is retained by the cage. The upper end of the bulb presses against a valve assembly which incorporates a soft metal seal.

When the quartzoid bulbs are manufactured, a small gas space is left inside the bulb so that if the bulb is subjected to heat, the liquid expands and the gas space diminishes. This will generate pressure inside the bulb and the bulb will shatter once a predetermined temperature (and hence pressure) is reached. Generally the operating temperature range permitted for these bulbs is 68°C to 93°C but the upper limit of temperature can be increased, this would depend upon the position where the sprinkler head or heads is to be sited. Quartzoid bulbs are manufactured in different colours, the colour indicates the temperature rating for the bulb.

e.g.	Rating	Colour
	68°C	*Red*
	80°C	*Yellow*
	93°C	*Green*

Once the bulb is shattered the valve assembly falls permitting water to be discharged from the head, which strikes the deflector plate and sprays over a considerable area.

When a head comes into operation the non-return alarm valve for the section opens and water flows to the sprinkler head. This non-return valve also uncovers the small bore alarm pipe lead and water passes through this small bore alarm pipe to a rubber diaphragm. The water pressure acts upon the diaphragm and this operates a switch which causes a break in the continuously live circuit. Alarms, both visible and audible, fitted in engine room, bridge and crew space are then automatically operated.

Stop valves, A and B (Fig. 8.22), are locked open and if either of these valves are inadvertently closed a switch will be operated that brings the alarms into operation. The alarm system can be tested by opening valve C which allows a delivery of water similar to that of one sprinkler head to flow to drain.

An electrically operated pump with a direct suction to the sea comes into operation when the fresh water charge in the pressure tank has been used up. This is arranged to operate automatically through the pressure relay.

A hose connection is also provided so that water can be supplied to the system from shore when the vessel is in dry dock.

High Pressure Water Spray System

This can be a completely separate system or it can be interconnected with the sprinkler system that is available for fire extinguishing in accommodation spaces (usually the latter).

The system incorporates an air vessel, fresh water pump and salt water pump all connected to piping which is led to sections, each section having its own shut-off valve and sprayer heads, which unlike the sprinker system have no quartzoid bulbs or valves but are open (Fig. 8.23).

With all section valves closed the system is full of fresh water under pressure from the compressed air in the air vessel. When a section valve is opened water will be discharged immediately from the open sprayer heads in that section, pressure drop in the system automatically starts the salt water pump which will continue to deliver water to the sprayers until the section valve is closed.

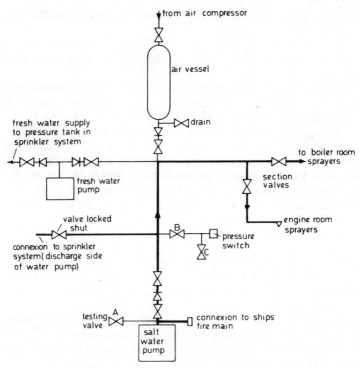

HIGH PRESSURE WATER SPRAY SYSTEM
Fig. 8.23

After use the system should be flushed out and recharged with clean fresh water.

The air vessel is incorporated into the system to prevent the pump cutting in if there is a slight leakage of water from the system.

To test: this should be carried out at weekly intervals, open *A*, close *B*, open *C*; the pump should automatically start and discharge from *A*. This avoids having to refill the system with fresh water.

MERCHANT SHIPPING (FIRE APPLIANCES) RULES

It is strongly recommended that students should obtain a copy of these rules and study them before attempting the DTp examinations. The following is an abbreviated extract.

Machinery Spaces Containing Oil-Fired Boilers or Oil-Burning Equipment

In every ship of Class I (*i.e.* a passenger ship engaged on voyages any of which are long international voyages) there shall be provided:

1. A fixed foam fire extinguishing installation operated from outside of the space and capable of giving a depth of foam of at least 150 mm in not more than five minutes over the largest single area over which oil fuel is liable to spread.

Such installations shall include mobile sprayers ready for immediate use in the firing area of the boiler and in the vicinity of the oil fuel unit. A pressure water spray system or fire smothering gas installation may be used as an alternative.

2. A 136-litre foam fire extinguisher (or 45 kg CO_2) capable of delivering foam to any part of the compartment.

3. Two portable fire extinguishers suitable for extinguishing oil fires.

4. A receptacle containing at least 0.3 m^3 of sand and a scoop.

5. Two fire hydrants, one port, one starboard, with hoses and nozzles (spray nozzles must also be provided).

Machinery Spaces Containing Internal Combustion Machinery

In every ship of Class I there should be provided:

1. A fixed foam fire extinguishing, water spray or smothering gas installation operated from outside of the machinery space if the main propulsion machinery is internal combustion or if the auxiliary diesel power is 746 kW or above.

2. One foam fire extinguisher of at least 45 litres capacity or a CO_2 fire extinguisher of at least 16 kg capacity.

3. One portable fire extinguisher suitable for extinguishing oil fires for each 746 kW (or part thereof) but not less than two such extinguishers or more than six.

4. Two fire hydrants, one port, one starboard, with hoses and nozzles (spray nozzles must also be provided).

Machinery Spaces Containing Steam Engines

1. Foam fire extinguishers each of at least 45 litres capacity or CO_2 fire extinguishers each of at least 16 kg capacity, sufficient in number to enable foam or CO_2 to be directed on to any part of the pressure lubrication system and on to any part of the casings enclosing pressure lubricated parts of turbines, engines or associated gearing. These would not be required if a fixed fire fighting installation similar to (1) for internal combustion machinery was provided.

2. One portable fire extinguisher suitable for extinguishing oil fires for each 746 kW (or part thereof) but not less than two such extinguishers or more than six.

3. Two fire hydrants, one port, one starboard, with hoses and nozzles (spray nozzles must also be provided).

Portable Fire Extinguishers

1. Those discharging fluid shall have a capacity of not more than 13.5 litres and not less than 9 litres.

2. CO_2 extinguishers shall have a capacity of not less than 3.2 kg.

3. Dry powder extinguishers shall have a capacity of not less than 4.6 kg.

International Shore Connection

An international shore connection must be provided to enable water to be supplied from another ship or from the shore to the fire main, and fixed provision shall be made to enable such a connection to be used on the port side and starboard side of the ship.

Cargo Spaces and Store Rooms

1. Every ship of Class I shall be provided with appliances whereby at least two powerful jets of water can be rapidly and simultaneously directed into any cargo space or store room.

2. Every ship of Class I of 1000 tonnes or over shall be provided with appliances whereby fire-smothering gas can be rapidly

conveyed by a permanent piping system into any compartment appropriated for the carriage of cargo. The volume of free gas shall be at least equal to 30 per cent of the gross volume of the largest hold in the ship which is capable of being effectively closed. Provided that steam may be substituted for fire smothering gas in any ship in which there are available boilers capable of evaporating 1.3 kg of steam per hour for each 1 m³ of the gross volume of the largest hold in the ship.

Fire Pumps

1. Every ship of Class I of 4,000 tonnes or over shall be provided with at least three fire pumps operated by power, and every such ship of under 4,000 tonnes with at least two such fire pumps.
2. In every ship of Class I fitted with main or auxiliary oil-fired boilers or internal combustion propelling machinery the arrangements of sea connections, pumps and the sources of power for operating them shall be such as will ensure that a fire in any one compartment will not put all the fire pumps out of action.

Water Pipes, Hydrants and Fire hoses

Every ship of Class I shall be provided with water pipes and hydrants. The diameter of the water pipes shall be sufficient to enable an adequate supply of water to be provided for the simultaneous operation of at least two fire hoses and for the projection thereby of two powerful jets of water. The number and position of the hydrants shall be such that at least two such jets may be directed into any part of the ship by means of two fire hoses each not exceeding 18 m in length, each jet being supplied from a separate hydrant. At least one fire hose shall be provided for each hydrant.

Firemen's Outfits

Every ship of Class I shall be provided with at least two firemen's outfits each consisting of
    (a) a safety lamp
    (b) a fireman's axe
    (c) (i) a breathing apparatus; or (ii) a smoke helmet; or (iii) a smoke mask.
    The outfits shall be kept in widely separated places.

BREATHING APPARATUS

Smoke Mask

This simple reliable unit consists of a foot operated bellows connected by hose to a face mask. A harness with lifeline attached accompanies it and it is essential that the signal code used must be fully understood by all personnel.

The main advantage with the smoke mask is that everyone can familiarise themselves with its operation by wearing and using the apparatus, no bottles have to be re-charged. In large vessels excessive hose length makes this type of unit unsuitable, the self

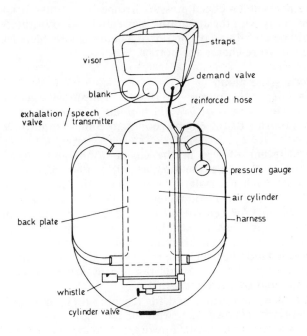

BREATHING APPARATUS
Fig. 8.24

contained type would be preferred. A major disadvantage is that the combination of hose and life-line could make things dangerous if sharp complex obstructions have to be negotiated, cutting or fouling of the hose and line could occur.

Self Contained

The minimum statutory capacity requirement is 1,200 litres of free air, most sets contain from 1200 to 1800 litres at a pressure of about 140 to 210 bar.

The set shown in Fig. 8.24 consists of an air cylinder mounted on a plastic back plate fitted with harness. A moulded rubber face mask incorporating a demand valve, exhalation valve/speech transmitter, head harness and visor is connected by high pressure reinforced hose from the demand valve to the air manifold. A pressure gauge and low pressure warning whistle, which gives audible warning to the wearer when 80% of the air has been used, completes the assembly.

To put it into operation the cylinder valve is opened and the wearer beathes, the demand valve supplies air according to his requirements at a reduced pressure irrespective of his work load.

Familiarity with the apparatus is essential and to facilitate this it would be useful to have on board a compressor which delivers oil free air to re-charge the bottles.

Emergency fire pump

This independent pump with its own prime mover, generally a diesel engine with own low flash point fuel supply, must be situated outside of the engine room and connected into the fire main.

In the event of fire in the engine room and subsequent evacuation and sealing, the emergency fire pump must be started and the engine room isolating valve in the fire main closed.

Fig. 8.25 shows a completely independent emergency fire pump system. The centrifugal fire pump and hydraulic motor would be completely submersible and irrespective of the height and draught of the vessel the pump would not require a priming device as it would be below the water level. Such an arrangement may also be used as a booster/priming device for a main fire pump situated on deck.

Safety is an important and far reaching topic and sea-going engineers will be conversant with the common sense aspects of safety, questions do arise, however, that are more searching than others and require more technical information.

e.g. How does oil vapour pressure affect flammability?

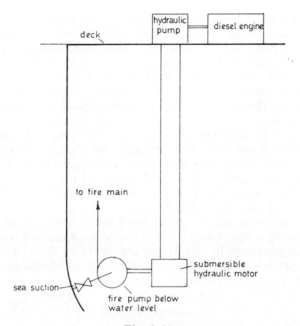

Fig. 8.25

Oils with high vapour pressure are those which are extremely volatile *e.g.* crude oil and petroleums. Hence, the higher the vapour pressure of the oil the greater the amount of flammable vapour given off and the greater the fire hazard.

e.g. How does explosive limit of oil affect flammability?

Explosive limits are 1. Lower explosive limit (LEL) 2. Higher explosive limit (HEL) and they are the percentage of oil vapour by volume with air, usually 1% to 10% respectively for most hydrocarbons. If the mixture is below the LEL or above the HEL it cannot ignite or explode.

Explosive limits are related to vapour pressure;

If vapour pressure is 0.05 bar then percentage by volume with air is $0.005 \times 100\% = 0.5\%$ (below the LEL).

e.g. How does oil vapour density affect safety?

Most petroleum vapours are heavier than air, hence in still air if a tanker is loading cargo some of the vapours could gravitate into the lower recesses of the vessel—*e.g.* accommodation and machinery spaces. P.V. valve arrangements usually vent the vapours at high velocity and to considerable height in order to minimise the risk.

e.g. How does heating of high viscosity oil affect safety?

For good atomisation fuel viscosity should be about 150 seconds Redwood N° 1 or less. With high viscosity oil it is necessary to heat the oil in order to reduce its viscosity.

Pressurised oil may be heated to a temperature above its flash point to achieve the necessary viscosity and obviously if a leakage of this hot pressurised oil occurred it could be extremely dangerous.

Fuel lines carrying this oil should not pass near to high temperature surfaces (*e.g.* exhaust manifolds) or electrical equipment. Ideally they should be jacketed, with jacket drains led to a safe place—a drain tank with level alarm.

e.g. How does the auto-ignition temperature of fuel and lubricating oil affect safety?

The auto-ignition temperature of the vapours of fuel and lubricating oil are much lower than those of vapours from the volatile petroleum liquids. Hence they are more likely to ignite if sprayed on to a hot surface. Remember it is the vapour which burns.

TEST EXAMPLES 8

Class 3

1. Sketch a cross section through a portable fire extinguisher suitable for use on oil fires. Identify the components.
2. State the component parts and associated equipment of a bellows type breathing apparatus.
3. Sketch and describe a smoke detector of the type fitted in an engine room, how is it tested?

TEST EXAMPLES 8

Class 2

1. Compare with reasons the merits and demerits of the following permanent fire extinguishing systems installed in machinery spaces:
   (a)   high pressure water spray,
   (b)   carbon dioxide smothering,
   (c)   chemical foam smothering.

2. Describe with sketches how the following portable fire extinguishers are operated:
   (a)   chemical foam,
   (b)   carbon dioxide.
   Explain how they extinguish fire.
   State with reasons for what type of fire each is most suited.

3. Sketch and describe a self-contained breathing apparatus. Give two advantages and two disadvantages of this equipment compared to the smoke helmet.
   State the signal system used when wearing breathing apparatus.

4. Describe with line diagrams a fixed carbon dioxide fire smothering system for an engine room.
   Explain the need for an action alarm stating when and how it operates.
   Give a reason for gang release and explain how this is achieved.

5. If a fire broke out in the engine room, explain how:
   (a)   the fuel supply could be shut off,
   (b)   the supply of air could be shut off,
   (c)   the fire could be dealt with from outside the engine room, giving a summary of all the facilities available for this purpose.

TEST EXAMPLES 8

Class 1

1. Describe, with sketches, an inert gas system using gas from the main uptakes.
   Explain:
   (a)   the scrubbing process and its purpose,
   (b)   safety devices.

2. Compare the advantages and the disadvantages of the following fixed fire extinguishing systems;
   (a)   high pressure water spray,
   (b)   carbon dioxide smothering,
   (c)   chemical foam smothering.

3. Differentiate between fixed temperature and rate of rise types of fire detector.
   Sketch and describe a fire detector of the rate of rise type and explain how a gradual rise of ambient temperature is accommodated.

4. With reference to fire or explosion explain the significance of the following properties of a flammable gas;
   (a)   combustion pressure,
   (b)   explosive limits,
   (c)   flashpoint,
   (d)   density.

5. Sketch the construction and describe the operation of the following types of fire detector;
   (a)   vapour products (ionisation),
   (b)   flame sensor (infra-red),
   (c)   heat sensor (rate of rise).
   Explain why use of all three types together is to be preferred to the use of one of these types alone.

CHAPTER 9

PUMPS AND PUMPING SYSTEMS

A ship's engine and pump room obviously contains a number of complex pipe arrangements. Bilge, ballast, oil fuel, sanitary water, etc., involving numerous pipe leads, cross connections, valves and so on. The pumps and equipment provided on a modern ship for these various duties are of all types and sizes.

Obviously then a description under the above heading must be drastically cut down and simplified. This chapter then attempts to simply pick out what are regarded as *essential* units or pipe groups and present them in a form suitable for *examination* needs. The work may seem somewhat disjointed but it is assumed that the student can utilise his background practical experience to join the various sections together towards a comprehensive picture.

Firstly the main types of pump in regular use are considered together with any relevant points. Associated equipment is then considered, *e.g.* oily-water separators, feed water injectors, etc. Lastly some pipe arrangements and fittings are presented, concluding with an attempted concise grouping of the rather lengthy rules and regulations appertaining to pumping systems. It should be stressed that these rules do not have to be memorised and are given only to allow the student to have some idea of the minimum requirements.

TYPES OF PUMPS

Classification

1. *Positive displacement pumps*, in which one or more chambers are alternately filled then emptied. These include reciprocating, screw, gear and water-ring types etc. They do not require a priming device, in fact they may be used as priming devices.

In general they would be used for small to medium discharge rates, they can pump fluids of a wide range of viscosity and can develop—especially in the case of the reciprocating pump—high pressure differentials if required.

2. *Dynamic pressure pumps* (*or roto-dynamic pumps*), in which a tangential acceleration is imparted to the fluid. These include centrifugal, axial and mixed flow types (the latter is part axial, part centrifugal). Depending upon supply head they may require a positive displacement pump as a priming device.

In general they would be used for medium to high discharge rates, they usually are confined to low viscosity fluids and generate only low to moderate pressure differentials.

Reciprocating Pumps

There are numerous forms of such pumps, both horizontal and vertical, used for all duties on ships. The reciprocating motion can be through connecting rod from electric motor drives or other forms, but still one of the most common forms is the direct steam drive.

The Weir Steam Pump

The steam end consists of a forged steel piston with either Ramsbottom type plain spring rings or Buckley type spring restriction rings, rings of cast iron with a vertical lateral clearance for the plain rings of about 70 μm and a butt gap clearance of about 140 μm when fitted. The cast iron steam cylinder has steam top and bottom from a bolted on valve chest which is provided with the required steam and exhaust valves and drain cocks. A lubricator for hand use is usually provided, filled with cylinder oil and graphite, but for superheated steam mechanical lubricators are usually used. A mechanical stroke counter is also sometimes fitted. The steam piston is bigger in diameter than the bucket to allow the pump to work at lower steam pressures than the discharge feed pressure (principle of differential areas) and as numerous sizes of pump are used the given sizes and clearances quoted here are based on a 150 mm bore pump, bigger pumps having proportionately larger clearances. A nickel steel piston rod and a brass or bronze bucket rod connect by screwing into a main steel crosshead and are locked by a steel taper pin. The steel valve gear levers have the fulcrum on a front stay and slide through a crosshead pin during vertical movement of the crosshead. The steel valve gear rod works off a ball crosshead between fulcrum and main crosshead, the lever movement butting against top and bottom adjustable nuts to transmit motion to the valve rod.

The full stroke of the pump must be utilised as short stroking produces ridges in the working bores. To adjust the strokes the valve spindle is screwed up until the piston is striking the top cover and then screwed down and locked to allow the piston to approach to within say 12 mm of the end cover. The process is repeated using the bottom nut and lock nut on the threaded spindle for the cylinder bottom.

The water end is of cast iron with a gunmetal bucket working in a brass or brone liner (cast iron throughout is used for oil pumps). The bucket usually has two grooves into which are fitted special ebonite (or tufnol) rings, the lateral clearance being about 220μm and the butt gap clearance about 800μm. The rings are cut and then heated in boiling water to make them flexible, the butt gap being adjusted by trying in the liner bore. When the correct butt gap is made the rings are cooled whilst sprung open to 9 mm butt gap so that the ring when fitted has the necessary compression. The double acting chamber has a twin unit valve chest at the front, each unit, one top and one bottom, having a suction and discharge valve set. The valves are spring loaded from valve guard plates, smaller old pumps usually employ flat brass plate Kinghorn type valves but modern larger pumps almost always employ group valves. Such valves are small circular valves, about five or seven in number, in a circular pattern, the valves being spring loaded from the guard plate. For heavy duty, say for example hot feed water, etc., the valves and seats are of stainless steel and are of the flat faced type. Each valve chest is usually provided with a small sentinel type relief valve on the top covers.

It is of course a requirement that a relief valve is fitted in the discharge pipe irrespective of the cover valves. The pump is also fitted with air pet cocks, drain plugs, air vessels, float control devices, suction and discharge valve chests, etc., as may be required for its duty, horizontal and vertical types are available for feed, oil fuel, ballast, bilge and service duties.

The Weir Type Valve Gear

The valve spindle driving rod is connected to a flat plain outside steam slide valve which works on, and is carefully bedded to, the flat back face of a round shuttle valve which distributes cylinder steam and exhaust. The slide valve, or auxiliary valve, has a vertical motion and the shuttle valve has an axial motion. The auxiliary valve is adjusted by liners so that with the auxiliary valve bolted up in place the shuttle valve can be *lightly* tapped across by hand. The shuttle valve works at its ends inside hollow bells, the bells being a smooth sliding fit over the shuttle. The bells have a slot across their back face into which slots a tongue piece from the end cover, the tongue piece can be rotated by a nut in the centre of the end cover (externally) which serves to turn the bells. The tongue piece spindle has a pointer outside the end cover, the pointer can be moved between two stops by moving the adjuster nut. Rotation of the bell serves to vary the opening to the bypass port so altering the quantity of *extra* steam supply. The inner face of the bell is bedded to an inner circular web, provided with slot or slots cut in to allow steam to pass into the cylinder formed between shuttle valve and bell at the end. With the end covers bolted up tight the bells should have an axial clearance of about 70μm to allow rotation of the bell by the adjuster nut when the pump is working.

The left hand pointer points up usually as it controls the pump upstroke while the right hand end indicator will point down.

The bells should only be used for starting the pump. When they are turned to the open position (indicator to letter O, cast on the end cover) steam can be admitted into the cylinder at any point in the stroke. When the pump is started the bells may be closed by turning them to the shut position (indicator to letter 'S', cast on the end cover). In this way the expansive property of the steam will then be utilised as cut off will take place at approximately $\frac{3}{4}$ stroke, this provides an economy. The bells must not be left open during normal running.

It is essential for all reciprocating pumps to maintain valves and rings, etc., in good order, this is applicable particularly to the shuttle valve gear. Regular skilled examination and attention can give efficient and reliable pumps.

Centrifugal Pumps
Impeller and Volute Casing

In single stage pumps a single impeller rotates in a casing of spiral or volute form and in multistage pumps two or more impellers are fitted on the same shaft. Fluid enters the impeller axially through the eye then by centrifugal action continues radially and discharges around the entire circumference. The fluid in passing through the impeller receives energy from the vanes giving an increase of pressure and velocity. The kinetic (velocity) energy of the discharging fluid is partly converted to pressure energy by suitable design of impeller vanes and casing. In some pumps *e.g.* turbine driven boiler feed pumps, diffusers are used. These consist of a ring of stationary guide vanes surrounding the impeller, the passage through the diffuser vanes is designed to change some of the velocity energy in the fluid to pressure energy. In double inlet pumps fluid enters from two sides to the impeller eye as if there were two impellers back to back giving twice the discharge at a given head. In multi-stage pumps the fluid from one impeller is discharged via suitable passages to the eye of the next impeller so that the total head developed (or discharge pressure) is the product of the head per stage and the number of stages, such a pump is often used for high pressure discharge at moderate speed (*e.g.* turbo-feed).

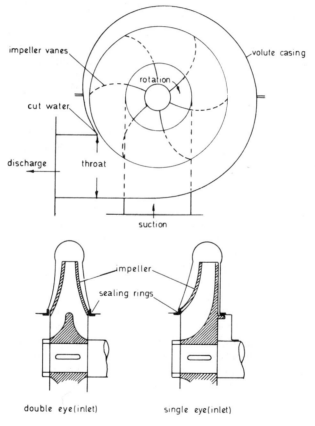

Fig. 9.1

A double inlet impeller and single inlet impeller for comparison, together with a volute casing are shown in Fig. 9.1. The impeller and volute casing design will depend on the required duty, *e.g.* head to lift, head to discharge (pressure), quantity, etc. A typical centrifugal bilge pump would give an output of about 30 kg of water in one second, 12 kW power, discharge up to 5 bar running at about 17 rev/s. The casing usually has the suction and discharge branches arranged at the back so impeller and spindle can be removed from the front without breaking pipe joints. The discharge branch is usually on the pump centre line so that the pump is not 'handed'. The number of impeller vanes is not fixed but usually there are six to ten. The volute casing is like a divergent nozzle which is wrapped around the impeller and serves two main functions (1) it enables velocity energy to be converted into pressure energy, the degree of conversion is governed mainly by the degree of diverence (2) it accommodates the gradual increase in quantity of fluid that builds at discharge from the circumference of the impeller. For the velocity to be constant the volute is made so that cross sectional pipe area increases uniformly from cut water to throat. With an impeller having six vanes then the cross sectional area of volute at No. 1 vane will be 1/6th of throat area as one vane is pumping 1/6th of the water quantity, similarly 1/3rd at No. 2 and so on, taking vanes in turn from cut water to throat. If the discharge were choked or blocked then the pump would merely churn water so that the fitting of a relief valve is not essential. A common fault for repair with these pumps is the increase of clearance due to wear at the bearing rim (or sealing ring) faces. This allows connection between suction and discharge so drastically reducing efficiency. On the larger pumps these faces are often brass strips on liners secured by countersunk screws, clearance adjustment is effected by adding further liners. On the smaller pumps the faces are made by sealing rings which are renewable. After any overhaul or clearance adjustments, care must be taken on re-assembly to make sure motor or impeller are not pulling on each other at the junction coupling.

In the smaller designs the shaft gland seal is by an ordinary stuffing box, water cooled, usually employing lead foil type packing. Great care must be taken on these packings as they are very prone to nip and score the shaft severely if not properly adjusted.

For larger types, a rotary packing is used. This consists of a fixed clamp ring on the shaft driving another ring cup, with packing rings on to the shaft, through driving pins. Ring cup and rings are free to slide along the shaft under the action of axial springs from the clamp ring. The cup ring presses on to a fixed ball ring which in turn sits in a ball socket joint in the back plate which bolts to the pump casting. Grease lubrication is provided to the face between ring cup and fixed ball ring, worked by spring or water pressure.

Fig. 9.2 shows diagrammatically a vertically arranged single inlet centrifugal pump. This is arranged with the casing split vertically one half has suction and discharge branches so that the impeller and shaft can be removed without breaking pipe joints. The impeller has a single eye (inlet), upward facing so that air locking is eliminated under operating conditions. Pressure in the space under the impeller ensures hydraulic balance.

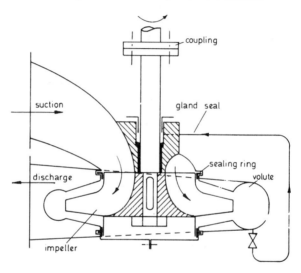

VERTICAL, SINGLE INLET, CENTRIFUGAL PUMP
(DRYSDALE)
Fig. 9.2

Centrifugal Pump Characteristics
Selection

This depends mainly upon duty and space available. Duty points: (1) Flow and total head requirements. This will govern the speed of rotation, impeller dimensions, number of impellers and type *e.g.* single or, double inlet (2) Range of temperature of fluid to be pumped. If suction capability is insufficient to accommodate supply conditions due for example to high inlet temperature cavitation can occur (3) Viscosity of the medium to be pumped (4) Type of medium, *e.g.* corrosive or non-corrosive, this would affect the choice of material (although for salt and fresh water the difference is often just the casing).

Materials for salt water could be, casing—gunmetal (cast iron for fresh water), impeller—aluminium bronze, shaft—stainless steel, casing bearing ring seals—leaded bronze. Space points: with vertically arranged pumps less floor space is required, this usually means that no hydraulic balance is necessary, impeller access is simple and no pipe joints have to be broken.

A typical engine room pump could be a vertical, in-line, overhung (*i.e.* suction and discharge pipes are in a straight line and the impeller is supported, or hung, from above), either base or frame mounted. From which the impeller can be removed without splitting the casing, breaking pipe joints or removing the electric motor.

Losses

Power supplied to the pump must take into account the various losses, these are made up to:

1. Friction loss in bearings and glands, surfaces of impeller and casing. Some impellers are highly polished to minimise friction loss.

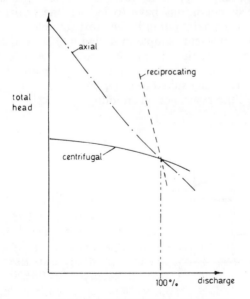

CHARACTERISTIC CURVES
Fig. 9.3

2. Head loss in pump due to shock at entry and exit to impeller vanes and eddies formed by vane edges.

3. Leakage loss in thrust balance devices, gland sealing, clearances between cut water and casing and bearing seals.

A characteristic curve for a centrifugal pump is obtained by operating the pump at rated speed with the suction open and the discharge valve shut. The discharge valve is then opened in stages to obtain different discharge rates and total heads (can be measured by discharge pressure gauge, suction head constant) corresponding to them. A typical curve is shown in Fig. 9.3. reciprocating and axial pump curves given for comparison.

Failure to deliver caused by loss of suction may be due to, insufficient supply head, air leakage suction pipe (*e.g.* valve open on empty bilge, etc), loss of priming facility or leaking shaft gland. Capacity reduction could be the result of a damaged sealing ring, leaking gland, obstruction (valve partly closed), incorrect rotational speed. Excessive vibration may be caused by either (1) loose coupling (2) loose impeller (3) bearing damaged (4) impeller imbalance.

Axial Flow Pump

When large capacity, wide variation of low lift head at constant speed, conditions have to be met the horizontal or vertically arranged axial pump is the most suitable.

The pump is efficient, simple in design and is available in a wide range of capacities. It can if required, be reversible in operation (a friction clutch between motor and pump would be required) and is ideally suited to scoop intake for condensers as it offers very little resistance when idling.

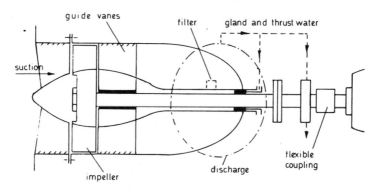

AXIAL FLOW PUMP
Fig. 9.4

Fig. 9.4 shows such a pump. Its casing would be cast iron or gun metal. Impeller, aluminium bronze. Guide vanes, gunmetal, these guide water without turbulence to the discharge. Pump shaft, stainless steel with solid and flexible couplings driven, if low head, by a relatively small prime mover at higher speeds than a comparable centrifugal pump. A water cooled thrust of the tilting pad type is required because of the considerable thrust generated (consider a propulsion system).

The mechanical seal is water cooled as is the composition bush for the shaft. The latter is via the multi-leaf filter, in the case of condenser circulating, because of the possible ingress of sand.

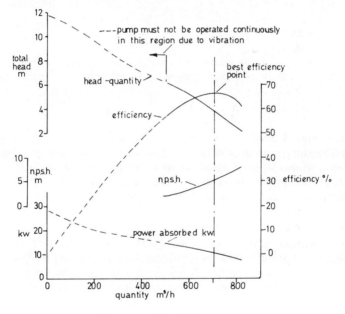

Fig. 9.5

Characteristic curves for an axial flow pump are given in Fig. 9.5. Careful study of these curves and comparison with those for a similar speed centrifugal pump given in Fig. 9.6 will greatly assist the reader to answer some of the questions asked, *e.g.* throttling the discharge valve, its effect on pressure, efficiency and power.

A mixed flow, *i.e.* part centrifugal part axial, pump for cargo duty with cryogenic carriers is shown in Fig. 9.7.

It is fitted, in this case, with a scroll (or screw) type of inducer to reduce n.p.s.h. (net positive suction head) requirement and

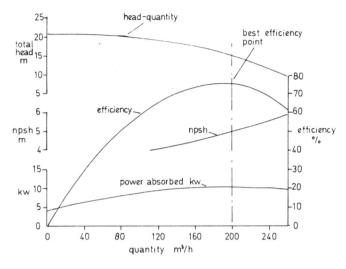

Fig. 9.6

eliminate the need for a stripping pump. Only one stage is shown in the diagram, in practice two or more vertically arranged stages would be used operated by the prime mover on the deck whilst the bell mouth suction at the bottom of the tank and the pump casing act as a long discharge pipe.

Cargo pumps

Centrifugal cargo pumps used, differ according to type of cargo, *e.g.* product tankers (crude oil, etc) would have a separate pump room with conventional centrifugal pumps, probably vertical overhung impeller, sometimes called barrel-type cargo pump installed. This double eye inlet pump with either a straight through or 90° suction—discharge angle with pipe connections in bottom half of casing has two external bearings above the impeller, the upper one takes all the hydraulic thrust and the lower acts as a radial load bearing. This pump has certain advantages over its counterparts, namely: (1) impeller can be sited lower in the pump room thus improving suction conditions and reducing stripping time. (2) Removal of impeller without disturbing pipe joints. (3) Easier access to bearings and shaft seal without removal of rotating elements.

Chemical, LPG, or multi-product tanker: here a separate pump is sited in each tank. Pumps driven through line shafting coupled to hydraulic motors on deck would be deep well, single

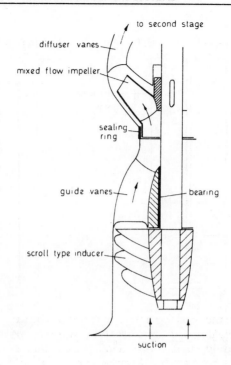

to second stage

diffuser vanes

mixed flow impeller

sealing ring

guide vanes — bearing

scroll type inducer

suction

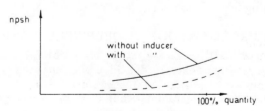

npsh

without inducer
with   "

100% quantity

CARGO PUMP
Fig. 9.7

or multi-stage with radial or mixed flow impellers respectively. Or, submerged pumps electrically or hydraulically driven with, usually, single elements. The line-shaft pump, despite some bearing problems, is proving the more popular, especially for LPG carriers.

Submersible pumps eliminate line shaft bearings, and gland problems but expensive problems could occur due to hydraulic fluid leakage into the cargo and vice-versa.

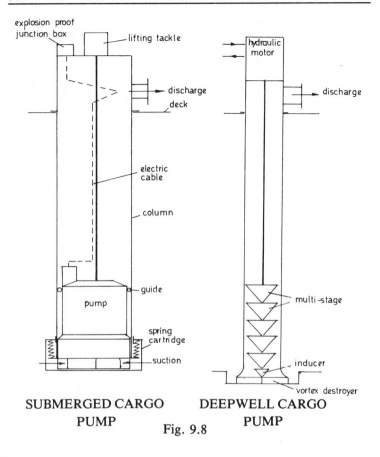

SUBMERGED CARGO
PUMP

Fig. 9.8

DEEPWELL CARGO
PUMP

Fig. 9.8 shows diagrammatically two of the cargo pump arrangements referred to above, the submerged electric motor driven pump rests on a spring cartridge which closes when the pump is raised and seals off the tank from the column.

Air extraction on most pumps is required, especially on all bilge pumps. Early designs of circulating pumps employed a steam ejector on the volute casing together with a steam jet into the casing to condense and prime, or a direct water priming valve. Later designs of centrifugal pump incorporated a separate air pump. In the first types the air is separated from the water in the suction chamber, it rises and is withdrawn by the air pump via a float operated valve. Twin single-acting air pumps are fitted, driven by worm and wheel from the pump spindle, and are crank driven. The pumps are capable of operating flooded should the float gear break down but in normal operation the flooded water suction closes the float valve and the air pumps idle. This design can be sketched fairly easily for examination requirements and is shown in the emergency bilge pump sketch in Fig. 9.12 (later). In the more modern designs the reciprocating air pumps are usually replaced by rotary types. In these designs the usual suction separating chamber and ball float are provided but the air connection from the top of the ball float chamber is taken to the rotary air pump which is directly driven by an extension of the motor spindle on top of the pump. The rotor revolves in a special variable shaped chamber which is supplied with fresh water from a reservoir in the air pump casing.

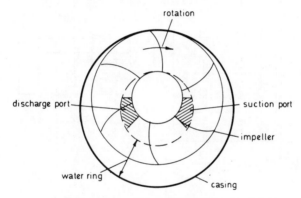

WATER RING AIR PUMP PRINCIPLE
Fig. 9.9

Due to the casing shape the water is made to flow from and towards the rotor centre during each revolution. The water motion is utilised to act as suction and discharge for the air through appropriate sets of ports. The rotor casing is continuously cooled by a closed water circuit from the pump discharge round the air pump jacket and returns to the pump suction. The air pump can be placed in or out of operation by a control cock on the front of the air pump casing. The principle of operation is referred to as the 'water ring principle'. Fig. 9.9 shows this in simplified form. As the impeller vanes pass the suction port air is drawn in and trapped between the water ring and the pump shaft. This 'slug' of air is carried around and delivered to the discharge port, hence this pump is a positive displacement type. In some ship plants all the priming connections for all pumps, etc., are led to a central exhausting system, this system under the operation of auto compressors functions to give priming from a central control station to all units in the engine room as required.

Central Priming System

Fig. 9.10 shows diagrammatically a central priming system arranged to give automatic priming to four pumps. The system can be used for as many pumps of the centrifugal type that would be used in an engine room.

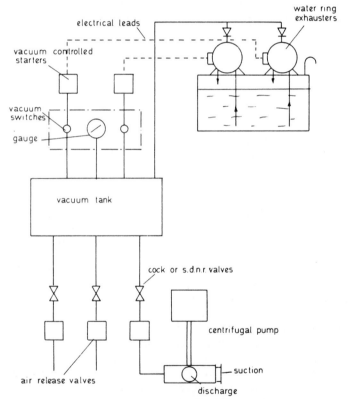

CENTRAL PRIMING SYSTEM
(WORTHINGTON-SIMPSON)
Fig. 9.10

Water ring exhausters maintain a vacuum condition between pre-set limits in the vacuum tank. Opening the priming cock, or s.d.n.r. valve, for a pump causes priming to take place. To prevent water entering the vacuum tank after priming, float operated 'air release' valves will automatically close.

For essential services a s.d.n.r. valve would be fitted instead of a priming cock so that if the valve is inadvertently left open, and due to mal-operation or a defect the vacuum in the tank is lost, air is not drawn into the pump and its suction lost with possible serious consequences to plant.

The advantages of the system are:

1. Saving in total power since each pump does not have its own exhauster or priming unit operating all the while the pump is operating.

2. Reduced capital cost.

3. Simplified maintenance.

4. Automatic—takes care of any minor leaks that may be present in the suction side of a centrifugal pump.

Two water ring type of exhausters mounted on top of a water supply tank are shown, one would act as a stand-by unit, but both could operate together in the event of heavy demand.

Gear pumps

These positive displacement pumps are usually motor driven through a chain or wheel drive. Control is either by a bypass valve for ac supply or shunt regulator if dc supply, and there are no suction or discharge valves so that in these respects the pump is similar to centrifugal pumps. The pump can also be arranged with wheels to operate in series for pressure groups. The two toothed wheels shown in Fig. 9.11 mesh together and are a close fit in the casing. The fluid is carried round between the teeth and the casing. Such pumps are fairly efficient and smooth running and are best suited to pump oil, particularly for boiler oil fuel pressure feed.

Screw Displacement Pumps

Considering Fig. 9.11 it is seen that the fluid enters the outer suction manifolds and passes through the meshing worm wheels, which are gear driven from a motor, to the central discharge manifold. Such pumps are quiet and reliable and are particularly suited to pumping all fluids, in particular oil. The pump can deal with large volumes of air whilst running smoothly and maintaining discharge pressure. It is well suited to tank draining and intermittent fluid supply such as may occur in lubricating oil supply systems to engines, with the vessel rolling.

Timing gears are fitted to some screw pumps to ensure that correct clearance is maintained at all times between the screws, thereby preventing overheating and possible seizure. Modern designs of screws preclude the use of timing gears, ensure smooth efficient simple operation, eliminate turbulence and vibration.

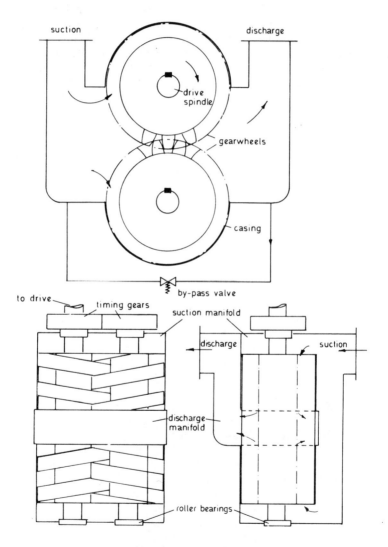

SCREW DISPLACEMENT PUMP
Fig. 9.11

Emergency Bilge Pump

The . function of this pump (Fig. 9.12) is to drain compartments adjacent to a damaged (holed) compartment. The pump is capable of working when completely submerged. The pump is a standard centrifugal pump with reciprocating or rotary air pumps. The motor is enclosed in an air bell so that even with the compartment full of water the compressed air in the bell prevents water gaining access to the motor. The motor is usually dc operated by a separate remote controlled electric circuit which is part of the vessels emergency essential electric circuit. The pump is designed to operate for long periods without attention and is also suitable for use as an emergency fire pump. This design is particularly suited for use in large passenger vessels giving outputs of about 60 kg/s.

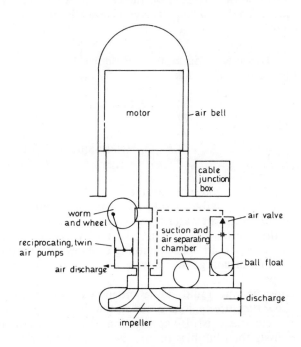

EMERGENCY BILGE PUMP
Fig. 9.12

COMPARISON OF PUMPS, SUCTION LIFT, CAVITATION, ETC.

Consider first the performance of a reciprocating pump. If the pump *could* create a perfect vacuum in the barrel it should *theoretically* be able to lift cold fresh water from a height of 10.3 m above the suction valve.

1.013 bar ~ 760 mm Mercury ~ 10.3 m water

Thus the pump lift depends on the barometer reading (for vacuum attainable) and also the fluid pumped *i.e.*, oil below a density of 1.0 will be capable of being lifted a greater amount. Also the fluid pumped should be cold as warm fluids tends to vaporise and destroy the vacuum. In *practice* a good reciprocating pump will lift cold water from about 8 m with a high barometer. As the temperature of the fluid rises the suction lift decreases so that at 94°C the pump will not draw water. Above this critical temperature water must be supplied from a head to increase the pressure on the suction valve and prevent vapour lock. The following figures give an indication of the above points:

Barometer 750 mm   Practical Lift 7.5 m
above figures for cold water.

Temperature	64°C	Practical Lift		3 m
,,	77°C	,,	,,	2.1 m
,,	94°C	,,	,,	0 m
	110°C	Head required		3 m
,,	123°C	,,	,,	6.7 m

above figures for a 760 mm barometer reading.

Air vessels are usually fitted to reciprocating pump discharge lines to ensure uniform water flow velocity in discharge lines so reducing the inertia head required. The vessel is merely a cylinder forming an air space damping cushion with fluid entry at one side and discharge over a weir at the other side, or via an internal pipe.

In pumps carrying liquids a phenomenon known as cavitation occurs. Low pressure regions occur in the flow at points where high local velocities exist. If vaporisation occurs due to these low pressure areas then bubbles occur, these expand as they move with the flow and collapse when they reach a high pressure region. Such formation and collapse of bubbles is very rapid and collapse near a surface can generate very high pressure hammer blows which results in pitting, noise, vibration, and fall off in the pump efficiency. This phenomenon is not usually very pronounced in reciprocating pumps. Incipient cavitation *i.e.* cavitation which is just beginning, can occur when suction lift capability cannnot meet supply requirements and the output reduces until the two coincide. Under these conditions of operation the pump runs noisily and cavitation damage can occur. By throttling the discharge, or reducing pump speed, rough running of the pump and possible damage can be avoided.

Super cavitation occurs when the vapour bubbles collapse within the liquid after the impeller.

Inducers

These are sometimes fitted to centrifugal pump impeller shafts at suction. Their purpose is generally to ensure the supply of fluid to the impeller is at sufficient pressure to avoid cavitation at impeller suction, or it enables the pump to operate with a lower net positive supply head. Different types are used either scroll, screw or propeller.

The propeller (like a stub bladed fan) inducer is fitted to super cavitating pumps, *i.e.* pumps where the cavitation occurs between the inducer and the impeller. Such pumps can operate at about one third of the net positive supply head normally required for conventional centrifugal pumps and they are suitable for LPG and LNG carriers.

Considering the previous remarks with respect to centrifugal pumps the following points are applicable: (1) the same remarks apply for pump suction head but as clearances in a fast running centrifugal pump are difficult to maintain then even with the good pump with facing clearances of a few millimetres it will probably lift about 7.3 m of cold water with a high barometer. (2) air vessels are rarely fitted as steady flow and air extraction is usual. (3) such pumps are very prone to cavitation especially at inlet to impellers and it may be advantageous to reduce the suction lift to prevent the formation of bubbles due to low pressure regions, incorrect attention to this point may cause severe cavitation and very poor pump performance.

Considering next the gear and screw displacement pumps then these pumps are also affected by changes of barometer pressure and fluid temperature. A reasonable mechanical clearance must be provided and any clearance will of course reduce the vacuum efficiency and hence suction head available. Summarising for these two types on the above three points it may be said that such good pumps will probably lift cold water from about 6.7 m with a high barometer, rarely need air vessels and are not specially prone to cavitation when correctly designed.

In a modern vessel most pumps would probably be motor driven centrifugal, with reciprocating, gear, screw displacement or turbo pumps only fitted for specialist individual duties. The discharge head attainable (or pressure of discharge) is virtually unlimited for a reciprocating pump. Provided a good steam pressure is available the principle of area differentials gives very high discharge pressures. For the other forms of pump, rotational speeds are increased to obtain higher discharge pressures up to a reasonable maximum, for really high pressures then impellers or wheels running in series are required. For example the maximum peripheral impeller speed is best fixed about 105 m/s from the stress viewpoint (although cavitation may be appreciable). A 200 mm impeller at 167 rev/s, a 120 mm impeller at 275 rev/s, or three compound 330 mm impellers running at 60 rev/s, would all produce 50 bar at peripheral speeds within 105 m/s, although the latter is preferable. The maximum head for series impellers is often fixed at about 170 m (16 bar) per stage, with a maximum of say nine stages, but these figures are by no means rigid.

ASSOCIATED EQUIPMENT AND SYSTEMS

It is proposed to consider a short selection of units and systems on which examination questions have been set.

Heat Exchanger
Thermodynamic Characteristics

$Q = U\theta A$ is the rate of heat transfer from one fluid to another in a heat exchanger, where Q is in watts.

U is the overall coefficient of heat transfer in W/m^2K, this depends upon the properties of the fluids, their speeds and the form of the heat exchanger surface.

θ is the logarithmic mean temperature difference in °C between the two fluids. θ is a maximum with counterflow.

A is the area of heat exchanger surface in m^2.

Fig. 9.10 shows some of the different flow patterns used in heat exchangers, counter flow is the best thermodynamically of the basic patterns. In practice most heat exchangers use mixed flow to obtain the best possible characteristics.

In the selection of a heat exchanger, certain points have to be considered, some are:

1. Quantity of fluid, maximum to minimum, to be cooled.
2. Range of inlet and outlet temperature of fluid to be cooled.
3. As above for the cooling medium.
4. Specific heat of the mediums.
5. Type of medium, corrosive or non-corrosive. Safety.
6. Operating pressures.
7. Maintenance, fouling, cleaning, access.
8. Position in system and associated pipework.
9. Cost, materials, streamline or turbulent flow.

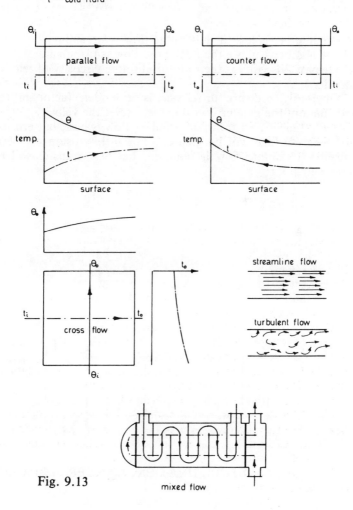

Fig. 9.13

Streamline and Turbulent Flow

In Fig. 9.13 simple diagrams show (1) the laminar, streamline flow of a fluid whose velocity variation is approximately parabolic. Being a maximum at the centre and zero where the fluid is in contact with the pipe or plate surface (2) turbulent flow of a fluid.

Whether flow is streamline or turbulent depends upon certain factors which are summed up by Reynold's number.

$$\text{Reynold's number} = \frac{\text{velocity of fluid flow} \times \text{pipe diameter}}{\text{kinematic viscosity}}$$

If the number is less than 2000 the flow is streamline.
If the number is more than 2500 the flow is turbulent.
(Kinematic viscosity is the ratio of absolute viscosity to relative density.)

Obviously pressure difference is a hidden factor in the calculation, the greater its value the greater the velocity.

For efficient heat transfer turbulent flow is best, but erosion of metal surface will be greatest. For little erosion of metal surface streamline flow is required, but heat transfer will be relatively poor.

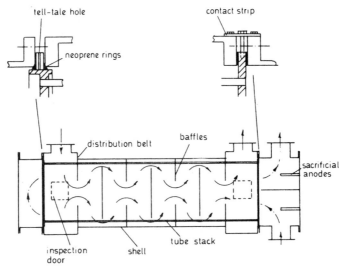

SHELL AND TUBE HEAT EXCHANGERS (Serck)
Fig. 9.14

Shell and Tube Type Heat Exchanger (Serck)

The shell (or cylinder) is usualy made of close grained cast iron, with surfaces machined as required. Gun metal or fabricated steel may be used as alternatives depending upon requirements. Inspection doors are fitted in the distribution belts.

End boxes with end access covers, are of the same material as the shell. Sacrificial anodes in the rod or plug form and an electrical contact strip are fitted to minimise corrosion.

The tube stack is made up of stress relieved aluminium brass tubes expanded into Naval brass tube plates, one plate is fixed as shown and the other is free to allow for expansion of the stack. Brass circular baffles give radial flow to the fluid and support to the tube stack.

In more recent designs of tube type heaters and coolers the guided flow concept has been introduced, *i.e.* a secondary heating, or cooling, surface in the form of radial fins integral with the tubes between which flow is guided radially, alternately out and in from section to section. This gives (1) greater heat transfer surface (2) better heat transfer (3) lower metal surface temperature (4) in the case of oil heaters less risk of oil cracking and hence fouling.

Plate Heat Exchangers

Fig. 9.15 shows diagrammatically the Alfa-Laval plate type heat exchanger. It consists of a variable number of gasketed, titanium (stainless steel or aluminium brass) plates, clamped together, between a closing pressure plate and a frame. The surface of the plates are corrugated to give strength and additional heat transfer surface. The most recent development is to use a herringbone pattern with vees pointing alternately up and down, touching in a criss-cross pattern. This gives additional support, allows pressure to be increased and plate thickness to be reduced.

Gaskets are usually Nitrile rubber bonded to the plate and arranged so that in the event of failure the two fluids cannot mix.

Principal advantages of the plate heat exchanger are:

1. Compact and space saving, virtually no head room is required.

2. Easily inspected and cleaned, all the pipe connections are at the frame plate hence they do not have to be disturbed when plates are dismantled.

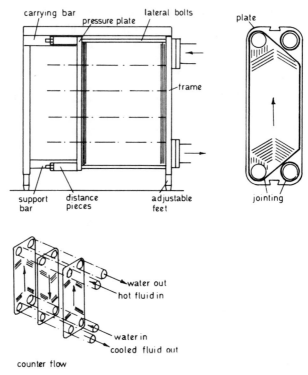

PLATE TYPE HEAT EXCHANGER (Alfa-Laval)
Fig. 9.15

3. Variable capacity, plate numbers can be altered to meet capacity requirements.

4. With titanium plates there is virtually no corrosion or erosion risk and turbulent flow (which is erosive) which takes place between the plates will increase heat transfer and enable fewer plates to be used.

Central Cooling Systems

These have been designed for diesel and steam plant. Fig. 9.16 shows diagrammatically the arrangement for a diesel engined installation.

Large, sea water cooled heat exchangers, one in operation the other stand-by, are the 'central coolers', they will have excess cooling capacity to allow for fouling. A controlled bypass of the fresh water to be cooled maintains it at a steady temperature of 35°C up to a maximum sea water temperature of 33°C. Sea

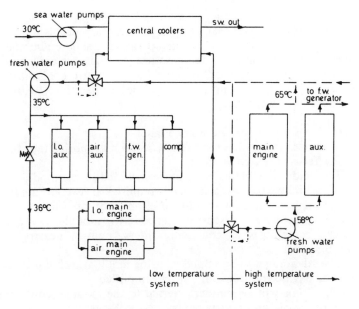

CENTRAL COOLING SYSTEM
Fig. 9.16

water temperature above 33°C will result in an increase in fresh water temperature.

The system is divided into low and high temperature zones. The low temperature zone contains the coolers which can be arranged in different ways to suit requirements. Automatic by-pass valves are arranged across each cooler unit which control the upstream water pressure keeping it constant irrespective of the number of coolers in use. The main advantages of using a central cooling system are:

1. Reduced maintenance. Due to the fresh water system having clean, treated water circulating. The cleaning of the system and component replacement are reduced to a minimum.

2. Fewer salt water pipes with attendant corrosion and fouling problems.

3. With titanium plate heat exchangers used in the central coolers cleaning of the coolers is simplified and corrosion reduced.

4. The higher water speeds possible in the fresh water system result in reduced pipe dimensions and installation costs.

5. The number of valves made of expensive material is greatly

reduced, also cheaper materials can be used throughout the fresh water system without fear of corrosion/erosion problems.

6. With a constant level of temperature being maintained, irrespective of sea water temperature, this gives stability and economy of operation of the machinery, *e.g.* no cold starting since part of the cooling system will be in operation. Reduced cylinder liner wear etc.

Modular Systems for Auxiliary Plant

Modular systems are used for items such as lubrication, fuel, boiler feed water, cooling, etc.

To decide what items have to be included in the module we need to know what performance is required of it. *e.g.* Fuel to a diesel engine: the fuel should be clean, free of water, at the correct pressure and viscosity. Hence in the module we require filters, centrifuges or coalescing filters, pumps, heaters and sensors.

The advantages to be gained by using modular techniques are:

1. The engine room layout will be simplified.

2. Pipe runs will be simple, external to the module, consisting only of supply and return.

3. Module is assembled in the workshop—this in itself has considerable advantage (a) The environment is easier to control, it should be clean dry and oil free. There should be reduced risk of damage to plant when the module is installed because no rust, scale, oil, waste, weld spatter, etc., would be present inside the module, which would have all open ended pipes blanked after satisfactory testing and examination, and they would remain blanked until they have to be connected to piping on board ship. This has the added advantage of reducing pre-commission cleaning time on board (b) The best possible arrangement of integral components for ease of maintenance coupled with shortest pipe runs can be achieved. This would be accomplished by designers and assemblers working in close collusion (c) The module can be easily tested and inspected.

4. Installation time at the shipbuilding yard would be reduced.

5. Standardisation with the least amount of material used, together with the best possible design for access, maintenance, reliability etc., results in economy.

Obviously standardisation does have its limitations. Units would be made in capacities of standard incremental quantities, the standard unit may not provide exactly for requirements. Also, the unit must not become so large that transport becomes a problem.

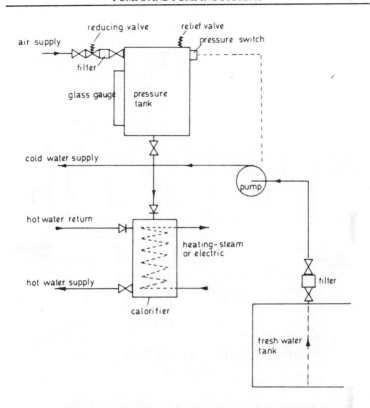

PRESSURISED FRESH WATER SYSTEM
(Pressure 1.3 to 2 bar at highest point in system)
Fig. 9.17

Automatic Domestic Water Supply Systems

For sanitary and fresh water supply modern vessels now usually employ automatic systems. Considering either system: this consists of a tank or reservoir for water supply. The pump discharge is led in and out of the bottom of the tank on its way to the piping system. The tank containing the water has an air space provided above the water. As the water is used up the pressure of air will drop. A pressure switch is connected to the tank, this switch is almost identical to that described in the refrigeration section so that when air pressure falls to say 2 bar the lead from the tank to the bellows serves to operate the switch so starting the pump. The pump builds up water quantity in the

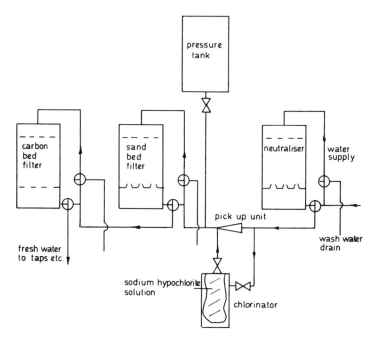

FRESH WATER TREATMENT PLANT
Fig. 9.18

tank until the air pressure is say 4 bar when the pressure switch serves to shut off the pump. The differential for cut in and out can be adjusted for reasonable running periods whilst maintaining a satisfactory pressure on sanitary and/or fresh water fittings.

Water Purification

For domestic purposes the water used must be slightly alkaline, sterilised, clear and pleasant tasting.
1. To give alkalinity and to improve the taste of insipid distilled water, carbonates of calcium and magnesium are used as a filter bed in a neutraliser.
2. To sterilise the water chlorine is used, this would normally be solutions of hypochlorite or possibly the powder calcium chloride. About 0.25 to 1 kg of chlorine would be required for every 1,000,000 kg of water.
3. To produce clear water it can be passed through a sand bed filter.

4. To improve taste a de-chlorination process is used. Chlorinated water is passed through an activated carbon filter bed which will absorb excess chlorine.

Neutraliser, sand bed filter and carbon bed filter can all have their flows reversed for cleaning purposes.

Hydraulic system

A centralised hydraulic system consisting of duplicated oil pumps, usually rotary reciprocating, accumulators, filters and an oil reservoir, fitted with pressure regulators which govern the pressure in different lines for different purposes is an economic, reliable and safe power distribution system.

Items that can be operated by such a system include: pumps *e.g.* submersible or line-shaft driven from deck motors, deck machinery, *e.g.* winches, windlass, cranes, derricks, hatch covers, ramps, water tight doors, bow thruster, etc.

The main advantages of a centralised hydraulic system are (1) smooth operation (2) infinitely variable speed control (3) self lubricating (4) intrinsically safe therefore useful for hazardous cargoes (5) centralised for ease of control.

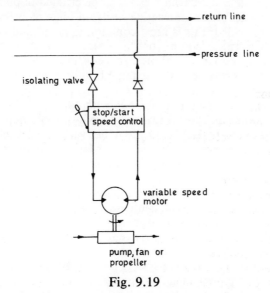

Fig. 9.19

Fig 9.19 shows in simple diagrammatical form how a controlled unit, pump, fan, etc, would be connected into the return and pressure lines which are connected to the centralised hydraulic system. The stop/start speed control may be fitted with a pilot line for remote operation and appropriate sensors would telemeter measurements to the control station.

PREVENTION OF POLLUTION OF THE SEA BY OIL

It is prohibited by law, based on the 1954 international convention to dump oil or oil-water polluted mixtures in port, harbour or within coastal limits of about 80 km. The zones have been increased to include 160 km coastal zones, and more, and to include whole seas as prohibited areas. Within time it can be said that it will be prohibited to dump such pollution from *any* vessel in *any* part of the world. The legal maximum oil particle discharge quantity is 100 parts per million of water, but this may also be reduced in the future. Improved tank cleaning plants have been made at all shore stations. However it may be said that from the operating engineers viewpoint at sea that he is not allowed to discharge any oil or contaminated water overboard. This means that unless a dump tank is utilised, which is quite feasible in oil tankers which can then be cleaned in port, then a separator suitable for extracting oil from bilge or ballast water must be provided, this is most common in cargo and passenger vessels. The rules require such a separator to be of sufficient design, size and construction. Provision must also be made to prevent over-pressure and discharge into confined spaces.

Avoidance of Pollution of the Sea with Oil
The manual on the avoidance of pollution of the sea by oil (DTp published by H.M.S.O.) together with current relevant M notices, are essential reading for Marine Engineers before attempting the examination. Some precautions to be observed when bunkering are:
1. All scuppers to be plugged so that in the event of a small spillage onto the deck it is contained and can be dealt with.
2. Drip trays must be placed under the ship-shore connection.
3. Good communication between ship and shore must be established and checked to regulate flow as desired.
4. Personnel operating the system must be fully conversant with the layout of pipes, tanks, valves etc.
5. Moorings and hose length should at all times be such that there is no possibility of stretching or crushing the hose.
6. Ensure blank at opposite end of cross-over pipe is securely in place.

7. Air pipes should be clear, soundings checked and depth indicators tested.

When transferring oil within the ship it should be ideally be done during the hours of daylight, the overboard discharge connections should be closed and secured, over-flow alarm should be tested and soundings taken at frequent intervals.

Using empty oil fuel tanks as ballast tanks should be avoided as far as possible, since the ballast will eventually have to be discharged.

Oil in Navigable Waters Act

It is an offence to discharge bilge water contaminated with more than 100 p.p.m. of fuel or lubricating oil in a prohibited zone. The international oil pollution chart shows the prohibited zones but generally it includes all waters within 160 km of the shore including territorial waters. When bilge water is discharged in a prohibited zone an entry must be made in the oil record book consisting of: (1) The quantity discharged (2) The source of the bilge water (3) The time of discharge (4) The ships position (5) The date. It must then be signed by the Master and Chief Engineer.

The Act requires that every British Ship of 80 tonnes and over registered in the United Kingdom which uses bunker fuel tanks for ballast water must be fitted with an oily-water separator.

Oily Water Separator

Various types of oily water separator have been produced over the years but most of the gravity types fall far short of the modern requirements. IMO have laid down requirements for separators and they are:

1. Oil-water separators for bilge and ballast applications should be capable of giving an effluent containing less than 100 p.p.m. of oil irrespective of the oil content (0 to 100%) of the feed supplied to the device.

2. Filtering systems are further required to provide an effluent of no more than 15 p.p.m. under all inlet conditions.

Most gravity types that have been installed in vessels will give effluents ranging from 50 to 1,500 p.p.m., the lower figure is probably an overestimate, 150 p.p.m. would probably be more realistic.

The type of pump used for delivering the oily-water mixture governs considerably the degree of contamination in the effluent. A large number of bilge pumps are centrifugal and they are often used as the supply pump to the separator. They churn

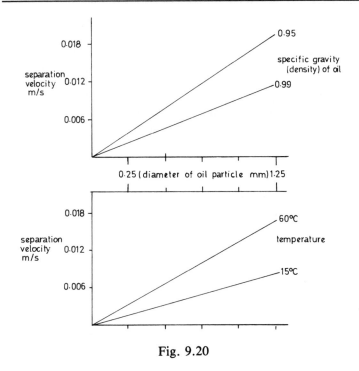

Fig. 9.20

the supply and produce small oil droplets (less than 200 μm) dispersed throughout the water so that the 100 ppm requirement cannot be met.

A positive displacement pump *e.g.* slow running double vane, screw, reciprocating or gear enables a much better performance to be achieved from the separator as they do not produce large quantities of small oil droplets.

The pumping mode is becoming important since it is claimed that with any kind of pump operating in the suction mode (*i.e.* pump after the separator) the IMO requirement of 15 p.p.m. or less can be met without the use of 2nd and 3rd stage filters or coalescers.

The graphs in Fig. 9.20 show clearly the effect of oil particle size and separation velocity thus further emphasising the importance of pump selection and mode, presence of oil coalescers (gather oil into larger droplets) and controlled flow within the separator. Oil density and mixture temperature also govern speed of separation and hence separator throughput.

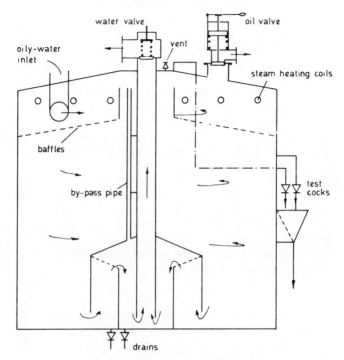

AUTOMATIC OILY-WATER SEPARATOR
Fig. 9.21

Automatic Oily-Water Separator

Fig. 9.21 shows the essential parts of an automatic separator. The operation is as follows:

Clean water is delivered to the separator through the oily-water inlet until discharge takes place out of the vent valve which is then closed. Oily-water is now delivered to the separator and when the pressure inside the separator reaches 2 bar approximately the water discharge valve automatically opens. The mixture circulates and flows across weirs and perforated baffles which assist in separating the oil and water. Oil will now accumulate at the top of the separator, and as the oily-water interface gradually moves down the oil discharge valve is automatically opened up. (See later for details).

A bypass pipe takes remaining traces of oil from the last separator stage up to the top of the separator.

Steam heating coils are provided in the oil space to reduce viscosity and assist separation, test cocks can be used to ascertain the levels of oil and water approximately as a check for the automatic detection. A spring loaded valve is usually fitted on both discharges but it is essential that a relief valve is provided on the shell or incoming mixture line to prevent overpressure and accidental discharge to a confined space or overboard under all working conditions. Such a relief valve should preferably be led back to the suction side of the supply pump or to an overflow tank. The usual working pressure for the separator is in the region of 2 bar, *i.e.* the pressure at which the spring loaded water discharge valve is set. The relief valve is set about 2½ bar approximately.

Fig. 9.22 shows a three stage separator which complies with IMO requirements. The first stage is as previously described for the automatic separator, the second and third stages are coalescers. The effluent from the first stage enters the bottom of the second stage and passes up the middle of the coalescer, the coalesced oil collects at the top and the water discharges at the bottom and then goes to the next stage.

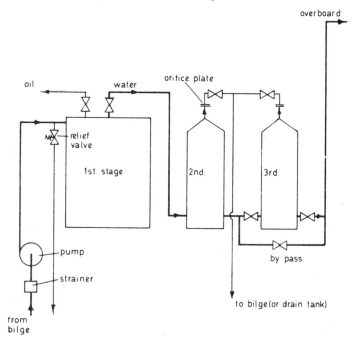

3-STAGE OILY-WATER SEPARATOR (Victor)
Fig. 9.22

Electric Separator Probe

This is rather a complex ac circuit and only the most simple operating principle is considered. Two sheathed probes are provided at the highest and lowest levels of the oil-water interface and a third probe is fitted low down in the clean water space, the latter acts as an emergency cut out should priming-over occur. The probes are connected to an ac circuit very similar to the dc Wheatstone Bridge principle. Two coils are energised from the supply and two condenser circuits complete the bridge, one condenser connected to the probe being the variable in the circuit. The probe and tank form two electrodes of the variable condenser. The capacitance depends on the dielectric constant of the material between (for given distance apart and electrode size). Thus the value of the capacitance depends on the material between probe and tank. The bridge when balanced in air would become unbalanced by change of capacitance in oil or water and the electrical signal could be magnified and relayed, similarly balance in oil would react to water, etc.

Automatic Valve Operation

The relay can be arranged to operate lights, alarms, etc., or preferably solenoid operation via air, steam or hydraulic servos for the operation of the appropriate oil or water discharge valves. With the lower probe in oil the unbalance due to capacitance change will function to open the oil valve and close the water valve, similarly the upper probe in water will serve to shut the oil valve and open the water valve.

The actual operation of automatic valve control combined with alarm and protection circuits can be considered by referring to Fig. 9.23.

Oil has the same effect as air. With the separator empty (both probes in air) the two probe indicator lamps will be out, oil discharge lamp on, main contactor energised, solenoid energised, pilot valve up, alarm bell ringing, pump tripped. When water enters the separator and reaches the lower probe the bell stops ringing and the lower probe indicator light comes on. When water reaches the upper probe its indicator light comes on, the water discharge light comes on and the oil discharge lamp goes out. The solenoid is de-energised and the pilot valve moves down. These conditions are reversed when oil pushes the interface down.

When oil build up occurs and pushes the oil-water interface down to the lower probe the solenoid is energised and the pilot

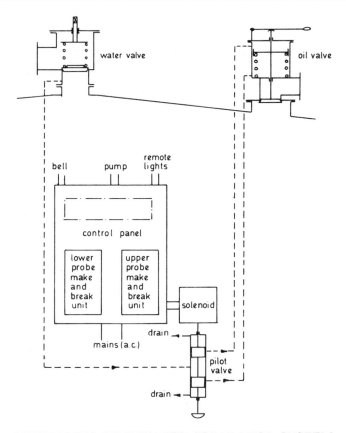

AUTOMATIC OILY-WATER SEPARATOR SYSTEM
Fig. 9.23

valve moves up. Clean water at 2 bar acts on top of the oil valve piston causing the valve to open. Pressure reduces, the water valve closes, and pressure reaches about $1\frac{1}{3}$ bar with the interface rising to the upper probe. The solenoid is now de-energised, the pilot valve moves down, clean water at $1\frac{1}{3}$ bar acts under the oil valve piston causing the valve to close, pressure starts to increase again.

With the main isolator shut the lower probe unit can be made to isolate and cut out the pump if oil reaches the danger level. With the main isolator open this action is shorted out so that the pump can be used for other duties. A float controlled air release arrangement can be fitted to give automatic air release from the shell.

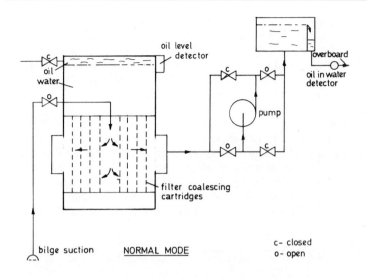

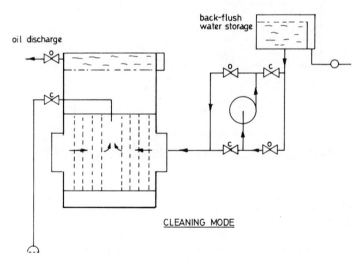

AUTOMATIC OILY-WATER SEPARATOR
Fig. 9.24.

The suction mode automatic oily-water separator shown in Fig. 9.24 can, it is claimed, reduce effluent level to 2 ppm of oil in the mixture or less. In order to achieve this low level the separator incorporates concentric cylindrical oil coalescing cartridges through which the oily-water mixture is drawn by a positive displacement pump. The coalesced oil rises to the top of the separator where its accumulation is detected by an oil-water interface probe. When in the normal mode a controller is constantly monitoring the oil-water interface level and the overboard discharge. In the event of the effluent exceeding set limit the process is stopped and alarm given.

When the oil-water interface reaches its lower level the controller changes the operation to one of cleaning by back flushing and oil discharge. The oil-water interface will then rise to the higher level when reversion to normal mode takes place.

By using an oily-water separator in the suction mode rather than the delivery mode (*i.e.* the pump after the separator not before) disintegration of the oily-water mixture prior to separation is achieved, thus improving separation efficiency.

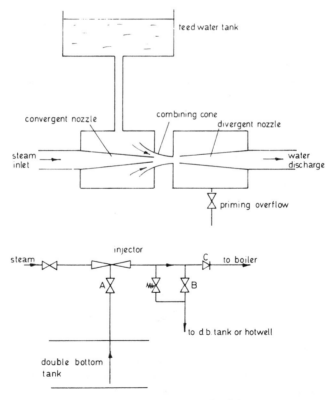

FEED WATER INJECTOR
Fig. 9.25

INJECTORS AND EJECTORS

The feed water injector could be used in place of a feed pump. It is rarely seen in marine practice but it is sometimes provided as a stand by feed supply device. Compared to a pump the injector has the advantage of no working parts but it has the disadvantage of being restricted to fairly cold water. Considering Fig. 9.25 and the theory of the injector.

The working steam expands through a convergent nozzle, losing pressure and gaining velocity so that it emerges at high velocity from the nozzle. It contacts the cold feed water from the feed tank and condenses and the resulting jet of entrained water is guided through the combining cone and has its maximum velocity at entrance to the diverging nozzle. The kinetic (velocity) energy of the jet is now converted to pressure energy again as it passes along the divergent nozzle it loses velocity and increases in pressure so that at exit the pressure is arranged to be higher than the boiler pressure so water will enter the boiler. Thus it can be seen that the principle of operation is conversion of energy. Ignoring temperature (energy) changes and losses and considering no rise of discharge pipe then the pressure and velocity energy of the entering steam together with the energy due to the head of entering water appears as pressure and velocity energy of the combined mass at discharge.

The feed tank need not be supplying from a head, *i.e.*, the injector will lift water but for given orifice sizes this reduces the discharge pressure from the injector. The orifice sizes are variable so that velocity and pressure energies are variable and the discharge pressure can be adjusted as required.

Fig. 9.25 also shows typical connections to a feed water injector. To put the injector into operation valves A and B would be opened, valve C closed, steam would then be supplied to the injector until it is primed and water is being delivered to the double bottom tank or the hotwell. Delivery would then be changed over to the boiler by opening C and closing B. This arrangement simplifies priming when the injector has to lift water and ensures that all the steam used is condensed.

Ejectors are used for bilge systems, evaporators and gas freeing systems on tankers etc. Their principle is similar to the injector but water is used instead of steam as the pumping medium. Ejectors consist of a convergent-divergent nozzle arrangement, similar to a Venturi, with a connection for pick up of the fluid to be discharged at the throat. Ejectors are simple, reliable, inexpensive, effective and virtually maintenance free.

SEWAGE AND SLUDGE

Present regulations relating to sewage in the U.K. are simply that no sewage must be discharged whilst the vessel is in port. Standards adopted by the U.S.A. and Canada are likely to become IMO recommendations, their main restriction is that the coliform count in the effluent discharged in restricted waters should not exceed 1000/100 ml.

Coliforms: this is the name given to a bacteria group found in the intestines. They are not normally harmful, except when they contain pathogenic colonies which can cause dysentry, typhoid, para-typhoid, etc.

Retention Systems

Their main advantage is simplicity in operation and virtually no maintenance, they comply with present regulations within the limit of their storage capacity. Since no sewage can be discharged in port, prolonged stays create a problem, this problem could be reduced by the use of a vacuum transportation system for toilets where only about 1 litre of water/flush is used compared to about 12 litres/flush for conventional types. Vacuum systems use smooth, small bore plastic pipes (except in fire hazard areas) which are relatively inexpensive, and because of the small amount of water used they are usually supplied with fresh water which keeps salt water out of accommodation spaces with obvious advantages.

With some retention systems the sewage is passed first through a comminutor, which macerates the solids giving greater surface area. The mix is then passed into a chlorine contact tank where it must remain for at least 20 minutes before discharge overboard.

Biological Treatment Plants

Plant description: raw sewage passes through a comminutor into the collection compartment. When the level in this compartment rises sufficiently, overflow of the liquid takes place into the treatment—Aeration compartment where the sewage is broken down by aerobic activation. Fluid in this compartment is continuously agitated by air which keeps the bacteriologically active sludge in suspension and supplies the necessary oxygen for purification.

The effluent is then pumped to a settlement compartment where the sludge settles out leaving treated effluent, which

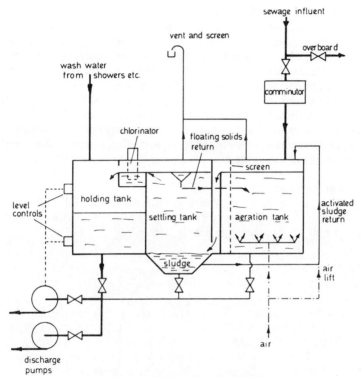

EXTENDED AERATION SEWAGE PLANT
Fig. 9.26

passes over a weir into the final compartment for chlorination before discharge overboard.

The settled sludge is continuously returned to the aeration compartment by an airlift pump.

Excess sludge builds up in the settlement chamber and this must be discharged at regular intervals, in port this may not be possible hence it should be pumped to a sullage tank for disposal later. By using an incinerator to deal with excess sludge a sullage tank may not be required.

With the extended aeration system it can be 5 to 14 days before the plant is fully operational because of the prolonged aeration of sewage necessary to produce the bacteria that carry out the purifying process. Hence, the plant should be kept operational at all times. It should be noted that oil or grease entering the system kills useful bacteria.

Chemical Treatment Plants

These are recirculation systems in which the sewage is macerated, chemically treated, then allowed to settle. The clear, sterilised, filtered liquid is returned to the sanitary system for further use and the solids are periodically discharged to a sullage tank or incinerator. The main advantages are (1) no necessity to discharge effluent or sludge in port or restricted waters (2) relatively small compact plant. However, chemical toilets are not always what they should be and with this relatively complex system increased maintenance is something which does not endear itself to engineers.

Sludge Incinerators

These are capable of dealing with waste oil, oil and water mixtures of up to 25% water content, rags, galley waste etc., and solid matter from sewage plants if required.

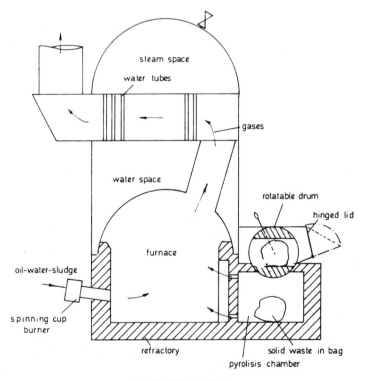

INCINERATOR
Fig. 9.27

Fig. 9.27 shows a small water tube type of boiler combined with incinerator plant in order to provide an economy.

Homogenous oil/water mixtures that have been formed by passing them through a comminutor—a kind of grinder, macerator, mixer which produces a fine well dispersed emulsion—are supplied to the rotating cup burner. Solid waste from the galley and accommodation, etc., would be collected in bags and placed in the chamber adjacent to the main combustion chamber, the loading system of which is self evident in the diagram. The loading arrangement incorporates a locking device which prevents the doors (loading and ash pit) being opened with the burner on. The solid waste goes through a process that may be described as pyrolysis, that is the application of heat. Hydrocarbon gases are formed, due to the low air supply to this compartment, which pass into the main chamber through a series of small holes and burn in the furnace. Dry ash remaining in the chamber has to be removed periodically through the ash pit door.

Solid matter from sewage systems could be incinerated in this unit, a connection would have to be made from the sewage plant to the pyrolysis chamber of the incinerator.

PIPE ARRANGEMENTS AND FITTINGS

Most of the details given are for cargo vessels as the tanker is virtually a whole pumping system within itself.

A Typical Bilge Pipe Arrangement

The arrangement as sketched satisfies the conditions required. The diagram should be considered in conjunction with the rules given later. For examination purposes it is advised that the student should, if asked, sketch and describe the bilge system and fittings with which he has been associated on a vessel at sea. In so doing he should be able to sketch the arrangement from memory and there should be no need to consider Fig. 9.28 further, it is presented merely for guidance.

Deep Tank Piping Arrangement

Referring to Fig. 9.29 it will be seen that the tank is arranged for filling with water ballast. In the early stages filling will be by means of the ballast pump discharge and later by gravity through the ballast pump suction chest, although if time is available gravity throughout is probably best. Final filling before closing the tank lid is best carried out by hose from the

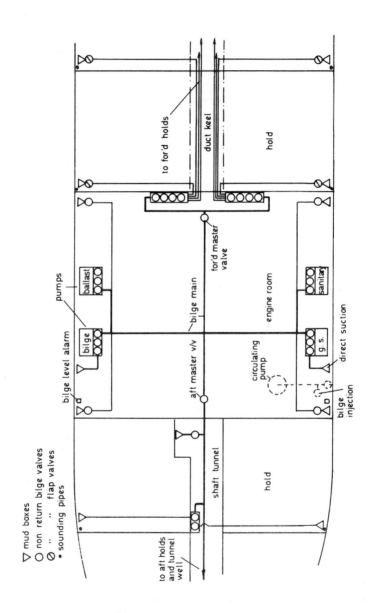

BILGE PIPE ARRANGEMENT
Fig. 9.28

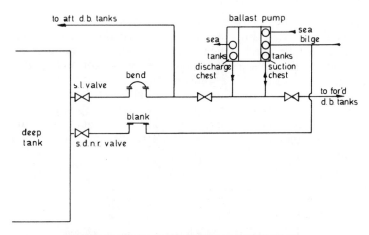

DEEP TANK PIPE ARRANGEMENTS

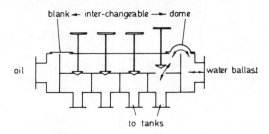

OIL-WATER BALLAST CHEST
Fig. 9.29

deck service line. When the tank is full the screw lift ballast valve is shut and the line is blanked off until the tank requires to be pumped out. When the tank is to be used for dry cargo the ballast line is blanked and the bilge line is open. Great care is necessary to avoid any mistakes being made and a rigid routine is advised. Clear explanatory notices are to be provided and all valves and fittings should be in good order and easily accessible.

Bilge Injection Valve

The bilge injection valve as sketched in Fig. 9.30 is one of the most important fittings in the machinery space. It is provided for use in the event of serious flooding in the machinery space. By closing in the main injection valve and opening up the bilge injection valve the largest pump (or pumps) in the engine room are drawing directly from the lowest point in the space, this action can remove large quantities of water. A doubler plate is welded to the skin, and machined usually after welding operations, the chest flange being bedded to the doubler and then studded in place. The joint is either spigot and jointing compound, or flat with a joint of canvas and red lead putty.

The diameter of the bilge injection valve is at least 2/3rds of the diameter of the main sea inlet. Valve spindles should be clear of the engine platform and valves and operating gear require regular examination and greasing, with cleaning of strum or strainer.

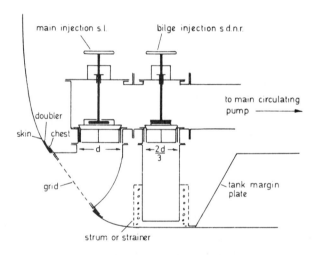

MAIN AND BILGE INJECTION VALVES
Fig. 9.30

Oil-Water Ballast Chest

This chest is a standard fitting on most cargo vessels, on the double bottom piping system. Normally all chests are open to oil fuel (bend) and blanked to water ballast. For ballast, or ballast prior to cleaning purposes, the bend and blank are as shown in the sketch (Fig. 9.30). This means that an error in opening the wrong valve would not in itself allow crossing of circuits.

As an alternative to this fitting, hollow one way discharge plug cocks or a system of interlock valves would be acceptable. Any system employed must prevent easy joining of oil and water circuits by accident.

SOME RULES RELATING TO PUMPING SYSTEMS
BILGE (vessels over 90 m long)

(1) A piping system and pumping plant should be provided to pump out and drain any adjacent to damage water-tight compartments (including tween decks) under all reasonable damage conditions. Efficient drainage should be provided especially to unusual form compartments and the piping system design should not allow flooding under damage conditions.

(2) Vessels shall have at least four independent power pumps connected to the main line. Ballast, sanitary, etc., are acceptable, also engine driven pump, provided they are of sufficient capacity and are connected to the main line.

(3) One such pump should be of the remote controlled submersible type *or* the power pumps and controls should be so placed so that one pump is always available under all reasonable damage conditions. Each pump should *where possible* be located in a separate watertight compartment.

(4) Pumps should be of the self priming type unless efficient priming devices are provided. The capacity of the pumps should give a water speed in the main line of not less than 2 m/s, and the capacity may be determined from a given empirical formula.

(5) Each pump should have a direct suction to the space in which it is situated, such suction to be at least the same bore as the bilge main. Not more than two such suctions are required and in the machinery space such suctions should be arranged one each side.

(6) Main engine circulating pumps shall have a direct suction (with non return valves), draining the lowest level in the machinery space, such suction at least 2/3rds of the diameter of the main sea inlet. In motor ships this should apply but direct suctions on other suitable pumps of equivalent capacity is acceptable.

(7) Bilge pipes should not be led through oil tanks or D.B. tanks. Joints should be flanged, pipes well secured and protected against damage. The pipes should be independent to the bilge systems only.

(8) Collision bulkheads should not be pierced below the margin line by more than one pipe, such pipe to be fitted with a screw down valve operated from above the bulkhead deck, valve chest being secured to the forward

side of the collision bulkhead (divided peaks may have two pipes).

(9)   Valves and cocks not forming part of a pipe system are not to be secured to watertight bulkhead. Pipes, cables, etc., passing through such a bulkhead are to be provided with watertight fittings to retain the integrity of the bulkhead. Connections attached to such bulkheads are to be made by screwed or welded studs, not by tap bolts passing through clearance holes.

(10) The bilge piping system is to be separate from cargo and oil fuel systems. Spindles to all master valves, bilge injection, etc., should be led above the engine room platform. All valves, extended spindles, etc., to be clearly marked and accessible at all times.

(11) Diameter of bilge suction lines in mm to be determined from given empirical formula. No bilge main under 65 mm bore and no branch under 50 mm or need be over 100 mm bore.

(12) Bilge valves should be one of the non return type. Valves, blanks, lock ups, etc., must be provided to prevent connection between sea and bilges or bilges and water ballast, etc., at the same time.

(13) Emergency bilge pumping systems if provided should be separate from the main system.

(14) Bilge pipes to be provided with mud boxes. Suction pipe ends should be enclosed in easily removable strum boxes, the holes through which should be approximately 10 mm diameter and their combined area not less than twice the area of the suction pipe.

(15) Sounding pipes where provided are to be as straight as possible, easily accessible, normally provided with closing plugs, machinery space pipes to have self closing cocks.

Note

One explicit rule, covered by the generalisation summary in Rule 1 given above, is considered worth repeating, in full, in view of a recent casualty:

Provision is to be made in every vessel to prevent the flooding of any watertight compartment served by a bilge suction pipe in the event of the pipe being severed or damaged, by collision or grounding, in any other watertight compartment. Where any part of such a pipe is situated nearer to the side of the ship than 1/5th of the midship breadth of the ship measured at the level of the deepest subdivision load water line, or in any duct keel, a non return valve shall be fitted to the pipe in the watertight compartment containing the open end of the pipe. (See Fig. 9.28).

Ballast
The only real requirement is that mentioned earlier, *i.e.*, no possibility of sea or ballast water gaining access to dry cargo or adjacent compartments. Bilge connections to pumps connected to ballast or sea must be non return valves or one way cocks. Lock up valves or blanks must prevent flooding or inadvertent pumping out of deep tanks, etc. Water ballast and oil fuel must be effectively isolated.

Oil Fuel Installations
These rules are somewhat lengthy and are mainly covered in other sections, *e.g.*, boilers, fuel testing, ship construction, etc. However, it is considered worth presenting that section of the rules regarding instructions to ships' engineers in full and then to present a *shortened extract* of *some* of the important rules not previously mentioned.

Instructions
(1) A plan and description of the oil piping arrangement should be clearly displayed.
(2) Escape of oil heated to or above the flashpoint is most dangerous, and may result in explosion or fire.
(3) After lighting burners, the torches *must* be fully extinguished by means of the appliances provided for that purpose.
(4) Cleanliness is essential to safety, no oil or other combustible substances should be allowed to accumulate in bilges or gutterways or on tank tops or boiler flats.
(5) Before any oil tank which has contained oil fuel is entered for any purpose the oil should be removed entirely, all oil vapour must also be carefully removed by steaming and efficient ventilation. Tests of the atmosphere in tanks or bunkers should be made to ensure safety before inspection or work in them is begun.

Extract
Boiler, settling tank and oil fuel unit spaces, etc., must be clean, have no combustible material, and have good access. Oil tanks, oil pumps, etc., should be fitted as far from boilers as is practicable and should be provided with trays and gutters, drain

cocks, etc., should be self closing and efficient sounding or indicating devices provided. Relief valves should be fitted to discharge to an overflow tank fitted with level alarms, filling stations should be isolated, well drained and ventilated. Every oil tank should have at least one air pipe, such air pipe or any overflow pipe system provided (preferably returning to an overflow tank with visual and sight returns) should have an aggregate area at least $1\frac{1}{4}$ times the aggregate area of the filling pipes. All means should be considered to prevent discharge of oil overboard.

Oil pipes and fittings should be of steel, suitably hydraulically tested. Oil units should be in duplicate and any oil pump should be isolated to the oil system only, provided with relief preferably back to the suction side, capable of being shut down from a remote control position, and provided with shut off isolating valves. Heating coil drains should be returned via an observation tank. Valves or cocks fitted to tanks in the machinery and boiler spaces should be capable of being operated from a remote position above the bulkhead deck. Ample ventilation and clearance spaces for circulation should be provided and no artificial type lights capable of igniting oil vapour are allowed. Ventilator dampers, etc., must have reliable operating gear clearly marked for shut and open positions.

Note

Essential features are care and cleanliness together with reliable overflow and isolating equipment. Particular care is advised during bunkering to avoid overflows (gravitating is always a safer process where practicable) and during tank cleaning, venting or inspection periods.

TEST EXAMPLES 9

Class 3
1. Make a diagrammatic sketch of a bilge pumping system itemising the main components.
2. Describe the passage of water through a centrifugal pump.
3. Describe an oily-water separator and state how you would check that it was working satisfactorily.

TEST EXAMPLES 9

Class 2

1. Sketch and describe a plate type heat exchanger.

   State one advantage and one disadvantage of this design compared to the tubular type;

2. Sketch and describe a pump other than the reciprocating or centrifugal type. Explain how it works. State with reasons, the duty for which it is most suited.

3. Sketch and describe a centrifugal bilge pump.

   Explain the need for a priming pump.

   Give one advantage and one disadvantage of the centrifugal pump compared to the direct acting pump for bilge duties.

4. Sketch the construction of an oily water separator.

   Explain how it functions in service.

   State the purpose and operation of all alarms or safety devices fitted to the separator.

5. Make a line diagram of a bilge pumping system for a dry cargo ship.

   Indicate the type and position of each valve fitted.

   In view of the possibility of collision, explain how the integrity of the bilge pumping system is ensured as far as possible.

TEST EXAMPLES 9

Class 1

1. Describe with a line diagram a hydrophore system, *i.e.*, a fresh water system incorporating an air reservoir.

    Describe how a drop in pressure actuates the fresh water pump.

    State two advantages of this system over the gravity head system.

2. Sketch a tubular oil cooler and explain how:
    (a)   differential expansion between the tubes and shell is accommodated,
    (b)   corrosion is controlled,
    (c)   automatic control of the oil temperatures is effected.

    State how by construction, operation and maintenance tube failure can be minimised.

3. Give a simple explanation of the nature and effect of cavitation in rotodynamic pumps.

    Describe with sketches a super-cavitating pump.
    State the purpose of such a pump and give an instance of current shipboard application.

4. Describe with sketches a centralised cooling system incorporating plate type heat exchangers.

    Explain the purpose of this system and how it is achieved.

5. Describe with sketches an axial flow pump.

    Explain its principle of operation.

    State what important advantage and serious disadvantage it possesses compared to other pumps.

    Explain the effects of throttling either the suction or discharge valve.

CHAPTER 10

LUBRICATION AND OIL PURIFICATION

Purification of fuel and lubricating oils on board ship is a widely practised and well known operation. Generally three methods are employed: Gravitation, filtration and centrifugal purification.

For the gravitation method, which is principally used for oil fuels, settling tanks are employed. When the oil is allowed to stand undisturbed in the tank, mediums of higher relative density than the oil gravitate to the bottom of the tank where they are discharged periodically through a manually operated sludge cock. The process of separation in a settling tank can be speeded up to a certain extent by heating the tank contents. If heating of the contents is possible, steam heating coils are generally used, but care must be taken not to heat the oil to too high a temperature. Fig. 10.1 shows a settling tank with the usual fittings provided.

In an examination these fittings should be itemised and a brief description of the function of each should be given thus:

Sludge valve or cock. Used for draining water and sludge from bottom of tank. It must be self-closing since if it were not, and it was left unattended, a dangerous situation could arise whereby the tank content could be drained into the oily bilge or sludge tank.

Dumping valve. This fitting can be used in the event of fire to dump the oil from an elevated settling tank to a double bottom tank which could possibly be below the level of the fire.

Exhaust steam from heating coils would be led to a steam trap, which ensures maximum utilisation of the heat content in the steam, then to an observation tank for oil detection.

Overflow pipe, etc. (The remainder should be completed in a similar way as an exercise by the student.)

Filtration of lubrication and fuel oils removes unwanted particles of material such as cotton threads, paint chippings, small pieces of metal, etc., which could cause damage to pumps and engines, from the oils. Filtration does not separate water from the oils, however, by pumping heated lubricating oil into a vacuum chamber, vaporisation of water can be achieved. Also, water repellant and water coalescing filter cartridges can be used which will cause separation of water from oil.

Many different types of filters are manufactured, the simplest being the wire mesh type which are fitted in pairs in the system of oil piping, which enables the operator to clean the filter not in use without shutting down the oil system. Others of a more complex nature can be cleaned whilst in operation and may be fitted singly in the oil piping system or again in pairs.

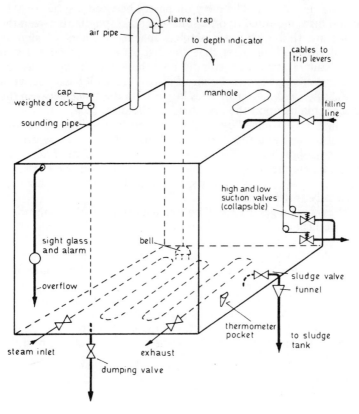

Fig. 10.1

FILTERS

Wire gauze type filters are made with coarse or fine mesh depending upon the positioning of the filter unit in the oil system. An example of this are the hot and cold oil filters fitted in oil burning and pumping installations, the coarse mesh suction filters are used for cold oil and the fine mesh discharge filters are used for the heated oil. The wire mesh type filter however is rarely made to filter out particles below 125 microns in size. If finer filtration is required, other types of filter unit are used, one such filter unit is the well known Auto-Klean strainer.

Auto-Klean Strainer (Fig. 10.2)

This is an improvement on the wire gauze strainer. It can be cleaned whilst in operation and it can filter out particles down to 25 microns in size. The dirty oil passes between a series of thin metal discs mounted upon a square central spindle. Between the discs are thin metal star shaped spacing washers of slightly smaller overall diameter than the discs. Cleaning blades, fitted to a square stationary spindle and the same thickness as the washers are between each pair of discs. As the oil passes between the discs, solid matter of sizes larger than the space between the discs remains upon the periphery of the disc stack.

The filter is cleaned by rotating the central spindle, this rotates the disc stack and the stationary cleaning blades scrape off the filtered solids which then settle to the bottom of the filter unit. Periodically the flow of oil through the filter unit is interrupted and the sludge well is cleaned out. To facilitate this the filters are generally fitted in pairs.

Pressure gauges are fitted before and after the filter unit, these give indication of the condition of the filter.

Fig. 10.2 illustrates an Auto-Klean filter unit of the type capable of filtering out particles down to 200 microns in size, this type can also be made to filter particles of under 75 microns, but the mechanical strength of the cleaning blades will be low. A more recent type of Auto-Klean strainer has the modified disc stack and cleaning blade arrangement shown in Fig. 10.3. With this modified disc stack particles of under 25 microns in size can be filtered out without impairing the mechanical strength of the cleaning blades.

Streamline Lubricating Oil Filter

The streamline filter consists of a two compartment pressure vessel containing a number of cylindrical filter cartridges. Each

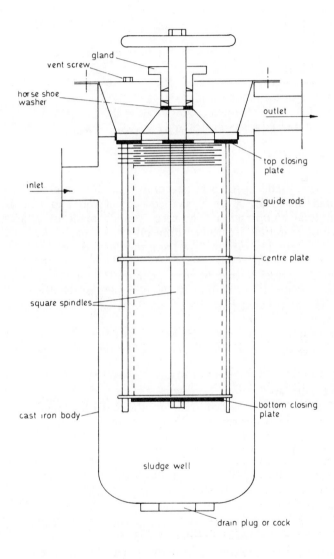

AUTO-KLEAN STRAINER
Fig. 10.2

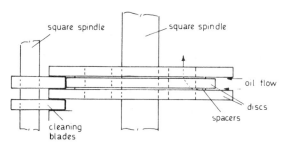

MODIFIED DISC STACK (Auto-Klean)
Fig. 10.3

cartridge is made up of a large number of thin annular discs
threaded on to an X or Y shaped section rod and held in
longitudinal compression. The discs can be made of a wide
variety of materials, for lubricating oil special paper discs are
generally used. The oil can flow from the dirty to the clean side
of the filter via the small spaces between the compressed discs
then up the spaces formed by the hole in the disc and the rod. In
this way the dirt is left behind on the periphery of the disc stack
and it is claimed that particles of the order of 1 micron can be
filtered out.

For cleaning, compressed air is generally used, by closing A
and B, and opening D and C reversal of flow results (see Fig.
10.4).

Filter Coalescers

These have been designed to replace the centrifugal method of
particulate and water removal from fuel and lubricating oils.

The unit consists of some form of pre-filter for particulate
removal followed by a compressed inorganic fibre coalescing
unit in which water is collected into larger globules.

Coalescing action is relatively complex but briefly, the
molecular attraction between the water droplets and the
inorganic fibres is greater than that between the oil and the
fibres. When the water globules are large enough they will move
with the stream out of the coalescing unit.

Downstream of the coalescing cartridges are P.T.F.E. coated,
stainless steel, water repelling screens that act as a final water
stripping stage. Water gravitates from them and from the outlet
of the coalescer cartridges into the well of the strainer body from
where it is periodically removed.

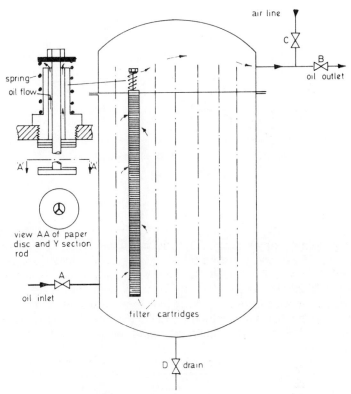

air line

C

B
oil outlet

spring

oil flow

A'   A'

view AA of paper
disc and Y section
rod

A

oil inlet

filter cartridges

D drain

STREAMLINE LUBRICATING OIL FILTER
Fig. 10.4

In modular form these units would have pumps, motors, alarms, indicators, water probes with automatic water dumping, heaters to lower the viscosity of the oil, together with the filtration system described above.

Lubricating Oil Filter-Coalescer

Lubricating oil in circulation round a closed system *e.g.*, turbine, generators, sterntubes etc., will absorb moisture from the atmosphere that will reduce the lubricating properties of the oil. Fig. 10.5, shows a filter-coalescer that will remove solid particles of three microns and above and also up to 99% of the water present in the oil.

Lubricating oil is pumped through the water coalescer filter cartridges which remove solids and coalesce (*i.e.* gather into

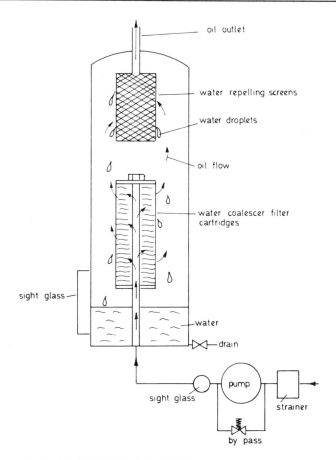

LUBRICATING OIL FILTER-COALESCER
Fig. 10.5

larger droplets) the free water droplets held in suspension in the oil. Most of the water then gravitates to the bottom of the body and the oil with the remaining water droplets passes to the water repelling screens, which permit passage of oil only. Water droplets which collect on the screens eventually settle to the bottom of the body.

To clean the unit, it must first be drained. Then the filter cartridges are renewed, the water repelling screens need not be touched.

A heater would be incorporated in the supply line which would heat the lubricating oil thus assisting separation.

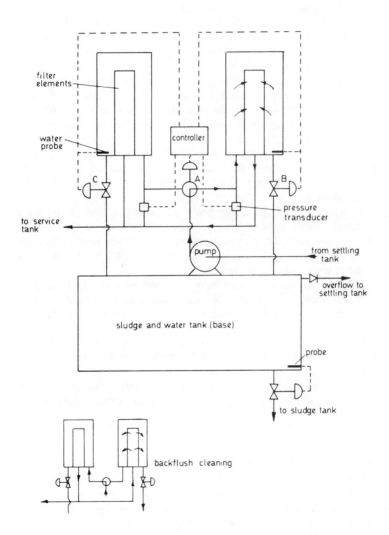

filter
elements

water
probe

controller

to service
tank

pressure
transducer

pump

from settling
tank

overflow to
settling tank

sludge and water tank (base)

probe

to sludge tank

backflush cleaning

AUTOMATIC OIL FILTER MODULE
Fig. 10.6

Oil Module (fuel or lubricating oil)

An automatic oil cleaning module comprising duplicated filter assembly, pumps and controls mounted on a water/sludge tank which serves as a base, is shown diagrammatically in Fig. 10.6.

In normal operation, dirty oil from the oil settling tank would be pumped through the filter to the service tank. Impurities collect on the outer surfaces of the filter and this results in an increase in pressure differences across the filter. When this pressure difference reaches the preset limit of about 0.4 bar a signal from the differential pressure switch to the controller starts the cleaning procedure. The controller sends signals to valves A and B which change over and open respectively so that the back-flush cleaning of the dirty filter as shown in Fig. 10.6 takes place for about 60 seconds. At the end of the cleaning period valve B closes and the system is back to normal operation.

If water enters the filter body its presence is detected by a water detection probe. A signal from the probe causes the valve B or C to open, depending upon which filter is in use, and the water is discharged into the sludge tank. When the water is completely discharged the valve automatically closes.

Sludge and water in the base tank are automatically located and discharged to a sludge storage tank. The relatively clean oil from the top of the base tank overflows into the settling tank for recycling.

A type of differential pressure device that could be used in the module is shown in Fig. 10.7. Increasing the spring force increases the pressure differential setting at which the plunger will operate a switch for the timed cleaning sequence. The synthetic rubber diaphragms at each end would resist attack from the oil.

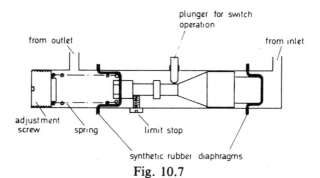

Fig. 10.7

CLARIFICATION AND SEPARATION

Clarification

The term clarification is used to describe separation of solids from a liquid. A centrifuge arranged to discharge a single liquid is called a clarifier.

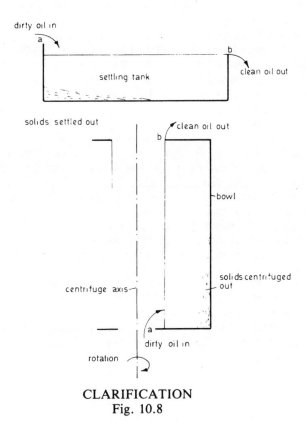

CLARIFICATION
Fig. 10.8

Fig. 10.8 shows clarification taking place in a gravity settling tank. Oil, containing solids, is fed into the tank at (a) and as the oil flows to (b) the solids present in the oil gravitate to the bottom of the tank. The heaviest solids deposit first at (a) and the lighter solids which are carried forward by the flow of the oil deposit nearer to (b).

A similar process takes place in the centrifugal clarifier, formed by rotating the settling tank analogy in Fig. 10.8 through

90° to give the lower figure in the diagram. Here, oil is fed in at (a) and is thrown by centrifugal force to the side of the rotating bowl. Solids present in the oil pass through the oil to the bowl side and accumulate there, the heavier solids depositing near the bottom of the bowl and the lighter solids towards the top. The similarity of the two methods of clarification, gravity and centrifugal, is self evident from the diagram.

Separation

The term separation is used to describe the separation of two liquids. In marine work these are usually oil and water. A centrifuge arranged for the separation and continuous discharge of two liquids is called a centrifugal separator.

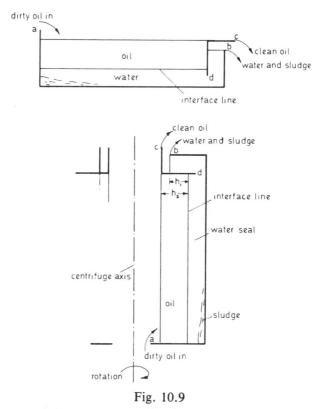

Fig. 10.9

In a purifier arranged to operate as a centrifugal separator any solids which are present will deposit upon the side of the bowl, hence clarification takes place at the same time as separation. In order for a purifier to operate as a centrifugal separator a water seal is necessary and this operates as follows:

Using the gravitation analogy Fig. 10.9, water is first fed into the tank at (a) until the level (b) is reached, overflow of the water will then take place at (b) and when this occurs the water supply is stopped, as any additional water added would not increase the level of the water above (b). Next oil is supplied into the tank at (a) and the oil will displace some of the water in the tank, the amount displaced depending upon the relative density of the oil. If overflow of oil takes place at (c) separation will occur, *i.e.*, water present in the oil will settle out causing overflow of an equal amount of water at (b) hence the quantity of water forming the seal remains constant. If however, when oil is supplied to the tank of sufficiently high relative density to cause the oil-water interface level (b) to reach (d), oil will be discharged at (b) and no oil will be discharged at (c). This is called loss of seal.

Rotating the settling tank analogy in Fig. 10.9 through 90° gives the lower figure in the diagram which shows separation taking place in a centrifugal separator, the principle being analogous to that of gravitational separation described above. Water is first delivered to the centrifuge and when discharge of water takes place at (b) the water supply is shut off and then oil is delivered at (a), some of the water is displaced and when oil and water are being separately and continuously discharged, the centrifugal separator is operational.

The water dam ring (or screws) is used to vary the position of (b) and the choice of dam ring should be such that the oil-water interface is as near as possible to (d) without oil discharge taking place at (b). This ensures as large a quantity of oil in the centrifugal separator as possible, thus for a given throughput rate the oil will be in the separator for as long a time as practicable, enabling the centrifugal force to give good separation and clarification.

The equilibrium equation for the centrifuge is:
$h_1 = h_2 \times$ oil density

Where h_1 is the head of water,
Where h_2 is the head of oil.

When oil of high relative density is to be passed through the centrifugal separator the dam ring which would be fitted will bring (b) closer to the axis of rotation increasing h_1 without altering h_2.

If oil of low relative density is to be passed through, the dam ring would have to be such that (b) is moved away from the axis of rotation reducing h_1 without altering h_2.

Control of the oil-water interface line, or equilibrium line, can be achieved in some purifiers by variation of back pressure, hence no dam ring would be required.

CENTRIFUGES

Two basic types of oil centrifuges are in marine use, the large diameter bowl type fitted with discs and the tubular bowl type without discs. Both types of centrifuge give good separation and clarification.

Action of Particles in a Disc Type Centrifuge

If oil flows in a streamline condition between two parallel plates its velocity varies between zero where it is in contact with the plate, to a maximum at the mid-point between the plates. Fig. 10.10 shows such a velocity variation.

Oil flows between two discs in a centrifuge is radially inward and up towards the clean oil outlet. Any particles in the oil will follow this general flow, but will also be acted upon by a radially outward centrifugal force. The magnitude of the force depends upon the mass of the particle, the speed squared and the radius at which the particle finds itself.

By referring to Fig. 10.10 it will be seen that any particles finding their way to the underside of a disc enter a region of zero velocity and they can then move, due to centrifugal force, down the underside of the disc and eventually into the sludge space of the bowl.

The important path taken by particles is that of the limit size particle, which is the smallest to be removed in the centrifuge. Particles smaller than this pass out with the clean oil. Some of the factors affecting the limit size particle would be:

1. Viscosity of the oil in the centrifuge, the higher its value the greater will be the viscous drag on the particles. Hence the oil should be pre-heated to as high a temperature as practicable.

2. Disc spacing, diameter and inclination to the vertical.

3. Speed of rotation of the purifier.

4. Throughput. If this is low the limit size particle will be small and the oil discharged cleaner. If throughput is great the limit size particle will be large. However, if the oil contains

appreciable quantities of water this would be effectively removed and this form of contamination could be the reason for operating at a high throughput.

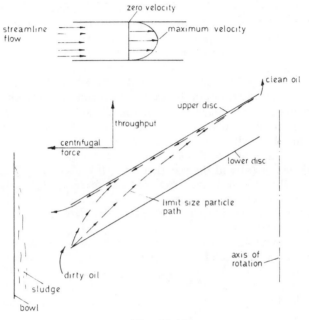

Fig. 10.10

De Laval Bowl Type Centrifuge

The stainless steel bowl of up to 0.6 m diameter is mounted on a tapered spindle, the lower part of which is fashioned into a sleeve which passes over a stationary spindle. The stationary spindle carries two ball races which are provided for the rotating spindle. These bearings, the upper one serving as a thrust bearing, give a high degree of flexibility.

A constant speed electric motor supplies the motive power for the oil suction and discharge pumps (if fitted) and the wheel and worm drive for the centrifuge bowl. The bowl rotates under operating conditions at 5,000 to 8,000 rev/min depending upon size. This gives a lower centrifugal settling force than is to be found in the tubular bowl type of centrifuge. To compensate for the lower centrifugal settling force, stainless steel conical discs carried by splines on the distributor are fitted to reduce the settling distance.

To operate the centrifuge as a purifier, it is first brought up to operating speed, supplied with fresh water to form the water seal and then the oil to be purified is delivered to the distributor by the inlet pump.

As the oil passes down the distributor it is rapidly brought up to the rotational speed of the purifier by the radial vanes provided for this purpose. The oil passes from the distributor through the space between the bottom plate and bowl to the supply holes.

From the supply holes the oil is fed to the spaces between discs through the distribution holes in the discs. Separation and clarification takes place between the discs, water and sludge moving radially outwards pass along the under surface of the discs and the purified oil moving radially inwards passes over the upper surface of the discs. Water and sludge are eventually discharged at (a) and the purified oil at (b). (See Fig. 10.11)

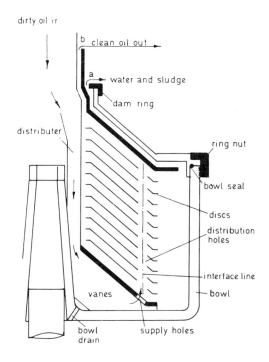

PURIFIER
Fig. 10.11

If the centrifuge is to be operated as a clarifier, no water seal is provided and the bottom plate and discs have no supply and distribution holes. Discharge of the clarified oil takes place at (b), sludge and solids collect upon the bowl wall. Since there is no water seal in a clarifier more bowl space is available for the oil, hence there will be available a greater centrifugal settling force due to the increased radii.

Fig. 10.12 shows a centrifuge arranged for clarification. The degree of diagrammatic simplification between it and the purifier should be noted by the student, and as an exercise in examination sketching it is recommended that the purifier should be drawn in a similar diagrammatic form.

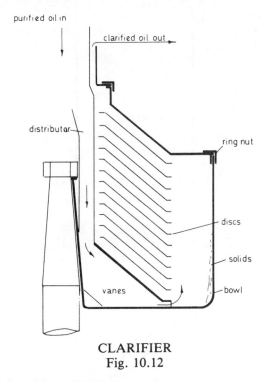

CLARIFIER
Fig. 10.12

Sharples Super-Centrifuge

Fig. 10.13 illustrates diagrammatically the Sharples super-centrifuge with 'one-pass' bowl, designed to replace the purifier-clarifier series combination used for the purification of residual oils. This purifier can also be used for the purification of lubricating and diesel oils.

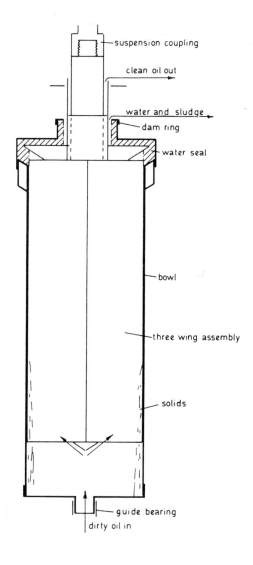

SUPER CENTRIFUGE
Fig. 10.13

It consists of a stainless steel tubular bowl about 110 mm diameter and 760 mm long supported at its upper end by a ball thrust bearing and flexible spindle assembly and guided at the bottom by a plain bearing. This arrangement permits the bowl to take up its own alignment.

An electric motor mounted upon the top of the purifier framework drives the bowl through a belt drive and this gives a bowl speed under operating conditions of about 15,000 rev/min. Suction and discharge pumps of the gear type, driven by the electric motor can be fitted, if required, thereby making the purifier and independent unit.

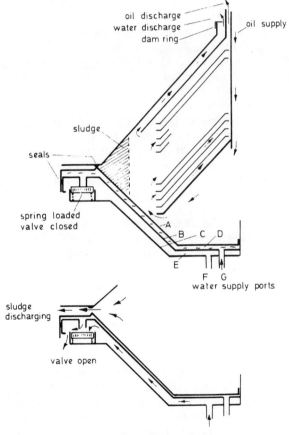

SELF-CLEANING PURIFIER
Fig. 10.14

A three wing assembly made of tinned or stainless steel, is fitted inside the bowl and is retained in position by spring clips. This assembly brings the oil rapidly up to bowl speed, thus ensuring that the oil is subjected to the maximum possible centrifugal settling force that the purifier is capable of producing.

At the top of the bowl a small annular space is provided and this space contains the water seal. By having a small water seal, all of the bowl space is available for the oil. This means that purification will be improved in this type of purifier compared with the type that has a water seal throughout the length of the bowl.

Self-Cleaning Purifier

Fig. 10.14, shows diagrammatically the method of sealing and sludge ejection for a self-cleaning purifier.

Bowl sections A, B and C, are all keyed to the central drive spindle, B and C, are secured so that they cannot move vertically whereas A is free.

The purifier is first brought up to operating speed and water is then supplied to space D through supply port G. Due to centrifugal force the water pressure in space D moves A vertically to form a seal at the bowl periphery. Water and then oil would next be supplied to the purifier in the usual way.

When the purifier requires to be cleared of sludge the oil supply is shut off and water supply is changed over from G to F supply port. The hydraulic pressure created in space E is sufficient to open the spring-loaded valves and the water from space D will—together with water from space E—be discharged and A will fall, the bowl seal will now be broken and the sludge ejection will take place.

CENTRIFUGAL PURIFICATION

Centrifugal Purification of Fuel Oils

For the purification of diesel fuel oil the single stage process is normally used. The diesel oil is delivered to a centrifugal purifier through a heater unit. If the oil is of low viscosity it may be purified efficiently without preheating. Oils of medium or high viscosity should be heated before purification in order to reduce their viscosity, this gives better clarification by reducing the viscous drag upon solid particles moving through the oil.

Purifier capacity depends upon various factors, grade of oil, purification temperature, type of impurities and degree of purification required. For diesel engines developing 3,000 kW to 10,000 kW a purifier having a capacity range of 2,200 to 8,200 litres per hour would be used. This would be sufficient to deal with a days supply of fuel in 8 hours.

For the purification of residual fuel oils the two stage process is commonly used. The residual fuel is heated in a supply tank to about 50°C to 60°C and is drawn from this tank by the purifier inlet pump. The inlet pump delivers the oil to a thermostatically controlled heater which raises the oil temperature to about 80°C and thence to the centrifugal purifier. The dry purified oil is then transferred to a centrifugal clarifier by the purifier discharge pump. After clarification the clarifier discharge pump delivers the oil to the daily service tank for engine use.

Centrifugal Purification of Lubricating Oils
Systems
Lubricating oil purifiers for diesel or turbine lubrication plants are normally arranged to operate on the continuous bypass system. In this system oil is drawn from the engine sump or drain tank by the purifier feed pump, delivered through a

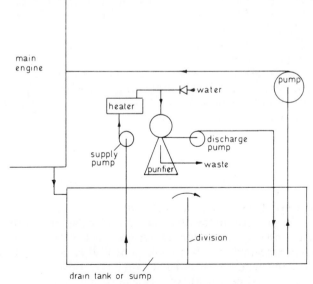

CONTINUOUS BYPASS SYSTEM
Fig. 10.15

heater to the purifier, then discharged after purification by the purifier discharge pump to the engine sump or main lubricating pump suction.

The system layout may vary slightly depending upon the engine arrangement, etc., but undoubtedly the best possible arrangement for the continuous bypass purification of lubricating oil is to take oil for the purifier from a point in the lubrication plant where the oil has passed through the engine, had time to settle, and therefore should be at its dirtiest. Then deliver the purified oil adjacent to the suction for the main lubricating oil pump. Fig. 10.15 illustrates a diagrammatic arrangement of the system.

Generally the layout of piping, tanks, etc., for the purifier permits operation on the batch system of purification if desired. In the batch system, the contents of the engine drain tank or sump would be discharged to a dirty oil tank and the drain tank or sump would be replenished with clean or new oil. The lubricating oil in the dirty oil tank can then be purified at leisure.

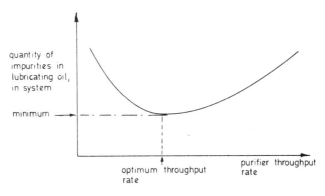

Fig. 10.16

Fig. 10.16, shows the variation of throughput rate of lubricating oil continuously bypassed to the purifier against the quantity of impurities in the system. The optimum purifier throughput rate is approximately one third of the maximum purifier throughput rate and it should be capable of dealing with the system oil content about twice every 24 hours. Maximum throughput rate would be used in the event of massive water contamination of the lubricating oil.

Under normal operation it is recommended that after shutting down the main engine the purifier should be kept running for about 12 hours in order to minimise corrosion due to acid vapours condensing as the engine cools down.

Water Wash

A feed pipe capable of supplying hot fresh water in a thin stream, intermittently or continuously as desired, should be fitted to the purifier oil inlet pipe. This hot water, fed in at approximately the same temperature as the oil, serves to sludge out some of the lighter dirt from the purifier bowl and wash out any acids.

In I.C. engines, the lubricating oil can become contaminated with sulphur combustion products that may combine with any water which is present in the oil to form sulphuric acid. Sulphuric acid can corrode cylinder liners and bearings, etc. In turbine installations, the lubricating oil, due to decomposition, may contain harmful acids which can cause corrosion. The acids formed in both cases are more soluble in water than in the lubricating oil, hence if a hot fresh water wash is put on to the purifier it has the effect of flushing out the acids present in the oil and reducing risk of corrosion. The purifier itself could be corroded by these acids and the water wash reduces this risk since the water seal is continually being replaced.

Detergent Oils

If it is considered necessary to water wash detergent lubricating oil the wash water supply must not exceed 1% of the total oil flow otherwise excessive depletion of detergent additives will occur, in addition, emulsion troubles may be created.

Steam Jet

By blowing steam into I.C. engine lubrication oil just prior to purification, coagulation of the colloidal carbon will occur. This enables the purifier to centrifuge this carbon out more effectively. This steam jet arrangement is *not* meant to serve as the preheating system for the lubricating oil, it is in addition to the oil heater provided for that purpose.

LUBRICATION

Manufacture of Lubricating Oil

Lubricating oil base stocks are obtained by fractional distillation of crude oil in vacuum distillation plant. The reader should refer to chapter two for details.

Crude oils are roughly classified into Paraffin base, which has a high lubricating oil content with a high pour point and high viscosity index and Asphalt base, which has a low lubricating oil content with a low pour point and low viscosity index. Lubricating oils refined from these bases would be subjected to various treatments to improve their properties, and they would be blended to produce a wide range of lubricating oils.

Compound Oil

From 5% to 25% of a non-mineral animal or vegetable oil may be added to a mineral (or mineral blend) oil to produce a compounded oil.

Oils which have to lubricate in the presence of water or steam are usually compounds of fatty animal oil and mineral oil, they tend to form a stable emulsion which adheres strongly to the metal surfaces. Fatty oils have a high load carrying capacity and if sulphurised they have extreme pressure (EP) property; used for cutting oils and running in of gearing.

It must be remembered that British Standards recommend that mineral oil only should be used for the lubrication of steam machinery as fatty oils contain acids which can cause corrosion in feed systems and boilers.

Lubricating Oil Additives

These are chemical compounds which are added for various reasons, mainly they would be added to give improved protection to the machinery and increased life to the oil by (a) giving the oil properties it does not have (b) replacing desirable properties that may have been removed during refining and improving those naturally found in the oil.

Among the additives used could be:

1. *Anti-oxidant*

Reduces oxidation rate of the oil. Oxidation rate doubles for approximately every 7°C rise in temperature and at temperatures above 80°C approximately oxidation rapidly reduces the life of the oil. Viscosity usually increases due to oxidation products and some of the products can help to stabilise foam, thereby preventing the formation of a good hydrodynamic layer of lubricant between the surfaces in a bearing and reducing the load carrying capacity. Oxidation products cause laquering on hot metal surfaces, they form sludge and possibly organic acids which can corrode bearings.

2. *Corrosion Inhibitor*

An alkaline additive is used to neutralise acidity formed in the oil and in the case of cylinder lubricants for diesel engines to neutralise sulphuric acids formed from fuel combustion.

The additive will increase the Total Base Number (TBN), prevent rusting of steel and corrosion of bearings.

3. *Detergents*

These keep metal surfaces clean by solubilising oil degradation products and coating metal surfaces, due to their polar nature, hindering the formation of deposits. They also neutralise acids.

4. *Dispersants*

These are high molecular weight organic molecules which stick to possible deposit making products and keep them in fine suspension by preventing small particles forming larger ones. At low temperatures they are more effective than detergents.

5. *Pour Point Depressant*

Added to keep oil fluid at low temperatures. The additive coats wax crystals as they form when temperature is reduced preventing the formation of larger crystals.

6. *Anti-foaming Additive*

When air is entrained into the oil, this could be due to low supply head or return lines not running full, etc., foaming could result which can lead to break down of the load carrying oil film in bearings.

An anti-foam or defoamant, acting like a conditioner in boiler water, is insoluble in the oil and finely dispersed throughout it. It may in time become soluble and the protection is lost.

7. *Viscosity Index Improver*

This is added to help maintain the viscosity of the oil as near constant with temperature variations as possible.

8. *Oiliness and Extreme Pressure Additives*

These reduce friction and wear. They may form chemically with the metal reaching welding temperature, a film which has a lower shear strength than the base metal, hence welding and tearing of the metal is prevented. These additives would be important during the running in of gearing.

Other additives could include emulsifying and de-mulsifying agents, tackiness agents and metal de-activators.

Lubrication Fundamentals

A lubricant will reduce friction and wear, it will keep metal surfaces clean by carrying away possible deposits and providing a seal to keep out dirt. A lubricating oil will carry away the heat generated in bearings and gears, etc., preventing overheating seizure and possible breakdown.

Bearing Lubrication

The addition of the slightest trace of lubricant to a bearing modifies the friction force appreciably. The two most important properties of a lubricant would be *oiliness* and *viscosity*. Oiliness is a form of bond between molecules of lubricant and material surface in which the lubricant is adsorbed by the material. The adsorbed film is very thin and once formed is very difficult to remove, which is most advantageous, in this respect colloidal suspension graphite is a very successful additive. If a layer of finite thickness lubricant exists without material contact, then friction is determined by viscosity, if the layer is only a few molecules thick then oiliness is the main factor. Viscosity is for liquids virtually as coefficient of friction is for solids.

$$F = \eta A \, \frac{\mathrm{d}v}{\mathrm{d}y}$$

where F is the viscous force required to move one plate over another with a velocity $\mathrm{d}v$ when the area of the plate is A, thickness of lubricant between surfaces $\mathrm{d}y$, η is viscosity coefficient.

Boundary friction is the condition between contact high spots (of a microscopic nature) while the low areas between are separated by a finite lubricant layer. In this state the thickness of the oil film is so small that oiliness becomes the predominant factor. This lubrication condition could be said to exist in some top end bearings, guides, etc.

Film lubrication, or hydrodynamic lubrication, is the condition whereby the bearing surfaces are completely separated by an oil layer. The load is taken completely by the oil film, the film thickness is greater at inlet (initial point in direction of rotation) than at outlet, the pressure at inlet increases quickly, remains fairly steady having a maximum value a little to the outlet side of bearing centre line, and then decreases quickly to zero at outlet. This form of lubrication is ideal but can only be satisfied in certain types of bearing, simple examples such as high speed journal bearings, as turbine bearings, or plane surfaces that can pivot to allow wedge oil film to allow for load, speed, viscosity, etc., effects, as in Michell bearings.

Using the variables of oil viscosity, relative speed of the bearing surfaces and pressure, Fig. 10.17 shows how the friction and form of lubrication alters in a journal bearing.

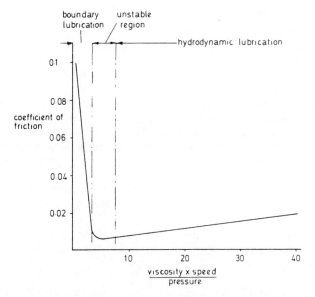

DIAGRAM FOR A JOURNAL BEARING
Fig. 10.17

Factors Affecting Hydrodynamic Lubrication
1. *Viscosity of the Lubricant*
The higher the viscosity the greater the tendency towards hydrodynamic lubrication. Obviously the type of lubricant—oil, water or grease—and the temperature are important. Temperature can be increased by insufficient lubricant circulating to remove the heat generated in a bearing—this could be caused by clearances being too small and/or insufficient supply of oil.

2. *Relative Speed of the Surfaces*
The higher the relative speed the greater the tendency towards hydrodynamic lubrication.

Increasing a journal or crankpin diameter and retaining the same rotational speed as before will increase relative speed.

In reciprocating engines the oscillatory motion of the crosshead and guide-shoe means that there is a tendency in these units towards boundary lubrication as the relative speed goes from a maximum to zero. This is one of the reasons why crosshead lubrication may be a problem.

3. *Bearing Clearance*

If this is too large the bearing 'knocks'. This impulsive loading increases pressure between the surfaces and can cause boundary lubrication. If the clearance is too small, overheating of the oil, boundary lubrication and possible seizure could result.

4. *Pressure, i.e. Bearing Load per Unit Area*

If this is high it can lead to boundary lubrication. If peak loads are high in the cylinder of a diesel, due to incorrect fuel injection timing or other reason, bearing pressure will increase.

Journal Bearings

Consider Fig. 10.18 in which the amount of clearance and pin shift movement have been much exagerated for clarity. When

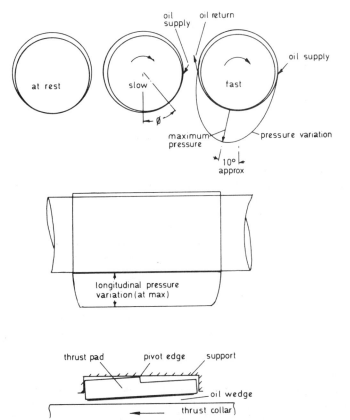

Fig. 10.18

movement first begins the pin climbs up the journal bearing *against* the direction of rotation, the friction angle is Φ. The layer of lubricant tends to be scraped off so boundary lubrication exists. As speed increases the oil is dragged behind the pin by viscous action until the oil film breaks through and separates the surfaces, the line of contact having moved *in the direction* of rotation, film lubrication exists. The variation of oil pressure circumferentially and longitudinally is as shown.

Michell Bearings

The bearing surface is divided up into a number of kidney shaped pads extending part or all the way round the surface, this principle being utilised in tunnel and thrust bearings.

The pads are prevented from moving circumferentially but are free to tilt and incline to the direction of motion. Such tilt allows a self adjusting oil film wedge giving full film lubrication. This film fully carries the load and allows pressures of 30 bar and shows a coefficient of friction value of 0.003.

Certain definitions and general points are now considered:

Scuffing

Breakdown of the oil film between surfaces causes instantaneous microscopic tack welding of a surface asperity nature. Further movement causes tearing out of the material and the resultant condition is known as scuffing. Most liable to be found when the lubrication film is difficult to maintain, for example on turbine gear teeth and in I.C. engine cylinder liners.

Extreme Pressure Lubricant

Special additives to the oil to maintain oil film under most severe load conditions and where film is difficult to maintain. Molybdenum disulphide (moly slip) additive is often used. Such lubricants are used to prevent scuffing.

Pitting

More a fatigue or a corrosion fatigue phenomena, usually the result of too high contact pressures giving minute cracking at contact surfaces.

Emulsion

Oil which is contaminated or has deteriorated in service will not separate easily from water and may cause an emulsion, in whole or in part. Emulsification is associated with precipitation of sludge at an increasing rate, such sludges are formed from accretion of resins and ashphaltenes. The oil should have a good demulsibility when new and should retain this in service.

Oxidation

A bearing oil subject to oxidation due to a high 'heat load' on the oil in circulation forms products in the oil which include polar compounds, for example the fatty acids such as oleic in which the acidic group is polar. Severe shaft and bearing corrosion can result. Polar substances have a molecular structure such that one part of the molecule is electrically negative with respect to the other part. This polar form tends to disperse one fluid in the other and stabilise the emulsion and tends to favour orientation at interfaces. Oxidation and corrosion products such as oxides of iron etc., stabilise emulsions. Anti-oxidation additives or inhibitors restrict polar molecule formation. Pure mineral oils normally have a high resistance to oxidation.

Typical Bearing Pressures

Crankpin bearings	91 bar (max)
Top end bearings	138 bar (max)
Guide shoes	5 bar (max)
Michell thrust bearing	30 bar (max)

Note that fluid film lubrication applies for most bearings of high speed engines but a guide shoe is a case of boundary lubrication.

Lacquering

Oxidation and corrosion products plus contamination products lead to deposit. On high temperature regions hard deposits form thin lacquer layers on pistons or heavier deposits for example on upper piston ring grooves of *I.C.* engines. Lacquer varnishes also form on piston skirts. On cooler surfaces sludge of a softer nature is more liable to be deposited.

Shipboard Lubricating Oil Tests

Qualitative oil tests carried out on board ship do not give a complete and accurate picture of the condition of the oil, this could only be obtained in a laboratory. However, they do give good enough indication of the condition of the oil to enable the user to decide when the oil should be replaced, or if some alteration in the cleaning procedure is considered necessary. Tests for alkalinity (or acidity), dispersiveness, contamination, water and viscosity are usual.

Samples of oil for analysis should be taken from the main supply line just before entry into the engine since it is the condition of the oil being supplied to the engine that is of the greatest importance.

Alkalinity Test

A drop of indicator solution is placed on to blotting paper and this is followed by a drop of sample oil placed at the centre of the drop of absorbed indicator. A colour change takes place in the area surrounding the oil spot, if it is red-acid, if blue/green-alkaline, if yellow/green-neutral.

Dispersiveness, Contamination and Water

A drop of oil is placed on to blotting paper and the shape colour and distribution of colour of the spot gives indication of oil condition. An irregular shape indicates water is present.

A uniform distribution of contaminants indicates good dispersiveness. If they are concentrated at the centre of the oil spot, dispersiveness is poor. If the colour of the spot is black, heavy contamination is the cause.

Viscosity Test

Four equal sized drops of oil, one used, one of the same grade unused, one with viscosity higher than and one with viscosity lower than the unused oil are placed in a line along the edge of an aluminium plate.

When sufficient time has elapsed so that they are all at room temperature the plate is inclined from the horizontal and when one of the oils has run down about 7.5 cm the plate is returned to the horizontal.

By comparing the distances travelled by the sample of used oil with the three reference oils an estimate of viscosity is possible. Obviously, if the distances travelled by used and unused oils of the same grade are equal there is no change in viscosity.

If the viscosity is reduced this could be due to dilution by distillate fuel. Heavy contamination due to carbon and oxidation would cause the viscosity to increase, as would contamination by heavy fuel oil. If variations in viscosity of 30% from initial viscosity are encountered the oil should be renewed.

A simple viscosity test of a similar nature to that described above known as the 'Mobil Flostick' test uses equal quantities of used and unused oils of the same grade in a testing device. Equal capacity reservoirs are filled with the oils which are allowed to reach room temperature, then the device is tilted from the horizontal and the oils flow down parallel channels. When the reference oil reaches a reference mark, the device is quickly returned to the horizontal and the distance travelled by the used oil in comparison to the unused oil gives a measure of viscosity.

Crackle Test for Water in Oil

If a sample of oil in a test tube is heated, any water droplets in the sample will cause a crackling noise due to the formation of steam bubbles—this test gives indication of small amounts of water being present. A simple settling test would be sufficient to detect large quantities of water in the oil.

Corrosion of White Metal Bearings

White metals are tin based, *i.e.* they have a larger proportion of tin in the alloy than any other metal. A typical composition could be 86% tin, 8.5% antimony, 5.5% copper.

In the presence of an electrolyte corrosion of the tin can occur forming extremely hard, brittle, stannous and stannic oxides (mainly stannic oxide SnO_2). These oxides are usually in the form of a grey to grey-black coloured surface layer on the white metal, either in local patches or completely covering the bearing. The hardness of this brittle oxide layer could be as high as twice that of steel and if it became detached, possibly due to fatigue failure, serious damage to bearing and journal surfaces could occur.

The formation of the oxide layer is accompanied by an upward growth from the white metal, which can considerably reduce clearance and could lead to overheating and seizure etc.

Factors which appear to contribute towards the formation of the tin oxides are:

1. Boundary lubrication, *e.g.* starting conditions.
2. Surface discontinuities.
3. Concentration of electrolyte, *e.g.* fresh or salt water or other contamination.
4. Oil temperature.
5. Stresses in the bearing metal.

Additives to the lubricating oil seem to offer some degree of protection, as does centrifuging and water washing of the oil.

Microbial degradation of lubricating oil

Bacterial attack of diesel engine lubricating oils, crankcase and cylinder, generally resulting in a smelly (not always) emulsion has occured with consequent damage to bearings, crankshafts, cylinders and piston rings.

This problem is still under investigation and has prompted many discussions in technical circles and papers.

Certain similar points emerge from the cases involved, they are:

1. Infections have usually taken place after water ingress into the oil — could even occur after condensation.

2. Evidence suggests that the microbes produce long chain organic acids.

3. Aerobic and/or anerobic bacteria have been detected.

4. Iron oxides in suspension, probably caused by corrosion, help to produce a tight emulsion in the oil which cannot be effectively removed by centrifuging.

5. Corrosion of the system can show two distinct phenomena (i) fine golden brown film on steelwork (ii) bearings and journals finely pitted.

Remedy and prevention

1. Burn oil (extreme case), clean out and disinfect system.

2. If oil is just beginning to show water separation difficulty, heat it in a tank for about two hours at 80 to 90°C in order to sterilise.

3. Prevent water entry into the oil.

4. Keep system and engine room clean, use disinfectant wash for tank tops and bilges, etc.

5. Treat P&J water with biocide.

6. Use P&J water additives which do not feed the microbes (Nitrogen and Phosphorous are, apparently, nutrients).

7. Use biocide in the oil.

8. Test lubricating oil and P&J water with prepared dip slides for the presence of bacteria.

GREASE

What it is

Semi-solid lubricant consisting of a high viscosity mineral oil and metallic soap with a filler.

Soaps are compounds of a metal base—calcium, sodium, aluminium—with fatty acids obtained from animal or vegetable fats.

Fillers are lead, zinc, graphite, molybdenum disulphite. Fillers enable grease to withstand shock and heavy loads.

What it does
  (1) Will stay put
  (2) Will lubricate
  (3) Will act as a seal
  (4) Useful for inaccessible parts.

What to use
  Calcium soap greases are water resistant and have a melting point of about 95°C and are suitable for low speeds. Sodium soap greases have a high melting point, about 200°C are suitable for high speeds but emulsify in water. Aluminium soap grease has a high load carrying capacity.

TEST EXAMPLES 10

Class 3
1. Explain why it is usually necessary to purify crankcase lubricating oil and how the purification is carried out.
2. Apart from providing lubrication to engine bearings, what other important function does lubricating oil perform?
3. If on passage you had reason to think that the lubricating oil in the main engine was contaminated can you state any simple checks which would help you come to a conclusion about the contamination.

TEST EXAMPLES 10

Class 2

1. Sketch a self-cleaning filter and describe its operation. Explain the function of magnetic filters. State why magnetic filters frequently complement self-cleaning filters in lubricating oil systems and why centrifuges do not render static filters redundant.

2. With reference to centrifugal separators:
   (a)   differentiate between the purpose and operation of purifiers and clarifiers,
   (b)   explain how these different roles are achieved,
   (c)   describe with sketches a self-cleaning arrangement.

3. Sketch and describe an oil centrifuge. Give a general explanation of the principles involved in the function of a centrifuge. State the adjustments made to the machine between handling oils of different densities.

4. Describe the operation of a differential pressure alarm fitted across an oil filter. Explain how such a device would be tested whilst the filter is in service.

5. Give two reasons why regular laboratory analysis of both main engine and auxiliary engine lubricating oil is desirable. State where and how representative samples of lubricating oil would be obtained from the systems. Describe the simple shipboard tests you could apply to determine:
   (a)   insoluble content,
   (b)   water content,
   (c)   acidity.

TEST EXAMPLES 10

Class 1

1. Describe a centrifugal oil purifier and explain in detail how separation occurs. Should a purifier be worked at its rated capacity if the maximum efficiency of separation is desired?

2. Sketch and describe a purifier and explain how the separation of dirt and water from oil is accomplished. What factors increase the speed and efficiency of the separation? Comment on the advantages and disadvantages of water washing lubricating oils.

3. Discuss the effects of water in lubricating oils and fuel oils. Explain how the presence of water can be detected and explain how water can be separated from oil by virtue of their different densities.

4. Sketch and describe three types of lubricating oil filters used aboard ship. Give reasons for using different types and relative positions in the system.

5. Explain the necessity for regular laboratory analysis of lubricating oils and the importance of obtaining a truly representative sample for this purpose. Without specialist equipment explain how to test for the following:

   (a)   sludge,
   (b)   water,
   (c)   acidity.

   State what effect each of these has on bearings and how it is countered.

CHAPTER 11

INSTRUMENTATION AND CONTROL

For the purposes of this chapter the material will be divided into four sections, namely:

Instruments—detecting elements (sensors) and measuring elements.

Telemetering—remote signal transmission and conversion (transduce).

Control Theory—basic concepts, pneumatic and electronic, of control actions.

Control Systems—application of control loops to marine circuits.

INSTRUMENTS

The range of such equipment is very wide because numerous variables require to be detected and measured. Classification is best made into temperature, pressure, level, flow and 'other' categories.

Temperature Measurement

Mechanical thermometry includes liquid in glass, filled system and bi-metallic types.

Mercury can be used within *liquid in glass* thermometers from −38°C to 366°C; if pressurised and contained in specially resistant glass the temperature range can be increased up to 600°C. Alcohol can be used for low temperature measurement (−80°C to 70°C) and pentane can be used down to −190°C.

Filled system thermometers utilise a bulb sensor, connecting capillary and bourdon tube measure element. The system is filled with a liquid (such as mercury), or a vapour (such as freon), or a gas (such as helium), under pressure.

Bi-metallic Thermometer

The principle of operation of this type is that of differential expansion of two different materials rigidly joined together, one on the other. Fig. 11.1 illustrates a typical design employed between $-40°C$ and $320°C$. The helix coils or uncoils with temperature variation and as one end is fixed the movement rotates shaft and pointer. Invar (36% Ni, 64% Fe) has a low coefficient of expansion and when welded to a Ni-Mo alloy gives a good bi-metallic strip.

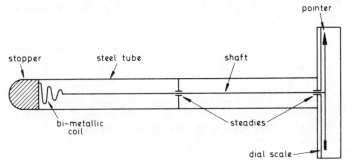

BI-METALLIC THERMOMETER
Fig. 11.1

Electrical thermometry includes resistance thermometers and thermocouples.

Resistance Thermometer

The electrical resistance of a metal varies with temperature

$$\varrho_\theta = \varrho_0(1 + \alpha\theta)$$

ϱ_θ is the specific resistance at temperature $\theta°C$
ϱ_0 is the specific resistance at temperature $0°C$
α is the temperature coefficient of resistance of the metal.

Fig. 11.2 illustrates a resistance thermometer utilising the Wheatstone bridge principle. $r_1 r_2$ is a variable resistance used for balance purposes; R_1, R_2 and R_3 are fixed resistors. At balance:

$$\frac{R_1 + r_2}{R_2 + r_1} = \frac{R_3 + r}{R_4 + r}$$

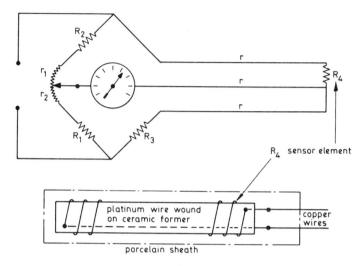

RESISTANCE THERMOMETER
Fig. 11.2

r is the equal resistance of each of the wires. Temperature alteration causes change in resistance and electrical unbalance. By use of the variable resistor r_1 r_2 balance can be restored (*i.e.* galvanometer reading returned to zero) and whilst this is being done another pointer can be moved simultaneously and automatically to give the temperature—this is a null balance method. Alternatively, the galvanometer can be calibrated directly in temperature units, so giving the temperature reading directly, in this case r_1 r_2 is not required. Platinum is the most suitable sensing wire element but copper and nickel wire are used in the range $-100°C$ to $200°C$. Tungsten, molybdenum and tantalum are used for high temperature pyrometry to $1200°C$, in protective atmospheres. Constantan can be used for the other resistances, if required, as its resistance varies negligibly with temperature variation. When the resistances utilise semi-conducting material, whose resistance decreases with temperature increase, the device is called a thermistor and there are many advantages in its use.

Thermocouple
Whenever the junctions formed of two dissimilar homogeneous materials are exposed to a temperature difference, an emf will be generated which is dependent on that temperature

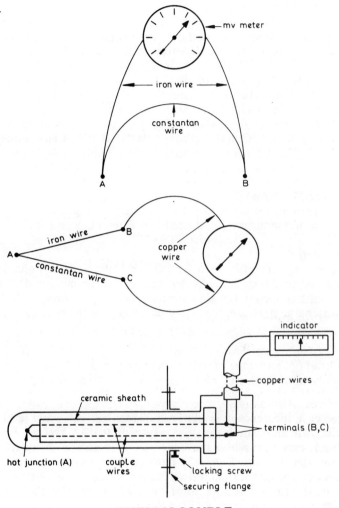

THERMOCOUPLE
Fig. 11.3

difference, the temperature level and the materials involved. This causes a current to flow in the circuit (Seebeck effect) and the two materials, usually metals, form the thermocouple. Fig. 11.3 (top sketch) shows a thermocouple consisting of two wires, one iron and one constantan, with a millivoltmeter coupled to the iron wire. If the junction A is heated to a higher temperature than junction B current will flow since the emf at one junction will be greater than the opposing emf at the other junction. The millivoltmeter will have calibrations directly in temperature values. A third wire can be introduced (middle sketch), where AB and AC form the couple wires. A will be the hot junction and B with C will form the cold junction. Providing the junctions B and C are maintained at the same temperature, the introduction of the third wire BC will not affect the emf generated. A copper ($+$) constantan ($-$) couple is used up to 350°C (constantan 40% Ni 60% Cu). An iron-constantan couple is used up to 850°C and a chromel (90% Ni 10% Cr)—alumel (94% Ni 2% Al) couple up to 1,200°C. Platinum—platinum plus 10% rhodium couples have been used to 1,400°C.

Pressure Measurement

The manometer is used for low pressures, the pressure gauge for high pressures and the dp cell for differential pressures.

Manometer

Essentially this instrument is a U tube, one limb of which is connected to the system whose pressure is to be measured, the other limb is open to the atmosphere. For low pressures, such as fan discharge pressure, etc. fresh water is used in the tube.

1 m³ of fresh water has a mass of 1 Mg and weighs 9.81×10^3N.
1 m head of fresh water exerts a pressure of 9.81×10^3N/m².
1 mm head of fresh water exerts a pressure of 9.81 N/m².

Hence a difference in level of say 20 mm between water levels in the two limbs indicates a pressure of 0.1862 kN/m². For higher pressures, such as scavenge belt air pressure for an I.C. engine, the fluid used would be mercury which has a relative density of 13.6. Hence a level difference of say 20 mm between mercury levels in the two limbs indicates a pressure of 3.532 kN/m².

A well type of mercury manometer is shown in Fig. 11.4. This instrument has a uniform bore glass tube which is small in internal diameter and when mercury is displaced from the well into the tube, the fall in level of the mercury in the well is so small it can be neglected. Pressure reading can be taken directly from the level of mercury in the tube. As volume displaced in the well equals volume displaced in the tube:

$$A \times x = a \times h$$

and by altering the ratio of the well and tube areas (A, a) the value of h (level variation in tube) can be made any multiple of x (level variation in well), so the instrument has a fixed scaling factor. The simple mercury barometer is essentially the same as the well manometer of Fig. 11.4 but with the top of the tube sealed, with a vacuum space down the tube to the mercury level. Normal atmosphere pressure is about 760 mm mercury (102 kN/m², 1.02 bar).

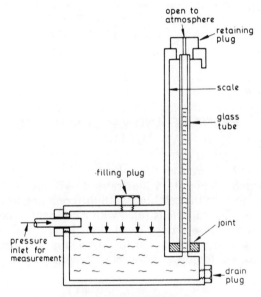

WELL MANOMETER
Fig. 11.4

Pressure Gauge (Bourdon)

The sensor element is the relay tube which is semi-elliptical in cross section. When this tube is subject to increased pressure it tends to unwind (straighten out) and this motion is transmitted to the gauge pointer via the linkage, quadrant and gear. If pressure is reduced the tube tends to wind (curl) up. This gauge is therefore suitable for measuring pressures above or below atmospheric. A diagrammatic sketch is shown in Fig. 11.5. The tube is generally made of phosphor bronze or stainless steel, as are other components except the case, which is usually brass or plastic material. The Bourdon sensor is often used as a transducer device in pneumatic control.

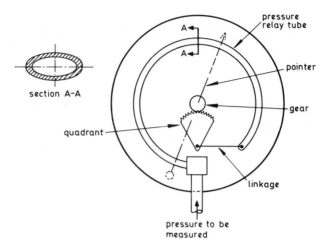

PRESSURE AND VACUUM GAUGE
Fig. 11.5

Differential Pressure Cell (dp cell)

The sketch of Fig. 11.6 illustrates a twin membrane sealed capsule secured in the cell body with different pressures applied at each side. The capsule is filled with a constant viscosity fluid (silicone) which also damps oscillation. Mechanical movement of the capsule is proportional to differential pressure. The dp cell is also used for flow and level measurements.

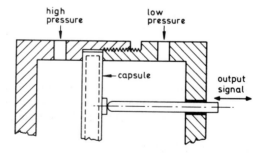

DIFFERENTIAL PRESSURE CELL
Fig. 11.6

Level Measurement

Direct methods include sight glasses, float devices and electrical probe elements (or photo-cells). Inferential methods involve any of the sensing devices used for pressure measurement such as manometers, pressure gauges, diaphragms, capsules, etc. Chapter 3 details various boiler water level indicators and it is only proposed to present one level measurement technique at this point.

Purge System

For small air flow rate, about one bubble per second, a pressure equal to that in a dip tube will be applied to the indicator, as shown in Fig. 11.7. This bubbler device is similar to the *pneumercator* as used for determination of tank liquid levels. Air supply to the open ended pipe in the tank will, in the steady state, have a pressure which is directly proportional to the depth level of liquid in the tank.

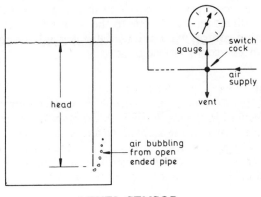

LEVEL SENSOR
Fig. 11.7

Flow Measurement

Quantity meters do not include time whilst flowmeters involve rate of flow; the latter are inferential *i.e.* volume inferred from velocity. One type of flowmeter will now be described.

Inferential-Differential Pressure

Consider Fig. 11.8:

The Bernoulli equation, incompressible flow for fluid of density ϱ, is:

$$\text{KE at } 1 + \text{PE at } 1 = \text{KE at } 2 + \text{PE at } 2$$

$$\tfrac{1}{2}v_1^2 + p_1/\varrho = \tfrac{1}{2}v_2^2 + p_2/\varrho \quad (a)$$

where KE is kinetic and PE potential energy. This also assumes unit mass, negligible friction and shock losses. The continuity equation is:

$$v_1A_1 = v_2A_2 \quad (b)$$

By substituting for v_2 from (b) in (a) and using mass flow rate ṁ as equal to ϱv_1A_1 then:

$$\dot{m} = k\sqrt{p}$$

where p is the pressure difference $(p_1 - p_2)$ and k is a meter constant. The venturi sensor, as sketched in Fig. 11.8, is the primary element and the pressure measuring device (such as a dp cell) is the secondary element. The measure scale will be non-linear for direct recorders, due to the square root relation, and telemetering-control will not be satisfactory unless a square root eliminator correcting device is fitted.

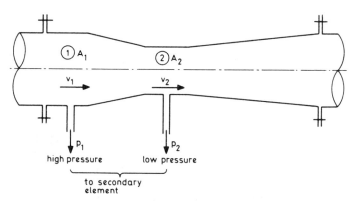

FLOW SENSOR (VENTURI)
Fig. 11.8

Other Measurement

Certain instruments are described elsewhere in the text *e.g.* viscometer, CO_2 recorder (Chapter 2), torsion meter (Chapter 6), etc.

Tachometer

The dc tachogenerator is a small precision generator driven by the shaft whose rotational speed is to be measured. Output voltage is directly proportional to speed and read-out is usually arranged to be a conventional voltmeter calibrated in terms of rotational speed. A digital counter can also be used (Fig. 11.9).

As the (ferrous) toothed wheel rotates each tooth alters the air gap and flux in a pick up coil (P) whose output pulses are amplified (A). Pulses pass through a timing gate (G), say one second opening period, and are counted on a digital counter (D) which scales (related to teeth number per revolution) and displays as revolutions per second. Alternatively rev/min readings can be arranged with different gate, or scale settings.

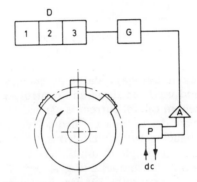

DIGITAL TACHOMETER
Fig. 11.9

Photo-Cell

Photo-conductive cells are constructed with a thin layer of semi-conductor material and their resistance varies with the incident light energy. They are used in some temperature sensors and flame failure devices.

Photo-emissive cells relay on the light energy providing energy to release electrons from a metallic cathode.

If visible light, which is radiation and hence energy, falls upon certain alkali metals—such as caesium---electrons will be emitted from the surface of the metal. Metals in general exhibit this characteristic but for most materials, the light required has a threshold wavelength in the ultra violet region so that visible light does not cause electron emission.

Light energy comes in packages called *photons* and the energy of the photons is used in doing work to remove the electrons and to give the electrons kinetic energy after escape from the metal.

Fig. 11.10 shows a simple photocell, visible light falls on the metal cathode from which electrons are emitted, they collect at

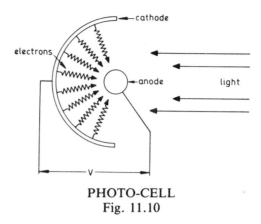

PHOTO-CELL
Fig. 11.10

the anode and in this way create a potential V which can then be amplified and used for alarm and control, etc.

In the vacuum cell all current is carried by photo electrons to the positive anode. In the gas filled cell emitted electrons ionise the gas, producing further electrons, so giving amplification. Secondary-emission (photo-multiplier) cells utilise a series of increasingly positive anodes and give high amplification.

Photo-transistors exhibit similar characteristics and small size and high amplification make their use particularly attractive especially when applied to counting systems *i.e.* digital tachometry.

Calibration

Instrument calibration and testing is specialised. Pneumatic instruments would be tested by master gauge, standard manometer or hydraulic deadweight tester and electrical instruments by standard resistors and potentiometers. Using a Bourdon calibration as example:

1. Zero (error) adjustment changes base point without changing the slope or shape of calibration curve. It is usually achieved by rotating the indicator pointer relative to the movement, linkage and element.

2. Multiplication (magnification) adjustment alters the slope without changing base point or shape. This is effected by altering the drive linkage length ratios between primary element and indicator pointer.

3. Angularity adjustment changes the curve shape without altering base point and alters scale calibration at the ends. This

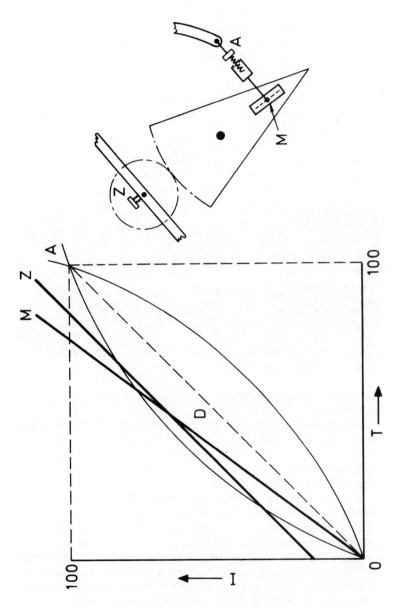

INSTRUMENT CALIBRATION
Fig. 11.11

error is minimised by ensuring that link arms are perpendicular with the pointer at mid scale.

Over the design range pointer movement bears a linear arrangement to pressure, and the scale is calibrated accordingly. Hysteresis—a vibration phenomena—is best eliminated by correctly meshed gearing and fitted pivots to reduce backlash, etc. Hysteresis of an instrument is the maximum difference between readings at given points moving up scale, to those taken when moving down scale *i.e.* hysteresis curves are plotted from up scale and down scale readings.

Fig. 11.11 shows calibration curves and adjustment for the Bourdon link type of instrument mechanism. Instrument readings (I), true values (T), desired result (D). Zero error and adjustment (Z), multiplication error and adjustment (M), angularity error and adjustment (A)—error curves or lines for actual values.

TELEMETERING

Telemetering may be defined as signal transmission over a considerable distance. The device at the measure point is called a transmitter with the receiver located at the recording or control centre. Telemetering may be involved with centralised instrumentation *i.e.* display, alarm scanning, data logging, etc. or with remote control devices, or both.

Centralised Instrumentation
Display

Essentially this aspect consists of centralised instrumentation in an air conditioned instrument and control room. Improved visual, audible and observation techniques are required. The data logger was the first step. Components are virtually all electronic (solid state devices working under air conditioned states are preferred) to fit in with standard equipment. Faults will be located by mimic board type diagnosis and replacement of printed card components rather than on the job repair.

In selecting alarm circuits great care must be taken in the preference choice utilised. Important circuits should be fitted with distinctive alarm indications and a quick and easy position location. Less important circuits can be fitted with a secondary importance alarm and isolating-locating system. The provision of too many alarms, not easily discriminated from each other, can cause confusion. Similar remarks apply to remote control room gauge boards where only really essential measurements should be *frequently* scanned.

The control room itself requires careful design with reference to comfort, lack of lighting glare, selective positioning of instruments for rapid viewing, correct placing of on-off and position and variable quantity indicators, improved instrument indication techiques, rapid control fault location and replacement, etc.

Various types of indicators and recorders are in use, for example: lights, dial gauges with pointer, colour strip movements, magnetic tapes, cathode ray (or GM) tubes, counters, charts, etc.

References are usually set on a pinboard and supply voltage stabilisation is usually necessary. Solid state devices give a high reliability rate.

Alarm Scanning; Data Logging; Terminology (Fig. 11.12)

The scanner normally covers up to about 200 points at the rate of about two points per second, 50 points per second are possible but are not normally utilised. Each measure point is selected in turn by automatically connecting the input terminals for presentation to the measuring circuit.

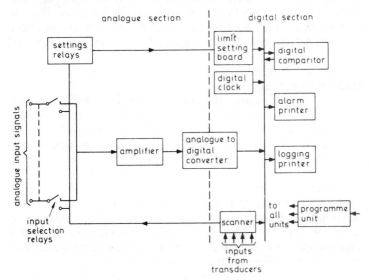

ALARM SCANNING AND DATA LOGGING
Fig. 11.12

Measurement

All analogue inputs are amplified from the low voltages produced by the instruments. This signal as a voltage representation of the measured value is translated in the analogue-to-digital converter to a numerical code form.

Display

The code signal is transferred to a strip printer or electronic type-writer, printing is selected for the various points at preset intervals, varying from virtually continuous for certain points, to reasonably long time intervals for others.

A second function is to compare digitally the analogue inputs with preset limit switches or pins in a patchboard and have lights on mimic diagrams to indicate alarms, in addition the excess deviation readings are presented on a separate alarm printer.

Programme

This is a pre-determined scanning routine which gives storage and actioning by the main programming unit. Print-out is timed by the special digital clock.

Equipment

Consists of solid-state silicon components on logic boards as printed circuits. Relays are hermetically sealed relay type on plug-in cards. Test board and replacement cards are provided for fault detection and replacement. Data loggers are sectional framework construction i.e. modules.

Analogue Representation

Where the measured quantity is converted in to another physical quantity *in a continuous way*. For example temperature converted into dc voltage by a thermocouple. Voltage is analogue of temperature. Useful for short term presentation *e.g.* manoeuvring, raising steam, etc.

Digital Representation

Where the measured quantity is represented by repeated individual increments *at given intervals*. For example a revolution counter which trips to alter the reading after each engine revolution. Useful for long term presentation *e.g.* 'full away' watchkeeping readings.

Scaling Unit

Most mechanical registers can record about two pulses per

second (maximum) without slip although the latest designs can reach 50 pulses per second. Electronic GM tubes can record 5,000 pulses per second so that the scalar functions to reduce output pulses to the register in the ratio 5,000:50.

Advantages of Data Logging
1. Reduces staff and number of instruments.
2. Provides continuous observation and fault alarm indication.
3. Provides accurate and regular operational data records.
4. Increases plant efficiency due to close operational margins.

Telemetering Components
Amplifier
   Used to step up the sensor low power signal for use in a high power actuator element. Two designs are given namely electronic and pneumatic (relay).
   The upper sketch of Fig. 11.13 shows a transistor amplifier of the common emitter type. A small change in input current signal produces a larger amplified change in load current. B, C, and E refer to base, collector and emitter respectively.

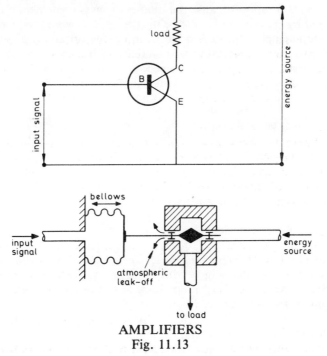

AMPLIFIERS
Fig. 11.13

The lower sketch of Fig. 11.13 illustrates a reverse acting pneumatic relay amplifier. Increase in the magnitude of the input signal air pressure reduces air flow from the pressure energy source and output pressure to load falls to a corresponding equilibrium value.

Transducer

A transducer converts the small sensing signal into a readily amplified output, usually in a different form. Designs can generally be simplified into three basic reversible types namely:

mechanical displacement ↔ pneumatic
mechanical displacement ↔ electrical
pneumatic ↔ electrical

A mechanical displacement → pneumatic type of transducer is the flapper nozzle device as shown in the later sketch, Fig. 11.16.

An electrical → pneumatic transducer is illustrated in Fig. 11.14. For an increase in current the created S pole to the left will be attracted up to the N pole of the magnet so giving a clockwise rotation because the moment arm is greater than that caused by the created N pole being attracted down on the S pole of the magnet. This action closes in on the nozzle so giving a higher output air pressure and increasing the feedback bellows force until equilibrium is achieved.

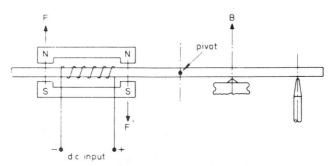

ELECTRO-PNEUMATIC TRANSDUCER
Fig. 11.14

Signal Media

Pneumatics or electrics are preferred although hydraulics are used in many steering gears.

Pneumatic systems generally have the advantages of lowest

first cost, inherent safety and proven reliability but they exhibit appreciable time lags and require clean air supplies.

Electrical-electronic systems have advantages of small component size, low power consumption and rapid response but generate some heat and are susceptible to variations in power supply.

CONTROL THEORY

This section is the basic requirement, deliberately brief and simple. A more detailed treatment is given in Volume 10 (Instrumentation and Control Systems).

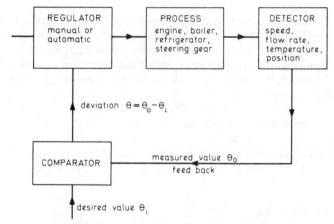

CLOSED LOOP CONTROL SYSTEM
Fig. 11.15

Terminology

Correct terminology is given in B.S. 1523: Part 1: 1967. BSRA have a recommended code of procedure booklet for marine instrumentation and control equipment.

A few simplified terms, related to Fig. 11.15 are now given.

Closed Loop Control System

Is one in which the control action is dependent upon the output. The system may be manually or automatically controlled. Fig. 11.15 shows the basic elements in a closed loop control system.

The measured value of the output is being fed back to the controller which compares this value with the desired value for the controlled condition and produces an output to alter the controlled condition if there is any deviation between the values. Measured Value; actual value of the controlled condition (symbol θ_o).

Desired Value; the value of the controlled condition that the operator desires to obtain. Examples, 2 rev/s, 25 degrees of helm, 55 bar, $-5°$, etc (symbol θ_i).

Set Value; is the value of the controlled condition to which the controller is set—this should normally be the desired value and for simplicity no distinction will be made between them.

Deviation (or error); is the difference between measured and desired values (symbol θ). Hence $\theta = \theta_1 - \theta_o$. This signal, probably converted into some suitable form such as voltage to hydraulic output or voltage to pneumatic output, etc., would be used to instigate corrective action—object to reduce the error to zero.

Offset; is sustained deviation.

Feedback; is the property of a closed loop control system which permits the output to be compared with the input to the system. Feedback will increase accuracy and reduce sensitivity.

Control Actions
Three basic actions will be described: (i) Proportional; (ii) Integral; (iii) Derivative.

Proportional Control (P)
A pneumatic type of proportional controller is shown diagrammatically in Fig. 11.16. A set value of pressure Ps is established in one bellows and the measured value of pressure Pm is fed into the opposing bellows (the measured value of pressure could be proportional to some measured variable such as temperature, flow, etc.) Any difference in these two pressures causes movement of the lower end of the flapper, alteration in air flow out of the nozzle and hence variation in output pressure Po to the control system.

If the upper end of the flapper was fixed, *i.e.* no proportional action bellows, then a slight deviation would cause output

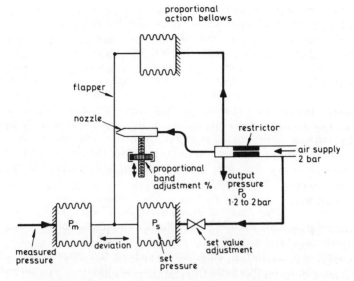

PNEUMATIC PROPORTIONAL CONTROLLER
Fig. 11.16

pressure Po to go from one extreme of its range to the other. This is simple proportional control [output pressure change Po and deviation (Pm – Ps)] with a very narrow proportional band width and high gain (gain = controller output change/deviation). Moving the nozzle down relative to the flapper increases the sensitivity and gain, and further narrows the proportional band width.

With output pressure Po acting in the proportional action bellows the top end of the flapper will always move in the opposite direction to the lower end, this reduces the sensitivity and widens the proportional band. When adjusting the controller to the plant the object would be to have minimum offset with stability, *i.e.* no hunting. Commencing with maximum proportional band setting (200 per cent) the set value control is moved away from and back to the desired setting (step input) and the effect on the controlled variable noted. Using incremental reductions of proportional band and for each reduction a step input, a point will be reached when oscillations of the controlled variable do not cease, a slight increase in proportional band setting to eliminate the oscillations gives optimum setting.

Proportional Plus Integral Control ($P + I$)

Proportional control will arrest a change and hold it steady but at a different point from the desired value. The difference between these values is called *offset*, which is different at each load; this is the shortcoming of proportional control. Offset can be reduced by increasing sensitivity (*i.e.* narrowing proportional band) but this can lead to hunting and instability. Integral (reset) action addition ($P + I$) gives arrest of the change and a reset to the desired value irrespective of load. Integral action will always be occurring whilst deviation exists. Controllers of this type have an adjustment to vary reset time, the shorter the time setting the greater the integral action. Too great an integral effect will cause *overshoot* past the desired value.

Proportional Plus Integral Plus Derivative Control ($P + I + D$)

Derivative action may be added as a damping action to reduce overshoot.

Derivative action is anticipatory where the sensed rate of change of deviation corrects to reduce likely deviation—it opposes the motion of the variable. Derivative action time, usually adjustable at the controller, has the effect that the longer the time setting the greater the derivative action.

Summary

(P) Proportional control: action of a controller whose output signal is proportional to the deviation.

i.e. Correction signal $\propto$ deviation.

(I) Integral control: action of a controller whose output signal changes at a rate which is proportional to the deviation.

i.e. Velocity of correction signal $\propto$ deviation.

Object: To reduce offset to zero.

(D) Derivative control: action of a controller whose output signal is proportional to the rate at which the deviation is changing.

i.e. Correction signal $\propto$ velocity of deviation.

Object: Gives quicker response and better damping.

(P) Single term controller.

($P + I$) or ($P + D$) Two term controller.

($P + I + D$) Three term controller.

Pneumatic Controller ($P + I + D$)

Fig. 11.17 shows in diagrammatic form a three term controller. Set value control and proportional band adjustment have been omitted for simplicity (see Fig. 11.16). Often,

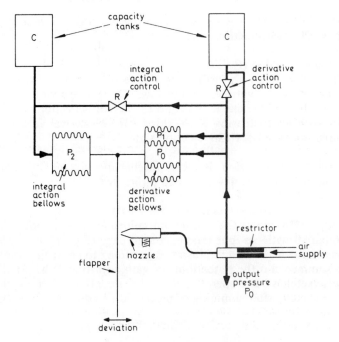

PNEUMATIC P + I + D CONTROLLER
Fig. 11.17

controller manufacturers produce a standard three term controller and the installer can adjust for type of control action necessary, *i.e.* either single, two or three term as required.

Approximate sizes are, restrictor about 0.2 mm bore, nozzle about 0.75 mm bore and flapper travel at nozzle about 0.05 mm. To ensure exact proportionality and linearity the effective flapper travel is reduced to near 0.02 mm, giving less sensitivity and wider proportional band, with negative feedback on the flapper due to the inner bellows and pressure P_0 acting on it. Note: Whichever way the bottom of the flapper is moved, by the deviation, if the top is moved in the opposite sense this is negative feedback, if in the same sense it is positive feedback.

Integral Added (P + I)

This is applied by adding positive feedback with pressure P_2 acting on the integral action bellows. Integral action time is the product of the capacity C and the resistance of the integral action control R, *i.e.* RC (note the similarity with electrical circuits). Increasing R by closing in the integral action control increases integral action time.

Derivative Added (P + D)

This is applied with further negative feedback with pressure P_1 acting on the derivative action bellows. Derivative action time is the product of the capacity C and the derivative action control resistance R. Increasing R by closing in the derivative action control increases derivative action time.

Note: Integral action is very rarely applied on its own. Derivative action is never applied on its own.

Electrical-Electronic Controller (P + I + D)

Fig. 11.18 shows the compound controller which should be compared with its pneumatic counterpart (Fig. 11.17). The upper part of the sketch illustrates grouping to controller (note the summer and the potentiometer gain adjustment) whilst the lower sketch is basic operational amplifier configuration. On the lower sketch, after summing of measured and desired value, the

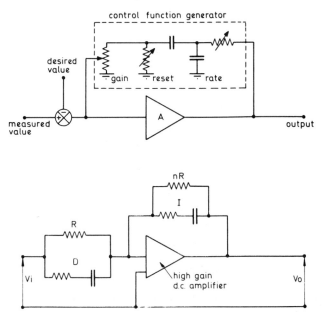

ELECTRICAL-ELECTRONIC CONTROLLER (P + I + D)
Fig. 11.18

input voltage is Vi. The gain adjustment is the factor n related to resistances R. The rate (derivative D) circuit is at input and the reset (Integral I) on the feedback line.

CONTROL SYSTEMS

One final controlling element, the diaphragm valve, one telemetering system, the electric telegraph, and three control circuits, fluid temperature control, automatic boiler control and bridge control of IC engine—are selected to illustrate principles involved.

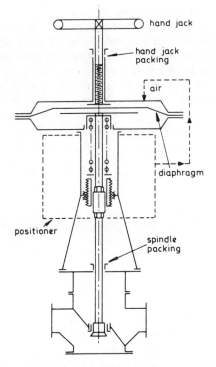

DIAPHRAGM VALVE
Fig. 11.19

Diaphragm Valve

The sketch (Fig. 11.19) illustrates such a valve used for controlling fuel quantity to burners of a boiler.

Control air acts on top of the synthetic rubber diaphragm, increasing air pressure causes the valve to move down permitting increased fuel supply to the burners.

If air supply to the diaphragm should cease then the valve will 'fail safe', *i.e.* it will close against the flow of the oil (Right to left in Fig. 11.19) and the burners will be extinguished. Hand regulation could be used by operating the hand jack.

A positioner would be used if:

(a) the valve is remote from the controller,

(b) there is a high pressure difference across the valve,

(c) the medium under control is viscous,

(d) the pressure on the gland is high.

In this case a flapper is fastened to the valve stem at one end and the other end operates against the nozzle whose air supply pressure acts on top of the diaphragm. The control air signal acts, via bellows and spring, between the two extremities of the flapper and fixes its position relative to the nozzle, dependent on magnitude of control pressure signal.

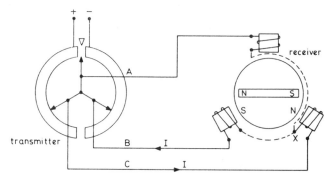

POSITION INDICATOR (ELECTRIC TELEGRAPH)
Fig. 11.20

Position Indicator (Electric Telegraph)

This device is inherently telemetering rather than a control system as such. Fig. 11.20 shows the system in equilibrium with equal dc currents (I) in line B and C and zero current in line A. The receiver rotor is locked by equal and opposite torques from the attractions on unlike pole faces. Assume the transmitter to be moved 30° clockwise. Current flows to the receiver from line C, subdivides at point X and equal currents return through lines A and B of magnitude I/2. This creates a strong N pole at fixed magnet X and two weak S poles at the other two fixed magnets.

The receiver indicator will therefore turn to the corresponding position *i.e.* 30° clockwise. Energy supply failure alarms are fitted.

As a telegraph, a bell can be activated until the hand lever on the receiver is moved to correspond with receiver position.

For clockwise (say ahead) rotation of the transmitter, line A will be carrying return current. If the engine driven speed tachogenerator is rotating in the correct direction its output can be arranged to be in the same sense as line A. A summed signal (additive) will maintain a 'wrong way alarm' in the isolated condition. Incorrect rotation of the engine will create signals in opposition which causes the alarm to be activated. The same applies for anticlockwise (say astern) rotation of the transmitter when line A will be carrying supply current.

Fluid Temperature Control

The arrangement sketched in Fig. 11.21 is single element for fresh water coolant temperature control applied to an auxiliary I.C. engine. It would be equally suitable for oil coolant or

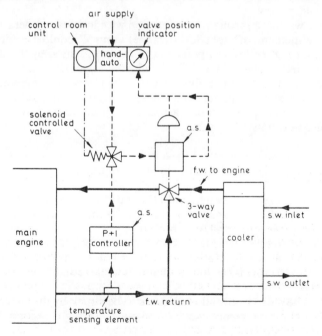

FLUID TEMPERATURE CONTROL
Fig. 11.21

lubricant (engine or gearbox) temperature control. Full flow of sea water is arranged through the cooler. A three way valve (two inlets, one outlet) operates to mix quantities of coolant, bypassing or going through the cooler, dependent on coolant return temperature.

With correct analysis of parameters, and careful valve selection, a simple single element control system can be utilised for most duties. A wax element activated valve gives a simple but fixed control (over say 10°C), by adjusting one outlet for the return coolant to the cooler with the other bypass to the engine. For large thermal variations, such as manoeuvring conditions, single element control may not meet requirements. 'Cascade control', involving one controller (the master) amending the set value of another controller (the slave) could then be used. The slave controller, sensing temperature of coolant leaving the cooler, would detect variations of sea temperature and adjust sea water flow accordingly. The master controller, sensing return temperature of coolant from engine or gearbox would if necessary amend the set value of the slave controller and so alter sea water flow.

For warming through, or operation with low sea temperatures the refinement of 'split level (range) control' could be added. Over a range of low temperatures of coolant, sensed by the slave controller, a lower magnitude signal would operate heat input to a coolant heater. At a given point, when coolant temperature had increased, the signal would close the heat control and for the rest of the range would operate to control sea water flow to the cooler in the usual way.

Automatic Boiler Control System

Refer to Fig. 11.22 for the lighting sequence:

1. The pressure switch initiates the start of the cycle. The switch is often arranged to cut in at about 1 bar below the working pressure and cut out at about 1/5 bar above the working pressure (this differential is adjustable).

2. The master initiating relay now allows 'air-on'. The air feedback confirms 'air-on' and allows a 30 second time delay to proceed.

3. The master now allows the arc to be struck by the electrode relay. The 'arc made' feedback signal allows a 3 second time delay to proceed.

4. The master now allows the fuel initiating signal to proceed. The solenoid valve allows fuel on to the burner. The 'fuel-on'

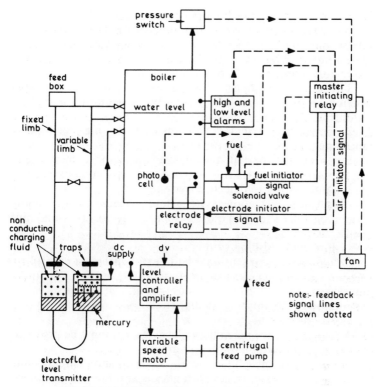

AUTOMATIC BOILER CONTROL SYSTEM
Fig. 11.22

feedback signal allows a 5 second time delay to proceed (this may be preceded by a fuel heating sequence for boiler oils).

5. The master now examines the photo electric cell. If in order the cycle is complete, if not then fuel is shut off, an alarm bell rings and the cycle is repeated.

Refer to Fig. 11.22 for emergency devices.

Obviously failure of any item in the above cycle causes shut down and alarm operation. In addition the following apply:

(a) High or low water levels initiate alarms and allow the master to interrupt and shut down the sequential system.

(b) Water level is controlled by an Electroflo type of feed regulator and controller. Sequential level resistors are immersed in conducting mercury or non-conducting fluid, so deciding pump speed by variable limbs level. The fixed limb level passes over a weir in the feed box.

Unattended Machinery Spaces

Essential requirements for unattended machinery spaces, *i.e.* particularly unmanned engine rooms during the night could be summarised thus:

1. Bridge control of propulsion machinery.

The bridge watchkeeper must be able to take emergency engine control action. Control and instrumentation must be as simple as possible.

2. Centralised control and instruments are required in machinery space.

Engineers may be called to the machinery space in emergency and controls must be easily reached and fully comprehensive.

3. Automatic fire detection system.

Alarm and detection system must operate very rapidly. Numerous well sited and quick response detectors (sensors) must be fitted.

4. Fire extinguishing system.

In addition to conventional hand extinguishers a control fire station remote from the machinery space is essential. The station must give control of emergency pumps, generators, valves, ventilators, extinguishing media, etc.

5. Alarm system.

A comprehensive machinery alarm system must be provided for control and accommodation areas.

6. Automatic bilge high level fluid alarms and pumping units.

Sensing devices in bilges with alarms and hand or automatic pump cut in devices must be provided.

7. Automatic start emergency generator.

Such a generator is best connected to separate emergency bus bars. The primary function is to give protection from electrical blackout conditions.

8. Local hand control of essential machinery.

9. Adequate settling tank storage capacity.

10. Regular testing and maintenance of instrumentation.

Bridge Control of IC Engine

To enable a direct reversing engine to be controlled from the bridge, basic procedure and safeguards must be built in to the control system.

The following shows some of the checks which may be incorporated in a system to protect the engine during starting and running.

1. Confirmation that the turning gear is disconnected.

2. Confirmation that the engine is running in the correct direction on air, before the fuel is applied.

3. Confirmation that the engine is accelerating on fuel before the starting air is cut off.

4. Alarm if a start is not confirmed within a reasonable period of time.

5. Speed limitation, *i.e.* avoidance of critical speed ranges or limits imposed by excessive jacket temperatures, etc.

6. Acceleration limiting to limit the rate at which the fuel is applied to give a safe torque or to prevent the fuel exceeding the air available from the turbo-blower.

7. Automatic rundown to half speed if, for example, the cylinder jacket temperature is too high.

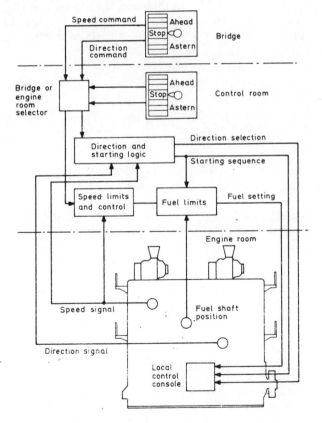

BRIDGE CONTROL: BLOCK DIAGRAM
Fig. 11.23.

8. Automatic stop if the lubricating oil pressure fails.

Other checks or alarms may be fitted if required.

A typical system is shown in block diagram form in Fig. 11.23.

The various signals may be electrical or pneumatic. Final connections to the engine are usually pneumatic cylinders which operate the engine controls. Selection of bridge or engine room control is made in the engine room, thus enabling the engineer to take control at any time, if required. When an electronic governor is fitted, the speed signal is generated by a tacho generator and the fuel quantity is measured by a position transducer fitted to the fuel control rack. When a hydraulic governor is fitted, speed is measured by a Watt type governor and hydraulically amplified. In this case, the blower and torque limits are usually incorporated into the governor. To protect the engine, the fuel limits are applied after the speed limits.

TEST EXAMPLES 11

Class 3

1. Describe the start up sequence of an automatic auxilliary boiler.
2. Describe a device which would automatically activate an alarm when the lubricating oil supply to an engine fails.
3. Explain the principle of operation of a pneumatic diaphragm activator.
4. List three automatically controlled systems in a ship's machinery space which need to be provided with alarms. State the consequences of an alarm failure in each system.

TEST EXAMPLES 11

Class 2

1. (a)   Sketch a diaphragm operated control valve of any design.
   (b)   State how flow changes are sensed.
   (c)   State how command signals are transmitted to actuators.
2. (a)   Explain why a pneumatic control system requires clean dry air.
   Explain how the following pollutants are dealt with:
   (b)   water,
   (c)   oil,
   (d)   dust and dirt,
3. (a)   Describe, with sketches, a bridge/engine room telegraph interconnecting gear.
   (b)   Explain how the system may operate a 'wrong way' alarm.
4. Describe, with sketches, instruments used for measuring the ambient temperature in the following spaces:
   (a)   refrigerated compartment,
   (b)   main machinery exhaust gas uptakes.

TEXT EXAMPLES 11

Class 1

1. Sketch diagrammatically an auxilliary boiler automatic combustion control system.
   Explain how it operates.
   Specify how 'fail safe' conditions are ensured.
2. With reference to automatic combustion control in auxiliary or main boilers state how:
   - (a) master controller follows steam pressure variations,
   - (b) and why pressure drop across the air registers is measured,
   - (c) air fuel ratio is adjusted.
3. (a) Sketch diagrammatically the arrangements to control lubricating oil temperature at cooler outlet by either of the following means:
       diaphragm actuated control valve as part of a closed loop system,
       or
       self operated valve of wax element type.
   - (b) Describe how the selected arrangement operates.
   - (c) Define, with reasons, where a control valve of the wax element type should be positioned to be effective.
4. With respect to shipboard control equipments, state:
   - (a) where an electronic system may be essential,
   - (b) the advantages of the electronic system over the other systems,
       and
   - (c) the disadvantages of the electronic system.

CHAPTER 12

MANAGEMENT

Collaboration between individuals for a common objective, with division of labour under a recognised leader, has been practised for centuries. Leadership requires some form of supportive group discipline. Social and organisational facets within the work environment were recognised at the beginning of the industrial revolution and have evolved this century. However, application of the scientific method—observation, data collection, analysis, classification, hypothesis, experimental verification, formulation of laws and use for prediction—to the work situation, is more recent. Such applications has resulted in a systematic approach leading to a recognised discipline—management.

Management is the knowledge of the (five) **processes** of **planning, organising, directing, co-ordinating** and **controlling**. This relates to machines, manpower, materials, method and money. Management by objectives, with targets and accountability, through line management and staff functions, is established practice.

GENERAL INDUSTRIAL MANAGEMENT

Overall organisation of an industrial concern is a complex structure involving personal interaction between individuals and their work situations. This usually requires work study of both time and method. Organisational study includes job analyses, flow diagrams and organisational charts with activities defined in terms of supervision, levels of authority, interrelation and coordination. A common result, for a large industrial enterprise, is the arrangement of divisions, each with a specific role involving the five processes of management. A typical set of divisions could be as follows:

Organisational Divisions
Purchasing:
Supply, ordering, inspection, stock control.
Production:
Drawings, materials, methods, progressing, production and quality control.
Personnel:
Selection, employment, health, safety, training, education, PR.
Development:
Research, design, standards, ergonomics, OR.
Marketing:
Storage, transport, packaging, selling, market research.
Finance:
Costing, budgets, capital, legal, accounting; essentially a control function.

Most of the terms considered above should be well understood including three such as stock control, quality control and ergonomics (human energy outputs). There are a number of other terms used in many stages of the management processes that are worthy of consideration.

Further Terminology
Queuing Theory:
Is applied to the case of a waiting line (persons, stores, vehicles, ships) delayed by a limited service availability. Often involves theories of probability, use of computers, and routeing (optimum paths).
Integrated Data Processing (IDP):
Utilises storage and speed characteristics of computers to handle complicated and lengthy data material, especially in finance divisions.
Linear Programming (LP)
Again utilises the computer to cover the mathematical relationships of many problems with a near linear characteristic for use in forecasts, etc. Extendable to non-linear.
Organisation and Methods (O&M)
An objective and analytic study of administrative office procedures aiming to improve performance and efficiency—and reduce paper work. To include behavioural techniques.
Operational Research (OR).
Essentially a planning-research technique. Applies mathematical techniques (computer assisted) to such as queuing theory and linear programming, detailed previously, and to critical path analysis, plant maintenance and replacement

policy, as considered later. OR aims to collate the best available data so as to provide management with statistics on relative advantages and disadvantages of all potential courses of action to allow efficient decision making. This can relate to a simple task such as economic selection of a single machine or, when linked to IDP, to the major financial strategies of large industrial or commercial companies.

OR is the ideal example of scientific method in operation as a management tool. Some specific examples can now be considered.

Some Practical Applications

Critical Path Analysis

A statistical planning path, utilising coded flow process charts, which arranges work in sequence to establish various project times and completion time overall (critical path). The aim is to establish the most economical overall project time by the most efficient use of resources.

Refer to Fig. 12.1:

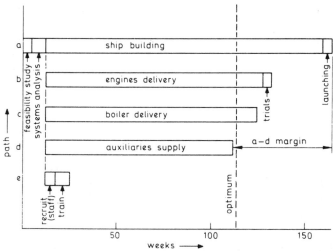

HYPOTHETICAL CRITICAL PATH CHART
Fig. 12.1

This flow process chart is purely illustrative of the technique and hypothetical in the sense that times may not be truly realistic—for example the 'fitting out' process has not been included, this will be necessary by extension or separate analysis.

Note the parallel paths for each operation within the original analysis, the critical path is a. (shipbuilding) as it is the 'bottleneck' preventing the earlier start of some other operations. Assume an alternative quote from another shipbuilder will reduce ship delivery (to the fitting out stage) by 50 weeks, but at a higher cost. A feasibility study may establish that this time saving may be advantageous in cost analysis for path a. By reducing the time of path a. other paths (b, c, d) can become critical and will have to be similarly analysed (for example, reduced delivery time but increased overtime). It may well be possible to arrive at an optimum completion time with new times for paths a, b, c, and d, virtually coincident (path e start can be delayed to 'close-up' to this optimum line). The final chart schedule could well show significant time reductions for overall completion at very little extra cost—the optimum.

Planned Maintenance

Such maintenance will delay the need for replacement and will reduce the risk of expensive breakdowns. Planned maintenance for motor vehicles, based on service at specific time or mileage intervals, is well known. Consider, as another example, part of the planned maintenance schedule for a large electric-driven pump supplying lubricating oil to engine plant (Table 12.1). Manufacturers data on pump, motor, fittings, installation date, etc. will be available in records for spare gear ordering. Pump running times will be recorded on plant performance log sheets.

Table 12.1 is illustrative only, the actual schedule detail will be dependent on company policy, pump type, duties, etc. Although words like *examine* are used consideration should be given to more precise wording to reduce variation between the work of individual maintenance personnel. It should be emphasised that planned maintenance in no way reduces the necessity for continuous checking of condition and performance. Terotechnology is total (life) maintenance of the ship plant in all its facets.

Replacement Policy

Will be dependent on planned maintenance but ultimately any decision on replacement would depend on financial considerations of increasing running costs, capital depreciation, sale value, inflation, etc. An exception to this approach is where components, particularly electronic, reduce only slightly in efficiency during their working life but fail suddenly at a particular time and are then useless. A timed replacement, during say shut-down periods, may prove less expensive then casual failure with expensive (and possibly dangerous) breakdown of plant operation. The timed replacement policy is established mathematically on probability calculations.

As an example consider the following analysis:

SCHEDULE	DATE	REPLACEMENTS	CLEARANCES	COMMENTS	SIGNATURE
1 month Clean and repack lubricant inserts, General tightness check on nuts					
3 month As for one month plus: examine and clean filters, renew joints when assembling					
6 month As for one and three months plus: examine and renew gland seals, clean motor, check starter box contacts and relays					
12 month As for one, three and six months plus: examine valve spindles and seats, re-pack valve glands. Examine bearings and shaft components, check and record radial and axial clearances. Insulation test and record. Examine for corrosion, including seatings					

TABLE 12.1

As an example consider the following analysis:

Failure in each succeeding year is 5%, 10%, 14%, 18% . . .
Average life of components $= 0.05 \times \frac{1}{2} + 0.10 \times 1\frac{1}{2} + \ldots = say 4$ years

Cost to replace random failure $= £150$
Cost on annual shut-down replacement $= £20$
Cost per component year on random failure $= 150/4 = £37.50$

Cost per component year on various replacement policies, in Table 12.2:

REPLACEMENT AFTER	YEARLY FAILURE PROBABILITY	CUMULATIVE PROBABILITY	REPLACEMENT COST TOTAL £	ANNUAL COST £
One Year	0.05	0.05	$150 \times 0.05 + 20$ $= 27.50$	27.50
Two Years	$0.05^2 + 0.10 = 0.1025$	0.1525	$150 \times 0.1525 + 20$ $= 42.88$	21.44
Three Years	$= 0.15$	0.3025	$= 65.38$	21.79
		0.508	$= 96.2$	24.05

TABLE 12.2

Minimum cost is achieved by replacement after two years. Clearly component life and random replacement cost are crucial factors. At sea the random replacement cost may well be very high if a significant part of the plant is affected by failure, also the risk factor is high, each makes a replacement policy especially attractive.

Ship Maintenance Costs

These are the largest item of operating costs. Fig. 12.2 indicates that they contribute over 70% of *controlled* operating costs for a given ship and would well be over 40% of *total* (direct and indirect, including such as marine insurance) operating costs.

Optimal Maintenance Policy

This is the best system for a given situation. The variation is from a repair only policy with no preventative maintenance on the one hand to a comprehensive and integrated fully preventative maintenance system on the other hand, based on accurate records and use of management'science.

Fig. 12.3 gives some idea of the parameters. Optimal is that which gives, with a specified amount of preventative maintenance, the minimum *total* cost of maintenance plus 'downtime'.

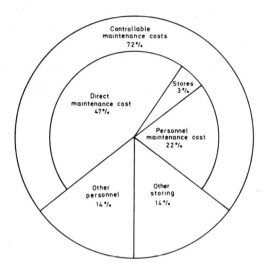

SHIP MAINTENANCE COSTS
Fig. 12.2

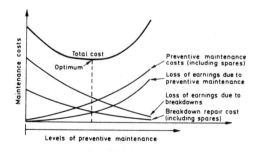

OPTIMAL MAINTENANCE
Fig. 12.3

Co-ordination

Processes relating to planning, control and organisation have been considered in some aspects, direction is equally involved with all activities, Co-ordination has not received significant attention here but is an important process. Co-ordination requires the essential factor of efficient two-way communications which must relate through divisions and cross-link between them. Instructions, information and reports must convey accurate, simple and clear details (see Report Writing, later).

ON-SHIP MANAGEMENT

The overall organisational management structure of the shipping company will vary but a typical 'tree' type divisional format may apply as shown in Fig. 12.4.

It will be noted from Fig. 12.4, in comparison to General Industrial Management (described previously), that Technical Services and Fleets (including development) replace Production and Marketing. The good management principle, *i.e* number of subordinates reporting to any executive should be limited, is readily attained by each sub-fleet manager only having responsibility for say six ships.

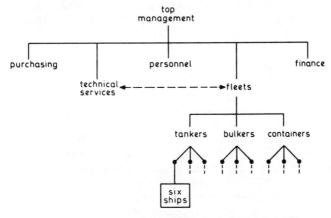

MANAGEMENT STRUCTURE (SHIPPING)
Fig. 12.4

Each individual ship is an independent unit with special management conditions, in which personnnel are in continuous close contact and whilst at sea have no external interaction, which can create human relationship problems. The increased automation, decreased crew-sizes and the trend to cost consciousness adds new dimensions. Planning is usually the responsibility of a small team of senior ship's officers, in liaison with company management, and requires the application of planned maintenance, replacement policies and some financial considerations. Organisation is departmentally based with a clearly defined structure, based to some extent on rank, which decides the directive process. Co-ordination and control are vital processes with the needs of good delegation, communication and personnel relations paramount.

Administration

For the Engineering Department the responsibility for this task lies primarily with the Chief Engineer Officer although a significant part is delegated to the Second Engineer Officer and certain other sub-departmental heads. The Chief Engineer Officer must ensure links with head office, between departments on ship and within his department. The Second Engineer Officer has an important role in delegation of engine room duties and responsibilities, control and recording of spares, maintenance schedules, etc. and, not least, effective personnel relations. The responsibility for efficient operation, firm leadership and good communications is an inherent requirement for senior ship managers. There is a developing trend to utilise committee structures, involving key officers and ratings, so as to improve decision making operations. This also allows more effective communications as the central 'hub' can relate closely to the peripheral 'wheel' with signal transmission via 'spokes' as well as around the 'rim'. 'On the job' training, to clearly defined objectives, is assuming increased importance on board ship.

REPORT WRITING

There is an important and increasing need for line managers to provide reports for consideration by top management and to write technical letters to external organisations. This becomes more vital at sea where senior ship management is remote from the central organisation of the company.

The importance of this aspect of the work of the marine engineer officer is recognised within the DTp Examinations. A common question in the Class One Engineering Knowledge examination paper requires a report to be written, usually from the Chief Engineer Officer to Head Office, on a selected technical topic. Class Two and Three are more likely to be directly concerned with 'on ship' management. Certain questions in these examinations, not specifically directed to report writing, do require however a knowledge of operational management principles—these are often related to safe practices.

Most students seem to have difficulty in writing mock letter reports or in presenting basic management routines. There is no 'model' answer to such examination questions. The following notes covering general use of English, examination requirements and specimen question-answer should be studied. The test examples at the end of this chapter should then be attempted, and preferably marked critically.

English Usage

1. The writer may well collect his thoughts by asking: 'what am I trying to say', 'what words will express it', 'can I put it clearly and briefly?'
2. A simple skeleton plan, of sequential ideas, may be listed.
3. Communication 'expert to expert' can include technical wording and information providing this is not overdone.
4. The 'shape' of a letter is important. A clear opening sentence, or short paragraph, is preferable to catch the immediate interest of the reader and to indicate what is to follow. The 'body' of the letter must follow a logical thought sequence—there is no objection to the use of a, b, c, etc., to define specific points, provided this makes the content more clear. The end of the letter should indicate some positive summary or conclusion.
5. Sentences should be short and well punctuated with compact paragraphs relating the main points.
6. Simple words should be used in place of more complicated words or phrases—join for integrate, send for despatch, about for respecting—walk for capable of locomotion, etc.
7. 'Robot like' references such as 'it is regretted', 'for your information', 'I am further to point out', etc., should not be used.
8. Verbosity, especially with adjectives (serious danger, unfilled vacancy), adverbs (to risk unduly, to enhance markedly) and prepositions (in terms of—about, until such time—until), is to be avoided.

9. The use of 'buzz words', *e.g.* maximise, optional, orientated, etc., is inclined to be showy.
10. Cliches (my grateful thanks, in this day and age), similes (as good as gold, works like a horse) and metaphors (hit for six, backed a winner) are best avoided.
11. A positive is preferable to double negative (not unnaturally, not unblack!).
12. Letter endings are best made 'yours faithfully' if the method of address is 'Dear Sir' and yours sincerely to a 'Dear Mr Smith' address. Subservient (your obedient servant) and somewhat ridicilous (at your convenience) remarks are not used.

Examination Requirements

a. The examiners look for clarity of expression, good punctuation, paragraphs, etc., *i.e.* English presentation is being assessed.
b. Technical accuracy is not so important, within reasonable limits.
c. Major details, without minor technical points, are required.
d. The experience of the candidate in matters of management, personnel relations, work study, etc., is part of the assessment.
e. The examiners attach particular importance to the following:
Machinery surveys: arranging, preparing, recording.
Safety equipment: certificates.
Planned maintenance: schedules, surveys.
Testing: machinery space lifting gear.
Oil in navigable waters act: instructions to staff.
Clean air act: instructions to staff.
Fire fighting: instructions and training for E.R. staff.
Fire fighting: co-operation between Deck and E.R. staff.
Training: engineer cadet training schedules.
Training: instructions to new junior officers.
Inspection: essential tests, etc., 24 hours before sailing on a strange vessel.
Performance: assessment of voyage records and test data.
New Ships: improved ventilation and equipment, suggestions.
Safety Schedules: day to day safety training.
Bunkering: information on bunker chits, stability during bunkering.
Crews: duties of staff, general purpose duties.

Ship maintenance: overall maintenance criteria for whole vessel.

Emergency conditions: machinery failures, operation.

Specimen Question

Write a letter to your company's Superintendent Engineer concerning the circumstances attending a fire in the boiler or machinery spaces. The letter should state the probable cause, action taken and suggest preventative measures.

The candidate should first ask himself the following questions and then answer accordingly (the same technique is applicable to most examination questions in the subject):

1. What happened . . . when?
2. What was the cause . . . effect?
3. How was the condition dealt with?
4. How can a re-occurrence be prevented?
5. Any other relevant comment?

Specimen answer

MV Eastern Glory,
c/o Foster Johns (Managers) Ltd.,
'Ocean View',
Brisbane,
Queensland,
AUSTRALIA. 10th November, 1986.

Chief Engineer Superintendent,
The Moss Line Ltd.,
Star House,
Leadenhall St.,
LONDON, W2 5MK.

Engine Room Fire, 5th November, 1986, at Sea

Dear Sir,

Further to my cable of the 5th November, I wish to confirm that the above vessel was stopped from 1500 hours to 2300 hours on that date, because of an Engine Room fire which required evacuation of this space for about five hours.

Due to an overflow when filling a settling tank, oil escaped on to the hot engine exhaust manifold causing a serious fire. The general fire alarm was sounded and the bridge informed but within two minutes the Engine Room was untenable and I ordered immediate evacuation.

At 1507 hours all Engine Room staff were accounted for, the Engine Room was sealed off and inert smothering gas injected. At 1800 hours an attempt was made to re-enter the Engine Room via the tunnel but without success. At 2000 hours the Engine Room was entered and small fires still burning were put out with portable extinguishers. No serious permanent damage was noted but the space was severely blackened. The machinery was prepared for sea and, before getting under way, all lagging was stripped from the manifolds.

The cause was established as a faulty tank indicating float and overflow gooseneck whose outflow was directed near the manifold. It is suggested that a mercury type level and alarm switch be fitted as a replacement and that the gooseneck be replaced by an overflow pipe (with sight glass) to an overflow tank. I ask for approval to put this work in hand immediately. In the meantime special care is being exercised in tank filling. A detailed damage report will be sent in the near future.

I would like to record the excellent behaviour of the Engine Room staff during the whole incident and the efficient communication between Deck and Engine departments. No injury occurred to personnel.

Yours faithfully,

William J. Hall (Chief Engineer)

Test Examples—Technique

An outline *framework*, as suggested method of answer, to three of the test examples at the end of this chapter is now presented for consideration before the reader proceeds to attempt the remaining test examples:

Class 3 Test Example No. 1
Fire location — accommodation, deck, engine (need to vary).
Advance warning (notice) and practice alarm (method).
Fire Stations — assembly, numbers, roll call.
Communications — central and remote.
Checking responsibilities (individual and collective).
Testing alarms and equipment.
Simulated attack on fire.
Emergency sealing arrangements — check.
Short seminar on effectiveness — feed back.

Class 2 Test Example No. 1

a. increased ignition potential—burning, welding, sparks, smoking.

b. increased combustible potential—waste, dirt, spillage.

c. increased air potential—draughts, openings, circulation.

d. increased space potential—open tanks, holds, stores.

Easier air and combustible access, less efficient sealing arrangements, more people/less co-ordination, reduced availability of immediate ship fire fighting services, etc.

Reduced a, b, c, d. Improved emergency arrangements, close liaison ship-shore personnel, ready access to sealing/opening facilities, fire patrol (24 hours), etc.

Class 1 Test Example No. 1

1. What major repairs?

   Precise nature, voyage effects, difficulties reaching port.

2. Why necessary after major refit?

   Possible cause, blame, deterioration on voyage.

3. Justification of shore labour?

   Scale of repair, time available, ship labour resources/facilities.

4. Justification of cost?

   Typical cost figures, estimates obtained, agents advice.

5. Balance costing?

   Survey in lieu of port time, cargo, voyage schedules.

6. Inspection?

   Classification Society, ship staff, work standards, expected outcomes.

Note

In cases where a report is on a subject likely to be used in subsequent legal actions (safety, law breaking, etc.), it is vitally important to present information very accurately with respect to time, date, names of personnel involved, etc.

TEST EXAMPLES 12

Class 3

1. Describe briefly how a practice fire drill should be carried out.
2. If a large item of machinery is to be lifted out of the engine room state what precautions should be taken to:
   (i)   prevent injury to any personnel,
   (ii)   prevent damage to either ship or the item being lifted.
3. Briefly describe a system aboard ship by which the spare gear can be monitored and an adequate supply be ensured for machinery repairs.
4. Explain what is meant by planned maintenance with respect to ship's machinery.

TEST EXAMPLES 12

Class 2

1. Give four common sources of fire in a vessel under repair in a yard.

   Explain why fire may spread more rapidly in a ship under repair in a yard than when at sea.

   Describe the precautions taken to minimise the possibility and effect of fire in a repair yard.

2. Explain what is meant by 'planned maintenance'.

   Give details of its application to the main lubricating oil pumps.

3. List the safe practices to be observed when personnel are:
   (a)   using lifting tackle,
   (b)   working beneath the floor plates,
   (c)   overhauling valves or renewing jointing in steam lines,
   (d)   dismantling machinery during rough weather,

4. (a) Explain the role of the Safety Officer in relation to the ship's Safety Committee.
   (b)   Outline the specific duties of this officer on board ship.

TEST EXAMPLES 12

Class 1

1. The ship's crew have conducted a series of combined lifeboat and fire drills over the period of the voyage.

   As Chief Engineer, make a brief report to the ship's management to explain the lessons learnt from these drills, proposing ways of improving the effectiveness of these emergency procedures.

2. Draft out a Chief Engineer's report to Head Office outlining a three month practical training programme on board ship for engineer cadets who have not been to sea before.

3. Your ship sustained a sudden and irrevocable loss of main propulsion power whilst entering port.

   As Chief Engineer, make a report to Head Office, explaining the cause of the failure.

4. Most foreign going cargo ships are required to possess a valid Safety Equipment Certificate renewed at intervals after survey of the safety equipment.

   (a)   Identify those items covered by the Safety Equipment Certificate which are usually the responsibility of the Chief Engineer.

   (b)   Suggest how the survey should be organised in order that it be completed with the least trouble and delay.

   (c)   Suggest how it can be ensured that this safety equipment is in a full state of readiness at all times.

SPECIMEN EXAMINATION QUESTIONS (DTp)
CLASS 3

Miscellaneous

1. A new valve spindle is to be ordered from ashore, make a simple sketch giving all the information you consider necessary for its manufacture.

2. What is the advantage of case hardening, how is it done, and give an example of a component which may have this treatment.

3. Explain why the water level in a boiler is very important.
   What might happen if the water level is allowed to drop significantly.
   What are the dangers of allowing the water level to rise significantly.

4. Water for boilers is usually kept as pure as reasonably possible. Give reasons why this is so.

5. State the precautions to be taken before entry into any enclosed space.
   What are the two main dangers.

6. When taking over a watch at sea, itemise the main points that should be checked.

7. Sketch and describe a smoke detector of the type fitted in an engine room, how is it tested?

8. Write brief comment on how the following can effect centrifugal pump performance:
   Wear rings
   Impeller erosion
   Gland sealing
   Shaft wear
   Speed

9. Explain how you would test an emergency fire pump. Where is this pump usually situated and why.

10. Describe some of the usual problems found in bilge pumping systems and explain what can be done to overcome them.

11. List the signs of damage or over straining which might be visible in a wire sling.

12. Itemise the safety precautions you would take before starting work on a steering gear motor.

13. A straight piece of fire main pipe on deck has corroded and needs to be renewed. After removing the corroded length of pipe the distance measured between the two adjoining flanges is 4m 37cm. The bore of the pipe is 10cm, flanges 20cm diameter and with 4 bolt holes 18mm diameter on 14.8cm PCD bolts off centre one end and on centre the other end.
Make a drawing suitable for giving to a shore firm to enable them to make the new piece of pipe.

14. Before lighting up an auxiliary oil fired boiler state the precautions to be taken.

15. Briefly describe a test for determining the tensile strength of a piece of steel.

16. Make a simple sketch of a boiler you are familiar with showing in section the main constructional parts.

17. Explain the function of the telemotor receiver in an electro-hydraulic steering gear system.

18. What are the dangers of letting a centrifugal pump run dry?

19. Briefly describe the smoke helmet type of breathing apparatus. Give one advantage and one disadvantage of this type.

20. State how you would test the main fire pump on a ship.

21. State the precautions you would take before dismantling an electric motor.

22. What dangers are increased if an engine room is allowed to become dirty?

23. Why is it important that a record of spares be kept on a ship?

24. State the two major chemical elements which make up fuel oil, and also give two other elements that may be found in fuel oil.

25. Sketch a screw down non-return valve in section, giving the material of each part.
Give an example where this type of valve is used in an engine room.

26. Describe how a tubular heat exchanger is cleaned.

27. Briefly describe why boiler water needs to be tested periodically, and state two of the tests.

28. Describe with the aid of a sketch if necessary a thermocouple, where would you expect this device to be fitted?

29. Sketch in section a 2 gallon foam type fire extinguisher itemising each part. On what type of fire is this type of extinguisher used?

30. State what precautions should be taken before entry into a cofferdam between a ballast tank and an oil tank.

31. Explain briefly the following terms which are often used with regard to engineering materials:
   (1) Annealed.
   (2) Case hardened.
   (3) Tempered.
   (4) Nitrided.

Give an example of two of the above.

32. Make a diagrammatic sketch of a bilge pumping system itemising the main components.

33. Explain the test procedure that should be carried out on an electro-hydraulic steering gear before leaving port.

34. Explain why it is necessary for a flexible coupling to be fitted between a medium speed main propulsion engine and a gearbox.

35. Make a drawing of a coupling bolt which would be suitable to give to an engineering firm so that some coupling bolts could be manufactured. The nominal diameter of the bolt is 70 mm and each flange is 75 mm thick.
The drawing should give all dimensions, material, etc.

36. For the following uses give a suitable material:
Diesel engine crankshaft.
Eye bolt used for lifting.
Oil heater tube nest.
Impeller for centrifugal sea water pump.
Diaphragm for pneumatically controlled valve.

37. Describe the basic refrigeration circuit for a compression type domestic refrigeration plant, what effect would a higher ambient temperature have on the unit?

38. With the aid of a simple sketch, explain how a watergauge fitted directly to a boiler is tested for accuracy when the boiler is steaming.

39. Why are positive displacement pumps usually fitted with relief valves, and why is this not usually the case with centrifugal pumps?

40. If a centrifugal bilge pump does not seem to be able to lower the level of water in the bilge state what should be checked.

DEPARTMENT OF TRANSPORT
EXAMINATION FOR CERTIFICATE OF COMPETENCY
CLASS 3 ENGINEER
ENGINEERING KNOWLEDGE (1)

Answer ALL questions
Time allowed, 2 hours

1. A new shaft has to be made for a sea water pump whose principal reference dimensions are as follows:
Overall length of shaft to be 525 mm.
The internal bore of the coupling flange is 40 mm.
The internal bore of the impeller is 32 mm.
Both impeller and coupling flange are keyed onto the shaft.
Make a sketch giving all necessary information for its manufacture.
You will have to make reasonable assumptions for all other dimensions.

2. Describe an oily water separator and state how you would check that it was working satisfactory.

3. State the material you would use for the following and state one of its main properties:
(a) Joint for flanged steam pipe.
(b) Spindle for sea water valve.
(c) Electrical contact in a starter.

4. Describe an electrically powered windlass, how is the motor protected from overload.

5. Before injecting CO_2 gas into an engine room to put out a fire, what is it necessary to do or check.

6. If it is necessary to enter a tank that has previously been filled with oil, explain how the tank can be gas freed, and what other precautions should be taken before entry.

7. Why is oil in boiler water considered dangerous, where does it usually come from and how can it be removed.

8. What pre-sea checks should be made on a steering gear and telemotor system.

9. Air compressors are prone to valve trouble, why is this and what can be done to limit this.

10. What items of hull and machinery should be checked in dry dock.

11. Your vessel develops a main engine defect that will necessitate assistance from a foreign repair yard (and possibly spares might have to be obtained by the repair yard from the UK). What information should you send ahead to the repair yard to help them.

12. With reference to a bank of batteries for emergency use, how would you:
(a) check that they are fully charged,
(b) keep them fully charged,
(c) what maintenance would you expect to do.

SPECIMEN EXAMINATION QUESTIONS (DTp)
CLASS 2

Miscellaneous

1. Sketch a compressed air system for use with pneumatic controls. Write notes on each component shown.

2. State the precautionary measures taken in the following instances: (a) employment of personnel in confined spaces with particular reference to duct keels, (b) heating of refrigerant bottles when charging a refrigeration plant, (c) use of spirit lamps when testing for refrigerant leakage.

3. Make a detailed sketch of a trailing collar and a brake as sometimes fitted to propeller shafting. Explain the purpose of the collar. Explain the purpose of the brake. Give one reason why both are needed on the same line of shafting.

4. State the risks to personnel when working: (a) beneath floor plates, (b) in refrigeration machinery spaces, (c) in an emergency battery room. For each case, give the appropriate safety measures to be taken.

5. Describe with sketches, any design of torsion meter for measuring the power transmitted between the main engine and the propeller. Explain how the power is measured and indicated.

6. Sketch and describe a Pilgrim nut for a propeller. Explain how it is used when fitting the propeller on to the shaft taper. State two advantages this type of nut has over a conventional propeller nut.

7. Describe how the following defects in a refrigeration system become apparent and are corrected: (a) undercharge, (b) overcharge, (c) oil in the condenser.

8. Give three causes for a semi-portable foam fire extinguisher failing to operate when required. State the chemical constituents used in this extinguisher and explain why it needs occasional recharging. Explain how staff are given practice in its use.

9. A bilge pump of the centrifugal type is found to be noticeably falling off in performance until it will barely empty the bilges although running continuously at its normal service speed. Give four common causes which individually or collectively will give rise to such a condition. Describe how each fault is traced, isolated or remedied by following a logical series of tests.

10. Describe the operation of the following portable extinguishers and, for each type, state the type of fire for which it is most suitable: (a) soda-acid, (b) chemical foam, (c) carbon dioxide.

11. Describe with sketches, two methods for remotely determining the quantity of liquid in a tank. Compare the accuracy of these methods and explain how the degree of accuracy can be maintained. State one possible source of error for each of the methods described.

12. Give two desirable properties and one undesirable property of each of the following metals: (a) brass, (b) cast iron, (c) mild steel. State for each of these metals one application in marine engineering where it is most suited.

13. If a fire broke out in the engine room, explain how: (a) the fuel supply could be shut off, (b) the supply of air could be shut off, (c) the fire could be dealt with from outside the engine room, giving a summary of all the facilities available for this purpose.

14. With reference to propeller shafts: (a) suggest, with reasons, the frequency at which shafts should be withdrawn for inspection, (b) state the defects that should be looked for during the inspection, (c) explain why some shafts require less frequent inspection than others, (d) explain why the introduction of the 'split' stern bearing has considerably reduced the normal frequency of dry docking the ship.

15. Give two indications that the main shaft bearings are unequally loaded at sea. Describe how the effect of unequal load distribution may be relieved whilst still at sea. Describe what remedial action will be taken in port.

16. State why a pneumatic control system requires clean dry air. Explain how the following air pollutants are dealt with: (a) water, (b) oil, (c) dust and dirt.

17. Give two indications other than excessive running, that a freon refrigeration plant is not operating satisfactorily. Suggest what the trouble may be and describe how it would be rectified.

18. Describe the operation of a differential pressure alarm fitted across an oil filter. Explain how such a device would be tested whilst the filter is in service.

19. Sketch a propeller shaft carried in either of the following stern tubes: (a) water lubricated, wood lined, (b) oil lubricated whitemetal lined. Describe major defects to which propeller shafts in (a) and (b) are susceptible. Explain the cause of these defects. State how these defects are dealt with.

20. With reference to multitubular oil coolers: (a) sketch a two pass cooler showing the direction of oil and coolant flow, (b) identify the materials of the components in (a), (c) give three serious faults to which (a) is prone, (d) state how the faults in (c) are inhibited.

21. With reference to centrifugal bilge pumps: (a) sketch a rotary air pump, (b) state why an air pump is fitted and how it works, (c) state why bilge pumps normally receive greater attention than other centrifugal pumps.

22. With reference to oily water separators: (a) sketch an automatic separator handling large quantities of contaminated water, (b) explain how it operates, (c) state what routine attention is needed to maintain satisfactory performance, (d) state how the maximum throughput is restricted and why this is important.

23. State why oxygen deficiencies may occur in certain spaces in ships. Describe the precautions taken before entry to any recently opened space. Describe with sketches a self-contained breathing apparatus. State how and why a bottle is checked before use and warning is given that a bottle is nearly exhausted.

24. With reference to centrifugal pumps used for handling large quantities of sea water: (a) suggest, with reasons, why the

pump need only be dismantled for inspection and overhaul at infrequent intervals, (b) state three common defects looked for during inspection, (c) describe why and how the impeller is sealed at the casing, (d) explain why the fineness of the clearance between casing and impeller is of less consequence with this pump than pumps for some other duties.

25. State the physical properties of materials used for the following components and give an explanation for the choice in each case: (a) safety valve or relief valve spring, (b) main engine bearing, (c) diesel engine crankshaft or high pressure turbine rotor.

26. State the physical properties of materials generally used for the following components and give an explanation for the choice in each case; (a) an oil cooler tube, (b) a ship-side valve chest, (c) an impeller of a centrifugal pump handling brine.

27. Define the meaning of the term 'coefficient of performance' in relation to refrigeration plant. Describe with sketches a refrigeration plant operating on the ammonia absorption cycle. State how its coefficient of performance compares with that of vapour compression systems.

28. With reference to hydraulic steering gears state: (a) what type of packing is used in the ram glands, (b) what emergency arrangements are provided to keep the main gear working, (c) how vertical movement of the rudder is accommodated.

29. Sketch a compressed air system for pneumatic controls labelling all the principal items. Describe with sketches an automatic drain on the air compressor. State what routine maintenance and tests are needed to keep the system fully operational.

30. Describe the tests to evaluate the following properties of oil: (a) viscosity, (b) closed flash point. Give representative results for a specified liquid fuel. Account for any inaccuracies in the tests.

31. With reference to a fixed carbon dioxide fire smothering system explain: (a) how rupture of the bursting disc on a gas cylinder does not result in loss of gas, (b) how the system is protected against accidental use, (c) why gang release is

necessary, how it functions and the necessary action it fails to operate.

32. Describe a test to determine the amount of water in lubricating oil. Give two ways whereby water can be extracted from the oil. Give three reasons why a significant quantity of water in lubricating oil is unacceptable.

33. Give a typical analysis of the dissolved solids in a sample of: (a) fresh water, (b) sea water. State which of these dissolved solids form scale when the water is heated and which cause corrosion.

34. Select the most suitable material for each of the following applications giving three good reasons for each choice: (a) cylinders of hydraulic steering gears, (b) tubes of salt water cooled oil coolers, (c) shells of unfired pressure vessels.

35. State what precautions are to be observed to avoid or contain any outbreak of fire arising from the following conditions on board a ship at a repair berth: (a) a length of the fire main dismantled, (b) power cables running across decks, (c) welding in confined spaces, (d) large quantities of rags and cotton waste deposited in temporary store rooms.

36. Sketch and describe a plate type heat exchanger. Explain how the fluids are separated and the effect of gasket thickness on performance. Give two good reasons for plate configuration and manufacture from titanium.

37. With reference to self-priming centrifugal pumps: (a) describe with sketches how air is excluded from the impeller eye, (b) describe with sketches how a liquid-ring priming pump operates, (c) state with reasons what parts of the priming pump require special attention during overhaul.

38. Draw a line diagram of any type of sewage system labelling the principal items and showing the direction of flow in all lines. Explain how the system works. State what advantage the system described has over other sewage systems.

39. Select the most suitable material for each of the following applications, giving three good reasons for each choice: (a)

shafts and impellers of centrifugal bilge pumps, (b) intermediate main shafts, (c) safety or relief valve springs.

40. Describe how you would instruct new personnel in the care and use of: (a) breathing apparatus, (b) CO_2 flooding system, (c) hoses and nozzles, (d) portable fire extinguishers.

41. Sketch and describe a centrifugal oil separator. How, and why, is a water wash used? Discuss 'batch purification' and 'continuous bypass' systems for lubricating oil.

42. Sketch and describe the following for a refrigerator unit: (a) compressor crankshaft gland seal, (b) pressure switch, (c) regulator.

43. Sketch and describe a thermo-electric pyrometer. State the various materials that can be used in its construction and give the approximate temperature ranges for which these materials are suitable. What arc the advantages and disadvantages of this instrument.

44. Sketch in diagrammatic form, and explain a refrigerating plant which utilises intermediate liquid cooling. State the refrigerating media used in this plant and the advantages of this type of system.

45. In what system of refrigeration is brine used? From what substances is it made? What is its freezing point? Why are the substances used? What density is used for the brine in circulation and how is testing carried out?

46. Describe a method of determining the calorific value of a fuel. What is meant by higher and lower calorific value. State the approximate calorific value of coal and fuel oil and explain any reason for the difference in values given.

Note:
Other specialist text books will need to be used to answer Section II (Electro technology) and Section III (Naval Architecture) questions given in the Class 2 specimen paper following.

DEPARTMENT OF TRANSPORT
EXAMINATION FOR CERTIFICATE OF COMPETENCY
CLASS 2 ENGINEER

ENGINEERING KNOWLEDGE — GENERAL

Time allowed: 3 hours

IMPORTANT
This paper consists of FOURTEEN questions divided into
THREE sections.

Candidates are required to attempt not more than TEN
questions as follows:

SECTION I (Questions 1-8)
Not more than SIX questions to be attempted in this section.

SECTION II (Questions 9-11)
Not more than TWO questions to be attempted in this section.

SECTION III (Questions 12-14)
Not more than TWO questions to be attempted in this section.

SECTION I
QUESTIONS 1-8
This section carries 60% of the total marks.
Not more than SIX questions to be attempted in this section.

1.   (i) Draw a line diagram of a zero
discharge sewage system in which the
water is recirculated and the solids
processed for disposal, labelling the
principal components and showing
the direction of flow in all lines.   (4 marks)

     (ii) Describe how the system operates.   (4 marks)

    (iii) Give reasons why this system might
be considered superior to that in
which the sterile water is discharged
overboard at sea.   (2 marks)

2. Give reasons why the following actions
   might help correct the fault if an electric
   salinometer registers an unacceptably high
   value for the distillate from a vacuum
   evaporator:

      (i) lower water level in evaporator,   (2 marks)
     (ii) increase flow rate through brine
           pump,   (2 marks)
    (iii) shut in coil inlet valve,   (2 marks)
    (iv) shut in vapour valve,   (2 marks)
     (v) Give reasons why salinity should be
         maintained at a consistently low
         value.   (2 marks)

3.   (i) Sketch in cross section, a pump other
         than of the reciprocating, centrifugal,
         or gear type.   (4 marks)
     (ii) Explain how it operates.   (4 marks)
    (iii) Suggest with reasons a shipboard
         application for which it is well suited. (2 marks)

4. With reference to rotary vane steering gear
   state:

      (i) how the fixed vanes are attached to
         the cylinder,   (2 marks)
     (ii) how the moving vanes are attached to
         the rotor,   (2 marks)
    (iii) how strength is imparted to the
         moving vanes to enable them to act
         as rudder stops,   (2 marks)
    (iv) how the vanes are sealed at the tips, (2 marks)
     (v) how rudder uplift is accommodated. (2 marks)

5.   (i) Sketch a hydraulic coupling between
         a medium speed diesel engine and
         reverse/reduction gear.   (4 marks)
     (ii) Describe how it operates.   (4 marks)
    (iii) State what advantages such couplings
         have over their friction, powder and
         magnetic counterparts.   (2 marks)

6. Describe with sketches circuit transducers
   for producing electrical or pneumatic
   signals to indicate:

      (i) main lubricating oil pressure,   (4 marks)
     (ii) cylinder jacket cooling temperature, (4 marks)
    (iii) State how each transducer is tested. (2 marks)

7.   (i) Suggest with reasons which of the
           following data is relevant and
           significant to the quality of fuel oil:
           viscosity,   Conradson number,
           pour point,   total base number,
           closed flash point,   octane number,
           open flash point,   specific gravity. (6 marks)
      (ii) Define the significance of lower and
           higher calorific value in assessing the
           standard of liquid fuel.   (4 marks)

8.   (i) Describe with sketches any one of the
           following portable fire extinguishers:
           chemical foam,
           carbon dioxide,
           dry powder.   (4 marks)
      (ii) Suggest why in certain instances
           carbon dioxide and dry powder can
           be more of a hazard than a help in
           untutored hands.   (2 marks)
     (iii) Suggest why dry powder is possibly
           more effective than carbon dioxide
           for switchboard fires.   (2 marks)
      (iv) State why chemical foam
           extinguishers occasionally require
           recharging even though they have not
           been used.   (2 marks)

SECTION II
QUESTIONS 9-11
This section carries 20% of the total marks.
Not more than TWO questions to be attempted in this section.

9. (i)   Distinguish between 'Primary cell'
          and 'Secondary cell' and between
          'acid cell' and 'alkaline cell'.   (5 marks)
    (ii) Describe how a battery of alkaline
          cells may be tested for its usefulness
          after a long storage and if found
          deficient how it can be remedied.   (5 marks)

10. (i)   Explain the meaning of single phasing
          in a.c. machinery.   (5 marks)
    (ii) State the dangers associated with
          single phasing and the protective
          devices normally fitted to counteract
          such dangers.   (5 marks)

11. (i)   State why incandescent lamps can be
          dimmed by simply regulating the
          applied voltage whereas this method
          cannot be used with gas discharge
          lamps.   (3 marks)
    (ii) State under what circumstances the
          assumption that, a lamp maintains
          it's value as long as it still functions,
          is wrong.   (3 marks)
    (iii) State FOUR factors which influence
          the life of gas discharge lamps.   (4 marks)

SECTION III
QUESTIONS 12-14
This section carries 20% of the total marks.
Not more than TWO questions to be attempted in this section.

12. With reference to solid propellers state:
    (i)   how badly damaged blade tips are
       restored,   (4 marks)
    (ii) why propellers need balancing from
        time to time,   (3 marks)
    (iii) why intense concentrated heat should
        not be applied to bosses.   (3 marks)

13.   (i)   Sketch in diagrammatic form a
       stabiliser unit in which the fins retract
       athwartships into a recess in the hull. (4 marks)
    (ii) Describe how the extension/retraction
        sequence is carried out.   (4 marks)
    (iii) Define how the action of fin
        stabilisers effects steering.   (2 marks)

14.   (i)   State how fresh water tanks are
       prepared for inspection.   (3 marks)
    (ii) State how the surface of the
        steelwork is treated prior to refilling. (2 marks)
    (iii) Give reasons for the manner of
        treatment employed in (ii).   (2 marks)
    (iv) Give reasons why fresh water from
        such tanks is quite suitable for human
        consumption and yet fresh water
        produced by evaporation of sea water
        is not necessarily suitable for such
        purposes.   (3 marks)

SPECIMEN EXAMINATION QUESTIONS (DTp)
CLASS 1

Miscellaneous

1. A rating has been badly burnt by a 'blow-back' from the oil fired auxiliary boiler. As Chief Engineer, make a full report to head office explaining the circumstances of the incident and the precautionary measures now taken to reduce the possibility of a similar occurence in the future.

2. Describe how the supervisory equipment for the control of machinery in a periodically unattended engine room is itself monitored for defects on individual channels and as a complete unit.

3. You were instructed to discontinue water treatment in the auxiliary boiler for a specified period of time. As Chief Engineer, make a full report to head office stating how the trial has been productive of information and data applicable to the improvement of boiler management.

4. With reference to a dock bottom inspection of a propeller shaft that is carried in a wood lined, water cooled, stern tube, state: (a) where corrosive action may be discovered, (b) the fault responsible for the wastage, (c) to what extent the wastage may be considered serious, (d) the defects associated with the keyways on the taper and how they arise, (e) why cavities between the liner and shaft may be considered serious.

5. In taking over a ship in a foreign port you are dissatisfied with your predecessor's report on the condition of the machinery. As Chief Engineer, write to head office expressing dissatisfaction with the report, making such amendments to it as you consider necessary.

6. Identify the chief causes of overheating in tunnel bearings and of vibration in main shafting. Explain why the siting of the engineer room amidships enhances these tendencies. State how overheating and vibration may be reduced or eliminated.

7. Explain why it is advisable to examine propeller shafts at regular intervals of time. Describe an examination of a solid shaft that is carried in a wood lined, water cooled bearing.

8. Sketch and describe a system for indicating remotely the propeller shaft speed. Explain how, with the system selected, inaccuracies occur and are kept to a minimum.

9. Compare the relative merits of infra red, ultra violet and combustion gas (ionisation) type fire detectors for use in machinery spaces. Explain why a combination of these types is more desirable than any one type individually.

10. Explain how the Prevention of Oil Pollution Act 1971 affects the normal operational practices conducted within shipboard machinery spaces. Describe: (a) measures taken to comply with the Act, (b) documentation involved.

11. Sketch and describe a flash type distillation plant. Describe the precautions taken to ensure the water is fit for drinking purposes.

12. Explain why radiographic and ultrasonic techniques are suitable for use during shipboard machinery inspection. Give two examples where such techniques are applicable. Describe either process in detail.

13. Explain in what manner and under what regulations the Chief Engineer is responsible for prevention of oil pollution at sea and in port. Describe the shipboard equipment installed to ensure that oil or oily water is not discharged overboard.

14. Sketch and describe a plate type cooler. Explain how leakage is prevented. State one advantage and one disadvantage it possesses over the tubular type.

15. Explain why the performance of a centrifugal sea water circulating pump 'falls off' in service. State two ways in which this 'fall off' is indicated. Describe how the pump may be restored to its original performance.

16. Explain why a carbon dioxide fixed fire smothering system requires periodical inspection and servicing. Describe the nature of this servicing. State two advantages and two disadvantages this system has over a fixed foam system.

17. Explain how the ingress of sea water is prevented in an oil lubricated stern bearing system. Should the system fail, describe

the corrective action possible whilst the vessel is afloat. State why two stern bearing oil header tanks are fitted in some instances.

18. Sketch and describe a method of measuring the pressure differential for fluid flow systems. State what are the effects of altering the orifice plate size of the position of the tapping points.

19. You have been advised that the amount of spare gear carried in the ship is to be reduced to just meet Classification Society's requirements. As Chief Engineer, make a report to head office requesting, with reasons, additional items for retention in the ship.

20. State what is the purpose of each of the following items in a machinery control system: (a) portable mercury manometer, (b) portable inclined-tube manometer, (c) portable temperature potentiometer, (d) compressor and vacuum pump. Describe in detail any two of these items.

21. Any proposal to operate a machinery space in the periodically unattended condition must take into account the dangers from fire, flooding and failure of supervisory equipment. Describe how the possibility of the latter two hazards may be minimised, detected and brought to the attention of the designated watchkeeper.

22. You have been asked for an explanation why your vessel's fuel consumption is significantly higher and its average sea speed correspondingly lower than that of a sister vessel. As Chief Engineer, make a report to head office giving in your opinion a full explanation for the discrepancy.

23. Make a simplified diagram of the operating gear for a controllable pitch propeller. Explain how the pitch is controlled and what happens if the control mechanism fails.

24. Give three reasons why axial flow pumps are particularly suitable for salt water circulation of steam condensers and similar large heat exchangers. Give one reason why this type of pump has a rather restricted shipboard application. Describe one further application for which the axial flow pump is well suited.

25. Explain how wear on bearing surfaces is effected by each of the following factors: (a) dissimilarity of the materials in the contact surfaces, (b) relative speed of sliding between the surfaces, (c) roughness of the surfaces, (d) incompatability of lubricant and bearing material. Describe how each effect may be identified during inspection. Suggest corrective action at either operational or maintenance stages.

26. In bunkering fuel in both double-bottom and deep tanks, describe: (a) the dangers present in the operation, (b) the precautions to be taken, (c) the legislation to be observed.

27. Make a three point comparison of the characteristics of centrifugal pumps with those of positive displacement rotary pumps. Suggest, with reasons, the type of pump most suited in each of the following instances: (a) main lubricating oil circulation, (b) domestic fresh water supply, (c) steering gear or stabiliser actuation.

28. Explain the problems involved in locating fire detector heads in machinery spaces. Describe the tests to check that the detecting system is functioning properly.

29. With particular reference to operational safety, elaborate on any two of the following statements and their implications: (a) the auto ignition temperatures of fuel and lubricating oils are lower than those of the lighter fractions, (b) the presence of oily residue in boilers is dangerous, (c) all electrical equipment is not intrinsically safe or flame proof, (d) static electricity is generated during any normal shipboard operation.

30. Sketch and describe a pump other than of the reciprocating, centrifugal, or gear type. Give two advantages it possesses over other types. Suggest one shipboard application for which it might be best suited.

31. Explain why a simple centrifugal type pump is unsuitable for bilge pumping duties. Sketch and describe how a centrifugal pump can be rendered suitable for such duties.

32. Explain why the fuel supply to the burners of a periodically unattended auxiliary boiler automatically cut-off in the alarm condition for low and a high water level, high steam

pressure, air failure and flame failure. Describe how and when you could safely test these devices.

33. Make a detailed sketch of the sealing arrangements for an oil-filled stern tube. Describe the common forms of seal failure. Explain how oil loss due to seal failure is restricted whilst on passage. Describe how the seals are restored to their original effectiveness. Give a reason other than the expense of oil loss why effective sealing is necessary.

34. With reference to ram type electro-hydraulic steering gears explain: (a) why four rams are provided in many instances, (b) with sketches the arrangement of the crosshead rapson slide and its principle of operation, (c) why the telemotor receiver is spring loaded and the effect on steering of spring failure.

35. Sketch and describe a fuel meter used with high viscosity fuel. Explain how it operates. Explain the value of the readings obtained and how they are used.

36. The necessity has arisen for the complete replenishment of the main lubricating oil system. As Chief Engineer report to head office justifying this heavy expenditure, explaining the temporary steps taken to avoid further trouble on voyage and suggesting permanent measures to avoid repetition.

37. With reference to main shaft bearings that are excessively loaded or very lightly loaded state for each condition what are the: (a) indications of the fault, (b) effects on adjacent bearings, (c) remedial steps. Explain why load distribution on main shaft bearings changes in service.

38. Compare the current methods of mounting propellers on their shafts. Sketch and describe a method of mounting a propeller on its shaft by 'hydraulic floating'. Give four good reasons why this method is considered superior to all others.

39. Give a reasoned opinion as to the accuracy of each of the following statements: (a) the smaller the particle size of dry powder the greater the fire extinguishing effect, (b) little advantage is gained in using carbon dioxide in preference to water unless the intensity of the fire is such as to render water ineffective, (c) low expansion foam is more effective than high expansion foam in many instances.

40. Compare the characteristics of centrifugal pumps with those of supercavitating pumps. Suggest with reasons the type of pump most suited for each of the following duties: (a) main sea water circulating, (b) crude oil cargo discharge, (c) toxic chemical cargo discharge.

41. Give a reasoned opinion as to the accuracy of each of the following statements: (a) the cooling effect of liquid inert gas is mainly responsible for its extinguishing efficiency, (b) carbon dioxide or inert combustion gas is preferable to steam for holds or machinery spaces, (c) dry powder extinguishes by chemical and physical means, (d) high expansion foam is not the most suitable smothering agent in most instances.

42. With reference to safety of personnel describe the precautions to be observed when: (a) effecting repairs in the crankcase or boiler furnace when the ship is rolling heavily, (b) cleaning engine components or clothing with compressed air, (c) painting in the shaft tunnel at sea, (d) using the engine room crane at sea.

43. With reference to heat exchangers define what is meant by the terms 'parallel flow' and 'contra flow'. Give two advantages and two disadvantages of each type of flow. State an application for which each is most suitable. Describe how the 'fall off' in efficiency of heat exchangers may be effectively countered.

44. Describe with sketches, the principle of operation of two of the following fire detection systems installed in periodically unattended machinery spaces: (a) infra red and ultra violet, (b) thermal, (c) ionisation chamber.

45. Explain why in many instances static filter units have replaced centrifuges for oil cleaning. Describe with a line diagram a static filter module for the total preparation of liquid fuel. State what standard of purification is achieved and how it is maintained in service.

46. Explain the mechanics of fatigue failure and state where it is likely to occur in marine engineering. Explain the contribution of the following conditions to fatigue failure: (a) corrosion, (b) alternating stress, (c) magnitude of stress, (d) frequency of load cycle. Identify the common signs of fatigue and state what steps are taken to avoid failure.

47. With reference to tubular heat exchangers explain: (a) how differential movement tubes and body is accommodated when the tube plates are rigidly located in the body, (b) how and why turbulence is imparted to fluid flow through the tubes, (c) why it has become possible to discard sacrificial anodes in sea water coolers, (d) what is meant by the term 'guided flow', with particular reference to oil heaters.

48. Give two reasons for sludge formation in main lubricating oil systems. Explain how bearing metal is attacked with particular reference to incompatibility between the oil and metal. Explain the role of additives and state what normal practices must be suspended in order to maintain treated oils in their optimum condition. Discuss the problems associated with the use of a multi-purpose lubricating oil.

49. Sketch and describe how cool and flow may be measured on a linear scale. Explan the principle of operation of the instrument concerned. Explain why the values recorded may vary from those expected from calculations.

50. In a particular case of collision and outbreak of fire the Court of Formal Investigation was not satisfied that proper co-ordination existed between engineering and deck departments. Discuss how a good measure of co-operation can be achieved paying particular attention to equipment with which both departments should be familiar.

Note:
Other specialist text books will need to be used to answer Section II (Electro technology) and Section III (Naval Architecture) questions given in the Class 1 specimen paper following.

DEPARTMENT OF TRANSPORT
EXAMINATION FOR CERTIFICATE OF COMPETENCY
CLASS 1 ENGINEER

ENGINEERING KNOWLEDGE — GENERAL

Time allowed: 3 hours

IMPORTANT
This paper consists of FOURTEEN questions divided into THREE sections.

Candidates are required to attempt not more than TEN questions as follows:

SECTION I (Questions 1-8)
Not more than SIX questions to be attempted in this section.

SECTION II (Questions 9-11)
Not more than TWO questions to be attempted in this section.

SECTION III (Questions 12-14)
Not more than TWO questions to be attempted in this section.

SECTION I
QUESTIONS 1-8
This section carries 60% of the total marks.
Not more than SIX questions to be attempted in this section.

1.   (i)   Give reasons why multi-additive and
           synthetic lubricants should not
           normally be passed through
           centrifuges.   (4 marks)
     (ii) State why centrifuge clutch slip
           should receive immediate attention
           for reasons other than overheating.   (3 marks)
     (iii) Explain why oil preheating greatly
           assists centrifuge performance.   (3 marks)

2. With reference to multi plate heat
exchangers state why:
    (i)   fluid pressure and temperature does
        not normally exceed 10 bar and
        150°C respectively,   (3 marks)
    (ii) preference for titanium and stainless
        steel plates is increasing,   (2 marks)
    (iii) carrying bars and clamping bolts are
        often much longer than pack
        thickness,   (2 marks)
    (iv) plates usually carry an impressed
        relief pattern.   (3 marks)

3.   (i)   Sketch a self contained totally
        submerged pump for emptying tanks
        of hazardous liquid chemical cargo. (4 marks)
    (ii) Explain why this pump is used for
        such services.   (3 marks)
    (iii) Identify the safety features
        incorporated in the pump design.   (3 marks)

4. With reference to hydraulic power systems
explain how the power units are able to
meet the following requirements:
    (i)   follow an infinitely variable pumping
        characteristic,   (3 marks)
    (ii) response to demand signal to be only
        marginally slower than electrical
        power systems,   (3 marks)
    (iii) full range of torque to be instantly
        available upon demand,   (3 marks)
    (iv) state why such a pump is to be
        preferred to a positive displacement
        pump with a controlled discharge. (1 mark)

5.   (i)   Identify those factors restricting the
        reliability of propeller shaft bearings. (3 marks)
    (ii) Define the limitations of white metal
        stern tube bearings.   (4 marks)
    (iii) State why the advantage of roller
        over plain bearings is lost in propeller
        shaft applications.   (3 marks)

6. With reference to the pressure sealing of
control valve spindles state why:
    (i)   tetrafluoroethylene packing is
        commonly used,   (4 marks)

      (ii) a considerable depth of packing is
           often employed,   (3 marks)
      (iii) bellow glands are sometimes fitted.   (3 marks)

7.   (i)   Give two reasons for sludge
           formation in main lubricating oil
           systems.   (2 marks)
      (ii) Explain how bearing metal is attacked
           with particular reference to
           incompatibility between oil and
           metal.   (4 marks)
      (iii) Define the role of additives and state
           what normal practice must be
           suspended in order to maintain
           treated oils in their optimum
           condition.   (4 marks)

8. With reference to fire fighting agents give
   two reasons why:
      (i)   dry powder is preferable to sand,   (2 marks)
      (ii) mechanical foam is preferable to
           chemical foam,   (2 marks)
      (iii) halon 1301 is preferable to carbon
           dioxide,   (4 marks)
      (iv) light water foam is preferable to high
           expansion foam.   (2 marks)

SECTION II
QUESTIONS 9-11
This section carries 20% of the total marks.
Not more than TWO questions to be attempted in this section.

9. With reference to electrical equipment in potentially flammable atmospheres aboard ships:

    (i) Explain why conventional equipment is considered to be hazardous. (3 marks)

    (ii) Explain the concept of intrinsic safety. (3 marks)

    (iii) Describe an intrinsically safe installation. (4 marks)

10. (i) Explain why automatic voltage regulation is required for an a.c. generator. (3 marks)

    (ii) Describe the main requirements for an automatic voltage regulator suitable for marine service. (3 marks)

    (iii) Briefly describe the operation of an automatic voltage regulator. (4 marks)

11. With reference to a.c. deck machinery:

    (i) State two forms of drive suitable for cargo working winches. (2 marks)

    (ii) Describe a drive suitable for a windlass. (5 marks)

    (iii) Describe the routine maintenance required for motor control equipment subjected to frequent starting. (3 marks)

SECTION III
QUESTIONS 12-14
This section carries 20% of the total marks.
Not more than TWO questions to be attempted in this section.

12.   (i) Describe with sketches how a keyless
           propeller is mounted on and released
           from the propeller shaft taper by
           'hydraulic floating'.   (5 marks)
     (ii) Evaluate the advantages 'hydraulic
           floating' possesses over dry 'push
           up'.   (3 marks)
    (iii) State what precautions need to be
           observed when mounting and
           releasing a propeller by 'hydraulic
           floating'.   (2 marks)

13. Bulbous protruberances at the fore foot
    provide permanent buoyancy.
      (i) Define with reasons the advantages
           gained from this additional buoyancy
           at the fore foot.   (2 marks)
     (ii) Suggest with reasons a further,
           equally important advantage gained
           from these appendages.   (3 marks)
    Bow flare provides temporary buoyancy.
    (iii) Define with reasons the advantage
           gained from this additional buoyancy
           in bow flare.   (3 marks)
     (iv) Suggest with reasons a further benefit
           gained from bow flare.   (2 marks)

14. Define with reasons the main purpose of
    each of the following practices:
      (i) electrical charge impressed into hulls,   (4 marks)
     (ii) emission of toxic biocides over the
           underwater surfaces of hulls,   (3 marks)
    (iii) shot blasting of underwater hull
           plating together with the application
           of 'self polishing' plant coatings.   (3 marks)

ACKNOWLEDGEMENT

   The Specimen Examination Questions and Specimen
Examination Papers appearing in this book are reproduced by
kind permission of the Controller of H.M. Stationery Office.

INDEX

A

Absorption type refrigerator 282
Accumulation of pressure test 97
Acid and basic processes 5
Acidity, fuel 62
Actuator servo-mechanisms 186
Aft end installations 217
Air, combustion 79
Air conditioning 286
Air in telemotors 181
Air register 80
Alarm scanning 453
Alignment of shafting 211
Alkalinity 145
Alternative stern gear 236
Aluminium 33
Amplifier, electrical 455
Amplifier, pneumatic (relay) 456
Amplifier, units (steering) 63
Analogues 455
Analysis, critical path 476
Analysis, flue gases 72
Analysis, fuel 64
Annealing 25
Anti-foams 161, 427
Anti-oxidant 426
Aromatics 48
Asbestos 35
Ash 62
Atomisers 79
Atoms 145
Auto-klean strainer 406
Automatic control, boiler 467
Automatic control, domestic
  water 377
Automatic control,
  refrigeration 276
Automatic control, sprinkler 336
Automatic control, stabiliser 207
Automatic control, steering 207
Automatic control, telegraph 467
Automatic control, temperature 465
Automatic 'fail safe' steering 195
Automatic oil filter module 411
Automatic water valve 280
Axial flow pump 358
Axial vibration 249

B

Babbitt metal 33
Balancing 245
Ball bearing 249
Ballast rules 399
Barometer, mercury 445
Battery system 284
BCF 312
Bearing lubrication 428
Bend test 20
Bessemer process 3
Bilge fittings, etc. 393
Bilge rules 397
Bi-metallic thermometer 441
Blackheart process 25
Blowdown valve 124
Blowing procedure, water
gauge 101
Boiler combustion chamber
  defects and repairs 121
Boiler combustion chamber
  girders 118
Boiler control system 467
Boiler corrosion 145
Boiler furnace defects
  and repairs 120
Boiler oil fuel systems 82
Boiler water treatment 154
Boilers, auxiliary packaged 125
Boilers, Cochran 110
Boilers, heat balance 77
Boilers, Scotch 114
Bomb calorimeter 58
Boundary lubrication 428
Bourdon pressure gauge 446
Brass 32
Brazing 42
Breathing apparatus 343
Bridge control IC engine 469
Brine 283
Brine circuits 284
Brine properties 285
Brinell test 13
Brittle fracture 16
Bronze 32
BTM 312
Bulk CO_2 system 331

Bypass valve   177

C

Calcium bicarbonate   152
Calcium sulphate   151
Calibration of instruments   450
Calorific values   57, 68
Carbon   5
Carbon dioxide   65, 153
Carbon residue   60
Carbonic acid   153
Cargo pump   360
Cascade control   466
Case hardening   26
Cast iron   5
Caustic embrittlement   148
Caustic soda treatment   156
Cavitation   368
Cell dp   446
Cementite   6
Centralised cooling system   374
Centralised instrumentation   452
Centralised priming system   364
Centrifugal casting   30
Centrifugal clarifier   419
Centrifugal compressor   272
Centrifugal pumps   353
Centrifugal purifier   418
Centrifugal purifier, super   420
Centrifuges   416
Cetane number   63
Charging system, telemotors   180
Charpy V notch   15
Chemical absorption CO_2
   recorder   74
Chemical treatment,
evaporators   130
Chemical treatment plant   392
Chromium   31
Clarification   413
Clean Air Act   76
Cleaning new boilers   162
Closed loop   457
CO_2 and water extinguisher   323
CO_2 flooding system   327
CO_2 flooding system, engine
   room   329
CO_2 portable fire extinguisher   321
CO_2 recorders   74
CO_2 refrigerant   258
Coagulants   159
Coalescers, filters   408
Cochran boiler   110
Cochran boiler, spheroid   113
Cochran exhaust gas boiler   114
Coefficient of performance   266

Coil type boiler   126
Combustion chamber defects   121
Combustion chamber girders   118
Combustion equipment   79, 86
Combustion gas detector   309
Combustion indications   78
Combustion of fuel   65
Comparison, steering gears   194
Compatibility of chemicals   85
Compound oil   426
Compressors, refrigerant   268
Condensate line treatment   161
Condenser, refrigerant   273
Conradson test   60
Continuous bypass system   423
Contraction of area, per cent   11
Control actions   458
Control, boiler system   467
Control, fluid temperature   465
Control, IC engine   469
Control loops   457
Control, management   474
Control, propeller pitch   237
Control, proportional   458
Control P + I   460
Control P + D   462
Control P + I + D   460
Control switch   277
Control systems   463
Control terminology   457
Control theory   457
Control valve   463
Control valve block   190
Control, viscosity   83
Controllable pitch propeller   237
Controller, electric-electronic   462
Controller, pneumatic   461
Controlling evaporator scale   130
Copper   32
Corrosion of boilers   145
Corrosion, electro-chemical   146
Corrosion, external   154
Corrosion fatigue   144
Corrosion, galvanic action   141, 148
Corrosion inhibitor   427
Corrosion, oils   147
Corrosion pitting   144
Corrosion, white metal
bearings   434
Cotton   35
Couplings and bolts   231
Counter flow   371
Crankcase oil dilution   64
Crankshaft alignment   216
Crankshaft deflections   220
Crankshaft stresses   228
Crankwebs   229

Creep test 17
Critical path analysis 476
Critical temperature 267
Cross flow 371
Cupro-Nickel 33

D

Dalton's laws 286
Dam ring 415
Data logging 455
Data processing 475
De-aeration 160
De-aluminification 144
Deep tank pipe arrangement 393
Deflection of shafts 222
De-humidifier 292
Density 51
Derivative control 460
Desired value 458
Detergent oil 425
Detuner 249
Deviation 458
Dew point 287
De-zincification 143
Diaphragm valve 463
Diecasting 29
Differential pressure cell 446
Digital 434
Digital tachometer 449
Direct expansion refrigerator 276
Dispersants 427
Display 454
Dissociation 76
Distillation 49
Downhand welding 41
Dry bulb temperature 288
Dry powder extinguisher 324
Dynamometer 240

E

Electrical control, stabiliser 202
Electrical control switch 277
Electrical-electronic controller 462
Electrical separator probe 385
Electrical steering gears 196
Electrical telegraph 464
Electrical telemotor 181
Electrical torsion meter 239
Electro-hydraulic steering
   gear 186, 193
Electro-pneumatic transducer 456
Elements in irons and steels 30
Elongation, per cent 11
Emergency batteries 189
Emergency bilge pump 367
Emergency steering 189
Emulsion 431
Engler scale 52

English usage 483
Entropy 265
EP additive 427
EP lubricant 431
Epoxy resin 35
Equations, combustion 65
Evaporator, diesel waste heat 135
Evaporator, double effect 135
Evaporator feed treatment 130
Evaporator heating element 134
Evaporator, refrigeration 274
Evaporator rules 133
Evaporator, simple vertical 132
Evaporator, single effect 129
Evaporator, single effect plant 135
Evaporator, two stage flash 135
Examination questions—
   Class Three miscellaneous 491
   Class Two miscellaneous 497
   Class One miscellaneous 508
   Class Three specimen paper 495
   Class Two specimen paper 503
   Class One specimen paper 515
Examination requirements 484
Examination technique 486
Exciter 197
Exhaust gas boiler, Cochran 114
Expansion valve, refrigerator 279
Explosion meter 87
Explosive limits 86
Explosive vapour concentration 86
Extended aeration sewage
plants 390

F

'Fail safe' steering system 195
Failure, steering units 189
Fatigue tests 18
Faults, refrigeration 264
Feedback 458
Feed pump 351
Feed water injector 389
Feed water treatment 131, 154
Ferrite 5
Filled system thermometers 440
Film lubrication 428
Filter, air 291
Filter, coalescers 408
Filtration 406
Fin gear 204
Fire alarm circuit 305
Fire appliances, rules 340
Fire detection methods 305
Fire detectors 304
Fire extinguishers 313
Fire extinguishing systems—
   CO_2 flooding 327, 329

Fire extinguishing systems—cont.
  Inert gas generator 333
  Mechanical foam 317, 318, 319
  Sprinkler 336
Fire point 62
Flame hardening 24
Flame temperatures 70
Flammability 69, 259
Flaps, stabiliser 205
Flash evaporator 135
Flash off 261
Flash point 55
Float valve, refrigerator 275
Flow measurement 447
Flow meter 447
Flow sensor 448
Flue gas loss 78
Fluid for telemotor 179
Fluid temperature control 465
Foam compound injection
  system 319
Foam, high expansion 320
Forging 30
Fork tiller 191
Forming of metals 28
Four ram steering gear 192
Freon 260
Freon compressor 269
Fresh water generator 135
Fretting corrosion 144
Fuel oil control valve 463
Fuel additives 71
Fuel, gaseous 84
Fuels 47

G
Galvanic action 141, 148
Galvanic series 142
Gas cutting 42
Gas explosive detector 87
Gas generator, fire 333
Gas torques 228
Gaseous fuels 84
Gear pumps 365
General industrial management 474
Girders, combustion chamber 118
Glass water gauge 99
Gland seals 233, 268
Graphitisation 143
Gravity ring 415
Grease 435
Grooving 122
Guided flow 373
Gyroscope 202

H
Halons 312

Hardening steel 23
Hardness salts 153
Hardness test 12, 167
Heat balance, boiler 77
Heat exchanger, plate 373
Heat exchanger, refrigeration 274
Heat exchanger, shell and tube 373
Heat pump 291
Heat sensors 305
Heat transfer 274, 297
Hele-Shaw pump 184
High expansion foam 320
Higher explosive limit 87
Hold ventilation 284
Humidity, relative, specific 286
Hunting gear 188
Hydraulic receiver 178
Hydraulic stabiliser control 202
Hydraulic test, boiler 123
Hydraulic transmitter 176
Hydrazine 160
Hydrazine test 171
Hydrocarbons 48
Hydrodynamic lubrication 428
Hydrogen 67
Hydrogen and hydroxyl ions 145
Hydrogen embrittlement 154

I
Ice 256
Ice making 284
Ignition delay 63
IMO rules 84, 195
Impeller 353
Incinerator 392
Incipient cavitation 369
Inducers 369
Induction hardening 27
Inert gas generator 333
Inert gas installation, tankers 334
Inertia force 246
Inertia torque 228
Inferential-differential pressure 447
Infra red detector 307
Instruments 440
Instruments, calibration 450
Insulation 293
Integral control 460
Integrated data processing 475
Intermediate liquid cooling 267
Intermediate shafts 226, 229
Ions 145
IP water in oil test 61
Izod test 15

J
Journal bearings 430

K

K-monel 33
Klinger reflex glass 105
Knock, engine cylinder 63

L

Lacquering 426, 432
LD process, metallurgy 3
Leuco reagent 169
Level measurement 446
Level sensor 447
Liquid level refrigerant
  control 274
Lime and soda treatment 155
Limits, explosive 86
Limits of flammability 69
Linear programming 475
Liner of tailshaft 230
Liquid fuels 47
Litmus paper 163
LNG 86, 294
Lower explosive limit 86
LPG 86, 294
Lub, oil filter-coalescer 408
Lub, oil filter, streamline 409
Lub, oil tests 432
Lubrication 425
Lubrication, bearings 428
Lubrication, fundamentals 427
Lubrication, oil additives 426

M

Magnesium chloride 150
Magnesium sulphate 151
Magnetic crack detection 22
Magnetic stop valve 280
Magnetic treatment 130
Magslip 202
Maintenance 479
Management, engine room 482
Management, general 474
Management, shipping 481
Manganese 30
Manometer, mercury and water 444
Manufacture, iron and steel 1
Materials, non-metallic 34
Mechanical straining-grooving 148
Mechanical type CO_2 recorder 75
Mercury barometer 444
Mercury in steel thermometer 440
Mercury manometer 444
Mercury thermometer 440
Methane 69
Michel bearings and thrust 242, 431
Miscellaneous examination
  questions—
  Class Three 491
  Class Two 497

Miscellaneous examination
  questions—cont.
  Class One 508
Mixed flow 371
Mixed flow pump 361
Modular systems 376
Modules 376
Molybdenum 31
Monel metal 33

N

Napthenes 48
Nessleriser 168
Nickel 31
Nitriding 26
Nitrile 34
Nitrogen 68
Non-destructive tests 20
Non-metallic materials 34
Normalising 25

O

O and M 475
Octane number 63
Offset 458
Ogee ring 110
Oil ballast chest 395
Oil burners 79
Oil for telemotors 179
Oil fuel additives 71
Oil fuel installation rules 399
Oil fuel settling tank 404
Oil fuel system, boiler 82
Oil in Navigable Waters Act 381
Oil lubricated sterntube 234
Oil module 412
Oil motor 203
Oil probe 385
Oil pump 186, 202
Oil purifier 418
Oil tests 432
Oily water separator 381
Oily water separator, automatic 383
Olefins 48
Open hearth process 2
Operational research 475
Optical telescope 214
Optimal maintenance policy 479
Organisation and method 475
Organisational divisions 481
OR technique 475
Orsat apparatus 72
Oxidation 432
Oxygen, dissolved 153
Oxygen in air 68
Oxygen in fuel 67
Oxygen test 169

P

Packaged auxiliary boiler   126
Paraffins   48
Parallel flow   371
Partial pressures   286
Pearlite   6
Penetrant tests   20
Pensky Marten flashpoint   56
Performance ratio, evaporators   129
Personnel relations   482
pH value   146
pH test   168
Phase changes   256
Phosphate treatment   157
Phosphorus   31
Photo-cell   450
Pig iron   2
Pilgrim wire alignment   220
Pitting   431
Pitting corrosion   144
Planned maintenance   477
Plastics   34
Pneumatic controller   458
Pneumatic controller action   458
Pneumercator   447
Pollution by oil   380
Polyelectrolytes   159
Polymers   34
Position indicator (telegraph)   464
Pour point   59
Pour point depressant   427
Powder type fire extinguisher   324
Power (amplifier) units   183
Pressure differential device   412
Pressure gauge, Bourdon   446
Pressure gauge, refrigerator   263
Pressure measurement   444
Pressurised FW system   377
Primary element   448
Proof stress   12
Propeller   237
Propeller, controllable pitch   237
Propeller shaft   226, 230
Propeller shaft and sterntube   232, 234
Properties of materials   7
Properties of refrigerants   259
Proportional band   459
Proportional control   458
P + I control   460
P + D control   462
P + I + D control   460
Psychrometric chart   289
PTFE   35
Pumps   350
Purge system   447
Purification of fuel oils   422
Purification of lub oils   423
Purifier, self cleaning   421

Q

Questions miscellaneous—
    Third class examination   491
    Second class examination   497
    First class examination   508
    Specimen examination paper—
    Third class   495
    Second class   503
    First class   515
Queueing theory   475

R

Radiography   22
Ram   186
Ram crosshead   188
Rapson slide   191
Rate of rise temperature
detector   305
Receiver (hydraulic) telemotor   178
Reciprocating compressor   268
Reciprocating mass   246
Reciprocating pumps   351
Red dye penetrant   22
Reducing valve   127
Redwood viscometer   52
Redwood viscosity scales   52
Refinery   49
Refrigerant, desirable
properties   259
Refrigerant insulation   293
Refrigerant oil   273
Refrigerants   259
Refrigeration   256
Refrigeration cycles   261
Refrigeration, absorption   281
Refrigerator compressors   268
Relative humidity   286
Relay   456
Remote engine control   469
Replacement policy   477
Report writing   482
Resistance thermometer   442
Retention system   390
Reynolds number   372
Rheostat   197
Roller bearing   244
Rotary compressor   271
Rotary vane steering unit   193
Rubber   35
Rudder motor   197
Rules, evaporators   133
Rules, fire appliances   340
Rules, pipe systems   397
Rules, safety valves   92
Rules, shafting   229
Rules, steering gears   200

S

Safety valve, full bore 98
Safety valve, full lift 97
Safety valve, improved
  high lift 93
Safety valve rules 92
Salinometer 163
Sand casting 28
Saybolt scales 52
Scale formation 151
Scale in evaporator 129
Scaling unit 454
Scotch boiler 114
Screw compressor 272
Scuffing 431
Screw displacement pump 365
Sea water analysis 150
Secondary element 448
Self cleaning purifier 421
Sensor, flow 448
Sensor, level 447
Sensor, pressure 445
Sensor, temperature 440
Separation 414
Servo-mechanisms 186
Set value 458
Settling tank 404
Sewage and sludge 390
Shafting alignment 212
Shafting rules 224
Shafting stresses 229
Ship management 481
Ship maintenance costs 479
Ship stabiliser 201
Sighting by light 213
Sighting by telescope 214
Signal media 456
Silicates 153
Silicon 30
Silicon nitride 35
Single motor steering gear 148
Sinuflo 112
Sludge incinerator 392
Smoke detector 307
Soda acid portable
  fire extinguisher 325
Sodium chloride 150
Sodium nitrate 162
Sootblower 108
Specific humidity 286
Specimen examination papers—
  Class Three 495
  Class Two 503
  Class One 515
Specimen examination questions—
  Class Three 491
  Class Two 497

  Class One 508
Specimen question - answer 485
Stabiliser 201
Steam jet atomiser 81
Steam jetting 425
Steering gear control 182
Steering gear control
  valve block 190
Steering gear, electric 196, 199
Steering gear, ram type 187, 192
Steering gear rules 200
Steering gear, single motor 199
Steering gear telemotor 178, 182
Steering gear, vane type 193
Steering gears 175
Steering gears, fail safe 195
Steering gears, types 186
Sterntube 232
Sterntube, oil lubricated 233
Sterntube, shaft 231
Sterntube, water lubricated 232
Stern gear, alternative 236
Stern gear, withdrawable 236
Stone vapour boiler 126
Storage temperature, refrigerant 294
Streamline flow 371
Streamline lub oil filter 409
Stress corrosion 143
Stresses, shafting 227
Sub-cooled liquid 260
Suction head 368
Sulphur 31
Supercavitation 369
Superheat control, refrigerant 279
Swirlyflo 112

T

Table of metals and uses 36
Tachometer 448
Tachometer, digital 449
Technique, examination 486
Telegraph (electrical) 464
Telemeter (transducer) system 175
Telemetering 452
Telemotor, electrical 182
Telemotor fluid 179
Telemotor, hydraulic 175
Temperature, dry and wet bulb 288
Temperature, fluid control 465
Temperature measurement 440
Temperature viscosity curves 54
Tempering 23
Tensile test 9
Terminology, control 457
Test, alkalinity 165
Test, boiler water 163
Test, chloride 166

Test, dissolved solids 163
Test examples 486
Test, hardness 12, 167
Test, oxygen 169
Test, phosphate 167
Test, sulphite 167
Testing of materials 9
Testing of materials,
  non-destructive 20
Thermal conductivity 294
Thermal conductivity type
  CO_2 recorder 74
Thermocouple 443
Thermodynamic cycles,
  refrigeration 265
Thermometer, bi-metallic 441
Thermometer, filled system 440
Thermometer, mercury 440
Thermometer, resistance 441
Thermostatic expansion valve 279
Thrust block 242
Thrust indicator 243
Thrust shaft 230
Tilting gear, stabiliser 205
Titanium 34
Torsional vibration 249
Torsionmeter 238
Toxic vapour concentration 86
Transducer, electro-pneumatic 45
Transmitter 176, 464
Transverse vibration 248
Treatment of metals 23
Treatment of metals, diagram 24
Tubes, Scotch boiler 117
Turbine alignment 219
Turning moment diagrams 227

U
Ultimate tensile strength 11
Ultrasonic jet atomiser 81
Ultrasonic testing 22
Unattended machinery spaces,
  safety 468
Usage of English 483

V
Valve, bypass 177
Valve, diaphragm 463
Valve, reducing 127
Valve block, steering gears ???
Vanadium 31
Vapour compression refrigeration
  system 261
Vapour concentration 86
Vaporising fluids 312
Vapour pressure 86

Variable delivery pumps 183, 185,
203
Vee block compressor 270
Venturi flow sensor 448
Vibration, axial 249
Vibration, damper 249
Vibration, torsional 249
Vibration, transverse 248
Vickers pyramid test 14
Viscometer 53
Viscosity 51
Viscosity control 83
Viscosity index 54
Viscosity scales 52
Volute casing 353

W
Wallsend-Howden atomiser 80
Ward Leonard steering gear 196
Waste heat boiler 110
Waste heat boiler, Cochran 110
Water in oil test 61
Water level indicator—
  Plate type 103
  Remote type 104
Water lubricated sterntube 232
Water manometer 444
Water purification 137
Water ring pump 363
Water spray system 336
Water valve, automatic 280
Water washing 425
Wax element valve 466
Weir pump 351
Weld preparation 41
Welding 35
Welding, blacksmith's forge 35
Welding, butt 41
Welding defects 40
Welding, downhand 41
Welding, heat affected zone 41
Welding, resistance 37
Wet bulb temperature 288
White metals 33
Work hardening 26
Work study 474

X
X-ray 22

Y
Yield stress 11
Young's modulus 12

Z
Zinc plates 148

REED'S MARINE ENGINEERING SERIES

Vol. 1   MATHEMATICS
Vol. 2   APPLIED MECHANICS
Vol. 3   APPLIED HEAT
Vol. 4   NAVAL ARCHITECTURE
Vol. 5   SHIP CONSTRUCTION
Vol. 6   BASIC ELECTROTECHNOLOGY
Vol. 7   ADVANCED ELECTROTECHNOLOGY
Vol. 8   GENERAL ENGINEERING KNOWLEDGE
Vol. 9   STEAM ENGINEERING KNOWLEDGE
Vol. 10   INSTRUMENTATION AND CONTROL SYSTEMS
Vol. 11   ENGINEERING DRAWING
Vol. 12   MOTOR ENGINEERING KNOWLEDGE

REED'S ENGINEERING KNOWLEDGE FOR DECK OFFICERS
REED'S MATHS TABLES AND ENGINEERING FORMULAE
REED'S MARINE DISTANCE TABLES
REED'S OCEAN NAVIGATOR
REED'S SEXTANT SIMPLIFIED
REED'S SKIPPERS HANDBOOK
REED'S COMMERCIAL SALVAGE PRACTICE
REED'S MARITIME METEOROLOGY
SEA TRANSPORT – OPERATION AND ECONOMICS

These books are obtainable from all good Nautical Booksellers
or direct from:

THOMAS REED PUBLICATIONS
The Barn, Ford Farm
Bradford Leigh
Bradford-on-Avon
Wiltshire BA15 2RP
United Kingdom

Tel: 01225 868821
Fax: 01225 868831

Email: tugsrus@abreed.demon.co.uk